HONDA
ACCORD/CIVIC/PRELUDE
1973-83 REPAIR MANUAL

CHILTON'S

D1306250

Senior Vice President	Ronald A. Hoxter
Publisher and Editor-In-Chief	Kerry A. Freeman, S.A.E.
Executive Editors	Dean F. Morgantini, S.A.E., W. Calvin Settle, Jr., S.A.E.
Managing Editor	Nick D'Andrea
Special Products Manager	Ken Grabowski, A.S.E., S.A.E.
Senior Editors	Jacques Gordon, Michael L. Grady, Debra McCall, Kevin M. G. Maher, Richard J. Rivele, S.A.E., Richard T. Smith, Jim Taylor, Ron Webb
Project Managers	Martin J. Gunther, Will Kessler, A.S.E., Richard Schwartz
Production Manager	Andrea Steiger
Product Systems Manager	Robert Maxey
Director of Manufacturing	Mike D'Imperio
Editor	Tony Tortorici

CHILTON BOOK COMPANY

Manufactured in USA
© 1994 Chilton Book Company
Chilton Way, Radnor, PA 19089
ISBN 0-8019-8591-9
Library of Congress Catalog Card No. 93-074293
3456789012   5432109876

Contents

Contents

SAFETY NOTICE

Proper service and repair procedures are vital to the safe, reliable operation of all motor vehicles, as well as the personal safety of those performing repairs. This manual outlines procedures for servicing and repairing vehicles using safe, effective methods. The procedures contain many NOTES, CAUTIONS, and WARNINGS which should be followed along with standard procedures to eliminate the possibility of personal injury or improper service which could damage the vehicle or compromise its safety.

It is important to note that the repair procedures and techniques, tools and parts for servicing motor vehicles, as well as the skill and experience of the individual performing the work vary widely. It is not possible to anticipate all of the conceivable ways or conditions under which vehicles may be serviced, or to provide cautions as to all of the possible hazards that may result. Standard and accepted safety precautions and equipment should be used when handling toxic or flammable fluids, and safety goggles or other protection should be used during cutting, grinding, chiseling, prying,or any other process that can cause material removal or projectiles.

Some procedures require the use of tools specially designed for a specific purpose. Before substituting another tool or procedure, you must be completely satisfied that neither your personal safety, nor the performance of the vehicle will be endangered.

Although information in this manual is based on industry sources and is complete as possible at the time of publication, the possibility exists that some car manufacturers made later changes which could not be included here. While striving for total accuracy, Chilton Book Company cannot assume responsibility for any errors, changes or omissions that may occur in the compilation of this data.

PART NUMBERS

Part numbers listed in this reference are not recommendation by Chilton for any product by brand name. They are references that can be used with interchange manuals and aftermarket supplier catalogs to locate each brand supplier's discrete part number.

SPECIAL TOOLS

Special tools are recommended by the vehicle manufacturer to perform their specific job. Use has been kept to a minimum, but where absolutely necessary, they are referred to in the text by the part number of the tool manufacturer. These tools can be purchased, under the appropriate part number, from your local dealer or regional distributor, or an equivalent tool can be purchased locally from a tool supplier or parts outlet. Before substituting any tool for the one recommended, read the SAFETY NOTICE at the top of this page.

ACKNOWLEDGMENTS

The Chilton Book Company expresses appreciation to Honda Motor Corporation for their generous assistance.

1

GENERAL INFORMATION AND MAINTENANCE

HOW TO USE THIS BOOK

Chilton's Repair manual for Honda models is intended to teach you more about the inner workings of your car and save you money on its upkeep. The first two sections will be used the most, since they contain maintenance and tune-up information and procedures. The following sections concern themselves with the more complex systems. Operating systems from engine through brakes are covered to the extent that we feel the average do-it-yourselfer should get involved as well as more complex procedures that will benefit both the advanced do-it-yourselfer mechanic as well as the professional. This book will explain such things as rebuilding the transaxle and it should be advised that the expertise required, and the investment in special tools makes this task uneconomical and unpractical for the novice mechanic. We will also tell you how to change your own brake pads and shoes, replace spark plugs, perform routine maintenance, and many more jobs that will save you money, give you personal satisfactions, and help you avoid problems.

A secondary purpose of this book is a reference guide for owners who want to understand their Honda and/or their mechanics better. In this case, no tools at all are required. Knowing just what a particular repair job requires in parts and labor time will allow you to evaluate whether or not you're getting a fair price quote and help decipher itemized bills from a repair shop.

Before attempting any repairs or service on your Honda, read through the entire procedure outlined in the appropriate section. This will give you the overall view of what tools and supplies will be required. There is nothing more frustrating than having to walk to the bus stop on Monday morning because you were short one gasket on Sunday afternoon. So read ahead and plan ahead. Each operation should be approached logically and all procedures thoroughly understood before attempting any work. Some special tools that may be required can often be rented from local automotive jobbers or places specializing in renting tools and equipment. Check the yellow pages of your phone book.

All sections contain adjustments, maintenance, removal and installation procedures, and overhaul procedures. When overhaul is not considered practical, we tell you how to remove the failed part and, then, how to install the new or rebuilt replacement. In this way, you at least save the labor costs. Backyard overhaul of some components (such as the alternator or water pump) is just not practical, but the removal and installation procedure is often simple and well within the capabilities of the average Honda owner.

Two basic mechanic's rules should be mentioned here. First, whenever the LEFT side of the Honda or engine is referred to, it is meant to specify the DRIVER'S side of the Honda. Conversely, the RIGHT side of the Honda means the PASSENGER'S side. Second, all screws and bolts are removed by turning counterclockwise, and tightened by turning clockwise.

Safety is always the most important rule. Constantly be aware of the dangers involved in working on or around an automobile and take proper precautions to avoid the risk of personal injury or damage to the Honda. See the section in this section, Servicing Your Vehicle Safely, and the SAFETY NOTICE on the acknowledgment page before attempting any service procedures and pay attention to the instructions provided. There are 3 common mistakes in mechanical work:

1. Incorrect order of assembly, disassembly or adjustment. When taking something apart or putting it together, doing things in the wrong order usually just costs you extra time; however, it CAN break something. Read the entire procedure before beginning disassembly. Do everything in the order in which the instructions say you should do it, even if you can't immediately see a reason for it. When you're taking apart something that is very intricate (for example a carburetor), you might want to draw a picture of how it looks when assembled at one point in order to make sure you get everything back in its proper position. We will supply exploded views whenever possible, but sometimes the job requires more attention to detail than an illustration provides. When making adjustments (especially tune-up adjustments), do them in order. One adjustment often affects another and you cannot expect satisfactory results unless each adjustment is made only when it cannot be changed by any other.

2. Overtorquing (or undertorquing) nuts and bolts. While it is more common for overtorquing to cause damage, under torquing can cause a fastener to vibrate loose and cause serious damage, especially when dealing with aluminum parts. Pay attention to torque specifications and utilize a torque wrench in assembly. If a torque figure is not available remember that, if you are using the right tool to do the job, you will probably not have to strain yourself to get a fastener tight enough. The pitch of most threads is so slight that the tension you put on the wrench will be multiplied many times in actual force on what you are tightening. A good example of how critical torque is can be seen in the case of spark plug installation, especially where you are putting the plug into an aluminum cylinder head. Too little torque can fail to crush the gasket, causing leakage of combustion gases and consequent overheating of the plug and engine parts. Too much torque can damage the threads or distort the plug, which changes the spark gap at the electrode. Since more and more manufacturers are using aluminum in their engine and chassis parts to save weight, a torque wrench should be in any serious do-it-yourselfer's tool box.

3. There are many commercial chemical products available for ensuring that fasteners won't come loose, even if they are not torqued just right (a very common brand is Loctite®). If you're worried about getting something together tight enough to hold, but loose enough to avoid mechanical damage during assembly, one of these products might offer substantial insurance. Read the label on the package and make sure the product is compatible with the materials, fluids, etc. involved before choosing one.

4. Crossthreading. This occurs when a part such as a bolt is screwed into a nut or casting at the wrong angle and forced, causing the threads to become damaged. Crossthreading is more likely to occur if access is difficult. It helps to clean and lubricate fasteners, and to start threading with the part to be installed going straight in, using your fingers. If you encounter resistance, unscrew the part and start over again at a different angle until it can be inserted and turned several times without much effort. Keep in mind that many parts, especially spark plugs, use tapered threads so

that gentle turning will automatically bring the part you're threading to the proper angle if you don't force it or resist a change in angle. Don't put a wrench on the part until it's been turned in a couple of times by hand. If you suddenly encounter resistance and the part has not seated fully, don't force it. Pull it back out and make sure it's clean and threading properly.

Always take your time and be patient; once you have some experience, working on your Honda will become an enjoyable hobby.

TOOLS AND EQUIPMENT

▶ **See Figures 1, 2, 3, 4, 5, 6, 7 and 8**

Naturally, without the proper tools and equipment it is impossible to properly service your vehicle. It would be impossible to catalog each tool that you would need to perform each or every operation in this book. It would also be unwise for the amateur to rush out and buy an expensive set of tools on the theory that he may need one or more of them at sometime.

The best approach is to proceed slowly, gathering together a good quality set of those tools that are used most frequently. Don't be misled by the low cost of bargain tools. It is far better to spend a little more for better quality. Forged wrenches, 6 or 12 point sockets and fine tooth ratchets are by far preferable to their less expensive counterparts. As any good mechanic can tell you, there are few worse experiences than trying to work on a Honda with bad tools. Your monetary savings will be far outweighed by frustration and mangled knuckles.

Certain tools, plus a basic ability to handle tools, are required to get started. A basic mechanics tool set, a torque wrench, and, for later models, a Torx® bits set. Torx® bits are hexlobular drivers which fit both inside and outside on special Torx® head fasteners used in various places on Honda vehicles.

Begin accumulating those tools that are used most frequently; those associated with routine maintenance and tune-up.

In addition to the normal assortment of screwdrivers and pliers you should have the following tools for routine maintenance jobs (your Honda, uses metric fasteners):

1. Metric wrenches, sockets and combination open end/box end wrenches in sizes from 3mm to 19mm; and a spark plug socket $^{13}/_{16}$"). If possible, buy various length socket drive extensions. One break in this department is that the metric sockets available in the U.S. will all fit the ratchet handles and extensions you may already have ($^{1}/_{4}$", $^{3}/_{8}$", and $^{1}/_{2}$" drive).

2. Jackstands for support.
3. Oil filter wrench.
4. Oil filter spout for pouring oil.

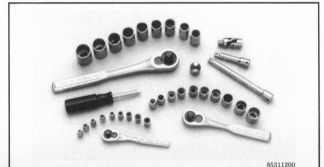

Fig. 1 All but the most basic procedure will require an assortment of ratchets and sockets

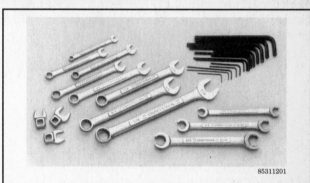

Fig. 2 In addition to ratchets, a good set of wrenches and hex keys will be necessary

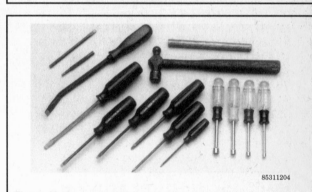

Fig. 3 Various screwdrivers, a hammer, chisels and prybars are necessary to have in your toolbox

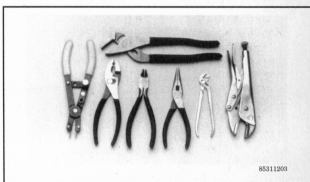

Fig. 4 An assortment of pliers will be handy, especially for old rusted parts and stripped bolt heads

5. Grease gun for chassis lubrication.
6. Hydrometer for checking the (old style) battery.
7. A container for draining oil.
8. Many rags for wiping up the inevitable mess.

In addition to the above items there are several others that are not absolutely necessary but handy to have around. These

Fig. 5 A hydraulic floor jack and a set of jackstands are essential for lifting and supporting the vehicle

include oil-absorbing material, a transmission funnel and the usual supply of lubricants, antifreeze and fluids, although these can be purchased as needed. This is a basic list for routine maintenance, but only your personal needs and desires can accurately determine your list of necessary tools.

The second list of tools is for tune-ups. While the tools involved here are slightly more sophisticated, they need not be outrageously expensive. There are several inexpensive tach/dwell meters on the market that are every bit as good for the average mechanic as a $100.00 professional model. Just be sure that it goes to at least 1,200-1,500 rpm on the tach scale and that it works on 4 cylinder engines. A basic list of tune-up equipment could include:

9. Tach/dwell meter.
10. Spark plug wrench.
11. Timing light (a DC light that works from the Honda's battery is best, although an AC light that plugs into 110V house current will suffice at some sacrifice in brightness).
12. Wire spark plug gauge/adjusting tools.
13. Set of feeler blades.

Here again, be guided by your own needs. A feeler blade will set the point gap as easily as dwell meter will read dwell, but slightly less accurately. And since you will need a tachometer anyway ... well, make your own decision.

In addition to these basic tools, there are several other tools and gauges you may find useful. These include:

14. A compression gauge. The screw-in type is slower to use, but eliminates the possibility of a faulty reading due to escaping pressure.

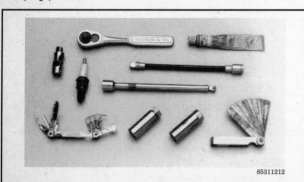

Fig. 6 A variety of tools and gauges are needed for spark plug service

Fig. 7 Many repairs will require the use of a torque wrench to assure the components are properly fastened

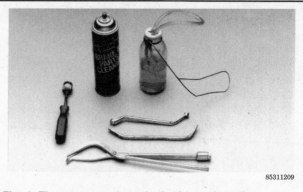

Fig. 8 The proper tools make brake work easier

15. A manifold vacuum gauge.
16. A test light.
17. An induction meter. This is used for determining whether or not there is current in a wire. These are handy for use if a wire is broken somewhere in a wiring harness.

As a final note, you will probably find a torque wrench necessary for all but the most basic work. The beam type models are perfectly adequate, although the newer click (breakaway) type are more precise and you don't have to crane your neck to see a torque reading in awkward situations. The breakaway torque wrenches are more expensive and should be recalibrated periodically.

Torque specification for each fastener will be given in the procedure in any case that a specific torque value is required. If no torque specifications are given, use the following values as a guide, based upon fastener size:

Bolts marked 6T
6mm bolt/nut: 5-7 ft. lbs.
8mm bolt/nut: 12-17 ft. lbs.
10mm bolt/nut: 23-34 ft. lbs.
12mm bolt/nut: 41-59 ft. lbs.
14mm bolt/nut: 56-76 ft. lbs.

Bolts marked 8T
6mm bolt/nut: 6-9 ft. lbs.
8mm bolt/nut: 13-20 ft. lbs.
10mm bolt/nut: 27-40 ft. lbs.
12mm bolt/nut: 46-69 ft. lbs.
14mm bolt/nut: 75-101 ft. lbs.

➡Special tools are occasionally necessary to perform a specific job or are recommended to make a job easier. Their use has been kept to a minimum. When a special tool is indicated, it will be referred to by manufacturer's part number, and, where possible, an illustration of the tool will be provided so that an equivalent tool may be used.

Some special tools are available commercially from major tool manufacturers. Others can be purchased through your Honda dealer.

SERVICING YOUR VEHICLE SAFELY

It is virtually impossible to anticipate all of the hazards involved with automotive maintenance and service, but care and common sense will prevent most accidents.

The rules of safety for mechanics range from "don't smoke around gasoline" to "use the proper tool for the job." The trick to avoiding injuries is to develop safe work habits and take every possible precaution.

Dos

• Do keep a fire extinguisher and first aid kit within easy reach.

• Do wear safety glasses or goggles when cutting, drilling or prying, even if you have 20-20 vision. If you wear glasses for the sake of vision, they should be made of hardened glass that can also serve as safety glasses, or wear safety goggles over your regular glasses.

• Do shield your eyes whenever you work around the battery. Batteries contain sulfuric acid; in case of contact with the eyes or skin, flush the area with water or a mixture of water and baking soda and get medical attention immediately.

• Do use safety stands for any under-car service. Jacks are for raising vehicles; safety stands are for making sure the vehicle stays raised until you want it to come down. Whenever the vehicle is raised, block the wheels remaining on the ground and set the parking brake.

• Do use adequate ventilation when working with any chemicals. Like carbon monoxide, the asbestos dust resulting from brake lining wear can be poisonous in sufficient quantities.

• Do disconnect the negative battery cable when working on the electrical system. The primary ignition system can contain up to 40,000 volts.

• Do follow manufacturer's directions whenever working with potentially hazardous materials. Both brake fluid and antifreeze are poisonous if taken internally.

• Do properly maintain your tools. Loose hammerheads, mushroomed punches and chisels, frayed or poorly grounded electrical cords, excessively worn screwdrivers, spread wrenches (open end), cracked sockets, slipping ratchets, or faulty droplight sockets can cause accidents.

• Do use the proper size and type of tool for the job being done.

• Do when possible, pull on a wrench handle rather than push on it, and adjust your stance to prevent a fall.

• Do be sure that adjustable wrenches are tightly adjusted on the nut or bolt and pulled so that the face is on the side of the fixed jaw.

• Do select a wrench or socket that fits the nut or bolt. The wrench or socket should sit straight, not cocked.

• Do strike squarely with a hammer — avoid glancing blows.

• Do set the parking brake and block the drive wheels if the work requires that the engine be running.

Don'ts

• Don't run an engine in a garage or anywhere else without proper ventilation — EVER! Carbon monoxide is poisonous; it takes a long time to leave the human body and you can build up a deadly supply of it in your system by simply breathing in a little every day. You may not realize you are slowly poisoning yourself. Always use power vents, windows, fans or open the garage doors.

• Don't work around moving parts while wearing a necktie or other loose clothing. Short sleeves are much safer than long, loose sleeves and hard-toed shoes with neoprene soles protect your toes and give a better grip on slippery surfaces. Jewelry such as watches, fancy belt buckles, beads or body adornment of any kind is not safe working around a vehicle. Long hair should be hidden under a hat or cap.

• Don't use pockets for toolboxes. A fall or bump can drive a screwdriver deep into you body. Even a wiping cloth hanging from the back pocket can wrap around a spinning shaft or fan.

• Don't smoke when working around gasoline, cleaning solvent or other flammable material.

• Don't smoke when working around the battery. When the battery is being charged, it gives off explosive hydrogen gas.

• Don't use gasoline to wash your hands; there are excellent soaps available. Gasoline may contain lead, and lead can enter the body through a cut, accumulating in the body until you are very ill. Gasoline also removes all the natural oils from the skin so that bone-dry hands will suck up oil and grease.

• Don't service the air conditioning system unless you are equipped with the necessary tools and training. The refrigerant, R-12, is extremely cold and when exposed to the air, will instantly freeze any surface it comes in contact with, including your eyes. Although the refrigerant is normally non-toxic, R-12 becomes a deadly poisonous gas in the presence of an open flame. One good whiff of the vapors from burning refrigerant can be fatal.

• Don't use screwdrivers for anything other than driving screws! A screwdriver used as a prying tool can snap when you least expect it, causing injuries. At the very least, you'll ruin a good screwdriver.

• Don't use a bumper jack (that little ratchet, scissors, or pantograph jack supplied with the vehicle) for anything other than changing a flat! These jacks are only intended for emergency use out on the road; they are NOT designed as a maintenance tool. If you are serious about maintaining your vehicle yourself, invest in a hydraulic floor jack of at least 1½ ton capacity, and at least two sturdy jackstands.

HISTORY

This repair manual for Honda's covers all the various model changes from 1973 through 1983. These are broken into model groups, Civic, Accord, and Prelude.
- Civic 1st generation: 1973-79
- Civic 2nd generation: 1980-83
- Accord 1st generation: 1976-81
- Accord 2nd generation: 1982-83
- Prelude 1st generation: 1979-82
- Prelude 2nd generation: 1983

SERIAL NUMBER IDENTIFICATION

Vehicle Identification (Chassis) Number

▶ See Figures 9, 10 and 11

Vehicle identification numbers are mounted on the top edge of the instrument panel and are visible from the outside. In addition, there is a Vehicle/Engine Identification plate under the hood on the hood mounting bracket on models built in 1974-78. On 1979-83 models, there are also identification plates located on the firewall and the rear door jam of the driver's door.

Fig. 9 The chassis number on the 1980 and later models is located on the rear door jam of the driver's side door

Fig. 10 Vehicle identification number-instrument panel

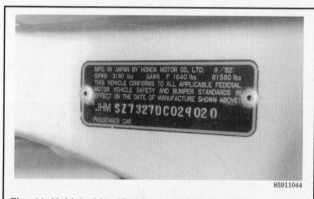

Fig. 11 Vehicle identification number-door jam

Engine Serial Number And Labels

▶ See Figures 12, 13, 14, 15, 16 and 17

The engine serial number is stamped on all vehicles. The first three digits indicate engine model identification. The remaining numbers refer to production sequence. This same number is also stamped onto the Vehicle/Engine Identification plate mounted on the hood bracket.

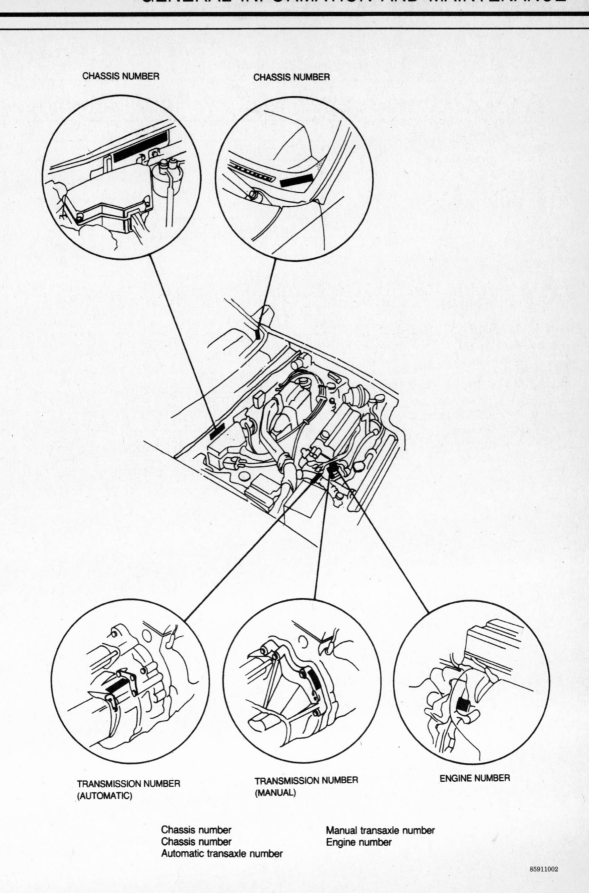

CHASSIS NUMBER

CHASSIS NUMBER

TRANSMISSION NUMBER
(AUTOMATIC)

TRANSMISSION NUMBER
(MANUAL)

ENGINE NUMBER

Chassis number
Chassis number
Automatic transaxle number

Manual transaxle number
Engine number

85911002

Fig. 12 View of the identification number locations

Engine Identification

Year	Model	Engine Displacement cc/liter	Engine Series Identification	No. of Cylinders	Fuel System
1973	Civic	1170/1.2	EB1	4	2 bbl.
1974	Civic 1200	1237/1.2	EB2	4	2 bbl.
1975	Civic 1200	1237/1.2	EB2	4	2 bbl.
	Civic CVCC	1487/1.5	ED1	4	3 bbl.
	Civic Wgn.	1487/1.5	ED3	4	3 bbl.
1976	Civic 1200	1237/1.2	EB2	4	2 bbl.
	Civic CVCC	1487/1.5	ED3	4	3 bbl.
	Civic Wgn.	1487/1.5	ED4	4	3 bbl.
	Accord	1600/1.6	EF1	4	3 bbl.
1977	Civic 1200	1237/1.2	EB2	4	2 bbl.
	Civic CVCC	1487/1.5	ED3	4	3 bbl.
	Civic Wgn.	1487/1.5	ED4	4	3 bbl.
	Accord	1600/1.6	EF1	4	3 bbl.
1978	Civic 1200	1237/1.2	EB2	4	2 bbl.
	Civic 1200	1237/1.2	EB3	4	2 bbl.
	Civic CVCC	1487/1.5	ED3	4	3 bbl.
	Civic Wgn.	1487/1.5	ED4	4	3 bbl.
	Accord	1600/1.6	EF1	4	3 bbl.
1979	Civic 1200	1237/1.2	EB2	4	2 bbl.
	Civic 1200	1237/1.2	EB3	4	2 bbl.
	Civic CVCC	1487/1.5	ED3	4	3 bbl.
	Civic Wgn.	1487/1.5	ED4	4	3 bbl.
	Accord	1751/1.8	EK1	4	3 bbl.
	Prelude	1751/1.8	EK1	4	3 bbl.
1980	Civic 1300	1335/1.3	EJ1	4	3 bbl.
	Civic CVCC	1487/1.5	EM1	4	3 bbl.
	Accord	1751/1.8	EK1	4	3 bbl.
	Prelude	1751/1.8	EK1	4	3 bbl.
1981	Civic 1300	1335/1.3	EJ1	4	3 bbl.
	Civic 1500	1487/1.5	EM1	4	3 bbl.
	Accord	1751/1.8	EK1	4	3 bbl.
	Prelude	1751/1.8	EK1	4	3 bbl.
1982	Civic 1300	1335/1.3	EJ1	4	3 bbl.
	Civic 1500	1487/1.5	EM1	4	3 bbl.
	Accord	1751/1.8	EK1	4	3 bbl.
	Prelude	1751/1.8	EK1	4	3 bbl.
1983	Civic 1300	1335/1.3	EJ1	4	3 bbl.
	Civic 1500	1487/1.5	EM1	4	3 bbl.
	Accord	1751/1.8	EK1	4	3 bbl.
	Prelude	1829/1.8	ES1	4	Dual Sidedraft

85911003

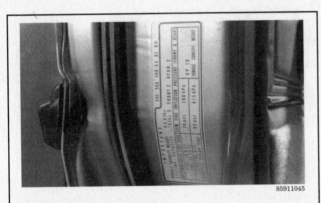

Fig. 13 Tire pressure label-door area

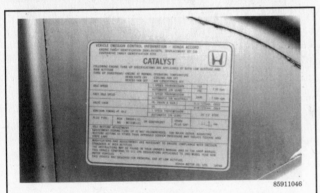

Fig. 14 Emission control information label-underhood

Fig. 15 Engine serial number-upper area under hood

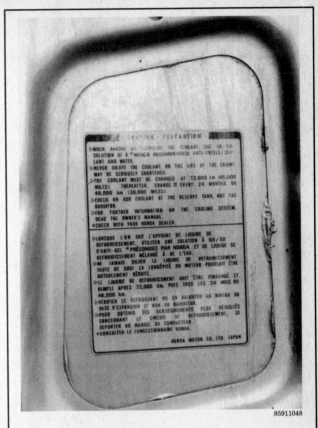

Fig. 16 Service information label-under hood

Fig. 17 Upper engine area view

Transaxle Serial Number

The transaxle serial number is stamped on the top of the transaxle/clutch case.

ROUTINE MAINTENANCE

Air Cleaner

REMOVAL & INSTALLATION

▶ See Figures 18, 19, 20, 21, 22, 23, 24, 25 and 26

The air cleaner element, housed above or to one side of the carburetor must be replaced every 12,000 miles (1973-74 models), 15,000 miles (1975-80 models), or 30,000 miles (1980-83 models).

1. To remove, unscrew the wing nut(s), bolts and/or spring clips from the air cleaner cover; on some models, it may be necessary to also remove a standard nut.

2. Remove the air cleaner cover and the air cleaner element.

3. Using a clean rag, clean out the air cleaner housing.

4. Using a new air cleaner element, reverse the removal procedures.

➡ Air cleaner elements are not interchangeable, although they may appear to be. Make sure you have the proper element for the year and model.

85911053

Fig. 20 Remove and replace the air filter element

85911054

Fig. 21 Remove the side hold down bolt on air cleaner assembly

85911051

Fig. 18 Remove the top wing nut on air cleaner assembly

85911055

Fig. 22 Remove the hold down screw on the air cleaner housing assembly

85911052

Fig. 19 Remove the side clamps on air cleaner assembly

Fig. 23 Remove and mark all vacuum hoses on air cleaner assembly

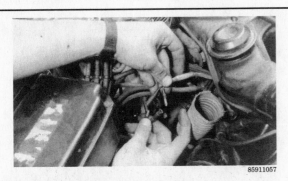

Fig. 24 Remove and mark all electrical connections, if equipped on the air cleaner assembly

Fig. 25 Remove all emission hoses on air cleaner assembly

Fig. 26 Remove the air cleaner assembly

Fuel Filter

All vehicles use a disposable type fuel filter which cannot be disassembled for cleaning. On 1973-74 models, the recommended replacement interval is 24,000 miles. On 1975-81 models, the filter is replaced after the first 15,000 miles, and every 30,000 miles thereafter. On 1982-83 models, the filter is replaced at 60,000 miles. Honda recommends that all rubber fuel hoses be replaced at the same time.

✳✳CAUTION

Before disconnecting any fuel lines, be sure to open the gas tank filler cap to relieve any pressure in the system. If this is not done, you may run the risk of being squirted with gasoline.

On 1975 CVCC Sedan models, the filter is located beneath a special access cover under the rear seat on the driver's side. The rear seat can be removed after removing the bolt at the rear center of the cushion and then pivoting the seat forward from the rear.

REMOVAL & INSTALLATION

Carbureted
▶ **See Figures 27, 28 and 29**

CIVIC 1973-75 — 1237CC (AIR) ENGINES

The filter, together with the electric fuel pump, are located in the recess.

1. Remove the four screws retaining the access cover to the floor and remove the cover.
2. Pinch the lines shut, loosen the hose clamps and remove the filter.
3. To install, use a new filter and reverse the removal procedures.

ACCORD (WAGON), 1976-81 CVCC AND 1975-81 PRELUDE

The filter is located under the rear of the vehicle, in front of the spare tire, together with the electrical fuel pump.

1. Raise and support the rear of the vehicle.
2. Clamp off the fuel lines on both sides of the fuel filter.
3. Loosen the hose clamps and work the hoses off by twisting, taking note of which hose is the inlet and which is the outlet.
4. Remove the fuel filter.

➡Some replacement filters have an arrow embossed or printed on the filter body, in which case you want to install the new filter with the arrow pointing in the direction of fuel flow.

FRONT — 1982-83 MODELS
▶ **See Figures 30, 31, 32, 33 and 34**

1. Depress the tang and unclip the filter.
2. Loosen the fuel line clamps and slide them back.
3. Using a twisting motion, remove the fuel lines from the filter.

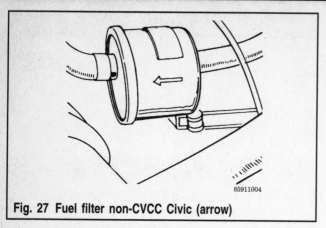

Fig. 27 Fuel filter non-CVCC Civic (arrow)

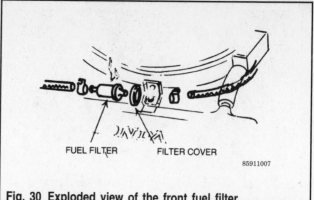

FUEL FILTER   FILTER COVER

Fig. 30 Exploded view of the front fuel filter

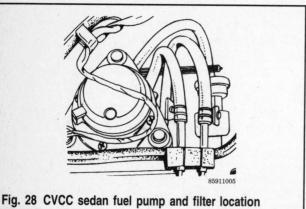

Fig. 28 CVCC sedan fuel pump and filter location

4. To install, use a new fuel filter and reverse the removal procedures. Start the engine and check for leaks.

REAR — 1982-83 MODELS

1. Raise and support the rear of the vehicle.
2. Push the fuel filter tab and release it from the holder.
3. Using two Fuel Line Clamp tools No. 07614-0050100 or equivalent, clamp off both fuel lines.
4. Loosen the fuel line clamps and slide them back.
5. Using a twisting motion, pull the fuel lines from the fuel filter, then, remove the filter.
6. To install, use a new filter and reverse the removal procedures. Start the engine and check for leaks.

Fig. 31 Removing the fuel filter hose clamp

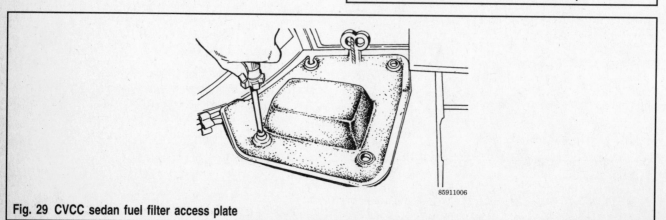

Fig. 29 CVCC sedan fuel filter access plate

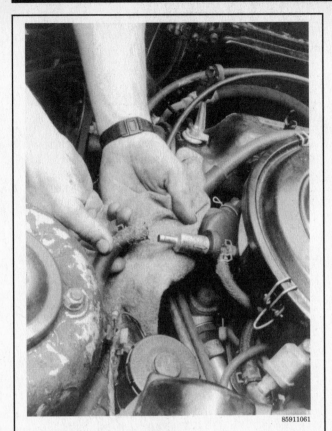

Fig. 32 Removing the fuel filter

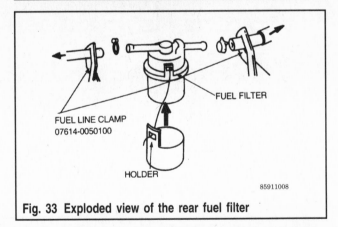

Fig. 33 Exploded view of the rear fuel filter

Positive Crankcase Ventilation (PCV)

The Honda is equipped with a Positive Crankcase Ventilation (PCV) system in which blow-by gas is returned to the combustion chamber through the intake manifold and/or the air cleaner.

REMOVAL & INSTALLATION

▶ See Figure 34

1. On 1973-75 models, squeeze the lower end of the drain tube and drain any oil or water which may have collected. Maintenance intervals are every 15,000 miles (1973-79 miles)

and 60,000 miles (1980-83 models). On 1976-82 models, remove the tube, invert and drain it; after all condensation has been drained, reinstall it.

2. Make sure that the intake manifold T-joint is clear. You first have to remove the air cleaner to where the joint is located. To clear the joint, pass the shank end of a drill of 0.9mm diameter through both ends (both orifices) of the joint.

3. Check for loose, disconnected or deteriorated tubes and replace if necessary. Make sure the hoses are clean inside, cleaning them with a safe solvent, if necessary. If the system has a condensation chamber attached to the bottom of the air cleaner, unscrew and remove the chamber, clean and replace it; when removing the top gasket from the chamber, note the angle of installation. Reinstall it in the same position to provide proper airflow.

4. The 1983 models use a regular PCV valve. Check the valve by pulling it out of the valve cover with the engine idling. Cover the open end of the valve with your finger so airflow is stopped. If the valve clicks, it is OK; if not, replace it.

For further information on the servicing of Honda emission control components, check Section 4.

Evaporative Charcoal Canister

The charcoal canister is part of the Evaporative Emission Control System. This system prevents the escape of raw gasoline vapors from the fuel tank and carburetor.

The charcoal canister is designed to absorb fuel vapors under certain conditions. For a more detailed description, see Section 4.

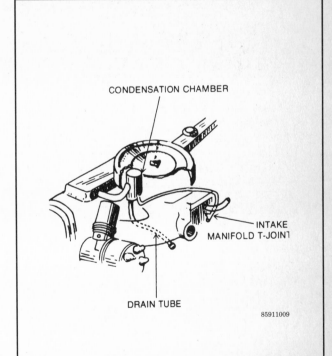

Fig. 34 Typical PCV system component locations-1973 model shown

The canister is a coffee can-sized object located in the engine compartment. Label the hoses leading to the canister before disconnecting them, then, remove the old canister from its mounting bracket and discard it. Install the new canister and connect the hoses as before.

SERVICING

Maintenance on the canister consists of testing and inspection at 12,000 mile intervals (1973-74 models), 15,000 mile intervals (1975-80 models) and replacement at 24,000 miles (1973-74 models) or 30,000 miles (1975-80 models). On the 1981-83 models, the canister does not require periodic replacement. The entire system requires a careful operational check with a vacuum gauge at 60,000 miles. See Section 4 for testing procedures.

Battery

FLUID LEVEL (EXCEPT MAINTENANCE FREE BATTERIES)

Check the battery electrolyte level at least once a month, or more often in hot weather or during periods of extended car operation. The level can be checked through the case on translucent polypropylene batteries; the cell caps must be removed on other models. The electrolyte level in each cell should be kept filled to the split ring inside, or the line marked on the outside of the case.

If the level is low, add only distilled water, or colorless, odorless drinking water, through the opening until the level is correct. Each cell is completely separate from the others, so each must be checked and filled individually.

If water is added in freezing weather, the car should be driven several miles to allow the water to mix with the electrolyte. Otherwise, the battery could freeze.

SPECIFIC GRAVITY (EXCEPT MAINTENANCE FREE BATTERIES)

▶ See Figures 35, 36 and 37

At least once a year, check the specific gravity of the battery. It should be between 1.20 in. Hg and 1.26 in. Hg at room temperature.

The specific gravity can be check with the use of an hydrometer, an inexpensive instrument available from many sources, including auto parts stores. The hydrometer has a squeeze bulb at one end and a nozzle at the other. Battery electrolyte is sucked into the hydrometer until the float is lifted from its seat. The specific gravity is then read by noting the position of the float. Generally, if after charging, the specific gravity between any two cells varies more than 50 points (0.50), the battery is bad and should be replaced.

It is not possible to check the specific gravity in this manner on sealed (maintenance free) batteries. Instead, the indicator built into the top of the case must be relied on to display any signs of battery deterioration. If the indicator is dark, the bat-

tery can be assumed to be OK. If the indicator is light, the specific gravity is low, and the battery should be charged or replaced.

CABLES AND CLAMPS

▶ See Figures 38, 39, 40, 41, 42, 43 and 44

Once a year, the battery terminals and the cable clamps should be cleaned. Loosen the clamps and remove the cables, negative cable first. On batteries with posts on top, the use of a puller specially made for the purpose is recommended. These are inexpensive, and available in auto parts stores. Side terminal battery cables are secured with a bolt.

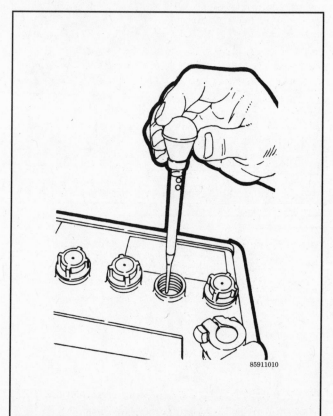

85911010

Fig. 35 An inexpensive hydrometer will quickly test the state of the charge of the battery

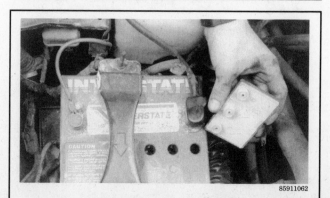

85911062

Fig. 36 Checking the fluid level in battery

Fig. 37 Checking the battery cables for corrosion

Clean the cable clamps and the battery terminal with a wire brush, battery tool, or small knife, until all corrosion, grease, etc., is removed and the metal is shiny. It is especially important to clean the inside of the clamp thoroughly, since a small deposit of foreign material or oxidation there will prevent a sound electrical connection and inhibit either starting or charging. Special tools are available for cleaning these parts, one type for conventional batteries and another type for side terminal batteries.

Before installing the cables, loosen the battery hold down clamp or strap, remove the battery and check the battery tray. Clear it of any debris, and check it for soundness. Rust should be wire brushed away, and the metal given a coat of anti-rust paint. Replace the battery and tighten the hold down clamp or strap securely, but be careful not to over tighten, which will crack the battery case.

Fig. 38 Battery maintenance items include baking soda to neutralize spilled acid and a post and terminal cleaner

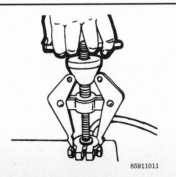

Fig. 39 Top terminal battery cables are easily removed with this inexpensive puller

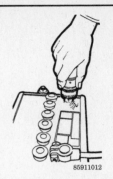

Fig. 40 Clean the battery posts with a wire terminal cleaner

Fig. 41 Clean the cable ends with a stiff cable cleaning tool

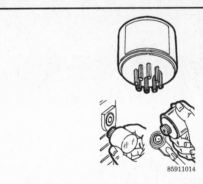

Fig. 42 Side terminal batteries require a special wire brush for cleaning

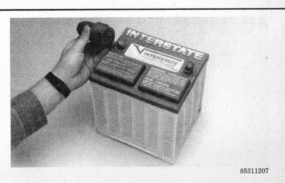

Fig. 43 The underside of this special battery tool has a wire brush to clean post terminals

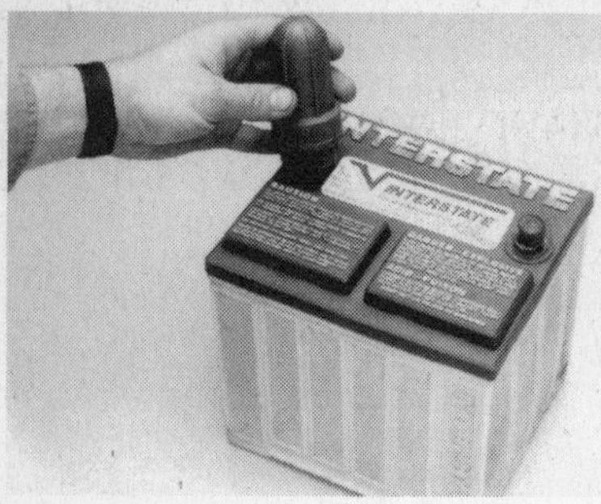

85311208

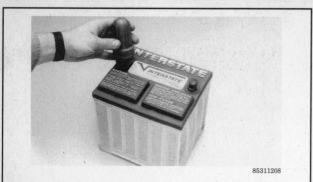

Fig. 44 Place the tool over the terminals and twist to clean the post

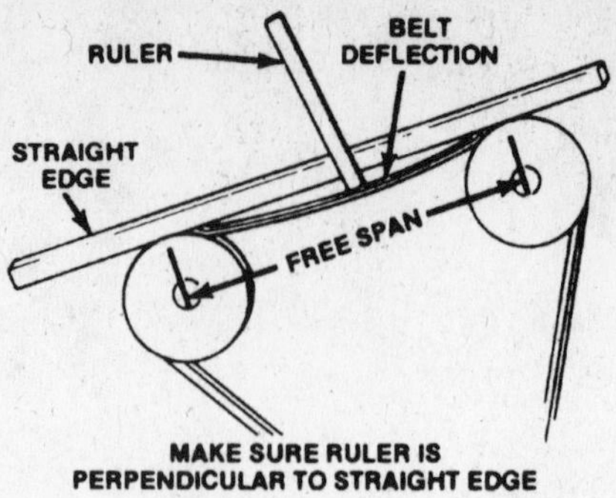

85911015

Fig. 45 Measuring belt deflection

After the clamps and terminals are clean, reinstall the cables, negative cable last; do not hammer on the clamps to install. Tighten the clamps securely, but do not distort them. Give the clamps and terminals a thin external coat of grease after installation, to retard corrosion.

Check the cables at the same time that the terminals are cleaned. If the cable insulation is cracked or broken, or if the ends are frayed, the cable should be replaced with a new cable of the same length and gauge.

CAUTION

Keep flame or sparks away from the battery; it gives off explosive hydrogen gas. Battery electrolyte contains sulfuric acid. If you should splash any on your skin or in your eyes, flush the affected area with plenty of clear water. If it lands in your eyes, get medical help immediately.

Belts

INSPECTION

See Figure 45

On the 1973-79 models, adjust the drive belt(s) after the first 3,000 miles, afterwards, inspect the belt(s) every 12,000 miles/12 months for evidence of wear such as cracking, fraying and/or incorrect tension; on the 1980-83 models, inspect the drive belt(s) every 30,000 miles/24 months. Determine the belt tension at a point halfway between the pulleys by pressing on the belt with moderate thumb pressure. The belt should deflect about 1/4″ over a 7-10″ span or 1/2″ over a 13-16″ span, at this point. If the deflection is found to be too much or too little, perform the tension adjustments.

CHECKING AND ADJUSTING TENSION

See Figures 46, 47, 48 and 49

Before adjusting, inspect the belt to see that it is not cracked or worn. Be sure that its surfaces are free of grease and oil.

1. Push down on the belt halfway between pulleys with moderate force. The belt should deflect approximately 1/2″. Deflection should be slightly less with a new belt as tension is lost rapidly for the first 1/2 hour or so of operation.
2. If the belt tension requires adjustment, loosen the adjusting link bolt and move the alternator with a pry bar positioned against the front of the alternator housing. On 1983 models, loosen the top mounting bolt and then turn the adjusting nut outboard of the alternator. This will reposition the alternator without prying.
3. When the belt tension is correct tighten the upper mounting bolt to about 16 ft. lbs. Recheck the tension, correcting the adjustment if necessary.

➡Do not apply pressure to any other part of the alternator.

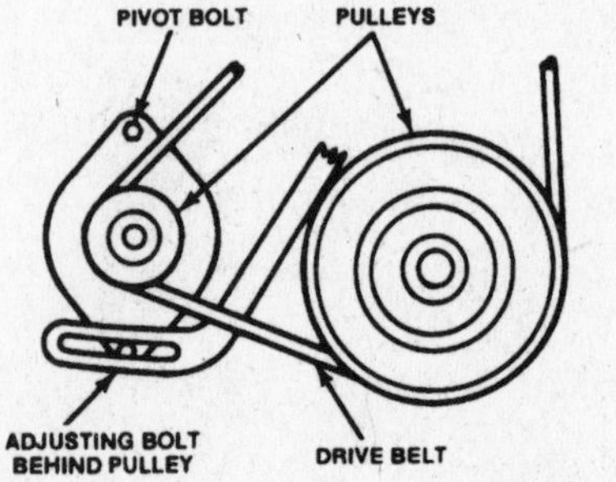

85911016

Fig. 46 Some accessories can be moved only if the pivot bolt is loosened

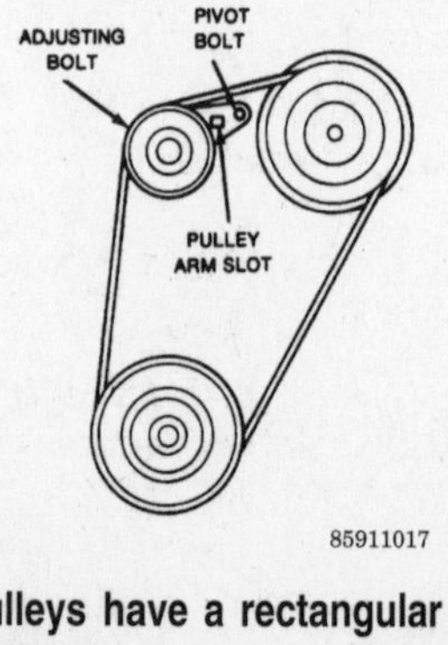

85911017

Fig. 47 Some pulleys have a rectangular slot to aid in moving the accessory

Fig. 48 Adjusting the typical drive belt

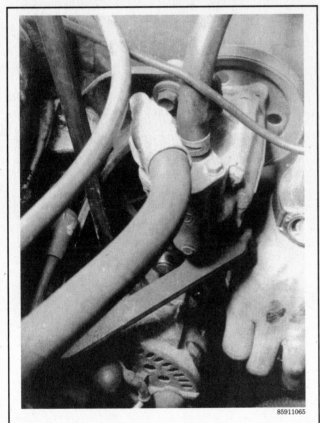

Fig. 49 Adjusting the alternator belt

REMOVAL & INSTALLATION

1. Loosen the component-to-mounting bracket bolts.
2. Rotate the component to relieve the tension on the drive belt.
3. Slip the drive belt from the component pulley and remove it from the engine.

➡If the engine uses more than one belt, it may be necessary to remove other belts that are in front of the one being removed.

4. To install, reverse the removal procedures. Adjust the component drive belt tension to specifications.

Hoses

The upper/lower radiator hoses and all heater hoses should be checked for deterioration, leaks and loose hose clamps every 15,000 miles/12 months (1973-79) or 30,000 miles/24 months (1980-83).

REMOVAL & INSTALLATION

▶ **See Figure 50**

1. Drain the cooling system.

✳✳CAUTION

When draining the coolant, keep in mind that cats and dogs are attracted by the ethylene glycol antifreeze, and are quite likely to drink any that is left in an uncovered container or in puddles on the ground. This will prove fatal in sufficient quantities. Always drain the coolant into a sealable container. Coolant should be reused unless it is contaminated or several years old.

2. Loosen the hose clamps at each end of the hose.
3. Working the hose back and forth, slide it off it's connection, then, install a new hose, if necessary.

➡When replacing the heater hoses, maintain a 1½″ clearance from any surface.

4. To install, reverse the removal procedures. Refill the cooling system.

➡Draw the hoses tight to prevent sagging or rubbing against other components; route the hoses through the clamps as installed originally. Always make sure that the hose clamps are beyond the component bead and placed in the center of the clamping surface before tightening them.

Fig. 50 Removing the heater hose clamps

Air Conditioning System

➡ R-12 refrigerant is a chlorofluorocarbon which, when released into the atmosphere, contributes to the depletion of the ozone layer in the upper atmosphere. Ozone filters out harmful radiation from the sun. Consult the laws in your area before servicing the air conditioning system. In some states it is illegal to perform repairs involving refrigerant unless the work is done by a certified technician and a recovery/recycling equipment meeting Society of Automotive Engineers (SAE) Standard J 1991 is used.

SAFETY WARNINGS

Because of the importance of the necessary safety precautions that must be exercised when working with air conditioning systems and R-12 refrigerant, a recap of the safety precautions are outlined.

• Avoid contact with a charged refrigeration system, even when working on another part of the air conditioning system or vehicle. If a heavy tool comes into contact with a section of copper tubing or a heat exchanger, it can easily cause the relatively soft material to rupture.

• When it is necessary to apply force to a fitting which contains refrigerant, as when checking that all system couplings are securely tightened, use a wrench on both parts of the fitting involved, if possible. This will avoid putting torque on the refrigerant tubing. It is advisable, when possible, to use tube or line wrenches when tightening these flare nut fittings.

• Discharge the system using a recovery/recycling station meeting Society of Automotive Engineers (SAE) Standard J 1991. Do not allow regrigerent to escape the system and enter the atmosphere.

• Never start a system without first verifying that both service valves are back-seated (if equipped) and that all fittings throughout the system are snugly connected.

• Avoid applying heat to any refrigerant line or storage vessel. Charging may be aided by using water heated to less than 125°F to warm the refrigerant container. Never allow a refrigerant storage container to sit out in the sun or near any other heat source, such as a radiator.

• Always wear goggles when working on a system to protect the eyes. If refrigerant contacts the eyes, it is advisable in all cases to see a physician as soon as possible.

• Frostbite from liquid refrigerant should be treated by first gradually warming the area with cool water, then, gently apply petroleum jelly. A physician should be consulted.

• Always keep the refrigerant drum fittings capped when not in use. Avoid any sudden shock to the drum, which might occur from dropping it or from banging a heavy tool against it. Never carry a drum in the passenger compartment of a vehicle.

• Always completely discharge the system before painting the vehicle (if paint is to be baked on), or before welding anywhere near the refrigerant lines.

➡Any repair work to an air conditioning system should be left to a professional. DO NOT, under any circumstances, attempt to loosen or tighten any fitting or perform any work other than that outlined here.

SYSTEM INSPECTION

Checking For Oil Leaks

Refrigerant leaks show up as oily areas on the various components because the compressor oil is transported around the entire system along with the refrigerant. Look for oily spots on all the hoses and lines, especially on the hose and tubing connections. If there are oily deposits, the system may have a leak, have it checked by a qualified repairman.

➡A small area of oil on the front of the compressor is normal and no cause for alarm.

Checking The Compressor Belt

Refer to the Drive Belt section in this section.

Keep The Condenser Clear

Periodically inspect the front of the condenser for bent fins or foreign material (dirt, bugs, leaves, etc.). If any cooling fins are bent, straighten them carefully with needlenose pliers. You can remove any debris with a stiff bristle brush or hose.

Operate The Air Conditioning System Periodically

A lot of air conditioning problems can be avoided by simply running the air conditioner at least once a week regardless of the season. Simply let the system run for a least 5 minutes a week (even in the winter) and you'll keep the internal parts lubricated as well as preventing the hoses from hardening.

Leak Testing the System
▶ See Figure 51

There are several methods of detecting leaks in an air conditioning system; among them, the two most popular are (1) halide leak detection or the open flame method and (2) electronic leak detector.

The Halide Leak Detection tool No. J-6084 or equivalent, is a torch like device which produces a yellow-green color when refrigerant is introduced into the flame at the burner. A purple or violet color indicates the presence of large amounts of refrigerant at the burner.

An Autobalance Refrigerant Leak Detector tool No. J-29547 or equivalent, is a small portable electronic device with an extended probe. With the unit activated, the probe is passed along those components of the system which contain refrigerant. If a leak is detected, the unit will sound an alarm signal or activate a display signal depending on the manufacturer's instructions as the design and function of the detection may vary significantly.

❋❋CAUTION

Care should be taken to operate either type of detector in well ventilated areas, so as to reduce the chance of personal injury, which may result from coming in contact with poisonous gases produced when R-12 is exposed to flame or electric spark.

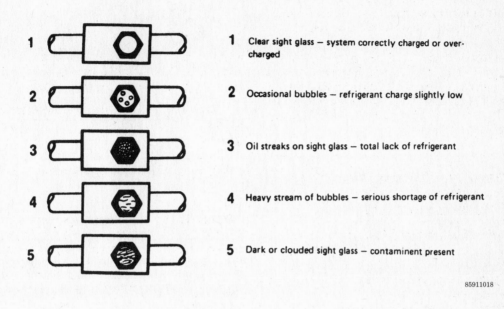

1 Clear sight glass – system correctly charged or over-
   charged

2 Occasional bubbles – refrigerant charge slightly low

3 Oil streaks on sight glass – total lack of refrigerant

4 Heavy stream of bubbles – serious shortage of refrigerant

5 Dark or clouded sight glass – contaminent present

85911018

Fig. 51 Sight glass inspection

GAUGE SETS

▶ **See Figure 52**

Most of the service work performed in air conditioning requires the use of a set of two gauges, one for the high (head) pressure side of the system, the other for the low (suction) side.

The low side gauge records both pressure and vacuum. Vacuum readings are calibrated from 0-30 in. Hg and the pressure graduations read from 0-60 psi.

The high side gauge measures pressure from 0-600 psi.

Both gauges are threaded into a manifold that contains two hand shut-off valves. Proper manipulation of these valves and the use of the attached test hoses allow the user to perform the following services:

1. Test high and low side pressures.
2. Remove air, moisture and/or contaminated refrigerant.

The manifold valves are designed so they have no direct effect on the gauge readings but serve only to provide for or cut off the flow of refrigerant through the manifold. During all testing and hook-up operations, the valves are kept in a Closed position to avoid disturbing the refrigeration system.

Service Valves
▶ **See Figure 53**

For the user to diagnose an air conditioning system, he or she must gain entrance to the system in order to observe the pressures; the type of terminal for this purpose is the Schrader valve.

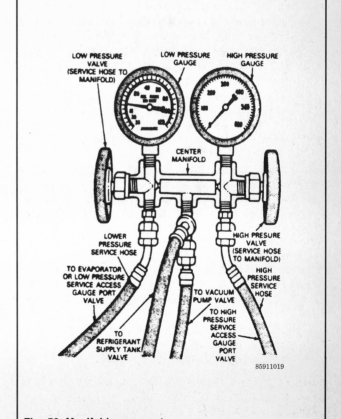

Fig. 52 Manifold gauge set

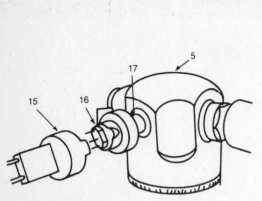

5. Accumulator
15. Electrical connector
16. Pressure cycling switch adjusting screw
17. "Schrader" type valve

85911021

Fig. 53 View of the A/C accumulator with the Schrader valve

The Schrader valve is similar to a tire valve stem and the process of connecting the test hoses is the same as threading a hand pump outlet hose to a bicycle tire. As the test hose is threaded to the service port the valve core is depressed, allowing the refrigerant to enter the test hose outlet. Removal of the test hose automatically closes the system.

Extreme caution must be observed when removing the test hoses from the Schrader valves as some refrigerant will normally escape, usually under high pressure; observe safety precautions.

Using the Manifold Gauges

The following are step-by-step procedures to guide the user to the correct gauge usage.

❊❊CAUTION

Wear goggles or face shield during all testing operations. Backseat hand shut-off type service valves.

1. Remove the caps from the high and low side service ports. Make sure both gauge valves are Closed.
2. Connect the low side test hose to the service valve that leads to the evaporator (located between the evaporator outlet and the compressor).
3. Attach the high side test hose to the service valve that leads to the condenser.
4. Mid-position the hand shutoff type service valves.
5. Start the engine allow it to warm-up. All testing of the system should be done after the engine and system has

reached normal operating temperatures (except when using certain charging stations).

6. Adjust the air conditioner controls to Max. Cold.
7. Observe the gauge readings. When the gauges are not being used it is a good idea to:
   a. Keep both hand valves in the Closed position.
   b. Attach both ends of the high and low service hoses to the manifold, if extra outlets are present on the manifold or plug them (if not).

DISCHARGING THE SYSTEM

Discharging the refrigerant from the air conditioning system should be performed by a qualified facility equipped with recovery/recycling equipment meeting Society of Automotive Engineers (SAE) Standard J 1991.

EVACUATING THE SYSTEM

Before charging any system it is necessary to purge the refrigerant and draw out the trapped moisture with a suitable vacuum pump. Failure to do so will result in ineffective charging and possible damage to the system.

1. Connect both service gauge hoses to the high and low service outlets. Connect a recovery/recharging station to the system as outlined in the information supplied with the unit in use.
2. Discharge the air conditioning system using the a recovery/recycling station. Do not allow the refrigerant to discharge into the atmosphere.
3. Install the center charging hose of the gauge set to the vacuum pump.
4. Operate the vacuum pump for at least one hour. If the system has been subjected to open conditions for a prolonged period of time, it may be necessary to pump the system down overnight. Refer to the System Sweep procedure.

➡**If the low pressure gauge does not show at least 28 in. Hg within 5 minutes, check the system for a leak or loose gauge connectors.**

5. Close the hand valves on the gauge manifold.
6. Turn Off the pump.
7. Observe the low pressure gauge to determine if the vacuum is holding. A vacuum drop may indicate a leak.

System Sweep

An efficient vacuum pump can remove all the air contained in a contaminated air conditioning system very quickly, because of its vapor state. Moisture, however, is far more difficult to remove because the vacuum must force the liquid to evaporate before it will be able to be removed from the system. If the system has become severely contaminated, as it might become after all the charge was lost in conjunction with vehicle accident damage, moisture removal is extremely time consuming. A vacuum pump could remove all of the moisture only if it were operated for 12 hours or more.

Under these conditions, sweeping the system with refrigerant will speed the process of moisture removal considerably. To sweep, follow the following procedure:

1. Connect the vacuum pump to the gauges, operate it until the vacuum ceases to increase, then, continue the operation for ten or more minutes.
2. Charge the system with 50% of its rated refrigerant capacity.
3. Operate the system at fast idle for 10 minutes.
4. Discharge the system using a recovery/recycling station.
5. Repeat (twice) the process of charging to 50% capacity, running the system for ten minutes, then, discharge it for a total of three sweeps.
6. Replace the drier.
7. Pump the system down as in Step 1.
8. Charge the system.

CHARGING

➡️**Charging the air conditioning system should be performed by a qualified facility equipped with recovery/recycling equipment meeting Society of Automotive Engineers (SAE) Standard J 1991.**

❋❋CAUTION

Never attempt to charge the system by opening the high pressure gauge control while the compressor is operating. The compressor accumulating pressure can burst the refrigerant container, causing severe personal injuries.

1. Start the engine, operate it with the choke Open and normal idle speed, then, position the air conditioning control lever Off.
2. Allow about 1 lb. of refrigerant to enter the system through the low side service fitting on the accumulator.
3. After the 1 lb. of refrigerant enters the system, position the control lever to Normal (the compressor will engage) and the blower motor on Hi speed; this operation will draw the remainder of the refrigerant into the system.

➡️**To speed up the operation, position a fan in front of the condenser; the lowering of the condenser temperature will allow refrigerant to enter the system faster.**

4. When the system is charged, turn Off the refrigerant source and allow the engine to run for 30 seconds to clear the lines and gauges.
5. With the engine running, remove the hose adapter from the accumulator service fitting (unscrew the hose quickly to prevent refrigerant from escaping).

❋❋CAUTION

Never remove the gauge line from the adapter when the line is connected to the system; always remove the line adapter from the service fitting first.

6. Replace the accumulator protective caps and turn the engine Off.

7. Using a leak detector, inspect the air conditioning system for leaks. If a leak is present, repair it.

Windshield Wipers

REPLACING WIPER BLADES

▶ **See Figures 54, 55, 56, 57 and 58**

For maximum effectiveness and longest element life, the windshield and wiper blades should be kept clean. Dirt, tree sap, road tar and etc. will cause streaking, smearing and blade deterioration, if left on the glass. It is advisable to wash the windshield carefully with a commercial glass cleaner at least once a month. Wipe off the rubber blades with the wet rag, afterwards.

If the blades are found to be cracked, broken or torn, they should be replaced immediately. Replacement intervals will vary with usage, although ozone deterioration usually limits blade life to about one year. If the wiper pattern is smeared, streaked or if the blade chatters across the glass, the elements should be replaced. It is easiest and most sensible to replace the elements in pairs.

1. To replace the blade elements, detach the wiper blade assembly from the arm or raise the wiper arm assemblies.
2. On some models, press together the two sides of the metal locking tab at one end of the assembly and slide the blade out. On other models, simply separate the rubber element from the wiper blade.

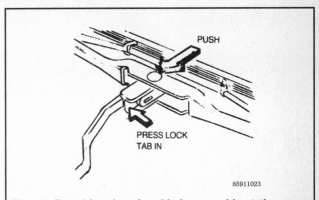

Fig. 54 Detaching the wiper blade assembly at the arm

Fig. 55 Release the retainer at the end of the blade by depressing the two halves of the clip

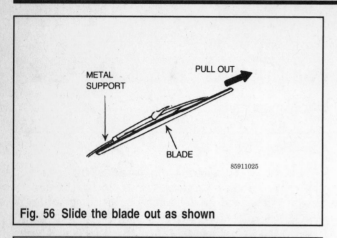

Fig. 56 Slide the blade out as shown

Fig. 57 Removing wiper blade retaining clip

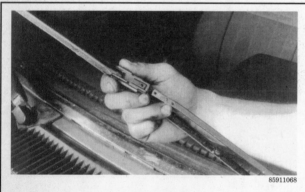

Fig. 58 Removing the wiper blade

3. Using a new rubber element, reverse the removal procedures.

➡️If using the locking tab type, slide the blade in until the locking click is heard.

Tires and Wheels

TIRE INFLATION

Tire inflation is the most ignored item of auto maintenance. Gasoline mileage can drop as much as 0.8% for every 1 psi of under inflation.

Two items should be a permanent fixture in every glove compartment: a tire pressure gauge and a tread depth gauge. Check the tire pressure (including the spare) regularly with a pocket type gauge. Kicking the tires won't tell you a thing, and the gauge on the service station air hose is notoriously inaccurate.

A plate located on the door or in glove box will tell the proper pressure for the tires. Ideally, inflation pressure should be checked when the tires are cool. When the air becomes heated it expands and the pressure increases. Every 10°F rise (or drop) in temperature means a difference of 1 psi, which also explains why the tire appears to lose air on a very cold night. When it is impossible to check the tires **Cold**, allow for pressure build-up due to heat. If the **Hot** pressure exceeds the **Cold** pressure by more than 15 psi, reduce vehicle speed, load or both. Otherwise internal heat is created in the tire. When the heat approaches the temperature at which the tire was cured, during manufacture, the tread can separate from the body.

✳✳CAUTION

Never counteract excessive pressure build-up by bleeding off air pressure (letting some air out). This will only further raise the tire operating temperature.

Before starting a long trip with lots of luggage, you can add about 2-4 psi to the tires to make them run cooler but never exceed the maximum inflation pressure on the side of the tire.

TIRE DESIGN

For maximum satisfaction, tires should be used in sets of five. Mixing of different types (radial, bias-belted, fiberglass belted) should be avoided.

Conventional bias tires are constructed so that the cords run bead-to-bead at an angle. This type of construction gives rigidity to both tread and sidewall.

Bias-belted tires are similar in construction to conventional bias ply tires. Belts run at an angle and also at a 90° angle to the bead, as in the radial tire. Tread life is improved considerably over the conventional bias tire. The radial tire differs in construction but instead of the carcass plies running at an angle of 90° to each other, they run at an angle of 90° to the bead. This gives the tread a great deal of flexibility and accounts for the characteristic bulge associated with radial tires.

If radial tires are used, tire sizes and wheel diameters should be selected to maintain ground clearance and tire load capacity equivalent to the minimum specified tire. Radial tires should always be used in sets of five but in an emergency, radial tires can be used with caution on the rear axle only. If this is done, both tires on the rear should be of radial design.

✳✳CAUTION

Radial tires should never be used on only the front axle.

Snow tires should not be operated at sustained speeds over 70 mph.

On four wheel drive vehicles, all tires must be of the same size, type and tread pattern, to provide even traction on loose surfaces, to prevent driveline bind when conventional four wheel drive is used and to prevent excessive wear on the center differential with full time four wheel drive.

TREAD DEPTH

▶ **See Figures 59, 60 and 61**

All tires made since 1968, have 8 built-in tread wear indicator bars that show up as ½″ wide smooth bands across the tire when ¹⁄₁₆″ of tread remains. The appearance of tread wear indicators means that the tires should be replaced. In fact, many states have laws prohibiting the use of tires with less than ¹⁄₁₆″ tread.

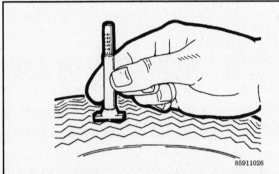

Fig. 59 Checking tread with an inexpensive depth gauge

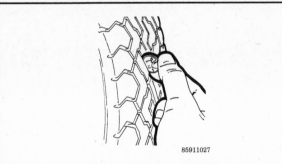

Fig. 60 Tread depth can be checked with a penny; when the top of Lincoln's head is visible, it's time for new tires

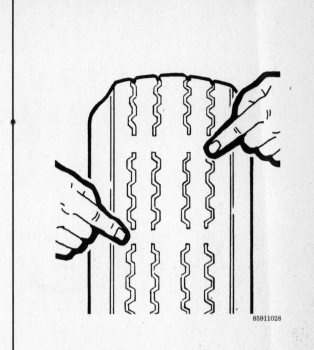

Fig. 61 Since 1968 wear indicators have been built into tires. When these bands become visible on the tire's surface, replace the tire

You can check your own tread depth with an inexpensive gauge or by using a Lincoln head penny. Slip the Lincoln penny into several tread grooves. If you can see the top of Lincoln's head in 2 adjacent grooves, the tires have less than ¹⁄₁₆″ tread left and should be replaced. You can measure snow tires in the same manner by using the 'tails' side of the Lincoln penny. If you can see the top of the Lincoln memorial, it's time to replace the snow tires.

TIRE ROTATION

▶ **See Figure 62**

Tires must be rotated periodically to equalize wear patterns that vary with a tire's position on the vehicle. Tires will also wear in an uneven way as the front steering/suspension system wears to the point where the alignment should be reset. Rotating the tires will ensure maximum life for the tires as a set, as you will not have to discard a tire early due to wear on only part of the tread.

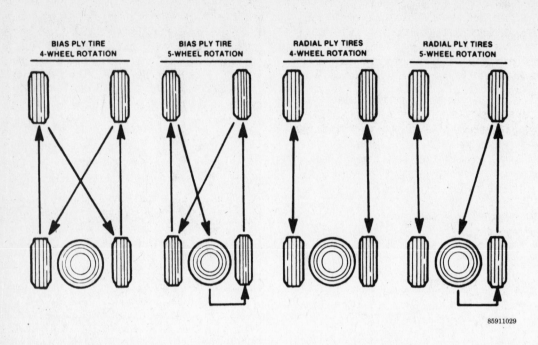

Fig. 62 Tire rotation diagrams

The cardinal rule to follow with radials is to make sure that they always roll in the same direction. This means that a tire used on the left side of the vehicle must not be switched to the right side and vice-versa. If a tire or tires is removed from a running position on the vehicle for a time for use as a spare or because of seasonal use of snow tires, make sure to clearly mark the wheel as to the side of the vehicle it was used on and to observe the mark when reinstalling the tire(s).

➡**Recently the cardinal rule has been re-written and tire manufacturers have begun recommending cross rotating radials. The best recommendation I can make, if your're not sure, is to check with the tire manufacturer of the tires currently on your Honda.**

TIRE STORAGE

Store the tires at proper inflation pressure if they are mounted on wheels. All tires should be kept in a cool, dry place. If they are stored in the garage or basement, do not let them stand on a concrete floor, set them on strips of wood.

FLUIDS AND LUBRICANTS

Fuel and Engine Oil Recommendations

FUEL

All 1973-79 Hondas are designed to run on regular gasoline. High octane (premium) gasoline is not required. This is permitted because the engines uses the CVCC combustion system, thereby avoiding the catalytic converter. The octane number is used as a measure of the anti-knock properties of a gasoline and the use of a higher octane gasoline than that which is necessary to prevent engine knock is simply a waste of money. If your Honda does knock (usually heard as a pinging noise), it is probably a matter of improper ignition timing, in which case you should check Section 2 for the proper adjustment procedure. You might also want to check that the EGR system is functioning properly (see Section 4).

The 1980-83 models use a catalytic converter even if the engine uses the CVCC system. This is because of increasingly stringent emissions standards. While unleaded gas is usually more expensive than leaded, there are many side benefits, including better fuel economy, less dirt in the engine oil and longer exhaust system life. Since the use of leaded fuel will damage the catalytic converter, it **does not pay** to attempt to bypass the narrow filler opening for the fuel tank and run the vehicle on leaded fuel. Little more than a single tankful will render the converter ineffective and may cause it to clog the exhaust system and affect engine operation.

You should be careful to use quality fuels having an octane rating of 86 when measured by the R/M method, which averages 'Research' and 'Motor' octane ratings. Too low an octane rating will produce combustion knock, which will prove to be damaging to the engine over a long period. Always buy fuel from a reputable dealer, preferably where a regular volume is pumped so that the fuel is always fresh.

OIL

♦ **See Figures 63 and 64**

When using engine oil, there are two types of ratings with which you should be familiar: viscosity and service (quality). There are several service ratings, resulting from tests established by the American Petroleum Institute. Use only SE rated oil or SF (for better fuel economy). SF oil passes SE requirements and also reduces fuel consumption. No other service ratings are acceptable.

Oil can be purchased with two types of viscosity ratings, single and multi-viscosity. Oil viscosity ratings are important because oil tends to thin out at high temperatures while getting too thick and stiff at low temperatures. Single viscosity oil, designated by only one number (SAE 30), varies in viscosity or thickness, a great deal over a wide range of temperatures. The single rating number comes from the fact that the oil is basically a single, straight grade of petroleum. A multi-viscosity oil rating is given as two numbers (for example: SAE 10W-40, the **W** standing for **winter**). Multi-viscosity oils slow changes in

viscosity with temperature. These changes occur with changes in engine temperature conditions, such as cold starts versus eventual engine warm-up and operation. The double designation refers to the fact that the oil behaves like straight 10W oil at 0°F and like straight 40W oil at 200°F. The desirable advantage of multi-viscosity oil is that it can maintain adequate thickness at high engine operating temperatures (when oil tends to get too thin) while it resists the tendency to thicken at very low temperatures. A straight 30 oil gets so thick near 0°F. that the engine will usually not crank fast enough to start. Because of its versatility, a multi-viscosity oil would be the more desirable choice.

When adding oil, try to use the same brand that's in the crankcase since not all oils are completely compatible with each other.

Engine

OIL LEVEL CHECK

♦ **See Figures 65, 66 and 67**

Checking the oil level is one of the simplest and most important checks. It should be done FREQUENTLY because low oil level can lead to oil pan or even engine overheating and eventual starvation of the oil pump. This can mean inadequate lubrication and *immediate, severe* engine damage. Because oil consumption patterns of an engine can change quickly and unexpectedly due to leakage or changes in the weather, check the oil every time you stop for fuel.

➡**If the engine has been running, allow it to rest for a few minutes until the oil accumulates in the sump, before checking the oil level.**

1. Raise the hood, pull the oil dipstick from the engine and wipe it clean.
2. Insert the dipstick into the engine until it is fully seated, then, remove it and check the reading.

➡**The oil level on all Hondas should register within the crosshatch design on the dipstick or between the two lines, depending on the type of stick.**

3. Oil is added through the capped opening of the rocker arm cover. Do not add oil if the level is significantly above the lower line or lower edge of the crosshatch. If the level is near

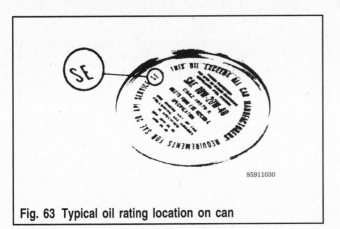

Fig. 63 Typical oil rating location on can

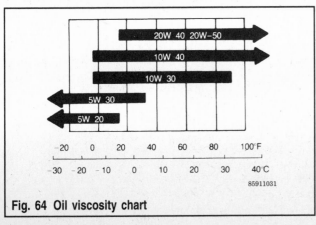

Fig. 64 Oil viscosity chart

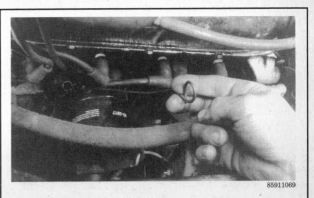

Fig. 65 Checking the engine oil

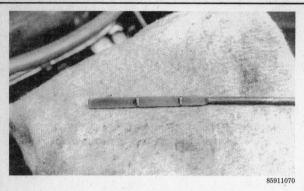

Fig. 66 Engine oil dipstick level marks

Fig. 67 Adding engine oil

or below the crosshatch or lower line, ADD oil but do not overfill. The length covered by the crosshatching on the dipstick is roughly equivalent to one quart of oil.

➡Refer to the "Engine Oil and Fuel Recommendations" in this section for the proper viscosity oil to use.

4. If oil has been added, replace the dipstick and recheck the level. It is important to avoid overfilling the crankcase because doing so will cause the oil to foam due to the motion of the crankshaft, affecting lubrication and may also harm the engine oil seals.

OIL AND FILTER CHANGE

▶ See Figures 68, 69, 70, 71, 72 and 73

After the initial 600 miles oil and filter change, the oil should be changed every 3,000 miles/3 months (severe conditions), 5,000 miles/6 months (1973-79) or 7,500 miles/6 months (1980-83), whichever comes first. The oil filter should be changed at every oil change! Remember the 'You can pay me now or pay me later' commercials you've seen on TV? If your going to skimp on anything, do let it be your intervals for changing oil. Be certain to use a high quality oil and filter.

1. Before changing the oil, see that the vehicle is situated on a flat surface with the engine warmed; warm oil will flow more freely from the oil pan.

2. Turn the engine Off, open the hood and remove the oil filler cap from the top of the engine valve cover.

✳✳CAUTION

Hot oil can burn you. Keep an inward pressure on the plug until the last thread is cleared, then, quickly remove it.

3. Place a container under the oil pan; large enough to catch the oil. A large, flat drain pan is the most desirable.

✳✳CAUTION

The EPA warns that prolonged contact with used engine oil may cause a number of skin disorders, including cancer! You should make every effort to minimize your exposure to used engine oil. Protective gloves should be worn when changing the oil. Wash your hands and any other exposed skin areas as soon as possible after exposure to used engine oil. Soap and water, or waterless hand cleaner should be used.

4. Remove the oil drain plug and allow the oil to drain completely. When the oil has finished draining, install the drain plug tight enough to prevent oil leakage, use a new washer (if necessary) on the plug.

➡Only oil filters which have an integral by-pass should be used when replacing the filter. Also note that before removing the filter it is advisable to have an oil filter wrench which is inexpensive and makes the job much easier.

5. Move the oil drain pan under the oil filter; the filter retains some oil which will drain when it is removed.

6. Using an oil filter wrench, loosen the filter, then, unscrew it by hand.

7. Using a clean cloth, wipe the filter mounting surface of the cylinder block. Apply a thin coat of clean oil to the new filter gasket and install the filter.

➡Hand-tighten the filter only; DO NOT use a wrench for tightening. If the filter has instruction printed on it as to how far it should be tightened (for example ½ or ¾ turn), mark the filter, then, tighten it accordingly.

8. Remove the drain pan from under the engine.

Fig. 68 Replacing the engine oil filter

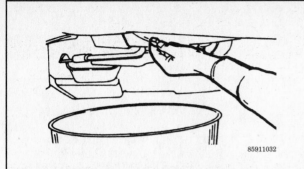

Fig. 69 By keeping inward pressure on the plug as you unscrew it, oil won't escape past the threads

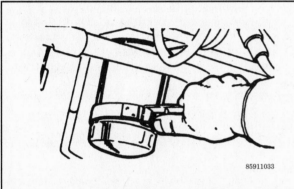

Fig. 70 Remove the oil filter with a strap wrench

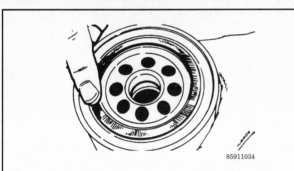

Fig. 71 Lubricate the gasket on the new filter with a clean engine oil. A dry gasket may not make a good seal and will allow the filter to leak

9. Add the correct amount of recommended oil into the oil filler hole on top of the valve cover. Be sure that the oil level registers near the full line on the oil dipstick.

10. Replace the filler cap, start the engine without touching the accelerator pedal and allow it to idle. The oil pressure light on the instrument panel should go out after a few seconds of running.

11. Run the engine for 1-2 minutes and check for leaks. Turn the engine Off, then, after a few minutes, recheck the oil level; add oil (if necessary). Be sure to check for oil leaks and

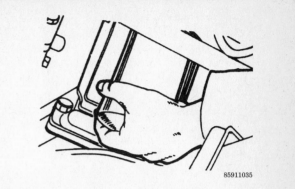

Fig. 72 Install the new oil filter by hand

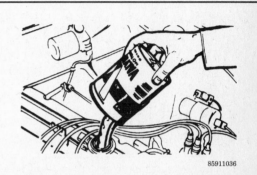

Fig. 73 Add oil through the capped opening in the cylinder head cover

fix any problems, as this is a common problem on early production models using the Japanese filter.

➡If the filter leaks lightly, gently turn it just a bit more but don't turn it really tight. If it still leaks, try another filter.

12. Recheck and/or refill the engine with oil.

Manual Transaxles

FLUID RECOMMENDATIONS

All manual transaxles use engine oil labeled for SE use. On the 1973-79 models, use 10W-40 oil. On the 1980-83 models 10W-30 or 10W-40 viscosity; the 10W-40 viscosity is the safer recommendation, especially driving frequency is at high speeds for prolonged periods in hot weather.

LEVEL CHECK

On the 1973-74 models, the transaxle fluid should be checked about once a month and replaced the first 3,000 miles, then, every 24,000 miles thereafter. On the 1975-79 models, replace the fluid at 15,000 miles, then, every 30,000 miles thereafter. On the 1980-83 models, replace the fluid every 30,000 miles.

The 1973-75 4-speed transaxle, uses a threaded dipstick with a crosshatch pattern. The dipstick is located beneath the battery. To check the fluid level, remove the dipstick, wipe it off and reinsert it ***without turning it inward.*** That is, make sure the threads on the dipstick itself are sitting on top of the threads in the transaxle housing. Approximately ¾ qt. will bring the fluid level from the ADD (lower) to the FULL (upper) line.

1976-77 Models

On the 1976-77 models, a special check bolt in the side of the transaxle is used.

1. To check the fluid level, turn the check bolt outward until fluid begins to flow from the transaxle or several turns, ***stopping the flat side of the bolt facing upwards.***

2. If fluid runs out, retighten the check bolt; if not, loosen the filler cap and pour oil in slowly until it begins to run out via the level check bolt. Then, tighten the bolt and filler cap.

All Other Models

1. Remove the oil level check bolt from the side of the transaxle. If oil runs out, retighten the bolt.

2. Loosen the filler cap and pour oil in slowly until it begins to run out via the level check bolt, then, tighten the bolt and filler cap.

DRAIN AND REFILL

▶ **See Figure 74**

1. Raise and support the front of the vehicle.
2. Place a fluid catch pan under the transaxle.
3. Remove the upper and lower plugs, then, drain the fluid.
4. Using a new washer, install the bottom plug. Refill the transaxle, until the oil is level with the upper filler plug hole.

Automatic Transaxles

FLUID RECOMMENDATIONS

All Hondamatics use Dexron®II automatic transmission fluid. Only Dexron®II is available today. It replaces straight Dexron® fluid which is the actual recommendation for older models and can be mixed with it.

85911073

Fig. 74 Drain plug for transaxle

LEVEL CHECK

On the 1973-74 models, the transaxle fluid should be checked about once a month and replaced after the first 3,000 miles (every 24,000 miles thereafter). On the 1975-79 models, replace the fluid at 15,000 miles, then, every 30,000 miles thereafter. On the 1980-83 models, replace the fluid every 30,000 miles.

The automatic transaxle, uses a threaded dipstick with a crosshatch pattern. The dipstick is located beneath the battery. To check the fluid level, remove the dipstick, wipe it clean and reinsert it ***without turning it inward.*** That is, make sure the threads on the dipstick itself are sitting on top of the threads in the transaxle housing. Approximately ¾ qt. will bring the fluid level from the ADD (lower) to the FULL (upper) line.

The fluid level is checked with the engine running. It is also necessary to warm up the transaxle by driving the vehicle a few miles, starting and stopping frequently.

1. Park the vehicle on level ground and let the engine idle with the transaxle in **Park**.

2. Unscrew the dipstick, wipe it clean and reinsert it. DO NOT SCREW IT IN, as this would result in an erroneous reading.

3. Using Dexron®II automatic transmission fluid, top off the transaxle, as necessary; add the fluid, if necessary, in small amounts, taking care not to overfill.

4. Recheck the transaxle oil level.

DRAIN AND REFILL

1. Drive the vehicle to bring the transaxle fluid up to operating temperatures.

2. Raise and support the front of the vehicle.

3. Place a fluid catch pan under the transaxle.

4. Remove the drain plug, located on the bottom of the transaxle housing, and drain the transaxle.

5. Using a new washer, install the drain plug. Using Dexron®II automatic transmission fluid refill the transaxle using the transaxle fluid dipstick hole until fluid reaches the Full mark on the dipstick; DO NOT overfill the transaxle.

➡**Be sure that the quantity of fluid you add is always slightly less than the specified quantity, due to the remaining fluid left in the transaxle housing recesses.**

Cooling System

FLUID RECOMMENDATIONS

Use a quality, ethylene-glycol based engine coolant specifically recommended for use with vehicles utilizing aluminum engine parts that are in contact with the coolant. Note that some coolants, although labeled for use in such vehicles, actually may fail to provide effective corrosion protection; if necessary, consult a professional mechanic. It is best to buy a top quality product that is known to work effectively under such conditions. Always add coolant mixed with the proper amount of clean water. Never add either water or coolant alone. Mix the coolant at a 50:50 ratio, unless this will not provide sufficient freeze protection. Consult the chart on the antifreeze container and utilize the proportions recommended for the lowest expected temperatures in your area.

LEVEL CHECK

To check the coolant level, simply discern whether the coolant is up to the **FULL** line on the expansion tank. Add coolant to the expansion tank if the level is low, being sure to mix it with clean water. Never add cold water or coolant to a hot engine as damage to both the cooling system and the engine could result.

The radiator cap should be removed only for the purpose of cleaning or draining the system.

✳✳CAUTION

The cooling system is under pressure when Hot. Removing the radiator cap when the engine is warm or overheated will cause coolant to spill or shoot out, possibly causing serious burns. The system should be allowed to cool before attempting removal of the radiator cap or hoses.

➡**If any coolant spills on painted portions of the body, rinse it off immediately.**

DRAIN AND REFILL

The radiator coolant should be changed every 24,000 miles (1973-74 models), 30,000 miles (1975-80 models) or 45,000 miles (1981-83 models); thereafter, replace every 24 months or 30,000 miles. When following this procedure, be sure to follow the same precautions as detailed in the **Coolant Level** section.

1. Remove the radiator cap.
2. Slide a fluid catch pan under the radiator. Loosen the drain bolt at the base of the radiator and drain the radiator. If equipped, loosen the drain bolt on the drain cock on the side of the block.

✳✳CAUTION

When draining the coolant, keep in mind that cats and dogs are attracted by the ethylene glycol antifreeze, and are quite likely to drink any that is left in an uncovered container or in puddles on the ground. This will prove fatal in sufficient quantity. Always drain the coolant into a sealable container. Coolant should be reused unless it is contaminated or several years old.

3. Drain the coolant in the reservoir tank by unclipping and disconnecting the hose.

➡**In cold weather the thermostat may be closed; it may be necessary to remove the thermostat to completely drain the engine.**

4. Mix a solution of 50% ethylene glycol (designed for use in aluminum engines) and 50% clean water. Use a stronger solution, as specified on the antifreeze container, if the climate in your area demands it. Tighten the drain bolt(s) and refill the radiator all the way to the filler mouth. Reconnect the overflow tank connecting tube.

5. Loosen the cooling system bleed bolt to purge air from the system. When coolant flows out of the bleed port, close the bolt and refill the radiator with coolant up to the mouth.

6. To purge any air trapped in other parts of the cooling system, set the heater control to **Hot**, start the engine, set it to fast idle and allow it to reach normal operating temperatures. DO NOT tighten the radiator cap and leave the heater control in the **Hot** position. When the engine reaches normal operating temperatures, top off the radiator and keep checking until the level stabilizes; then, refill the coolant reservoir to the **Full** mark and make sure that the radiator cap is properly tightened.

FLUSHING AND CLEANING THE SYSTEM

▶ **See Figures 75 and 76**

1. Refer to the "Thermostat, Removal & Installation" procedures in Section 3 and remove the thermostat from the engine.
2. Using a high pressure water hose, force fresh water into the thermostat housing opening, allowing the water to backflush into the engine, heater and radiator. Back-flush the system until the water flowing from the radiator hose is clear.
3. After cleaning, reverse the removal procedures. Refill the cooling system with fresh coolant.

Brake and Clutch Master Cylinder

FLUID RECOMMENDATIONS

Use only DOT 3 or DOT 4 specification brake fluid from a tightly sealed container. If you are unsure of the condition of the fluid (whether or not it has been tightly sealed), use new fluid rather than taking a chance of introducing moisture into the system. It is critically important that the fluid meet the specification so the heat generated by modern disc brakes will not cause it to boil and reduce braking performance. Fluid must be moisture free for the same reason.

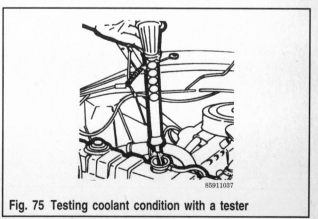

85911037

Fig. 75 Testing coolant condition with a tester

Fig. 76 Removing and inspecting the radiator cap. Always check radiator when engine is cold

LEVEL CHECK

Brake and clutch master cylinder fluid level should be checked every few weeks for indication of leaks or low fluid level due to normal wear of the brake lining. Infrequent topping-off will be required in normal use because of this wear.

On all Hondas there is a fill line on the brake fluid reservoir(s) as well as an arrow on the reservoir cap(s) which should face forward when installed. When adding brake fluid, the following precautions should be observed:

1. Use only recommended brake fluid: DOT 3 or DOT 4; SAE J 1703b HD type.
2. Never reuse brake fluid and never use fluid that is dirty, cloudy or has air bubbles.
3. Store brake fluid in a clean dry place in the original container. Cap tightly and do not puncture a breather hole in the container.
4. Carefully remove any dirt from around the master cylinder reservoir cap before opening.
5. Take special care not to spill the fluid. The painted surface of the vehicle will be damaged by brake fluid.

Power Steering Pump

FLUID RECOMMENDATIONS

Only genuine Honda power steering fluid or a known equivalent may be used when adding fluid. Honda says that

ATF or fluids manufactured for use in other brands of vehicles by their manufacturers or independents are not compatible with the Honda power steering system. The use of any other fluid will cause the seals to swell and create leaks.

RESERVOIR LEVEL CHECK

▶ **See Figure 77**

The fluid in the power steering reservoir should be checked every few weeks for indications of leaks or low fluid level. Check the fluid with the engine cold and the vehicle parked on a level spot. The level should be between the upper and lower marks. Fluid need not be added right away unless it has dropped almost to the lower mark. DO NOT overfill the reservoir.

Manual Steering Gear

INSPECTION

The manual steering used on Hondas is of the rack and pinion design. This unit is packed with grease and therefore does not require a periodic fluid level check. However, inspect the box and associated rubber boot-type seals for obvious grease leaks or torn boots for 1973-78 models: 5,000 miles, then, at every 10,000 mile increments; for the 1979 models: 5,000 miles, 15,000 miles, then, at 15,000, then, at every 15,000 mile increments; for 1980-83 models: 15,000 miles, 30,000 miles, then, at 30,000 mile increments. Make repairs as necessary.

FLUID RECOMMENDATIONS

Repack with about 2 oz. of multipurpose grease.

Chassis Greasing

All the suspension fittings on the Hondas covered by this guide are permanently lubricated. However, at the time when the steering box is inspected for grease leakage (see the item directly above), inspect the suspension and steering joints for

Fig. 77 Checking the power steering fluid

grease leakage and/or torn rubber boots and make repairs as necessary.

Body Lubrication

Lubricate all locks and hinges with multi-purpose grease every 6000 miles or 6 months.

Rear Wheel Bearings — 2WD Only

To check the wheel bearings for basic problems, jack up each wheel to clear the ground. Hold the wheel and shake it to check the bearings for any play. Also rotate the wheel to check for any roughness. If any play is felt or there is noticeable roughness, the bearing may have to be replaced. Adjust the bearing; then, if play is still present, replace the bearing.

➡**Over tightening the spindle nuts will cause excessive bearing friction and will result in rough wheel rotation and eventual bearing failure. Therefore, follow the procedures given in Section 8 exactly, using the proper procedures and tools.**

REMOVAL PACKING AND INSTALLATION

✳✳CAUTION

Brake shoes contain asbestos, which has been determined to be a cancer causing agent. Never clean the brake surfaces with compressed air! Avoid inhaling any dust from any brake surface! When cleaning brake surfaces, use a commercially available brake cleaning fluid.

All Models
▶ **See Figures 78, 79, 80, 81, 82 and 83**

1. Slightly loosen the rear wheel lug nuts. Raise and support the rear of the vehicle.
2. Release the parking brake. Remove the rear wheel assembly.
3. Remove the rear wheel grease cap, the cotter pin, the spindle nut retainer, the spindle nut, the thrust washer and the outer wheel bearing.
4. Pull the brake drum from the wheel spindle.
5. Using a hammer and a drift punch, drive the outer bearing race from the hub.

➡**When removing the bearing races, use a criss-cross pattern to avoid cocking the race in the hub bore.**

6. Turn the hub over and drive the inner bearing race and grease seal from the hub; discard the grease seal.
7. Using solvent, clean the bearings, races and the hub. Using compressed air, blow dry the components.

8. Using the Bearing Driver tool No. 07949-6110000, 07749-0010000 or equivalent, and the Driver Attachment tool No. 07946-6920100 or equivalent, drive the bearing races into the hub until they seat against the shoulders.
9. Using Multipurpose grease, pack the wheel hub and the wheel bearings, also, lightly coat the lips of the grease seal. Install the inner bearing into the hub.
10. Using a mallet, tap the grease seal (using a criss-cross method) into the rear of the hub until it is flush with it.
11. To install the hub, reverse the removal procedures. To adjust the spindle nut, perform the following procedures:
   a. Rotate the brake drum and torque the spindle nut to 18 ft. lbs.
   b. Loosen the spindle nut and retorque to 3 ft. lbs.
   c. Install the spindle nut retainer and align a slot with the hole in the spindle.

➡**If the cotter pin holes do not align, tighten the nut slightly until they do.**

   d. Using a new cotter pin, install it through the spindle nut retainer.
12. To complete the installation, fill the grease cap with multi-purpose grease and reverse the removal procedures.

85911076

Fig. 78 Removing the grease cap on wheel bearings

85911077

Fig. 79 Removing the grease cap gasket on wheel bearings

Fig. 80 Removing the cotter pin on wheel bearings

Fig. 82 Removing the outer wheel bearing

Fig. 81 Removing the washer and wheel bearing nut

❶ Tighten spindle nut to 2.5 ± 0.5 kg-m (18 ± 4 lb-ft) and rotate brake drum by hand.

❷ Loosen spindle nut.

❸ Now tighten nut to specified torque of 0.5 kg-m (3 lb-ft).

❹ Set pin holder so slots will be as close as possible to hole in spindle.

❺ Tighten spindle nut just enough to align slot and hole, then secure with a new cotter pin.

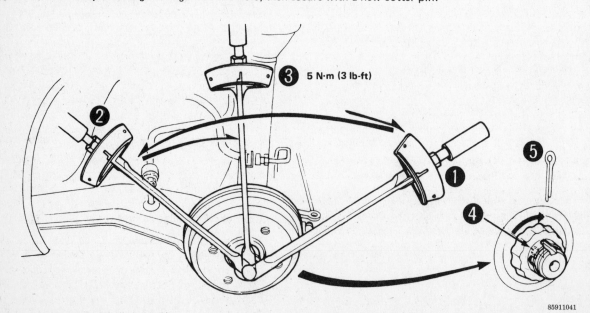

Fig. 83 Spindle nut adjustment procedure

TRAILER TOWING

➡**Although Honda's can be used for light trailer hauling, it is generally considered not to be a good choice in heavy applications.**

General Recommendations

Your car was primarily designed to carry passengers and cargo. It is important to remember that towing a trailer will place additional loads on your vehicle's engine, drive train, steering, braking and other systems. However, if you find it necessary to tow a trailer, using the proper equipment is a must.

Local laws may require specific equipment such as trailer brakes or fender mounted mirrors. Check your local laws.

Trailer Weight

The weight of the trailer is the most important factor. A good weight-to-horsepower ratio is about 35:1, 35 lbs. of GCW (Gross Combined Weight) for every horsepower your engine develops. Multiply the engine's rated horsepower by 35 and subtract the weight of the car passengers and luggage. The result is the approximate ideal maximum weight you should tow, although a numerically higher axle ratio can help compensate for heavier weight.

Hitch Weight

Figure the hitch weight to select a proper hitch. Hitch weight is usually 9-11% of the trailer gross weight and should be measured with the trailer loaded. Hitches fall into three types: those that mount on the frame and rear bumper or the bolt-on or weld-on distribution type used for larger trailers. Axle mounted or clamp-on bumper hitches should never be used.

Check the gross weight rating of your trailer. Tongue weight is usually figured as 10% of gross trailer weight. Therefore, a trailer with a maximum gross weight of 2,000 lb. will have a maximum tongue weight of 200 lb. Class I trailers fall into this category. Class II trailers are those with a gross weight rating of 2,000-3,500 lb., while Class III trailers fall into the 3,500-6,000 lb. category. Class IV trailers are those over 6,000 lb. and are for use with fifth wheel trucks, only.

When you've determined the hitch that you'll need, follow the manufacturer's installation instructions, exactly, especially when it comes to fastener torques. The hitch will be subjected to a lot of stress and good hitches come with hardened bolts. Never substitute an inferior bolt for a hardened bolt.

Cooling

ENGINE

One of the most common, if not THE most common, problems associated with trailer towing is engine overheating.

If you have a standard cooling system, without an expansion tank, you'll definitely need to get an aftermarket expansion tank kit, preferably one with at least a 2 quart capacity. These kits are easily installed on the radiator's overflow hose, and come with a pressure cap designed for expansion tanks.

Another helpful accessory is a Flex Fan. These fans are large diameter units are designed to provide more airflow at low speeds, with blades that have deeply cupped surfaces. The blades then flex, or flatten out, at high speed, when less cooling air is needed. These fans are far lighter in weight than stock fans, requiring less horsepower to drive them. Also, they are far quieter than stock fans.

If you do decide to replace your stock fan with a flex fan, note that if your car has a fan clutch, a spacer between the flex fan and water pump hub will be needed.

Aftermarket engine oil coolers are helpful for prolonging engine oil life and reducing overall engine temperatures. Both of these factors increase engine life.

While not absolutely necessary in towing Class I and some Class II trailers, they are recommended for heavier Class II and all Class III towing.

Engine oil cooler systems consist of an adapter, screwed on in place of the oil filter, a remote filter mounting and a multi-tube, finned heat exchanger, which is mounted in front of the radiator or air conditioning condenser.

TRANSMISSION

An automatic transmission is usually recommended for trailer towing. Modern automatics have proven reliable and, of course, easy to operate, in trailer towing.

The increased load of a trailer, however, causes an increase in the temperature of the automatic transmission fluid. Heat is the worst enemy of an automatic transmission. As the temperature of the fluid increases, the life of the fluid decreases.

It is essential, therefore, that you install an automatic transmission cooler.

The cooler, which consists of a multi-tube, finned heat exchanger, is usually installed in front of the radiator or air conditioning compressor, and hooked inline with the transmission cooler tank inlet line. Follow the cooler manufacturer's installation instructions.

Select a cooler of at least adequate capacity, based upon the combined gross weights of the car and trailer.

Cooler manufacturers recommend that you use an aftermarket cooler in addition to, and not instead of, the present cooling tank in your radiator. If you do want to use it in place of the radiator cooling tank, get a cooler at least two sizes larger than normally necessary.

➡**A transmission cooler can, sometimes, cause slow or harsh shifting in the transmission during cold weather, until the fluid has a chance to come up to normal operating temperature. Some coolers can be purchased with or retrofitted with a temperature bypass valve which will allow fluid flow through the cooler only when the fluid has reached operating temperature, or above.**

Handling A Trailer

Towing a trailer with ease and safety requires a certain amount of experience. It's a good idea to learn the feel of a trailer by practicing turning, stopping and backing in an open area such as an empty parking lot.

PUSHING AND TOWING

If your Honda's rear axle is operable, you can tow your vehicle with the rear wheels on the ground. Due to its front wheel drive, the Honda is a relatively easy vehicle to tow with the front wheels up. Before doing so, you should release the parking brake.

If the rear axle is defective, the vehicle must then be towed with the rear wheels off the ground. Before attempting this, a dolly should be placed under the front wheels. If a dolly is not available, and you still have to tow it with the rear wheels up, then you should first shift the transaxle into Neutral and then lock the steering wheel so that the front wheels are pointing straight ahead. In such a position, the vehicle must not be towed at speeds above 35 mph or for more than short distances (50 miles). *It's critically important that you observe these limitations to prevent damage to your transaxle due to inadequate lubrication.*

JUMP STARTING

Hondas equipped with a manual transaxle can be push-started. Make sure that the bumpers match as otherwise a damaged bumper and/or fender could result from push-starting. To push-start your Honda, turn the ignition switch **ON**, push the clutch in, and select 2nd or 3rd gear. Depress the accelerator pedal to set the choke as you normally would, *then, release it.* As the vehicle picks up speed (10-15 mph), slowly release the clutch pedal until the engine fires up.

If your vehicle is equipped with an automatic transaxle, it cannot be push-started. Shifting the transaxle into gear has absolutely no effect until the transmission oil pump, driven by the engine, begins to run.

JACKING

▶ **See Figures 84, 85, 86 and 87**

Your Honda comes equipped with a scissors jack. This jack is fine for changing a flat tire or other operations where you do not have to go beneath the vehicle. There are four lifting points where this jack may be used: one behind each front wheel well and one in front of each rear wheel well in reinforced sheet metal brackets beneath the rocker panels.

A more convenient way of jacking is the use of a garage or floor jack. You may use the floor jack beneath any of the four scissors jacking points or you can raise either the entire front or entire rear of the vehicle using the special jacking brackets beneath the front center or rear center of the vehicle. On station wagon models, the rear of the vehicle may be jacked beneath the center of the rear axle beam.

The following safety points cannot be overemphasized:
• Always block the opposite wheel or wheels to keep the vehicle from rolling off the jack.
• When raising the front of the vehicle, firmly apply the parking brake.
• When raising the rear of the vehicle, place the transaxle in Low or Reverse gear.
• Always use jack stands to support the vehicle when you are working underneath. Place the stands beneath the scissors jacking brackets. Before climbing underneath, rock the vehicle a bit to make sure it is firmly supported.

If you are going to have your Honda serviced on a garage hoist, make sure the four hoist platform pads are placed beneath the scissors jacking brackets. These brackets are reinforced and will support the weight of the entire vehicle.

85911050

Fig. 84 Typical front lift points-note position of jack pads

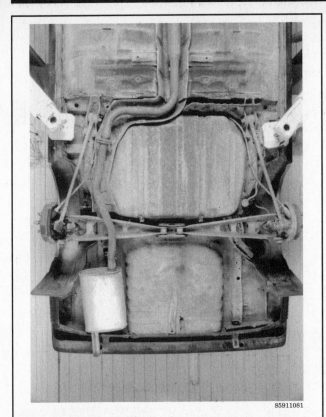

Fig. 85 Typical rear lift points-note position of jack pads

Fig. 86 A hydraulic floor jack and jackstands are essential for safely lifting and supporting your vehicle

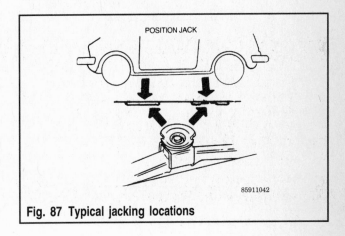

Fig. 87 Typical jacking locations

CAPACITIES

Year	Model	Engine Displacement (cc)	Engine Crankcase With Filter	Without Filter	Transmission (pts.) 4-Spd	5-Spd	Auto. ①	Drive Axle (pts.)	Fuel Tank (gal.)	Cooling System (qts.)
1973	Civic	1170	3.8	3.2	5.2	—	5.2	—	10.0	4.2
1974	Civic 1200	1237	3.8	3.2	5.2	—	5.2	—	10.0	4.2
1975	Civic 1200	1237	3.8	3.2	5.2	—	5.2	—	10.0	4.2
	Civic CVCC	1487	3.8	3.2	5.2	5.2	5.2	—	10.6④	4.2
1976	Civic 1200	1237	3.8	3.2	5.2	—	5.2	—	10.0	4.2
	Civic CVCC	1487	3.8	3.2	5.2	5.2	5.2	—	10.6④	4.2
	Accord	1600	3.8	3.2	5.2	5.2	5.2	—	13.2	4.2
1977	Civic 1200	1237	3.8	3.2	5.2	—	5.2	—	10.6	4.2
	Civic CVCC	1487	3.8	3.2	5.2	5.2	5.2	—	10.6④	4.2
	Accord	1600	3.8	3.2	5.2	5.2	5.2	—	13.2	4.2
1978	Civic 1200	1237	3.8	3.2	5.2	—	5.2	—	10.6	4.2
	Civic CVCC	1487	3.8	3.2	5.2	5.2	5.2	—	10.6④	4.2
	Accord	1600	3.8	3.2	5.2	5.2	5.2	—	13.2	4.2
1979	Civic 1200	1237	3.8	3.2	5.2	—	5.2	—	10.6	4.8
	Civic CVCC	1487	3.8	3.2	5.2	5.6	5.2	—	10.6④	4.8
	Accord	1751	3.8	3.2	5.2	5.2	5.2	—	13.2	6.4
	Prelude	1751	3.8	3.2	5.2	5.2	5.2	—	13.2	6.0
1980	Civic 1300	1335	3.8	3.2	4.8	5.2	5.2	—	10.8	5.2
	Civic CVCC	1487	3.8	3.2	4.8	5.2	5.2	—	10.8	5.2
	Accord	1751	3.8	3.2	5.0	5.0	5.2	—	13.2	6.4
	Prelude	1751	3.8	3.2	5.0	5.0	5.2	—	13.2	6.0
1981	Civic	1335 1487	3.8	3.2	5.2	5.2	5.2	—	10.8②	4.8③
	Accord	1751	3.8	3.2	5.0	5.0	5.2	—	13.2	6.4
	Prelude	1751	3.7	3.2	5.0	5.0	5.2	—	13.2	6.0
1982	Civic	1335 1487	3.7	3.2	5.2	5.2	5.2	—	10.8②	4.8③
	Accord	1751	3.7	3.2	5.0	5.0	5.2	—	15.8②	6.0
	Prelude	1751	3.7	3.2	5.0	5.0	5.2	—	13.2	6.0
1983	Civic	1335 1487	3.7	3.2	5.2	5.2	5.2	—	10.4②	4.8③
	Accord	1751	3.7	3.2	5.0	5.0	6.0	—	15.8	6.0
	Prelude	1829	3.7	3.2	—	5.0	5.8	—	15.9	6.3

① Does not include torque converter
② 4-dr. sedan: 12.1
③ 1335cc: 4.0
④ Station Wagon: 11.0

85911C02

2

ENGINE PERFORMANCE AND TUNE-UP

TUNE-UP PROCEDURES

The procedures in this section are specifically intended for your Honda and intended to be as basic and complete as possible.

Spark Plugs

▶ See Figures 1 and 2

➡The spark plugs should be replaced every 15,000 miles (1973-79) or 30,000 miles (1980-83).

Most people know that the spark plug ignites the air/fuel mixture in the cylinder, which in turn forces the piston downward, turning the crankshaft. This action turns the drivetrain (clutch, transaxle, drive axles) and moves the vehicle. What many people do not know, however, is that spark plugs should be chosen according to the type of driving done. The plug with a long insulator nose retains heat long enough to burn off oil and combustion deposits under light engine load conditions. A short-nosed plug dissipates heat rapidly and prevents pre-ignition and detonation under heavily loaded conditions. Under normal driving conditions, a standard plug is just fine.

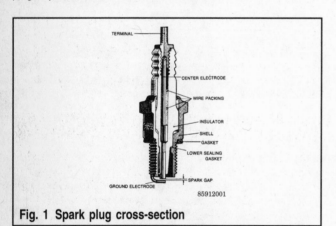

Fig. 1 Spark plug cross-section

Fig. 2 Spark plug information label on valve cover

Spark plug life is largely governed by operating conditions and varies accordingly. To ensure peak performance, inspect the plugs every 10,000-15,000 miles. Faulty or excessively worn plugs should be replaced immediately. It is also helpful to check plugs for types of deposit and degree of electrode wear, as an indication of engine operating condition. Excessive or oily deposits could be an indication of real engine trouble, it would be wise to investigate the problem thoroughly and make sure the cause is found and corrected.

REMOVAL & INSTALLATION

▶ See Figures 3, 4, 5, 6 and 7

1. Disconnect the negative battery cable. Place a piece of masking tape around each spark plug wire and number it according to its corresponding cylinder.
2. Pull the wire from the spark plug, grasping the wire by the end of the rubber boot and twisting off. It is recommended that the spark plugs be replaced one at a time. This will help prevent installing the wires in the incorrect order.

➡Avoid spark plug removal while the engine is Hot. Since the cylinder head spark plug threads are aluminum, the spark plug becomes tight due to the different coefficients of heat expansion. If a plug is too tight to be removed even while the engine is Cold, apply a solvent around the plug followed with an application of oil once the solvent has penetrated the threads. Do this only when the engine is Cold.

3. Loosen each spark plug with a ¹³/₁₆″ spark plug socket. When the plug has been loosened a few turns, stop to clean any material from around the spark plug holes; compressed air is preferred. If air is not available, simply use a rag to clean the area.

➡In no case should foreign material be allowed to enter the cylinders. Severe damage could result.

4. Remove and inspect the spark plugs; if necessary, clean them.
   To install:
5. Inspect and set the spark plug gap to specifications. Refer to the "Tune-Up Specifications Chart" listed in this Section.
6. Oil the spark plug threads and hand tighten them into the cylinder head. Torque the spark plugs into the cylinder head to 13 ft. lbs.

➡It's a good idea to apply an anti-seize compound on the threads of the spark plugs before installing them. DO NOT over-tighten them because of the aluminum cylinder heads.

7. Connect the wires to the plugs, making sure that each is securely fitted. Reconnect the battery cable.

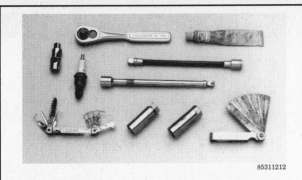

Fig. 3 A variety of tools and gauges are needed for spark plug service

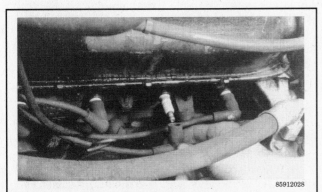

Fig. 4 Mark and remove the spark plug wire

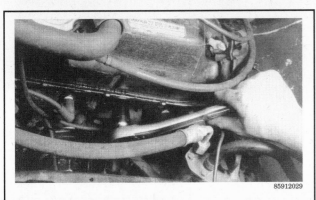

Fig. 5 Removing the spark plug

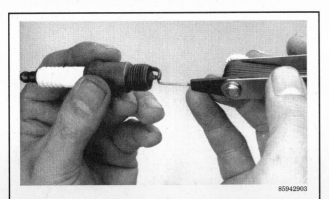

Fig. 6 Checking the spark plug gap with a feeler gauge

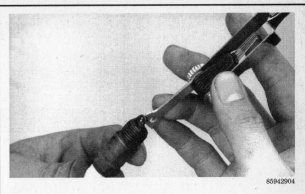

Fig. 7 Adjusting the spark plug gap

INSPECTION AND CLEANING

Before attempting to clean and re-gap plugs be sure that the electrode ends are not worn or damaged and that the insulators (the white porcelain covering) are not cracked; replace the plug if this condition exists.

Clean reusable plugs with a small file or a wire brush. The plug gap should be checked and readjusted, if necessary, by bending the ground electrode with a spark plug gapping tool.

→**DO NOT use a flat gauge to check plug gap. An incorrect reading will result; use a wire gauge only. Also, replace the plugs one at a time, keeping the ignition wires connected to those plugs you're not working on. This will avoid confusion about how to reconnect the plug wires according to the firing order.**

Spark Plug Wires

Spark plug wires do a critical job for your vehicle's ignition system. They transmit the very, very tiny amounts of current that fire the spark plugs at an extremely high voltage. Voltage is high at the plugs because the spark must actually leap the plug gap, something which requires tremendous electrical pressure or **voltage**. Electricity has great difficulty in traveling through air or air/fuel mixture. In fact, the mixture will not transmit electricity at all in its natural state. The tremendous voltage at the plug's center electrode actually pumps electrons into the air, **ionizing** it before the spark can travel to the ground electrode. The required voltage is especially high because of the pressure generated in the cylinders during the compression stroke.

Since the coil's ability to increase the voltage in the ignition system is traded in direct proportion for decreased amperage or current flow, there is little room for loss of current due to poor ignition wires. To make matters worse, the high voltage existing throughout the wires naturally tends to create a corona effect and loss of both current and voltage.

All this is worth knowing for one simple reason, it pays to buy quality ignition wires with a metallic conductor and it pays to inspect wires frequently for either cracked or brittle insulation. A most common symptom of ignition wires that are starting to give out is poor performance or difficult starting in wet weather that improves after the engine warms up or when the weather clears. You can confirm this problem by watching the engine run in the dark. If you see a lot of blue sparking around the wires, replace them. At this time, it is also a good idea to inspect the distributor cap and rotor, replace them, if there is any sign of cracking or carbon **tracking**. These are paths of burnt plastic, usually beginning at a crack or groove, where sparks may have been leaping from the center of the cap to ground.

Note too that you may be able to improve ignition performance by purchasing either resistor wires or resistor spark plugs for improved performance of your radio. You do not need to purchase components with the **resistor** designation in both cases!

If you have an ignition problem that seems to come and go, yet the insulation on the outside of the ignition wires is still good, it may pay to have your vehicle run on an ignition scope or diagnostic system. The scope readings will sometimes reveal high resistance in the conductor at the center of each wire. You can also use an ohmmeter to measure the resistance of the wire from end to end; it should not exceed 25,000Ω.

Ignition wires are most easily replaced one at a time. Make sure to very carefully insert wires all the way into the cap and onto the ends of the plugs; make sure all insulator boots are installed all the way onto the cap or plugs.

Firing Orders

▶ **See Figures 8, 9 and 10**

➡**To avoid confusion, remove and tag the wires one at a time, for replacement.**

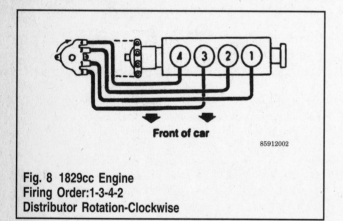

85912002

Fig. 8 1829cc Engine
Firing Order:1-3-4-2
Distributor Rotation-Clockwise

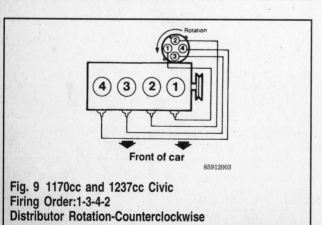

85912003

Fig. 9 1170cc and 1237cc Civic
Firing Order:1-3-4-2
Distributor Rotation-Counterclockwise

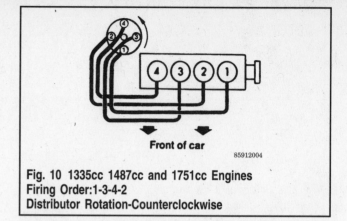

85912004

Fig. 10 1335cc 1487cc and 1751cc Engines
Firing Order:1-3-4-2
Distributor Rotation-Counterclockwise

Breaker Points and Condenser

▶ **See Figures 11 and 12**

The points and condenser function as a circuit breaker for the primary circuit of the ignition system. They are used on 1973-79 models, which do not have a catalytic converter. The ignition coil must boost the 12V of electrical pressure supplied to it by the battery to about 20,000V in order to fire the spark plugs. To do this, the coil depends on the points and condenser for assistance.

The coil has a primary and a secondary circuit. When the ignition key is turned to the **ON** position, the battery supplies voltage to the primary side of the coil which passes the voltage on to the points. The points are connected to ground to complete the primary circuit. As the cam in the distributor turns, the points open and the primary circuit collapses. The magnetic force in the primary circuit of the coil cuts through the secondary circuit and increases the voltage in the secondary circuit to a level that is sufficient to fire the spark plugs. If this electrical charge was not transferred elsewhere, the material on the contacts of the points would melt and that all-important gap between the contacts would start to change. If this gap is not maintained, the points will not break the primary circuit abruptly enough. If the primary circuit is not broken properly, the secondary circuit will not have enough voltage to fire the spark plugs.

The function of the condenser is to absorb the excessive voltage from the coil which jumps across the points when they open. This prevents the points from becoming pitted or burned.

There are two ways to check breaker point gap: with a feeler gauge or with a dwell meter. Either way the points are set, you are adjusting the amount of time (in degrees of distributor rotation) that the points remain open. If the points are adjusted with a feeler gauge, you are setting the maximum amount the points will open when the rubbing block on the points is on a high point of the distributor cam. When you adjust the points with a dwell meter, you are measuring the number of degrees (of distributor cam rotation) that the points will remain closed before they start to open as the distributor cam approaches the rubbing block of the points.

If you still do not understand how the points function, take a friend, go outside and remove the distributor cap from your engine. Have your friend operate the starter (make sure the

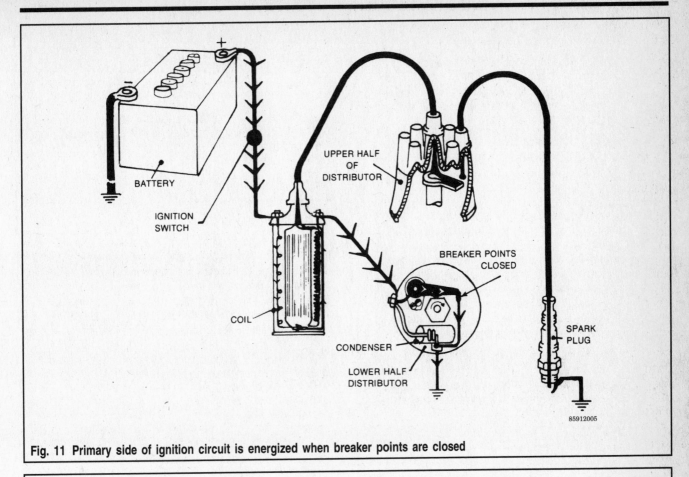

Fig. 11 Primary side of ignition circuit is energized when breaker points are closed

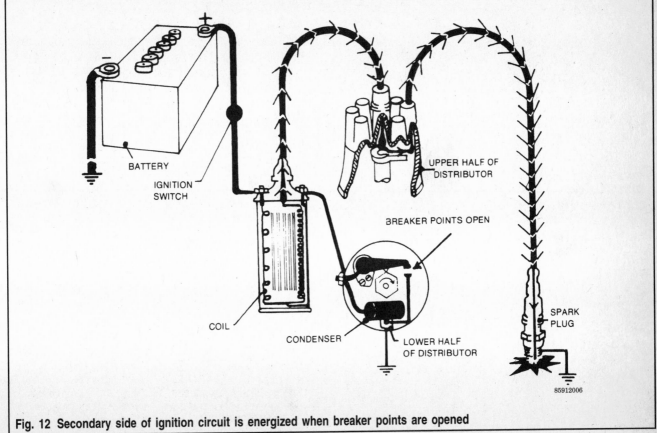

Fig. 12 Secondary side of ignition circuit is energized when breaker points are opened

transaxle is not in gear) as you look at the exposed parts of the distributor.

➡️There are two rules that should always be followed when adjusting or replacing points. The points and condenser are a matched set; never replace one without replacing the other. If the points are adjusted, the timing must also be adjusted.

INSPECTION

▸ **See Figures 13 and 14**

1. Disconnect the high tension wire from the coil.
2. Unfasten the two retaining clips to remove the distributor cap.
3. Remove the rotor from the distributor shaft by pulling it straight up. Examine the condition of the rotor. If it is cracked or the metallic tip is excessively burned, replace it.
4. Pry the breaker points open with a screwdriver and examine the condition of the contact points. If the points are excessively worn, burned or pitted, they should be replaced.

➡️Contact points which have been used for several thousand miles will have a gray, rough surface but this is not necessarily an indication that they are malfunctioning. The roughness between the points matches so that a large contact area is maintained.

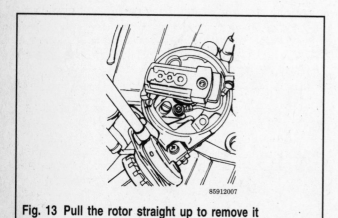

Fig. 13 Pull the rotor straight up to remove it

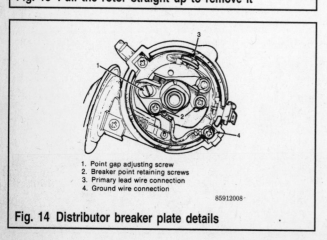

1. Point gap adjusting screw
2. Breaker point retaining screws
3. Primary lead wire connection
4. Ground wire connection

Fig. 14 Distributor breaker plate details

5. If the points are in good condition, polish them with a point file.

➡️DO NOT use emery cloth or sandpaper as they may leave particles on the points which could cause them to arc.

After polishing the points, refer to the section following the breaker point replacement procedures for proper adjustment. If the points need replacing, refer to the following procedure.

REMOVAL & INSTALLATION

▸ **See Figure 15**

1. Remove the small nut from the terminal screw located in the side of the distributor housing and remove the nut, screw, condenser wire and primary wire from the terminal. Remove the terminal from the slot in the distributor housing.
2. Remove the screw(s) which attaches the condenser to the outside of the distributor housing (most models) or to the breaker plate inside the distributor (CVCC Hondamatic models) and the condenser.
3. Using a Phillips head screwdriver, remove the ground wire-to-breaker point assembly screw and lift the end of the ground wire out of the way.
4. Remove the two point assembly-to-breaker plate screws and the point assembly.

➡️When removing or installing the point assembly screws, use a magnetic or locking screwdriver; trying to locate one of these tiny screws after you have dropped it can be an excruciating affair.

5. Wipe all dirt and grease from the distributor plate and cam with a lint-free cloth. Apply a small amount of heat resistant lubricant to the distributor cam. Although the lube is supplied with most breaker point kits, you can buy it at any auto store if necessary.
6. Properly position the new points on the breaker plate of the distributor and secure with the two point screws. Attach the ground wire, with its screw, to the breaker plate assembly. Screw the condenser to its proper position on the distributor housing or breaker plate.
7. Fit the terminal into the distributor housing notch, attach the condenser and primary wires to the terminal screw, then, fasten with the nut.

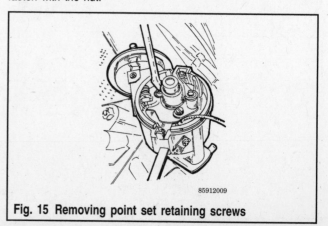

Fig. 15 Removing point set retaining screws

DWELL ADJUSTMENT

Dwell or cam angle refers to the amount of time the points remain closed and is measured in degrees of distributor rotation. Dwell will vary according to the point gap, since dwell is a function of point gap. If the point gap is too wide, they open gradually, and dwell angle (the time they remain closed) is small. This wide gap causes excessive arcing at the points, leading to point burning. The insufficient dwell does not give the coil sufficient time to build up maximum energy, so coil output decreases.

If the point gap is too small, dwell is increased, the idle becomes rough and starting is difficult. When setting points, remember: the wider the point opening, the smaller the dwell or the smaller the point opening, the larger the dwell. When connecting a dwell meter, connect one negative lead (black) to a good ground on the engine and the positive lead (red) to the negative or distributor side of the coil. This terminal is easy to find, look for the terminal which has the small wire that leads to the distributor.

Feeler Gauge Method
▶ See Figure 16

1. Rotate the crankshaft pulley until the point gap is at its greatest (where the rubbing block is on the high point of the cam lobe). This can be accomplished by using either a remote starter switch or by rotating the crankshaft pulley by hand.
2. Using a 0.018-0.022″ feeler gauge between the points, a slight drag should be felt.
3. If no drag is felt or the feeler gauge cannot be inserted, loosen, but do not remove the two breaker point set screws.
4. Adjust the points as follows:
   a. Using a screwdriver, insert it through the hole in the breaker point assembly and into the notch provided on the breaker plate.
   b. Twist the screwdriver to open or close the points.
   c. When the correct gap has been obtained, retighten the point set screws.
5. Recheck the point gap to be sure that it did not change when the breaker point attaching screws were tightened.
6. Align the rotor with the distributor shaft and push the rotor onto the shaft until it is fully seated.
7. Reinstall the distributor cap and the coil high tension wire.

Dwell Meter Method

1. Install a dwell/tach according to the manufacturer's instructions.
2. Warm the engine and read the dwell meter; running at the specified idle speed.
3. If the point dwell is not within specifications, turn the engine **OFF** and adjust the point gap. Remember, increasing the point gap decreases the dwell angle and vice-versa.
4. Check the dwell reading again and adjust it as required.

Electronic Ignition

All 1980-83 vehicles are equipped with a magnetic pulse type electronic ignition system. This system eliminates the points and condenser, it requires no periodic maintenance.

The electronic ignition system uses a magnetic pulse/igniter distributor and a conventional ignition coil. The distributor cap, rotor, advance mechanism (vacuum and centrifugal) and secondary ignition wires are also of standard design. The distributor contains the stator, reluctor and pulse generator (pick-up coil) and igniter assembly.

During operation, the teeth of the reluctor align with the stator, a signal is generated by the pulse generator (pick-up coil) and sent to the igniter (module). The module, upon receiving the signal, opens the primary of the ignition coil. As the primary magnetic field collapses, a high voltage surge is developed in the secondary windings of the coil. This high voltage surge travels from the coil to the distributor cap and rotor through the secondary ignition wires to the spark plugs.

➡**The electronic ignition system on your Honda requires special handling. Unlike conventional ignition systems, it is very sensitive to abrupt changes in voltage or voltage applied in the wrong direction electrically. Observe the precautions listed below to prevent expensive system damage!**

1. Always disconnect the battery cables before doing repair work on the electronic ignition system.
2. Always double check the markings on the battery and the routing of the cables before making connections, especially if the battery has been removed and might have been reinstalled in the opposite position. Hooking the battery connections up backwards will cause current to flow through the electronic ignition system in an improper way and may immediately damage it. Be careful, also when jumping the vehicle's battery with another for the same reasons.

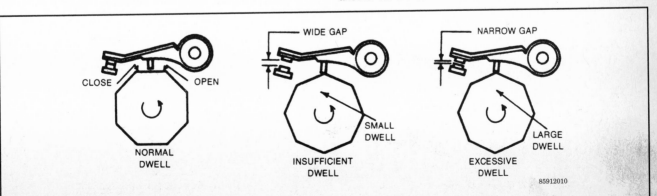

Fig. 16 Dwell angle as a function of point gap

3. Do not allow the wires connected to the pulse generator to touch other ignition wiring connections.

4. Abnormal voltage pulses may damage the system. Therefore, be sure to disconnect the battery before doing any work on the vehicle that is of an electrical nature. This includes charging the battery and replacing small bulbs.

5. Connect any electrical tachometer to the negative (-) terminal of the ignition coil — **not to any other connection!**

6. Always double check any connection (you are making) involving the ignition system before reconnecting the battery and putting the system into operation.

7. When cranking the engine for compression testing or similar purposes, disconnect the coil wire at the distributor.

RELUCTOR GAP ADJUSTMENT

▶ **See Figures 17, 18, 19 and 20**

1. Remove the distributor cap and the rotor.

2. Turn the crankshaft to align the reluctor points with the stator ends.

3. Using a non-metallic feeler gauge, check the air reluctor-to-stator air gaps; they must be equal.

4. To adjust, loosen the stator-to-distributor screws, adjust the stator-to-reluctor air gaps and tighten the screws.

5. Recheck the air gaps.

Fig. 17 Removing the coil wire from the distributor cap

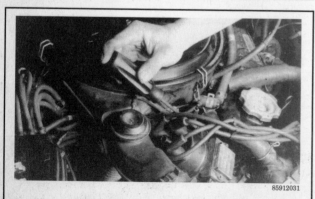

Fig. 18 Removing the distributor cap hold-down screw

Fig. 19 Removing the distributor cap (remove the 2 hold-down screws)

Fig. 20 Removing the distributor rotor (rotor lifts off)

PARTS REPLACEMENT

Retailers often offer Tune-Up kits consisting of a pick-up coil, igniter unit (if used), reluctor, rotor and distributor cap.

Reluctor

▶ **See Figure 21**

1. Disconnect the negative battery terminal.

2. Remove the distributor cap and the rotor.

3. Using two medium pry bars, pry the reluctor from the distributor shaft; be careful not to damage the reluctor or stator.

➡**When installing the reluctor, be sure the manufacturer's number is facing upward.**

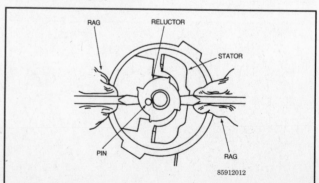

Fig. 21 Removing the reluctor from the distributor assembly

4. To install, push the reluctor onto the distributor shaft. When installing the reluctor roll pin, be sure to position the pin gap facing away from the distributor shaft.

Pickup Coil

1. Refer to the Reluctor Removal & Installation procedures in this section and remove the reluctor.
2. Disconnect the electrical connector from the pickup coil.
3. Remove the pickup coil-to-distributor screws and pull the pickup coil from the distributor.
4. To install, use a new pickup coil (if necessary) and reverse the removal procedures.

Igniter Unit
▶ **See Figures 22 and 23**

On the Accord (1983), Prelude (1983), Toyo Denso introduced an igniter unit which is installed on the side of the distributor housing.

1. Disconnect the negative battery terminal.
2. Remove the igniter cover-to-distributor screws and the cover.
3. Pull the igniter unit from the distributor.
4. If necessary, perform the Igniter Unit Troubleshooting procedures in this section.
5. Using silicone grease, apply it to the connector housing.
6. To install, reverse the removal procedures.

Rotor

1. Remove the distributor cap.
2. Pull the rotor from the distributor shaft.

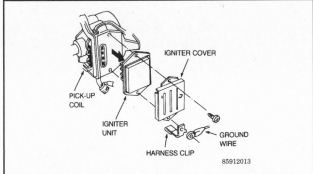

Fig. 22 Removing the igniter unit from the distributor-Toyo Denso model

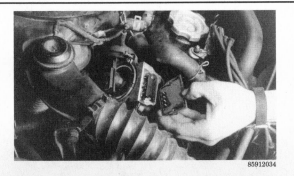

Fig. 23 Removing the igniter unit cover from the distributor

3. Inspect the rotor burns and damage; if necessary, replace it. It may be necessary to lightly file the tip.
4. To install, apply a light coat of silicone grease to the rotor tip, align the rotor with the distributor shaft and push it into place and reverse the removal procedures.

TROUBLESHOOTING

▶ **See Figure 24**

Use a quality electrical multimeter — a tester which will measure voltage and resistance precisely.

1. To verify that the electronic ignition system is malfunctioning, first carefully pull the coil wire out of the coil. Then, hold the wire so that the metal parts of the coil tower and wire are ¼" apart. Have someone crank the engine with the ignition switch so the ignition will be turned **ON**. If there is spark, the electronic ignition system is working, proceed with routine checks for spark at the plugs and inspection of the ignition wires, cap and rotor to be certain the rest of the ignition system is operable. If there is a large, fat spark, reconnect the coil high tension wire securely; if there is no spark or if the spark is weak, proceed with the tests below.

2. With the ignition switch still **ON**, switch the multimeter into the 12V range. Connect the ground (black) lead of the meter to a good, clean ground that is not covered with paint. Connect the positive lead to the positive (+) terminal of the coil. The voltage should be approximately 12V — the same as the battery. If not, look for problems in the wiring connector at the coil or somewhere in the wiring between the ignition switch and the coil.

3. On 1973-83 models, disconnect the coil high tension lead, this time at the distributor end. Ground the high tension lead securely. Connect the voltmeter across the (+) and (-) connectors of the coil, with the black or negative lead at the (-) connector. Set the meter on a scale that will read less than 5V precisely. Have someone crank the engine with the key; the reading must be 1-3V. If the reading is within the specified range, check the coil primary and secondary resistance as in Step 4. Otherwise, proceed with Step 5.

4. On all models, turn the ignition switch **OFF**. Set your meter to read resistance (Ohms). Choose a scale that will measure the resistance specified effectively. Make sure the coil is at approximately 70°F (21°C). On all models, connect the two meter probes to the two primary (small) terminals of the coil. On 1973-83 models, these are the two small connectors

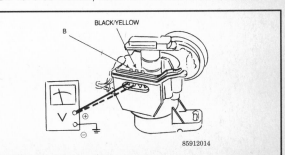

Fig. 24 Toyo Denso type distributor assembly-measure the voltage at each of the terminals on the left side-the igniter unit continunity is measured between the same two terminals

that use nuts to retain the coil wires. Read the resistance; it must be 1.0-1.3Ω (1980), 1.06-1.24Ω (1981-83). Now read the secondary resistance. Connect the meter probes between the (+) primary terminal and the large, secondary connector — the coil tower on all models 1973-83. This resistance must be 7,400-11,000Ω on models (1973-83). If any test is failed, replace the coil. If all tests were passed, check the spark plug wire resistance by disconnecting each wire at both ends and connecting a probe from the meter to either end of the wire. Resistance must be no more than 25,000Ω. Otherwise, the wire must be replaced. Remember to check the coil-to-distributor wire as well as the individual plug wires. Check the wires one at a time to avoid mixing up the firing order.

5. Note the locations for the blue and black/yellow connectors. Disconnect the lead wires from the igniter unit. Turn the ignition switch **ON**. Measure voltage between the blue wire and a good, clean ground. Do the same for the black/yellow wire. In both cases, battery voltage MUST be present at both connectors. Otherwise, trace the wiring back through the ignition switch to find the problem. Turn the ignition switch **OFF**. Now, measure the resistance in the igniter with the meter set to the **R x 100** scale. Connect the positive probe onto the black/yellow distributor terminal and the negative onto the blue distributor terminal. There must be continuity. Now, reverse the probes so that the positive probe is on the blue terminal and the negative probe is on the black/yellow. There must be NO continuity with the probes in this position. If the continuity test is failed either way, replace the igniter. Proceed with Step 6.

6. Connect the ohmmeter probes between the blue wire and green wire distributor terminals. Pick-up coil resistance must be approximately 750Ω. Otherwise, replace the pick-up coil.

DIAGNOSIS AND TESTING

Igniter Unit Test
▶ See Figures 25 and 26

1983 ACCORD AND PRELUDE (WITH HITACHI TYPE)

1. Disconnect lead wires from igniter unit.
2. Using a voltmeter, check the voltage between blue wire and body ground, then, black/yellow wire to body ground, with ignition switch **ON**. There should be battery voltage.
3. If no voltage, check wiring to igniter unit.

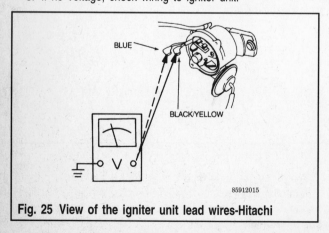

Fig. 25 View of the igniter unit lead wires-Hitachi

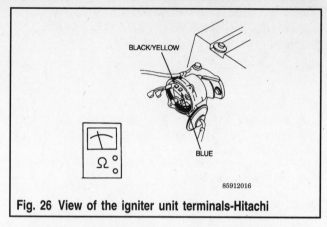

Fig. 26 View of the igniter unit terminals-Hitachi

4. Using a ohmmeter, set the scale on the **R x 100** position, disconnect the lead wires and check the continuity.
5. Place the positive (red) probe on the black/yellow wire terminal and negative (black) probe on the blue wire terminal; no continuity should be read on ohmmeter.
6. Place the positive (red) probe on the blue wire terminal and negative (black) probe on the black/yellow wire terminal; continuity should be read on the ohmmeter.
7. If ohmmeter readings are not as specified in Steps 5 and 6, replace igniter unit.

1983 ACCORD AND PRELUDE (WITH TOYO DENSO TYPE)
▶ See Figures 27 and 28

1. Disconnect lead wires from igniter unit.
2. Using a voltmeter, check the voltage between the blue wire and ground, then, the black/yellow wire to ground, with the ignition switch **ON**; there should be battery voltage.
3. If no voltage, check wiring to igniter unit.
4. Using an ohmmeter, set the scale on the **R x 100** position, disconnect the lead wires and check the continuity between the igniter unit terminals.
5. Place probes of meter to black/yellow wire terminal and blue wire terminal. No continuity should be read on ohmmeter.
6. Reverse the meter probes. Continuity should be read on ohmmeter.

➡**Polarity may change with different meters. Determine polarity of your ohmmeter before conducting this test.**

7. If ohmmeter readings are not as specified in Steps 2 and 3, replace igniter unit.

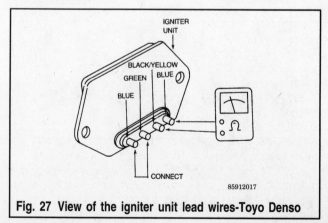

Fig. 27 View of the igniter unit lead wires-Toyo Denso

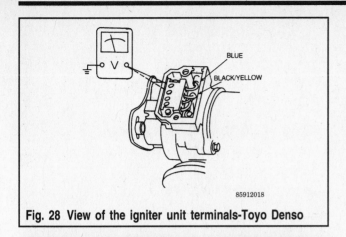

Fig. 28 View of the igniter unit terminals-Toyo Denso

Ignition Timing

Ignition timing is the measurement, in degrees of crankshaft rotation, at the instant the spark plugs in the cylinders fire, in relation to the location of the piston, while the piston is on its compression stroke.

Ideally, the air/fuel mixture in the cylinder will be ignited (by the spark plug) and just beginning its rapid expansion as the piston passes top dead center (TDC) of the compression stroke. If this happens, the piston will be beginning the power stroke just as the compressed (by the movement of the piston) and ignited (by the spark plug) air/fuel mixture starts to expand. The expansion of the air/fuel mixture will force the piston down on the power stroke and turn the crankshaft.

It takes a fraction of a second for the spark from the plug to completely ignite the mixture in the cylinder. Because of this, the spark plug must fire before the piston reaches TDC, if the mixture is to be completely ignited as the piston passes TDC. This measurement is given in degrees (of crankshaft rotation) before the piston reaches top dead center (BTDC). If the ignition timing setting is 6° BTDC, this means that the spark plug must fire at a time when the piston for that cylinder is 6° BTDC of its compression stroke. However, this only holds true while your engine is at idle speed.

As you accelerate from idle, the speed of your engine (rpm) increases. The increase in rpm means that the pistons are now traveling up and down much faster. Because of this, the spark plugs will have to fire even sooner if the mixture is to be completely ignited as the piston passes TDC. To accomplish this, the distributor incorporates means to advance the timing of the spark as engine speed increases.

The distributor has two means of advancing the ignition timing. One is called centrifugal advance and is actuated by weights in the distributor. The other is called vacuum advance and is controlled in that large circular housing on the side of the distributor.

In addition, some Honda distributors have a vacuum retard mechanism which is contained in the same housing on the side of the distributor as the vacuum advance. Models having two hoses going to the distributor vacuum housing have both vacuum advance and retard. The function of this mechanism is to regulate the timing of the ignition spark under certain engine conditions. This causes more complete burning of the air/fuel mixture in the cylinder and consequently lowers exhaust emissions.

If ignition timing is set too far advanced (BTDC), the ignition and burning of the air/fuel mixture in the cylinder will try to oppose the motion of the piston in the cylinder while it is still traveling upward. This causes engine **ping**. If the ignition timing is too far retarded (after, or ATDC), the piston will have already started down on the power stroke when the air/fuel mixture ignites and expands. This will cause the piston to be forced down with much less potency. This will result in rough engine performance and lack of power and gas mileage.

CHECKING AND ADJUSTING

▶ See Figure 29

Honda recommends that the ignition timing be checked at 12,000 mile intervals (1973-74), 15,000 mile intervals (1975-78) or when problems are suspected (1979-82). On 1983 models, check the timing and adjust (if necessary) every 60,000 miles.

➡**If the vehicle is equipped with a conventional ignition system, the timing should always be adjusted after installing new points or adjusting the dwell angle.**

On all non-CVCC engines, the timing marks are located on the crankshaft pulley, with a pointer on the timing belt cover. All are visible from the driver's side of the engine compartment. On all CVCC engines, the timing marks are located on the flywheel (manual transaxle) or torque converter drive plate (automatic transaxle), with a pointer on the rear of the cylinder block. All are visible from the front right side of the engine compartment after removing a special rubber access plug in the timing mark window. In all cases, the timing is checked with the engine warmed to operating temperature (176°F), idling in Neutral (manual transaxle) or Drive (automatic transaxle), and with all vacuum hoses connected.

1. Stop the engine and install a tachometer to the engine. The positive lead connects to the distributor side terminal of the ignition coil and the negative lead to a good ground, such as an engine bolt.

➡**On some models you will have to pull back the rubber ignition coil cover to reveal the terminals.**

2. Following the manufacturers instructions, install a timing light to the engine. The positive and negative leads connect to their corresponding battery terminals and the spark plug lead to No. 1 spark plug. The No. 1 spark plug is the one at the driver's side of the engine compartment.

Fig. 29 Install timing light and checking ignition timing

3. Make sure that all wires are clear of the cooling fan and hot exhaust manifolds.

4. Set the parking brake and block the front wheels. Start the engine. Check that the idle speed is set to specifications with the transaxle in **Neutral** (manual transaxle) or **Drive** (automatic transaxle).

5. If the distributor is equipped with a vacuum advance mechanism, disconnect the hose(s), plug it (them) and reinstall on the vacuum advance.

➡️**Any engine speed other than specified, the distributor advance or retard mechanisms will actuate, leading to an erroneous timing adjustment.**

6. Point the timing light at the timing marks.

➡️**On Non-CVCC, align the pointer with the F or red notch on the crankshaft pulley. On CVCC engines, align the pointer with the red notch on the flywheel or torque converter drive plate (except on vehicles where the timing specification is TDC in which case the T or white notch is used).**

7. If necessary to adjust the timing, loosen the distributor holddown (clamp) bolt(s) and/or nut, then, slowly rotate the distributor in the required direction while observing the timing marks.

❄️❄️CAUTION

DO NOT grasp the top of the distributor cap while the engine is running, as you might get a nasty shock. Instead, grab the distributor housing to rotate.

8. To complete the adjustment operation, tighten the holddown bolt, taking care not to disturb the adjustment. If equipped with a vacuum advance mechanism, unplug and reinstall the hose(s).

➡️**Some models are equipped with two bolts, others are equipped with a bolt and a nut, which may be loosened to adjust ignition timing. If there is a smaller bolt on the underside of the distributor swivel mounting plate, it should not be loosened, unless you cannot obtain a satisfactory adjustment using the upper bolt. Its purpose is to provide an extra range of adjustment, such as in cases where the distributor was removed and then installed one tooth off.**

Valve Arrangements

All valves are identified, starting from the front (camshaft sprocket) of the engine to the rear; Intake-I, Exhaust-E and Auxiliary-A.

NON-CVCC (1973-78)

Right Side: **I-I-I-I** (front-to-rear)
Left Side: **E-E-E-E** (front-to-rear)

1976-81 ACCORD, 1975-83 CIVIC CVCC AND 1979-81 PRELUDE

Right Side: **I-E-E-I-I-E-E-I** (front-to-rear)
Left Side: **A-A-A-A** (front-to-rear)

1982-83 ACCORD AND 1982 PRELUDE

Right Side: **E-I-E-I-I-E-I-E** (front-to-rear)
Left Side: **A-A-A-A** (front-to-rear)

1983 PRELUDE

Right Side: **I-I-I-I-I-I-I-I** (front-to-rear)
Left Side: **A-E-A-E-E-A-E-A** (front-to-rear)

Valve Lash

◆ **See Figures 30, 31 and 32**

Valve adjustment is one factor which determines how far the intake and exhaust valves will open into the cylinder. If the valve clearance is too large, part of the lift of the camshaft will be used up in removing the excessive clearance, thus the valves will not be opened far enough. This condition has several effects. The valve train components will emit a tapping noise as they take up the excessive clearance and also as they shut very abruptly. Also, the engine will perform poorly, as the valves will not cause the engine to breathe in the normal manner. Finally, the carburetor will produce a richer than normal mixture, increasing emissions and, possibly, fouling spark plugs over a great length of time.

If the valve clearance is too small, the intake and exhaust valves will not fully seat on the cylinder head when they close. When a valve seats on the cylinder head it does two things: it seals the combustion chamber so none of the gases in the cylinder can escape and it cools itself by transferring some of the heat it absorbed from the combustion process through the cylinder head and into the engine cooling system. Also, the change in valve timing that occurs will lean out the mixture, causing hesitation and possible burning of the valves. Therefore, if the valve clearance is too small, the engine will run poorly (due to gases escaping from the combustion chamber

85912036

Fig. 30 Removing the valve cover to adjust the valves

Fig. 31 Identify the valve arrangement

Fig. 32 Adjust the valves

and lean mixture) and the valves will tend to overheat and warp (since they cannot transfer heat unless they are touching the seat in the cylinder head).

Honda recommends that the valve clearance be checked at 12,000 mile intervals (1973-74 models) or 15,000 mile intervals (1975-83 models).

➡**While all valve adjustments must be as accurate as possible, it is better to have the valve adjustment slightly loose than slightly tight, as burned valves may result from overly tight adjustments. Valves that are only slightly loose will not damage the engine.**

NON-CVCC MODELS — 1973-78

1. Adjust the valves when the engine is **Cold**, 100°F (38°C) or less.
2. Remove the valve cover and align the TDC (Top Dead Center) mark on the crankshaft pulley with the index mark on the timing belt cover. The TDC notch is the one immediately following the 5° BTDC (red) notch used for setting ignition timing.
3. When the No. 1 cylinder is at TDC on the compression stroke, check and adjust the following valves (numbered from the crankshaft pulley end of the engine):
   • Intake — Nos. 1 and 2 cylinders
   • Exhaust — Nos. 1 and 3 cylinders

To adjust the valves, perform the following procedures:
4. Using a feeler gauge, check the valve clearance between the tip of the rocker arm and the top of the valve; there should be a slight drag on the feeler gauge.
   a. If there is no drag or the gauge cannot be inserted, loosen the valve adjusting screw locknut.
   b. Using a screwdriver, turn the adjusting screw to obtain the proper clearance.
   c. Hold the adjusting screw and tighten the locknut.
   d. Recheck the clearance before reinstalling the valve cover.
5. Rotate the crankshaft 360°, position the No. 4 piston on TDC its compression stroke, then, check and/or adjust the following valves by performing the procedures in Step 3.
   • Intake — Nos. 3 and 4 cylinders.
   • Exhaust — Nos. 2 and 4 cylinders.
6. To install the valve cover, use a new gasket, sealant (if necessary) and reverse the removal procedures.

CVCC MODELS

1975-78
▶ See Figure 33

The engine must be **Cold** (cylinder head temperature below 100°F) before performing this procedure.
1. Remove the valve cover.
2. From the front of the engine, take a look at the forward face of the camshaft timing belt gear. When the No. 1 cylinder is at Top Dead Center (TDC), the keyway for the woodruff key retaining the timing gear to the camshaft will be facing upward. On 1976-78 models, the word **UP** will be at the top of the gear. Double-check this by checking the distributor rotor position. Using a piece of chalk or crayon, mark the No. 1 spark plug wire position on the distributor cap; then, remove the cap and check that the rotor faces that mark.
3. With the No. 1 cylinder at the TDC of it compression stroke, adjust the following valves (numbered from the crankshaft pulley end of the engine):
   • Intake — Nos. 1 and 2 cylinders.
   • Auxiliary — Nos. 1 and 2 cylinders.
   • Exhaust — Nos. 1 and 3 cylinders. Adjust the valves as follows:
   a. Using a feeler gauge, position it between the tip of the rocker arm and the top of the valve; there should be a slight drag on the feeler gauge.

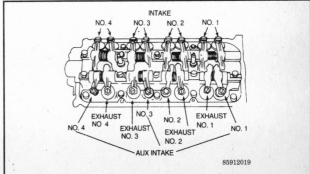

Fig. 33 Location of the intake, exhaust and auxiliary valves on the CVCC engines-others are similar

b. If there is no drag or if the gauge cannot be inserted, loosen the valve adjusting screw locknut.

c. Using a screwdriver, turn the adjusting screw to obtain the proper clearance.

d. Hold the adjusting screw and tighten the locknut.

e. Recheck the clearance before reinstalling the valve cover.

4. Rotate the crankshaft 360° to position the No. 4 cylinder on the TDC of its compression stroke; this will correspond to an 180° movement of the distributor rotor and camshaft timing gear. The rotor will now be pointing opposite the mark made for the No. 1 cylinder. The camshaft timing gear keyway or **UP** mark will now be at the bottom (6 o'clock position). Adjust the remaining valves:

- Intake — Nos. 3 and 4 cylinders.
- Auxiliary Intake — Nos. 3 and 4 cylinders.
- Exhaust — Nos. 2 and 4 cylinders.

1979-83 MODELS

▶ **See Figures 34, 35, 36 and 37**

Be aware the engines for this time period vary in the location of the intake, exhaust and auxiliary (intake) valves (see valve arrangements). Exhaust valves align with the exhaust manifold tubes and the intake valves with intake tubes.

➡**The valves cannot be adjusted until the engine has cooled to below 100°F (38°C).**

1. Remove the valve cover.

2. Using a wrench on the crankshaft pulley bolt, rotate the crankshaft until the No. 1 cylinder is on TDC of its compression stroke; the **UP**, round mark or semicircular cut in the bottom of the opening on the rear of the camshaft pulley aligns with the small mark on the rear of the timing belt housing and the two TDC marks on the rear of the pulley align with the cylinder head surface.

3. To double check the engine's position, perform the following procedures:

a. Remove the distributor cap; the distributor rotor should align with the No. 1 plug wire.

b. Adjust all of the valves for No. 1 cylinder.

➡**On Civics, the intake and auxiliary valves are adjusted to 0.13-0.18mm and exhaust valves to 0.18-0.23mm. On Preludes and Accords, the intakes are adjusted to 0.13-0.18mm and the exhausts to 0.25-0.30mm.**

c. Loosen the locknut. Using a flat feeler gauge, place it between the top of the valve and the adjusting stud. If the clearance is under, rotate the stud outward with a screwdriver until the blade can be inserted between the two items, then, tighten the stud very gently just until it touches the gauge. A slight drag on the gauge should be felt by moving the gauge in and out — it must not be pinched between the two parts. Hold the position of the stud with a screwdriver, then, tighten the locknut securely but not extremely tight — 14 ft. lbs. is the recommended torque (10 ft. lbs. for the auxiliary valve, which are smaller). Slide the gauge in and out to make sure the required clearance has been main-

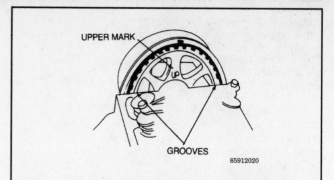

Fig. 34 Positioning the camshaft to adjust the valves for No. 1 cylinder-1979-83 engines

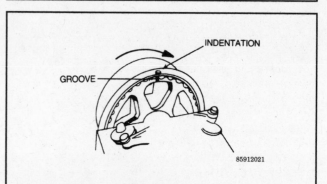

Fig. 35 Positioning the camshaft to adjust the valves for No. 3 cylinder-1979-83 engines

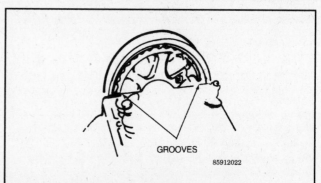

Fig. 36 Positioning the camshaft to adjust the valves for No. 4 cylinder-1979-83 engines

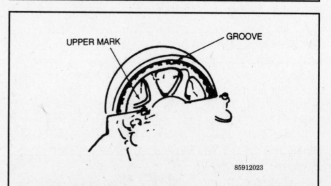

Fig. 37 Positioning the camshaft to adjust the valves for No. 2 cylinder-1979-83 engines

tained. If not, readjust the valve. Repeat the procedure for the remaining No. 1 cylinder valves.

➡**As the work progresses, keep double checking that you are using the proper gauge for the type of valve being adjusted.**

4. Rotate the crankshaft counterclockwise 180° (the camshaft turns 90°). Now, the TDC groove on the outer edge of the camshaft pulley should be aligned with the indentation on the timing belt cover. The distributor rotor will point to the No. 3 cylinder plug wire; the No. 3 cylinder should be on TDC of its compression stroke. Perform the same adjustment procedures as you did for the No. 1 cylinder.

5. Rotate the crankshaft counterclockwise 180°. Now the TDC grooves will again be visible and the distributor rotor will point to No. 4 cylinder's plug wire. The No. 4 cylinder should be at the TDC of its compression stroke. Perform the same adjustment procedures as you did for the No. 1 cylinder.

6. Rotate the crankshaft counterclockwise 180°, until the mark on the rear of the pulley aligns with the indentation on the belt cover and the distributor rotor points to No. 2 plug wire. The **UP** mark should also be visible, on the left side of the camshaft pulley. Perform the same adjustment procedures as you did for the No. 1 cylinder.

7. To install the valve cover, use a new gasket, sealant (if necessary) and reverse the removal procedures. Torque to 9 ft. lbs. For high valve covers, which use just two, crown type nuts, torque them evenly in several stages to 7 ft. lbs.

Idle Speed and Mixture Adjustment

This section contains only adjustments which apply to engine tune-up — namely, idle speed and mixture adjustments. Descriptions of the carburetors used and complete adjustment procedures can be found in Section 5.

Idle speed and mixture adjustment is the last step in any tune-up. Prior to making the final carburetor adjustments, make sure that the spark plugs, points and condenser (if used), dwell angle, ignition timing and valve clearance have all been checked, serviced and adjusted (if necessary). If any of these tune-up items have been overlooked, it may be difficult to obtain a proper adjustment.

➡**All adjustments must be made with the engine fully warmed to operating temperatures.**

CARBURETED MODELS

Civic 1170cc — Hitachi 2-bbl (1973)

1. Set the parking brake and block the front wheels.
2. Turn the headlights **ON** and the cooling fan **OFF**.
3. From the radiator base, on the engine side, disconnect the electrical leads from either the cooling fan motor or the thermoswitch (screwed into the base of the radiator).
4. If equipped with a manual transaxle, position the shift selector in **Neutral**; if equipped with a Hondamatic transaxle, position the shift selector to **gear 1**.
5. From the carburetor, remove the limiter cap and turn the idle mixture screw counterclockwise, until engine speed drops, then, turn the idle speed screw in the reverse direction (clock-

wise) until the engine reaches its highest rpm; if the idle speed is higher than specifications, repeat Steps 2 and 5.
6. Continue to turn the idle mixture screw clockwise to obtain the specified rpm drop:
   4-speed — 40 rpm.
   Hondamatic — 20 rpm.
7. Replace the limiter cap and reconnect the cooling fan lines.

Non-CVCC Civic — Hitachi 2-bbl (1974-77)

1. Set the parking brake and block the front wheels.
2. Turn the headlights **ON** and the radiator cooling fan **OFF**. To make sure that the cooling fan is turned **OFF** while you are making your adjustments, disconnect the fan leads.

✳✳CAUTION

DO NOT leave the cooling fan leads disconnected for any longer than necessary, as the engine may overheat.

3. If equipped with a manual transaxle, position the shift selector in **Neutral**; if equipped with a Hondamatic transaxle, position in shift selector in **gear 1**.
4. From the carburetor, remove the plastic limiter cap from the idle mixture screw.
5. Using a tachometer, connect it to the engine with the positive lead connected to the distributor side (terminal) of the coil and the negative lead to a good ground. On 1976 models, disconnect the breather hose from the valve cover.
6. Start the engine. To adjust, turn the mixture screw (turn counterclockwise to richen), then, the idle speed screw for the best quality idle at 870 rpm (manual transaxle) or 770 rpm (automatic transaxle in gear).
7. Turn the idle mixture screw (clockwise), until the idle speed drops to 800 rpm (manual transaxle) or 750 rpm (automatic transaxle in gear).
8. Replace the limiter cap, connect the cooling fan and disconnect the tachometer.

CVCC Models — Keihin 3-bbl (1977-79)

1. Apply the parking brake and block the front wheels.
2. Start the engine and allow it to reach normal operating temperatures, the cooling fan should turn **ON**.

➡**If the fan does not turn ON, load the electrical system (for purposes of adjusting the idle speed), by turning the high speed heater blower ON instead. Do not have both the cooling fan and heater blower operating simultaneously, as this will load the engine too much and lower the idle speed abnormally.**

3. Turn the headlights **ON**. Position the transaxle's shift selector in **Neutral** (manual transaxle) or in **2nd (Hi) Gear** (Hondamatic).
4. Using a tachometer, connect it to the engine with the positive lead connected to the distributor side (terminal) of the coil and the negative lead to a good ground.
5. Remove the plastic cap from the idle mixture screw. Start the engine and rotate the idle mixture screw counterclockwise (rich), until the highest rpm is achieved. Then, adjust the idle speed screw to 910 rpm (manual transaxle) or 810 rpm (automatic transaxle in 2nd gear).

6. Finally, lean out the idle mixture (turn mixture screw clockwise) until the idle speed drops to 700 rpm (manual transaxle) or 650 rpm (automatic transaxle in 2nd gear).

➡**If the idle speed cannot be adjusted properly, check and/or adjust the throttle cable.**

7. Replace the limiter cap (make sure the pointer is facing 180° away from the boss on the carburetor base) and disconnect the tachometer.

Carbureted Engines (1980-83)
▶ **See Figure 38**

Changes in the carburetors have made the adjustment of the idle mixture impossible without a propane enrichment system not available to the general public. The idle speed may be adjusted as follows:

1. Operate the engine until normal operating temperatures are reached.
2. Remove the vacuum hose from the intake air control diaphragm and clamp the hose end.
3. Using a tachometer, connect it to the engine.
4. With the headlights, heater blower, rear window defroster, cooling fan and air conditioner **OFF**, adjust the idle speed by turning the throttle stop screw to the rpm listed in the **Tune-Up Specifications** or underhood sticker.

CVCC Models — Keihin 3-bbl (1980-82)
▶ **See Figures 39, 40 and 41**

➡**This procedure requires a propane enrichment kit, and, for California cars, a special tool for fuel/air mixture adjustment.**

1. Start the engine and warm it up to normal operating temperature. The cooling fan will come on.
2. Remove the vacuum tube from the intake air control diaphragm and plug the tube end.
3. Connect a tachometer.
4. Check the idle speed with the headlights, cooling fan and air conditioner OFF. Adjust the idle speed if necessary, by turning the throttle stop screw. Idle speed should be set to the specifications found in the Tune-Up Specifications Chart or on the emission control decal in the engine compartment.
5. Remove the air cleaner intake tube from the air duct on the radiator bulkhead.
6. Insert the tube of the propane enrichment kit into the intake tube about 4 inches.

Fig. 38 Common mixture adjustment plug on carburetor assembly

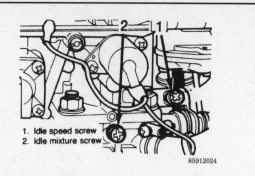
1. Idle speed screw
2. Idle mixture screw

Fig. 39 Idle speed and mixture screws-Keihin 3 bbl carburetor

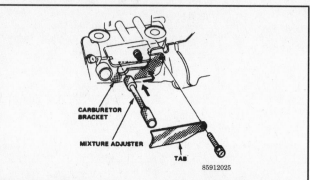
CARBURETOR BRACKET
MIXTURE ADJUSTER
TAB

Fig. 40 Using special tool for mixture adjustment on California models

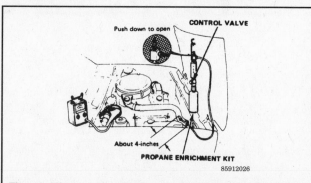
Push down to open
CONTROL VALVE
About 4-inches
PROPANE ENRICHMENT KIT

Fig. 41 Mixture adjustment using propane enrichment method

7. With the engine idling, depress the push button on top of the propane device, then slowly open the propane control valve to obtain maximum engine speed. Engine speed should increase as the percentage of injected propane increases.

➡**Open the propane control valve slowly; a sudden burst of propane may stall the engine.**

a. If the engine speed does not increase, the mixture screw is improperly adjusted. Go to Step 8.
b. If the engine speed increase, go to Step 9.
8. Lean out the mixture until the idle speed (with propane on) increases. On California cars remove the screws on the right side of the carburetor then swing the tab out of the way. Insert the mixture adjuster all the way to the right and slip it

onto mixture the screw. Turn the mixture screw clockwise to lean out the mixture as required.

➡ **49 States models still have the normal mixture screw. No special tools are required for mixture adjustment.**

a. If the speed increase matched the specification, go to Step 11.

b. If the speed increase is out of specification, go to Step 9.

9. Check the speed increase against the specifications. If adjustment is required, adjust the engine speed to the propane enriched maximum rpm by turning the mixture screw. Turn it clockwise to increase; counterclockwise to decrease. Again, adjust the propane control valve for maximum engine speed.

10. Close the propane control valve and recheck the idle speed.

➡ **Run the engine at 2500 rpm for 10 seconds to stabilize the condition.**

a. If the idle speed is as specified (Step 4) go to Step 12.

b. If the idle speed is not as specified (Step 4), go to Step 11.

11. Recheck the idle speed and, if necessary, adjust it by turning the throttle stop screw, then repeat Steps 7-10.

12. Remove the propane enrichment kit and reconnect the air cleaner intake tube on the radiator bulkhead.

13. On 49 States cars, install the limiter cap with the pointer 180° away from the boss on the carburetor body. On California cars, remove the mixture adjuster, then push the tab back into place and install the screw.

14. If the car is equipped with air conditioning, recheck the idle speed with the air conditioning on. The speed should still be within specifications. If the speed is outside the specification, remove the rubber cap on the idle boost diaphragm and adjust it by turning the adjusting screw.

CVCC Models — Keihin 3-bbl (1983 Models)

➡ **This procedure requires a propane enrichment kit.**

1. Start the engine and warm it up to normal operating temperature. The cooling fan will come on.

2. Remove the vacuum hose from the intake air control diaphragm and clamp the hose end.

3. Connect a tachometer to the engine as per the manufacturer's instructions.

4. Check the idle speed with the headlights, heater blower, rear window defroster, cooling fan and the air conditioner OFF. Idle speed should be set to specifications according to the Tune-Up Specifications Chart or the emission control decal in the engine compartment.

5. Adjust the idle speed if necessary with the throttle stop screw.

a. On the Prelude with automatic transmission, remove the frequency solenoid valve and the control valve. Disconnect the vacuum tubes and connect the lower hose to the air control valve.

b. On the Accord with automatic transmission, remove the air filter from the frequency solenoid valve and plug the

opening in the solenoid valve. On all models, insert the tube of the propane enrichment kit into the air intake tube about 4 inches.

6. With the engine idling, depress the push button on top of the propane device, then slowly open the propane control valve to obtain maximum engine speed. Engine speed should increase as the percentage of the propane injected goes up.

➡ **Open the propane control valve slowly; a sudden burst of propane may stall the engine.**

7. Remove the air cleaner. Disconnect the vacuum hose from the fast idle unloader. Remove the bolts holding the throttle opener bracket to the rear edge of the carburetor.

8. On the Accord and Civic models, remove the carburetor nuts and washers. Remove the brake booster hose and throttle cable from their brackets. Lift the carburetor off the studs and tilt it backwards. Remove the throttle opener screw and bracket.

9. Remove the mixture adjusting screw cap from the throttle opener bracket. Reinstall the bracket. Using new O-rings on the insulator and new gaskets on the heat shield, install the carburetor.

10. Reconnect the vacuum hose to the fast idle unloader.

11. Install the air cleaner, start the engine and warm it to normal operating temperature. The cooling fan will come on.

12. Disconnect and plug the vacuum hose from the intake air control diaphragm.

13. On the Prelude models, label and disconnect all the lines from the carburetors. Disconnect the throttle cable and the vacuum hose from the throttle opener diaphragm. Disconnect the automatic choke lead. Drain the coolant and disconnect hoses. Remove the carburetors.

✳✳CAUTION

When draining the coolant, keep in mind that cats and dogs are attracted by the ethylene glycol antifreeze, and are quite likely to drink any that is left in an uncovered container or in puddles on the ground. This will prove fatal in sufficient quantity. Always drain the coolant into a sealable container. Coolant should be reused unless it is contaminated or several years old.

14. Place a drill stop on a 3mm drill bit, 3mm from end. Drill through the center of the mixture screw plug. Screw a 5mm sheet metal screw into the plug. Grab the screw head with a pair of pliers and remove the plug. Reinstall the carburetors in the reverse order of removal and refill the cooling system.

15. On all models, install the propane enrichment kit and recheck the maximum propane enriched rpm. If the enriched rpm is too low, lean out the mixture. If it is too high, enrich the mixture. Turn the mixture screw clockwise to increase rpm; counterclockwise to decrease rpm.

16. Run the engine for about 10 seconds to stabilize the mixture. Close the propane control valve and recheck the idle speed. Repeat the procedure until the idle rpm is correct. Remove the propane enrichment kit and reconnect the air cleaner intake tube.

Keihin Dual Sidedraft (1983 Prelude)

➡This procedure requires a propane enrichment kit. Check that carburetors are synchronized properly before making idle speed and mixture inspection. It will also be necessary to remove the ECU fuse from the fuse box for at least 10 seconds to reset the control unit, after this procedure is complete.

1. Start engine and warm up to normal operating temperature. Cooling fan will come on.
2. Remove vacuum hose from intake air control diaphragm and clamp hose end.
3. Connect tachometer. Check that the fast idle lever is not seated against the fast idle cam.

➡If the fast idle lever is seated against the fast idle cam, it may be necessary to replace the left carburetor.

4. Check idle speed with all accessories turned off. Idle speed should be 800 ± 50 rpm (750 ± 50 rpm on automatic transmission in gear). Adjust idle speed, if necessary, by turning throttle stop screw.

➡If the idle speed is excessively high, check the throttle control.

5. On automatic cars only, remove attaching bolt, then remove frequency solenoid valve and air control valve. Disconnect the two prong connector from the EACV and disconnect the hose from the vacuum hose manifold, then cap the hose end.
6. Disconnect vacuum tubes and connect lower hose to air control valve. Disconnect the vacuum hose from the air conditioning idle boost throttle controller. Disconnect the air cleaner intake tube from the air intake duct.
7. Insert propane enrichment hose into opening of intake tube about 4".

➡It is not necessary to disconnect intake tube. Opening for the tube is just behind right headlight. Check that propane bottle has adequate gas before beginning test.

8. With engine idling, depress push button on top of propane device, then slowly open propane control valve to obtain maximum engine speed. Engine speed should increase as percentage of propane injected goes up.

➡Open propane control valve slowly. Sudden burst of propane may stall engine.

9. Propane enrichment maximum rpm:
   - 1983 manual transmission — 45 ± 25 rpm.
   - 1983 automatic transmission — 110 ± 25 rpm (in D3 or D4).
10. If engine speed does not increase per specification, remove carburetor.

11. Place a drill stop on a ⅛" drill bit, then drill through center of mixture screw hole plug.

➡If drilled deeper than this measurement, damage to mixture adjusting screw may result from bit. On the later models, remove the mixture adjusting screw hole caps, by pulling them straight out.

12. Screw a 5mm sheet metal screw into hole plug.
13. Grab screw head with a pair of pliers and remove hole plug.
14. Reinstall carburetor.
15. Start engine and warm up to normal operating temperature. Cooling fan will come on.
16. Recheck maximum propane enriched rpm. If mixture is rich, turn both mixture screws ¼ turn counterclockwise.
17. Close propane control valve.
18. Run engine at 2500 rpm for 1800 seconds to stabilize mixture conditions, then check idle speed. Adjust idle speed, if necessary.
19. Disconnect upper #22 vacuum hose from air leak solenoid valve at air jet controller stay, and plug end of hose, than connect a vacuum gauge to solenoid valve.
20. With engine idling, depress push button on top of propane device, then slowly open propane control valve and check vacuum. Vacuum should be available.
21. If no vacuum, inspect air leak solenoid valve.
22. Inspect thermovalve.
23. Remove propane enrichment kit and reconnect connector.
24. Install new plugs into idle mixture screw holes.

Tailpipe Emission Inspection

CARBURETED MODELS

1. Perform Steps 1-2 of the Propane Enrichment Procedure as outlined in this section. If necessary adjust the idle speed. On Accord and Civic models, disconnect the air cleaner intake tube from the air duct on the radiator bulkhead.
2. Warm up and calibrate the CO meter according to the manufacturer's instructions.
3. Check the idle CO with the headlights, heater blower, rear window defroster, cooling fan and the air conditioner off. The CO reading should be 0.1% maximum. If the CO level is correct go to Step 4. If the CO level is not correct, remove the idle mixture plug as described in the Propane Enrichment Procedure and adjust the mixture screws to obtain the proper CO meter reading.
4. Recheck the idle speed and adjust it if necessary by turning the throttle stop screw. Recheck the CO level and adjust, if necessary. On Prelude models, check and adjust the propane enriched rpm according the Propane Enrichment Procedure above.

GASOLINE ENGINE TUNE-UP SPECIFICATIONS

Year	Model	Engine Displacement (cc)	Spark Plugs Type	Gap (in.)	Ignition Timing (deg.) MT	AT	Compression (psi)	Fuel Pump (psi)	Idle Speed (rpm) MT	AT	Valve Clearance In. ⑧	Ex.
1973	Civic	1170	B-6ES ⑨	.030	TDC ①	TDC ①	N.A.	2.5	750–850	700–800	0.005–0.007	0.005–0.007
1974	Civic 1200	1237	B-6ES ⑨	.030	5B ①	5B ①	N.A.	2.5	750–850	700–800	0.004–0.006	0.004–0.006
1975	Civic 1200	1237	B-6ES ⑨	.030	7B ①	7B ①	N.A.	2.5	750–850	700–800	0.004–0.006	0.004–0.006
	Civic CVCC	1487	B-6ES ⑨	.030	TDC	3A	N.A.	2.5	800–900	700–800	0.005–0.007	0.005–0.007
1976	Civic 1200	1237	B-6ES ⑨	.030	7B ①	7B ①	N.A.	2.5	750–850	700–800	0.004–0.006	0.004–0.006
	Civic CVCC	1487	B-6ES ⑨	.030	2B ⑩	2B ⑪	N.A.	2.5	800–900	700–800	0.005–0.007	0.005–0.007
	Accord	1600	B-6ES ⑨	.030	6B	2B	N.A.	2.5	800–900	700–800	0.005–0.007	0.005–0.007
1977	Civic 1200	1237	B-6ES ⑨	.030	7B ①	7B ①	N.A.	2.5	750–850	700–800	0.004–0.006	0.004–0.006
	Civic CVCC	1487	B-6ES ⑨	.030	2B ⑩	2B ⑪	N.A.	2.5	800–900	700–800	0.005–0.007	0.005–0.007
	Accord	1600	B-6ES ⑦	.030	6B	2B	N.A.	2.5	800–900	700–800	0.005–0.007	0.005–0.007
1978	Civic 1200	1237	B-6ES ⑨	.030	7B ①	7B ①	N.A.	2.5	750–850	700–800	0.004–0.006	0.004–0.006
	Civic CVCC	1487	B-6ES ⑨	.030	2B ⑩	2B ⑪	N.A.	2.5	800–900	700–800	0.005–0.007	0.005–0.007
	Accord	1600	B-6ES ⑨	.030	6B	2B	N.A.	2.5	800–900	700–800	0.005–0.007	0.005–0.007
1979	Civic 1200	1237	B-6ES ⑨	.030	2B ①	2B ①	N.A.	2.5	650–750	600–700	0.004–0.006	0.004–0.006
	Civic CVCC	1487	B-6EB ⑨	.030	2B	6B	N.A.	2.5	650–750	600–700	0.005–0.007	0.007–0.009
	Accord	1751	B-7EB	.030	6B ⑫	4B ⑫	190	2.5	650–750 ①	650–750 ②	0.005–0.007	0.010–0.012
	Prelude	1751	B-7EB	.030	6B ⑫	4B ⑬	190	2.5	650–750 ①	650–750 ②	0.005–0.007	0.010–0.012
1980	Civic 1300	1335	B6EB-11	.042	2B ③	TDC	180	2.5	700–800	700–800	0.005–0.007	0.007–0.009
	Civic CVCC	1487	B7EB-11	.042	15B ⑭	TDC	180	2.5	700–800	700–800	0.005–0.007	0.007–0.009
	Accord	1751	B-7EB	.030	4B	TDC	190	2.5	750–850 ①	750–850 ②	0.005–0.007	0.010–0.012
	Prelude	1751	B-7EB	.030	4B	TDC	190	2.5	750–850 ①	750–850 ②	0.005–0.007	0.010–0.012

GASOLINE ENGINE TUNE-UP SPECIFICATIONS

Year	Model	Engine Displacement (cc)	Spark Plugs Type	Gap (in.)	Ignition Timing (deg.) MT	AT	Compression (psi)	Fuel Pump (psi)	Idle Speed (rpm) MT	AT	Valve Clearance In. ⑧	Ex.
1981	Civic	1487	B6EB-11	.042	10B	2A	180	2.5	700–800 ①	700–800 ②	0.005–0.007	0.007–0.009
	Civic 1300	1335	B6EB-11	.042	2B ③	—	180	2.5	700–800 ①	—	0.005–0.007	0.007–0.009
	Accord	1751	BR6EB-L11	.042	TDC ⑦	TDC	190	2.5	750–850 ①	750–850 ②	0.005–0.007	0.010–0.012
	Prelude	1751	B6EB-L11	.042	TDC ⑦	TDC	190	2.5	750–850 ①	750–850 ②	0.005–0.007	0.010–0.012
1982	Civic 1300	1335	BR6EB-11	.042	20B ③	—	210	2.5	650–750 ①	—	0.005–0.007	0.007–0.009
	Civic 1500	1487	BR6EB-11	.042	18B ③	18B ③	190	2.5	650–750 ①	650–750 ②	0.005–0.007	0.007–0.009
	Accord	1751	BR6EB-L11	.042	16B ④	16B	190	2.5	750–850 ①	750–850 ②	0.005–0.007	0.010–0.012
	Prelude	1751	BR6EB-L11	.042	12B ⑤	16B	190	2.5	700–800 ①	700–800 ②	0.005–0.007	0.010–0.012
1983	Civic 1300	1335	BR6EB-11	.042	18B ⑥③	—	210	2.5	600–750 ①	—	0.005–0.007	0.007–0.009
	Civic 1500	1487	BR6EB-11	.042	18B ③	18B	210 ③	2.5	650–750 ①	650–750 ②	0.005–0.007	0.007–0.009
	Accord	1751	BR6EB-L11	.042	16B ④③	16B ③	195	2.5	700–800 ①	650–750 ②	0.005–0.007	0.010–0.012
	Prelude	1829	BUR6EB-11	.042	10B ④③	12B ③	215	2.5	750–850 ①	700–800 ②	0.005–0.007	0.010–0.012

NOTE: The underhood specifications sticker often reflects tune-up specification changes in production. Sticker figures must be used if they disagree with those in this chart.

TDC—Top Dead Center
B—Before Top Dead Center
A—After Top Dead Center
—Not applicable
NA—Not available
① In neutral, with headlights on
② In drive range, with headlights on
③ Aim timing light at red mark on fly wheel or torque converter drive plate with the distributor vacuum hose connected at the specified idle speed.

④ Calif.: 12B
⑤ Std.: Calif. 16B
  MT: 20B, AT: 15B
⑥ 4 speed: 20B
⑦ Aim timing light at white mark
⑧ Auxiliary valve, all except 1342cc and 1488cc: 0.005–0.007
  1342cc and 1488cc: 0.007–0.009

⑨ Ignition point: gap: .020
  dwell: 49–55
⑩ Sedan with 5 speed from engine number 2500001 and up: 6B
⑪ Station Wagon: TDC
⑫ California and high altitude: TDC
⑬ California and high altitude: 2B
⑭ Station Wagon 49 states: 10B

85912C1a

3

ENGINE
AND
ENGINE
OVERHAUL

ENGINE ELECTRICAL

Ignition Coil

TESTING

1973-83

▶ See Figure 1

1. Turn the ignition switch **OFF**.
2. Disconnect the primary and the secondary wiring connectors from the ignition coil.
3. Using an ohmmeter, inspect the resistance between the primary terminals; the resistance should be 3.42-4.18Ω @ 70°F (1973-75), 1.35-1.65Ω @ 70°F (1976-78), 1.78-2.08Ω @ 70°F (1979-80) or 1.06-1.24Ω @ 70°F (1981-83). If the resistance measured does not agree with the desired reading, replace the ignition coil.

➡**The resistance will vary with the coil's temperature.**

4. Using an ohmmeter, inspect the resistance between the primary positive (+) terminal and the **secondary** wiring terminal; the resistance should be 6,400-9,600Ω @ 70°F (1973-75), 8,000-12,000Ω @ 70°F (1976-78), 8,800-13,200Ω @ 70°F (1979-80) or 7,400-11,000Ω @ 70°F (1981-83). If the measured resistance does not agree with the desired readings, replace the ignition coil.

REMOVAL & INSTALLATION

1. Disconnect the negative battery cable. Turn the ignition switch **OFF**.
2. Disconnect the primary and the secondary wiring connectors from the ignition coil.
3. Remove the ignition coil-to-mount screws and the coil from the vehicle.
4. To install, reverse the removal procedures.

Distributor

The distributor is bevel gear driven by the camshaft on 1973-83 engines except Prelude. On the 1983 Prelude the distributor is driven directly by the camshaft.

All distributors utilize centrifugal advance mechanisms to advance ignition timing as engine speed increases. Centrifugal advance is controlled by a pair of weights located under the breaker plate. As the distributor shaft spins faster, the weights are affected by centrifugal force and move away from the shaft, advancing the timing.

In addition, all distributors use some kind of vacuum ignition control, although this varies from model to model.

Vacuum advance works as follows: When the engine is operating under low load conditions (light acceleration), the vacuum diaphragm moves the breaker plate in the opposite direction of distributor rotation, thereby advancing the timing.

Vacuum retard, on the other hand, is actuated when the engine is operating under high vacuum conditions (deceleration or idle), and moves the breaker plate in the same direction of rotation as the distributor, thereby retarding the spark. On models equipped with both vacuum advance and retard, both these ignition characteristics are true. You can always tell a dual diaphragm distributor by its two hoses.

REMOVAL & INSTALLATION

Breaker Point Type

ENGINE UNDISTURBED

▶ See Figures 2, 3 and 4

1. Disconnect the negative battery terminal from the battery.
2. Disconnect the high tension (distributor-to-coil) lead and the primary leads, then, move them out of the way.
3. At the distributor cap, unsnap the retaining clamps. Remove the distributor cap and move it out of the way.
4. To position the No. 1 piston at the TDC of its compression stroke, perform the following procedures:
   a. Locate the No. 1 spark plug wire position on the distributor cap and align the cap with the housing.
   b. Using a piece of chalk, mark the No. 1 cylinder position on the distributor housing.

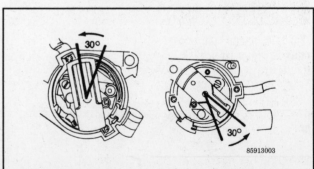

Fig. 1 Testing the secondary winding resistance of the ignition coil

85913002

Fig. 2 Upon installation the rotor will turn 30 degrees. Allow for this when installing the distributor assembly.

85913003

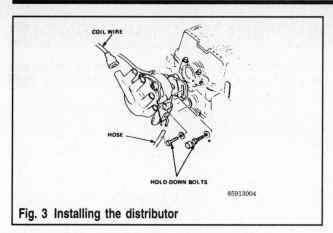

Fig. 3 Installing the distributor

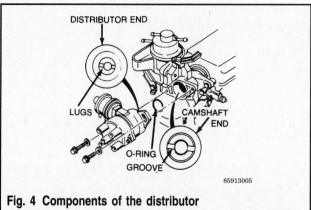

Fig. 4 Components of the distributor

c. Using a wrench on the crankshaft pulley, rotate the crankshaft until the distributor rotor aligns with the mark on the distributor housing.

5. Using a piece of chalk, mark distributor rotor-to-housing position and the distributor housing-to-engine position. When this is done, the mark on the distributor housing should be aligned with the rotor tip and the engine block mark.

➡This aligning procedure is very important because the distributor must be reinstalled in the exact location from which it was removed, if correct ignition timing is to be maintained.

6. Note the position of the vacuum line(s) on the vacuum diaphragm with masking tape, then, disconnect the line(s) from the vacuum unit.

7. Remove the distributor holddown bolts and the distributor from the engine.

✳✳WARNING

DO NOT disturb the engine while the distributor is removed. If you attempt to start the engine with the distributor removed, you will have to retime the engine.

8. To install, place the rotor on the distributor shaft and align the tip of the rotor with the line that you made on the distributor housing.

9. With the rotor and housing aligned, insert the distributor into the engine while aligning the mark on the housing with the mark on the block or extension housing.

➡Since the distributor pinion gear has helical teeth, the rotor will turn slightly as the distributor gear meshes with the camshaft gear. Allow for this when installing the distributor by aligning the mark on the distributor with the mark on the block but positioning the tip of the rotor slightly to the side of the mark on the distributor.

10. When the distributor is fully seated in the engine, install and tighten the distributor holddown bolts.

11. To complete the installation, reverse the removal procedures. If necessary, refer to Section 2 to check and/or adjust the ignition timing.

INSTALLATION WHEN ENGINE HAS BEEN DISTURBED

If the engine was cranked with the distributor removed, it will be necessary to retime the engine. If you have installed the distributor incorrectly and you have found that, for that reason, the engine will not start, remove the distributor from the engine and start from scratch.

1. To position the engine on the correct firing position, perform the following procedures:

   a. Remove the No. 1 spark plug from the engine.

   b. Using a clean rag, insert it into the spark plug hole.

   c. Using a wrench on the crankshaft pulley bolt, rotate the engine until the compression blows the rag from the No. 1 cylinder. Check and/or align the engine's timing mark(s); this is the TDC of the No. 1 cylinder's compression stroke.

2. Align the rotor with the No. 1 cylinder position on the distributor housing.

3. Carefully insert the distributor into the cylinder head opening with the holddown bolt slot aligned with the distributor mounting hole in the cylinder head, then, secure the plate at the center of the adjusting slot. The rotor head must face No. 1 cylinder.

➡Since the distributor pinion gear has helical teeth, the rotor will turn slightly as the gear on the distributor meshes with the gear on the camshaft. Allow for this when installing the distributor by positioning the tip of the rotor to the side of the protrusion.

4. To complete the installation, reverse the removal procedures. If necessary, refer to Section 2 to check and/or adjust the ignition timing. Inspect and adjust the point gap.

Electronic Ignition Type
▶ See Figures 5 and 6

1. Using masking tape, remove the spark plug wires from the cap and number them for installation as they are removed.

2. Disconnect the vacuum hoses, the primary wire and the high tension wire.

3. Remove the holddown bolt(s) and pull the distributor from the head.

4. Crank the engine until No. 1 piston is at TDC of its compression stroke.

5. Using a new O-ring, install it on the distributor housing.

6. Align the raised mark on the lower part of the distributor housing with the punch mark on the distributor gear shaft. Insert the distributor into the head and the rotor will turn to No.

Fig. 5 Removing the vacuum hose form the distributor vacuum advance unit

Fig. 6 Removing the hold-down bolt form the distributor assembly

1 firing position. Loosely install the holddown bolt(s). Tighten the bolt(s) temporarily and replace the cap.

7. Connect all wires and hoses.
8. Start the engine and adjust the ignition timing.

Alternator

The alternator converts the mechanical energy which is supplied by the drive belt into electrical energy by electromagnetic induction. When the ignition switch is turned **ON**, current flows from the battery, through the charging system light or ammeter, to the voltage regulator and finally to the alternator. When the engine is started, the drive belt turns the rotating field (rotor) in the stationary windings (stator), inducing alternating current. This alternating current is converted into usable direct current by the diode rectifier. Most of this current is used to charge the battery and power the electrical components of the vehicle. A small part is returned to the field windings of the alternator enabling it to increase its output. When the current in the field windings reaches a predetermined control voltage, the voltage regulator grounds the circuit, preventing any further increase. The cycle is continued so that the voltage remains constant.

On early non-CVCC models, the alternator is located beneath the distributor toward the rear of the engine compartment. On all other models, the alternator is located near the No. 1 spark plug at the front of the engine compartment. On models equipped with air conditioning, the alternator is mounted on a special vibration absorbing bracket at the driver's side of the engine compartment.

PRECAUTIONS

1. Observe the proper polarity of the battery connections by making sure that the positive (+) and negative (-) terminal connections are not reversed. Misconnection will allow current to flow in the reverse direction, resulting in damaged diodes and an overheated wire harness.
2. Never ground or short out any alternator or alternator regulator terminals.
3. Never operate the alternator with any of its or the battery's leads disconnected.
4. Always remove the battery or disconnect its output lead while charging it.
5. Always disconnect the ground cable when replacing any electrical components.
6. Never subject the alternator to excessive heat or dampness.
7. Never use arc welding equipment with the alternator connected.

REMOVAL & INSTALLATION

▶ **See Figure 7**

1. Disconnect the negative (-) battery terminal.
2. Disconnect the wire(s) and/or harness connector from the rear of the alternator.
3. Remove the alternator-to-bracket bolts, the V-belt and the alternator assembly from the engine.
4. To install, reverse the removal procedure. Adjust the alternator belt tension according to the "Belt Tension Adjustment" section below. Torque the lower alternator-to-bracket bolt(s) to 33 ft. lbs. and the upper adjusting nut/bolt to 17 ft. lbs.

BELT TENSION ADJUSTMENT

The initial inspection and adjustment to the alternator drive belt should be performed after the first 3,000 miles or if the alternator has been moved for any reason. Afterwards, you should inspect the belt tension every 12,000 miles (1973-78), 15,000 miles (1977-79) or 30,000 miles (1980-83). Before adjusting, inspect the belt to see that it is not cracked or worn. Be sure that its surfaces are free of grease and oil.

1. Push down on the belt halfway between pulleys with a force of about 24 lbs. The belt should deflect 12-17mm.
2. If the belt tension requires adjustment, loosen the adjusting link bolt and move the alternator with a pry bar positioned against the front of the alternator housing.

✳✳WARNING

Do not apply pressure to any other part of the alternator.

3. After obtaining the proper tension, tighten the adjusting link. Do not overtighten the belt; damage to the alternator bearings could result.

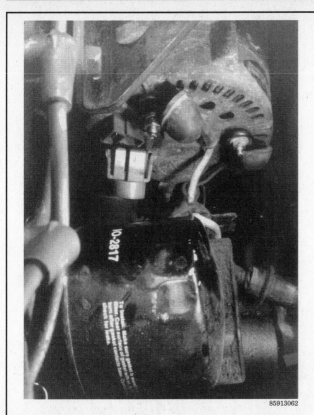

Fig. 7 Rear view of alternator connections. Always disconnect before starting this repair.

Regulator

The regulator is a device which controls the output of the alternator. If the regulator did not limit the voltage output of the alternator, the excessive output could burn out components of the electrical system, as well as the alternator itself.

REMOVAL & INSTALLATION

Except 1982-83 Accord

The regulator is inside the engine compartment, attached to the right fenderwell just above the battery.
1. Disconnect the negative (-) terminal from the battery.
2. Remove and label the regulator terminal lead wires to avoid confusion during installation.
3. Remove the regulator retaining bolts and the regulator from the vehicle.
4. To install, reverse the removal procedure.

1982-83 Accord
▶ See Figure 8

1. Disconnect the negative (-) terminal from the battery.
2. Remove the four main fuse plate retaining bolts and the main fuse plate to gain access to the solid state regulator.

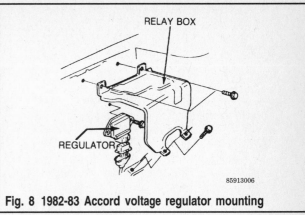

Fig. 8 1982-83 Accord voltage regulator mounting

3. Remove the regulator terminal plug from the regulator.
4. Unscrew the regulator retaining bolts and remove the regulator from the vehicle.
5. To install, reverse the removal procedure.

Battery

REMOVAL & INSTALLATION

The battery is located in the engine compartment on all models.
1. Make sure the ignition switch is turned **OFF**.
2. Disconnect the negative battery cable (1st), then, the positive cable from the battery.
3. Remove the battery holddown clamp nuts, the clamp and the battery from the vehicle.
4. To install, reverse the removal procedures; be sure the battery is seated correctly on the battery tray.

➡**Before installing the battery, it would be a wise idea to clean the battery posts and the terminal connectors.**

5. Install the positive battery cable (1st), then, the negative battery cable. Coat the battery terminals with a non-metallic grease; this will keep the terminals from oxidizing.

Starter

The starter is located on the firewall side of the engine block, adjacent to the flywheel or torque converter housing. On 1170cc and 1237cc models, use a direct drive type starter, while the CVCC uses a gear reduction starter. Otherwise, the two units are similar in operation and service. Both starters are 4-pole, series wound, DC units to which an outboard solenoid is mounted. When the ignition switch is turned to the start position, the solenoid armature is drawn in, engaging the starter pinion with the flywheel. When the starter pinion and flywheel are fully engaged, the solenoid armature closes the main contacts for the starter, causing the starter to crank the engine. When the engine starts, the increased speed of the flywheel causes the gear to overrun the starter clutch and rotor. The gear continues in full mesh until the ignition is switched from the start to the on position, interrupting the starter current. The shift lever spring then returns the gear to its neutral position.

REMOVAL & INSTALLATION

▶ See Figures 9 and 10

1. Disconnect the negative battery terminal and the starter motor cable at the positive terminal.
2. Disconnect the starter motor cable from the motor.
3. Remove the starter motor by loosening the two attaching bolts. On CVCC models, the bolts attach from opposing ends of the starter.
4. To install, reverse the removal procedures. Torque the starter-to-engine bolts to 29-36 ft. lbs. and make sure that all wires are securely connected.

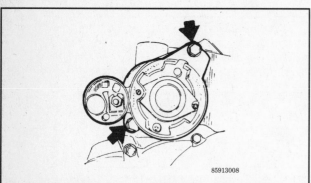

85913008

Fig. 9 Non CVCC engine starter showing mounting bolts (arrows)

85913063

Fig. 10 Rear view of starter assembly connections. Always disconnect the battery before starting this repair.

STARTER DRIVE REPLACEMENT

Hitachi And Nippondenso Direct Drive Types

▶ See Figures 11, 12 and 13

1. Remove the solenoid by loosening and removing the attaching bolts.
2. Remove the two brush holder plate retaining screws from the rear cover. Also pry off the rear dust cover along with the clip and thrust washer(s).
3. Remove the two through-bolts from the rear cover and lightly tap the rear cover with a mallet to remove it.
4. Remove the four carbon brushes from the brush holder and the brush holder.
5. Separate the yoke from the case. The yoke is provided with a hole for positioning, into which the gear case lock pin is inserted.
6. Pull the yoke assembly from the gear case, being sure to carefully detach the shift lever from the pinion.
7. Remove the armature unit from the yoke casing and the field coil.
8. To remove the pinion gear from the armature, first set the armature on end with the pinion end facing upward and pull the clutch stop collar downward toward the pinion. Remove the pinion stop clip, then, pull the pinion stop and gears from the armature shaft as a unit.
9. To assemble and install the starter motor, reverse the disassembly and removal procedures. Be sure to install new clips, be careful of the installation direction of the shift lever.

Nippondenso Reduction Gear Type

These starters come in 1.0 and 1.4 KW sizes and are used on various models, the larger power rating on the larger engines. They may be identified in two ways. This starter uses a double reduction set of pinion gears and has a very wide reduction gear housing. Also, its solenoid is housed entirely within the housing of the starter, rather than in an externally visible unit.

1. Remove the solenoid end cover. Pull out the solenoid. There is a spring on the shaft and a steel ball at the end of the shaft.
2. Remove the through bolts retaining the end frame to the motor and solenoid housing.
3. Remove the end frame. The over-running clutch assembly complete with drive gear can be removed. The idler and motor pinion gears can be removed separately. The idler gear retains five steel roller bearings.
4. The clutch assembly is held together by a circlip. Push down on the gear against the spring inside the clutch assembly and remove the circlip with a circlip expander. Slide the stopper ring, gear, spring and washer out of the clutch assembly.
5. To assemble, reverse the disassembly procedures. The stopper ring is installed with the smaller end with the lip towards the clutch. Be sure that the steel ball is in place at the end of the solenoid shaft. Grease all sliding surfaces of the solenoid before reassembly.

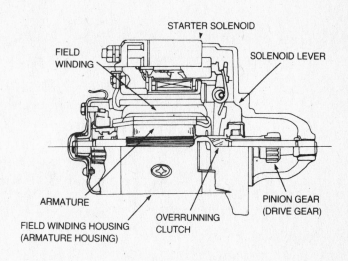

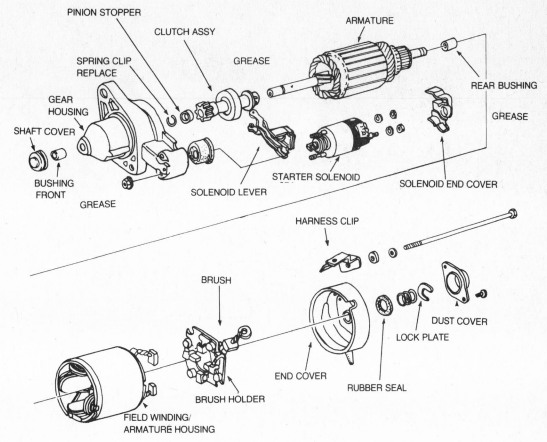

Fig. 11 Exploded view of the Nippondenso direct-drive starter motor

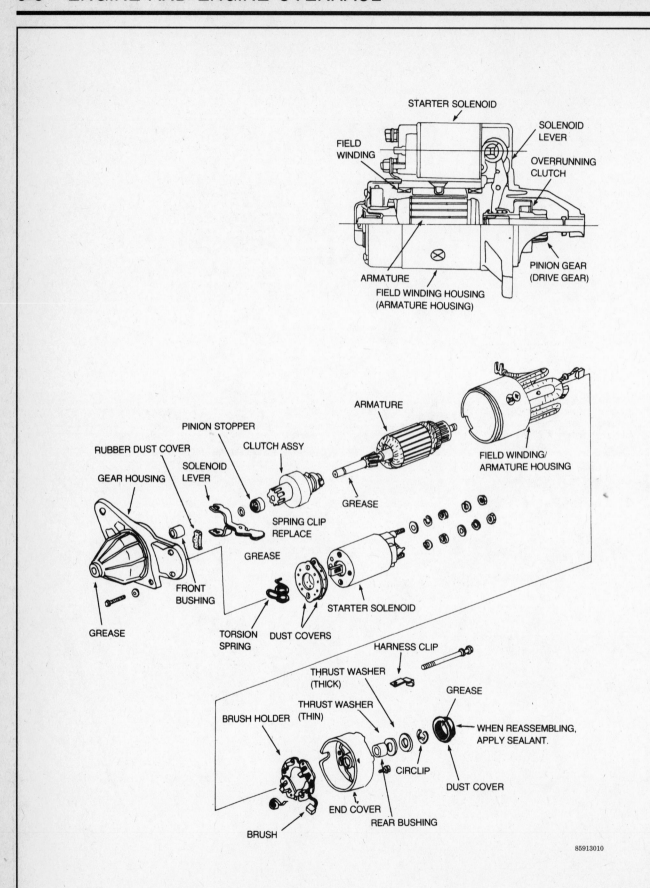

Fig. 12 Exploded view of the Hitachi direct-drive starter motor

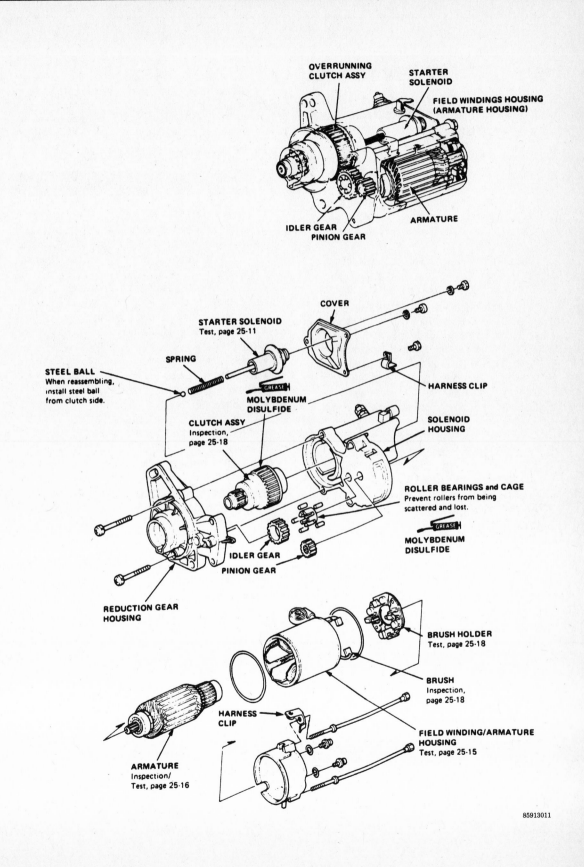

Fig. 13 Exploded view of the Nippondenso reduction gear type starter

ENGINE MECHANICAL

Design

The engines used in the Honda Civic, Accord and Prelude are water cooled, overhead cam, transversely mounted, inline four cylinder powerplants. They can be divided into two different engine families; CVCC and non-CVCC.

The non-CVCC engines have been offered in two different displacements; 1170cc (1973 only), and 1237cc (1974-79). These engines are somewhat unusual in that both the engine and the cylinder head are aluminum. The cylinder head is a crossflow design. The block uses sleeved cylinder liners and a main bearing girdle to add rigidity to the block. The engine uses five main bearings.

The CVCC (Compound Vortex Controlled Combustion) engine is unique in that its cylinder head is equipped with three valves per cylinder, instead of the usual two. Besides the intake and exhaust valve, each cylinder has an auxiliary intake valve which is much smaller than the regular intake valve. This auxiliary intake valve has its own separate precombustion chamber (adjacent to the main chamber with a crossover passage), its own intake manifold passages and carburetor circuit.

Briefly, what happens is this; at the beginning of the intake stroke, a small but very rich mixture is introduced into the precombustion chamber, while next door in the main combustion chamber, a large but very lean mixture makes its debut. At the end of the compression stroke, ignition occurs. The spark plug, located in the precombustion chamber, easily ignites the rich auxiliary mixture and this ignition spreads out into the main combustion chamber, where the large lean mixture is ignited. This two-stage combustion process allows the engine to operate efficiently with a much leaner overall air/fuel ratio. So, whereas the 1975 and later non-CVCC engines require a belt driven air injection system to control pollutants, the CVCC accomplishes this internally and gets better gas mileage.

On the 1983 models, Honda decided to improve engine breathing by replacing the single large main intake valve with a pair of smaller ones. This allows a much greater total intake valve area than a single valve and it also permits intake valve timing to be staggered slightly. This gave Honda engineers a unique opportunity to design air swirl into the combustion process. Such swirl not only tends to reduce engine knock but improves combustion speed and therefore engine efficiency, especially at low speeds. These engines retain the auxiliary intake valve on the exhaust side of the head.

Engine Overhaul Tips

Most engine overhaul procedures are fairly standard. In addition to specific parts replacement procedures and complete specifications for your individual engine, this section also is a guide to accepted rebuilding procedures. Examples of standard rebuilding practices are shown and should be used along with specific details concerning your particular engine.

Competent and accurate machine shop services will ensure maximum performance, reliability and engine life.

In most instances, it is more profitable for the do-it-yourself mechanic to remove, clean and inspect the component, buy the necessary parts and deliver these to a shop for actual machine work.

On the other hand, much of the rebuilding work (crankshaft, block, bearings, pistons, rods and other components) is well within the scope of the do-it-yourself mechanic.

Tools

The tools required for an engine overhaul or parts replacement will depend on the depth of your involvement. With a few exceptions, they will be the tools found in a mechanic's tool kit (see Section 1). More in-depth work will require any or all of the following:
• a dial indicator (reading in thousandths) mounted on a universal base
• micrometers and telescope gauges
• jaw and screw-type pullers
• scraper
• valve spring compressor
• ring groove cleaner
• piston ring expander and compressor
• ridge reamer
• cylinder hone or glaze breaker
• Plastigage®
• engine stand

Use of most of these tools is illustrated in this section. Many can be rented for a one-time use from a local parts jobber or tool supply house specializing in automotive work.

Occasionally, the use of special tools is called for. See the information on Special Tools and the Safety Notice in the front of this book substituting another tool.

Inspection Techniques

Procedures and specifications are given in this section for inspecting, cleaning and assessing the wear limits of most major components. Other procedures such as Magnaflux® and Zyglo® can be used to locate material flaws and stress cracks. Magnaflux® is a magnetic process applicable only to ferrous materials. The Zyglo® process coats the material with a fluorescent dye penetrant and can be used on any material. Check for suspected surface cracks can be more readily made using spot check dye. The dye is sprayed onto the suspected area, wiped off and the area sprayed with a developer. Cracks will show up brightly.

Precautions

Aluminum has become extremely popular for use in engines, due to its low weight. Observe the following precautions when handling aluminum parts:
• Never hot tank aluminum parts (the caustic hot-tank solution will eat the aluminum).
• Remove all aluminum parts (identification tag, etc.) from engine pats prior to hot-tanking.

• Always coat threads lightly with engine oil or anti-seize compounds before installation, to prevent seizure.

• Never over-torque bolts or spark plugs, especially in aluminum threads.

Stripped threads in any component can be repaired using any of several commercial repair kits (Heli-Coil®, Microdot®, Keenserts®, etc.).

When assembling the engine, any parts that will be in frictional contact must be prelubed to provide lubrication at initial start-up. Any product specifically formulated for this purpose can be used but engine oil is not recommended as a prelube.

When semi-permanent (locked, but removable) installation of bolts or nuts is desired, threads should be cleaned and coated with Loctite® or other similar, commercial non-hardening sealant.

Repairing Damaged Threads

▶ **See Figures 14, 15, 16, 17 and 18**

Several methods of repairing damaged threads are available. Heli-Coil® (shown here), Keenserts® and Microdot® are among the most widely used. All involved basically the same principle — drilling out stripped threads, tapping the hole and installing a pre-wound insert — making welding, plugging and oversize fasteners unnecessary.

Two types of thread repair inserts are usually supplied: a standard type for most Inch Coarse, Inch Fine, Metric Coarse and Metric Fine thread sizes and a spark plug type to fit most spark plug port sizes. Consult the individual manufacturer's catalog to determine exact applications. Typical thread repair kits will contain a selection of prewound threaded inserts, a tap (corresponding to the outside diameter threads of the insert) and an installation tool. Spark plug inserts usually differ because they require a tap equipped with pilot threads and a combined reamer/tap section. Most manufacturers also supply blister-packed thread repair inserts separately in addition to a master kit containing a variety of taps and inserts plus installation tools.

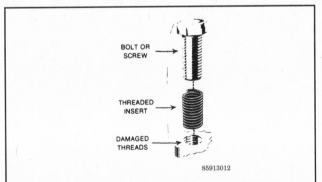

Fig. 14 Damaged bolt holes can be repaired with thread repair inserts

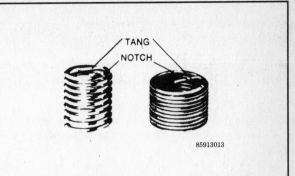

Fig. 15 Standard thread repair insert (left) and spark plug thread insert (right)

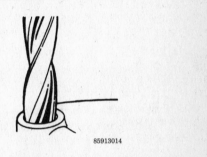

Fig. 16 Drill out the damaged threads with specified drill. Drill completely through the hole or to the bottom of a blind hole.

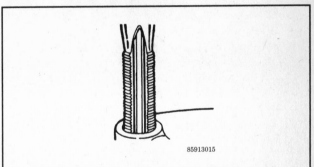

Fig. 17 With the tap supplied, tap the hole to receive the thread insert. Keep the tap well oiled and back it out frequently to avoid clogging threads

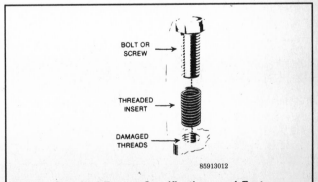

Fig. 18 Standard Torque Specifications and Fastener Markings

Before effecting a repair to a threaded hole, remove any snapped, broken or damaged bolts or studs. Penetrating oil can be used to free frozen threads; the offending item can be removed with locking pliers or with a screw or stud extractor. After the hole is clear, the thread can be repaired.

CHECKING ENGINE COMPRESSION

A noticeable lack of engine power, excessive oil consumption and/or poor fuel mileage measured over an extended period are all indicators of internal engine wear. Worn piston rings, scored or worn cylinder bores, blown head gaskets, sticking or burnt valves and worn valve seats are all possible culprits here. A check of each cylinder's compression will help you locate the problems.

As mentioned in the 'Tools and Equipment' section of Section 1, a screw-in type compression gauge is more accurate than the type you simply hold against the spark plug hole, although it takes slightly longer to use. It's worth it to obtain a more accurate reading. Follow the procedures below for gasoline engines.

Gasoline Engines

1. Warm the engine to normal operating temperatures.
2. Label and disconnect all spark plug wires at the plugs. Remove all spark plugs from the engine.

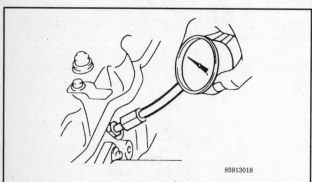

85913018

Fig. 19 The screw-in type compression gauge is more accurate

3. Disconnect the high tension lead from the ignition coil.

4. On carbureted vehicles, fully open the throttle either by operating the carburetor throttle linkage by hand or by having an assistant 'floor' the accelerator pedal.
5. Screw the compression gauge into the No. 1 spark plug hole until the fitting is snug.

➡**Be careful not to crossthread the plug hole. On aluminum cylinder heads use extra care, as the threads in these heads are easily ruined.**

6. Ask an assistant to depress the accelerator pedal fully. Then, while you read the compression gauge, ask the assistant to crank the engine two or three times in short bursts using the ignition switch.
7. Read the compression gauge at the end of each series of cranks and record the highest of these readings. Repeat this procedure for each of the engine's cylinders. Compare the highest reading of each cylinder to the compression pressure specifications in the "Tune-Up Specifications" chart in Section 2. The specs in this chart are maximum values.

➡**A cylinder's compression pressure is usually acceptable if it is not less than 80% of maximum. The difference between each cylinder should be no more than 12-14 pounds.**

8. If a cylinder is unusually low, pour a tablespoon of clean engine oil into the cylinder through the spark plug hole and repeat the compression test. If the compression comes up after adding the oil, it appears that the cylinder's piston rings or bore are damaged or worn. If the pressure remains low, the valves may not be seating properly (a valve job is needed) or the head gasket may be blown near that cylinder. If compression in any two adjacent cylinders is low and if the addition of oil doesn't help the compression, there is leakage past the head gasket. Oil and coolant water in the combustion chamber can result from this problem. There may be evidence of water droplets on the engine dipstick when a head gasket has blown.

GENERAL ENGINE SPECIFICATIONS

Year	Model	Engine Displacement (cc)	Net Horsepower (@ rpm)	Net Torque (@ rpm)	Bore × Stroke (in.)	Compression Ratio	Oil Pressure (@ rpm)
1973	Civic	1170	50 @ 5000	59 @ 3000	2.76 × 2.99	8.3:1	55 @ 5000
1974	Civic 1200	1237	63 @ 5000	77 @ 3000	2.83 × 3.23	7.9:1	55 @ 5000
1975	Civic 1200	1237	63 @ 5000	77 @ 3000	2.83 × 3.23	7.9:1	55 @ 5000
	Civic CVCC	1487	52 @ 5000	68 @ 3000	2.91 × 3.41	8.0:1	55 @ 5000
1976	Civic 1200	1237	63 @ 5000	77 @ 3000	2.83 × 3.23	7.9:1	55 @ 5000
	Civic CVCC	1487	52 @ 5000	68 @ 3000	2.91 × 3.41	7.9:1	55 @ 5000
	Accord	1600	68 @ 5000	85 @ 3000	2.91 × 3.66	8.2:1	55 @ 5000
1977	Civic 1200	1237	63 @ 5000	77 @ 3000	2.83 × 3.23	7.9:1	55 @ 5000
	Civic CVCC	1487	52 @ 5000	68 @ 3000	2.91 × 3.41	7.9:1	55 @ 5000
	Accord	1600	68 @ 5000	85 @ 3000	2.91 × 3.66	8.2:1	55 @ 5000
1978	Civic 1200	1237	63 @ 5000	77 @ 3000	2.83 × 3.23	7.9:1	55 @ 5000
	Civic CVCC	1487	52 @ 5000	68 @ 3000	2.91 × 3.41	7.9:1	55 @ 5000
	Accord	1600	68 @ 5000	85 @ 3000	2.91 × 3.66	8.2:1	55 @ 5000
1979	Civic 1200	1237	63 @ 5000	77 @ 3000	2.83 × 3.23	7.9:1	55 @ 5000
	Civic CVCC	1487	52 @ 5000	68 @ 3000	2.91 × 3.41	7.9:1	55 @ 5000
	Accord	1751	72 @ 4500	94 @ 3000	3.03 × 3.70	8.0:1	55 @ 5000
	Prelude	1751	72 @ 4500	94 @ 3000	3.03 × 3.70	8.0:1	55 @ 5000
1980	Civic 1300	1335	68 @ 5000	77 @ 3000	2.83 × 3.23	7.9:1	55 @ 5000
	Civic CVCC	1487	52 @ 5000	68 @ 3000	2.91 × 3.41	7.9:1	55 @ 5000
	Accord	1751	72 @ 4500	94 @ 3000	3.03 × 3.70	8.0:1	55 @ 5000
	Prelude	1751	72 @ 4500	94 @ 3000	3.03 × 3.70	8.0:1	55 @ 5000
1981	Civic 1300	1335	60 @ 5500	68 @ 4000	2.83 × 3.23	7.9:1	50 @ 2000
	Civic 1500	1487	63 @ 5000	77 @ 3000	2.91 × 3.41	9.9:1	50 @ 2000
	Accord	1751	72 @ 4500	94 @ 3000	3.03 × 3.70	8.8:1	50 @ 2000
	Prelude	1751	72 @ 4500	94 @ 3000	3.03 × 3.70	8.8:1	50 @ 2000
1982	Civic 1300	1335	60 @ 5500	68 @ 4000	2.83 × 3.23	9.3:1	50 @ 2000
	Civic 1500	1487	63 @ 5000	77 @ 3000	2.91 × 3.41	9.3:1	50 @ 2000
	Accord	1751	72 @ 4500	94 @ 3000	3.03 × 3.70	8.8:1	50 @ 2000
	Prelude	1751	72 @ 4500	94 @ 3000	3.03 × 3.70	8.8:1	50 @ 2000
1983	Civic 1300	1335	60 @ 5500	68 @ 4000	2.83 × 3.23	9.3:1	50 @ 2000
	Civic 1500	1487	63 @ 5000	77 @ 3000	2.91 × 3.41	9.3:1	50 @ 2000
	Accord	1751	75 @ 4500	96 @ 3000	3.03 × 3.70	8.8:1	50 @ 2000
	Prelude	1829	100 @ 5000	104 @ 4000	3.15 × 3.58	9.4:1	60 @ 1500

NOTE: Horsepower and torque are SAE net figures. They are measured at the rear of the transmission with all accessories installed and operating. Since the figures vary when a given engine is installed in different models, some are representative rather than exact.

85913C01

CRANKSHAFT AND CONNECTING ROD SPECIFICATIONS

All measurements are given in inches.

| Year | Engine Displacement (cc) | Crankshaft | | | | Connecting Rod | | |
		Main Brg. Journal Dia.	Main Brg. Oil Clearance	Shaft End-play	Thrust on No.	Journal Diameter	Oil Clearance	Side Clearance
1973	1170	1.9685–1.9673	0.0009–0.0017	0.0039–0.0138	3	1.5736–1.5748	0.0008–0.0015	0.0079–0.0177
1974	1237	1.9685–1.9673	0.0009–0.0017	0.0039–0.0138	3	1.5736–1.5748	0.0008–0.0015	0.0059–0.0118
1975	1237	1.9685–1.9673	0.0009–0.0017	0.0039–0.0138	3	1.5736–1.5748	0.0008–0.0015	0.0059–0.0118
	1487	1.9687–1.9697	0.0010–0.0021	0.0039–0.0138	3	1.6525–1.6535	0.0008–0.0015	0.0059–0.0118
1976	1237	1.9685–1.9673	0.0009–0.0017	0.0039–0.0138	3	1.5736–1.5748	0.0008–0.0015	0.0059–0.0118
	1487	1.9687–1.9697	0.0010–0.0021	0.0039–0.0138	3	1.6525–1.6535	0.0008–0.0015	0.0059–0.0118
	1600	1.9687–1.9697	0.0010–0.0021	0.0039–0.0138	3	1.6525–1.6535	0.0008–0.0015	0.0059–0.0118
1977	1237	1.9685–1.9673	0.0009–0.0017	0.0039–0.0138	3	1.5736–1.5748	0.0008–0.0015	0.0059–0.0118
	1487	1.9687–1.9697	0.0010–0.0021	0.0039–0.0138	3	1.6525–1.6535	0.0008–0.0015	0.0059–0.0118
	1600	1.9687–1.9697	0.0010–0.0021	0.0039–0.0138	3	1.6525–1.6535	0.0008–0.0015	0.0059–0.0118
1978	1237	1.9685–1.9673	0.0009–0.0017	0.0039–0.0138	3	1.5736–1.5748	0.0008–0.0015	0.0059–0.0118
	1487	1.9687–1.9697	0.0010–0.0021	0.0039–0.0138	3	1.6525–1.6535	0.0008–0.0015	0.0059–0.0118
	1600	1.9687–1.9697	0.0010–0.0021	0.0039–0.0138	3	1.6525–1.6535	0.0008–0.0015	0.0059–0.0118
1979	1237	1.9687–1.9697	0.0009–0.0017	0.0040–0.0140	3	1.5739–1.5748	0.0008–0.0015	0.0059–0.0118
	1487	1.9687–1.9697	0.0010–0.0022	0.0040–0.0140	3	1.6526–1.6535	0.0008–0.0015	0.006–0.012
	1751	1.9687–1.9697	0.0010–0.0022	0.0040–0.0140	3	1.6525–1.6535	0.0008–0.0015	0.006–0.012
1980	1335	1.9687–1.9697	0.0010–0.0022	0.0040–0.0140	3	1.5739–1.5748	0.0008–0.0015	0.006–0.012
	1487	1.9687–1.9697	0.0010–0.0022	0.0040–0.0140	3	1.6526–1.6535	0.0008–0.0015	0.006–0.012
	1751	1.9687–1.9697	0.0010–0.0022	0.0040–0.0140	3	1.6525–1.6535	0.0008–0.0015	0.006–0.012
1981	1335	1.9676–1.9685	0.0009–0.0017	0.0040–0.0140	3	1.5739–1.5748	0.0008–0.0015	0.006–0.012
	1487	1.9687–1.9803	0.0010–0.0022	0.0040–0.0140	3	1.6525–1.6535	0.0008–0.0015	0.006–0.012
	1751	1.9687–1.9697	0.0010–0.0022	0.0040–0.0140	3	1.6525–1.6535	0.0008–0.0015	0.006–0.012

85913C02

CRANKSHAFT AND CONNECTING ROD SPECIFICATIONS

All measurements are given in inches.

| Year | Engine Displacement (cc) | Crankshaft | | | | Connecting Rod | | |
		Main Brg. Journal Dia.	Main Brg. Oil Clearance	Shaft End-play	Thrust on No.	Journal Diameter	Oil Clearance	Side Clearance
1982	1335	1.9676–1.9685	0.0009–0.0017	0.0040–0.0140	3	1.5739–1.5748	0.0006–0.0015	0.006–0.012
	1487	1.9687–1.9803	0.0010–0.0022	0.0040–0.0140	3	1.6525–1.6535	0.0008–0.0015	0.006–0.012
	1751	1.9687–1.9697	0.0010–0.0022	0.0040–0.0140	3	1.6525–1.6535	0.0008–0.0015	0.006–0.012
1983	1335	1.9676–1.9685	0.0009–0.0017	0.0040–0.0140	3	1.5739–1.5748	0.0008–0.0015	0.006–0.012
	1487	1.9687–1.9803	0.0010–0.0022	0.0040–0.0140	3	1.6525–1.6535	0.0008–0.0015	0.006–0.012
	1751	1.9687–1.9697	0.0010–0.0022	0.0040–0.0140	3	1.6525–1.6535	0.0008–0.0015	0.006–0.012
	1829	1.9687–1.9697	0.0010–0.0022	0.0040–0.0140	3	1.7707–1.7717	0.0006–0.0015	0.006–0.012

85913Ca2

TORQUE SPECIFICATIONS
All readings in ft. lbs.

Year	Engine Displacement (cc)	Cylinder Head Bolts ①	Main Bearing Bolts	Rod Bearing Bolts	Crankshaft Pulley Bolts	Flywheel Bolts	Manifold Intake	Manifold Exhaust	Spark Plugs
1973	1170	③	27–31	18–21	61	34–38	13–17	13–17	15
1974	1237	37–42	27–31	18–21	61	34–38	13–17	13–17	15
1975	1237	37–42	27–31	18–21	61	34–38	13–17	13–17	15
	1487	40–47	30–35	18–21	61	34–38	15–18	15–18	15
1976	1237	37–42	27–31	18–21	61	34–38	13–17	13–17	15
	1487	40–47	30–35	18–21	61	34–38	15–18	15–18	15
	1600	40–47	30–35	18–21	61	34–38	15–18	15–18	15
1977	1237	37–42	27–31	18–21	61	34–38	13–17	13–17	15
	1487	40–47	30–35	18–21	61	34–38	15–18	15–18	15
	1600	40–47	30–35	18–21	61	34–38	15–18	15–18	15
1978	1237	37–42	27–31	18–21	61	34–38	13–17	13–17	15
	1487	40–47	30–35	18–21	61	34–38	15–18	15–18	15
	1600	40–47	30–35	18–21	61	34–38	15–18	15–18	15
1979	1237	37–42	27–31	18–21	61	34–38	13–17	13–17	15
	1487	33	29	21	61	51	18	18	15
	1751	43	48	23	61	51	18	18	15
1980	1335	43	29–33	21	80	51	18	18	13
	1487	43	29–33	21	80	51	18	18	13
	1751	43	48	23	80	51	18	18	13
1981	1335	43	29–33	21	80	51	18	18	13
	1487	43	29–33	21	80	51	18	18	13
	1751	43	48	23	80	51	18	18	13
1982	1335	43	29–33	21	80	51	18	18	13
	1487	43	29–33	21	80	51	18	18	13
	1751	43	48	21	80	51	18	18	13
1983	1335	43	29–33	21	80	51	18	18	13
	1487	43	29–33	21	80	51	18	18	13
	1751	43	48	21	80	51	18	18	13
	1829	49	48	23	83	76 ②	16	22	13

① 2-Step procedure; see text
② Auto Trans: 54
③ To engine number EB 1-1019949:
  30–35 ft. lbs.
  From engine number EB 1-1019950:
  37–42 ft. lbs.

85913C03

VALVE SPECIFICATIONS

Year	Engine Displacement (cc)	Seat Angle (deg.)	Face Angle (deg.)	Spring Test Pressure (lbs.)	Spring Installed Height (in.)	Stem-to-Guide Clearance in. ①		Stem Diameter in. ①	
						In.	Ex.	In.	Ex.
1973	1170	45	45	NA	⑧	0.005–0.007	0.005–0.007	0.2591–0.2594	0.2579–0.2583
1974	1237	45	45	NA	⑧	0.005–0.007	0.005–0.007	0.2591–0.2594	0.2579–0.2583
1975	1237	45	45	NA	⑧	0.005–0.007	0.005–0.007	0.2591–0.2594	0.2579–0.2583
	1487	45	45	NA	⑦	0.0004–0.0016	0.0020–0.0031	0.2592–0.2596	0.2580–0.2584
1976	1237	45	45	NA	⑧	0.005–0.007	0.005–0.007	0.2591–0.2594	0.2579–0.2583
	1487	45	45	NA	⑦	0.0004–0.0016	0.0020–0.0031	0.2592–0.2596	0.2580–0.2584
	1600	45	45	NA	⑦	0.0004–0.0016	0.0020–0.0031	0.2592–0.2596	0.2580–0.2584
1977	1237	45	45	NA	⑧	0.005–0.007	0.005–0.007	0.2591–0.2594	0.2579–0.2583
	1487	45	45	NA	⑦	0.0004–0.0016	0.0020–0.0031	0.2592–0.2596	0.2580–0.2584
	1600	45	45	NA	⑦	0.0004–0.0016	0.0020–0.0031	0.2592–0.2596	0.2580–0.2584
1978	1237	45	45	NA	⑧	0.005–0.007	0.005–0.007	0.2591–0.2594	0.2579–0.2583
	1487	45	45	NA	⑦	0.0004–0.0016	0.0020–0.0031	0.2592–0.2596	0.2580–0.2584
	1600	45	45	NA	⑦	0.0004–0.0016	0.0020–0.0031	0.2592–0.2596	0.2580–0.2584
1979	1237	45	45	NA	⑧	0.005–0.007	0.005–0.007	0.2591–0.2594	0.2579–0.2583
	1487	45	45	NA	⑥	0.0004–0.0016	0.0020–0.0031	0.2592–0.2596	0.2580–0.2584
	1751	45	45	NA	⑤	0.001–0.002	0.002–0.004	0.2748–0.2751	0.2732–0.2736
1980	1335	45	45	NA	②	0.0008–0.0020	0.0008–0.0037	0.2591–0.2594	0.2574–0.2578
	1487	45	45	NA	②	0.0008–0.0020	0.0008–0.0037	0.2591–0.2594	0.2574–0.2578
	1751	45	45	NA	⑤	0.001–0.002	0.002–0.004	0.2748–0.2751	0.2732–0.2736
1981	1335	45	45	NA	②	0.0008–0.0020	0.0008–0.0037	0.2591–0.2594	0.2574–0.2578
	1487	45	45	NA	②	0.0008–0.0020	0.0008–0.0037	0.2591–0.2594	0.2574–0.2578
	1751	45	45	NA	⑤	0.001–0.002	0.002–0.004	0.2748–0.2751	0.2732–0.2736

85913C04

VALVE SPECIFICATIONS

Year	Engine Displacement (cc)	Seat Angle (deg.)	Face Angle (deg.)	Spring Test Pressure (lbs.)	Spring Installed Height (in.)	Stem-to-Guide Clearance in. ①		Stem Diameter in. ①	
						In.	Ex.	In.	Ex.
1982	1335	45	45	NA	②	0.0008–0.0020	0.0025–0.0037	0.2591–0.2594	0.2574–0.2578
	1487	45	45	NA	②	0.0008–0.0020	0.0025–0.0037	0.2591–0.2594	0.2574–0.2578
	1751	45	45	NA	③	0.001–0.002	0.002–0.004	0.2748–0.2751	0.2732–0.2736
1983	1335	45	45	NA	②	0.0008–0.0020	0.0025–0.0037	0.2591–0.2594	0.2574–0.2578
	1487	45	45	NA	②	0.0008–0.0020	0.0025–0.0037	0.2591–0.2594	0.2574–0.2578
	1751	45	45	NA	③	0.001–0.002	0.002–0.004	0.2748–0.2751	0.2732–0.2736
	1829	45	45	NA	④	0.001–0.002	0.002–0.004	0.2591–0.2594	0.2736–0.2736

NA—Not available
① Jet Valve: 0.0009–0.0023
② 1335cc, 1487cc:
  Intake & Exhaust inner: 1.402
  Intake & Exhaust outer: 1.488
  Auxiliary: 0.906
③ 1751cc:
  Intake & Exhaust inner: 1.402
  Intake & Exhaust outer: 1.488
  Auxiliary: 0.984
④ 1829cc, 1955cc:
  Intake: 1.660
  Exhaust inner: 1.460
  Exhaust outer: 1.670
  Auxiliary: 0.984 carbureted

⑤ 1751cc: (1979–80)
  Intake inner: 1.000
  Exhaust inner: 1.031
  Intake outer: 1.094
  Exhaust outer: 1.109
  Auxiliary: 0.875
⑥ 1487cc: (1979)
  Intake inner: 1.401
  Exhaust inner: 1.358
  Intake outer: 1.488
  Exhaust outer: 1.437
  Auxiliary: 0.906

⑦ 1487cc, 1600cc: (1975–78)
  Inner: 1.358
  Outer: 1.437
  Auxiliary: 0.906
⑧ 1170cc, 1237cc: (1973–79)
  Inner: 1.6535
  Outer: 1.5728

85913Ca4

PISTON AND RING SPECIFICATIONS

All measurements are given in inches.

Year	Engine Displacement (cc)	Piston Clearance	Ring Gap		Ring Side Clearance			Oil Control
			Top Compression	Bottom Compression	Oil Control	Top Compression	Bottom Compression	
1973	1170	0.0012–0.0039	0.008–0.016	0.008–0.016	0.008–0.035	0.0008–0.0018	0.0008–0.0018	Snug
1974	1237	0.0012–0.0039	0.010–0.016	0.010–0.016	0.011–0.034	0.0008–0.0018	0.0008–0.0018	Snug
1975	1237	0.0012–0.0039	0.010–0.016	0.010–0.016	0.011–0.034	0.0008–0.0018	0.0008–0.0018	Snug
	1487	0.0012–0.0039	0.008–0.016	0.008–0.016	0.008–0.035	0.0008–0.0018	0.0008–0.0018	Snug
1976	1237	0.0012–0.0039	0.010–0.016	0.010–0.016	0.011–0.034	0.0008–0.0018	0.0008–0.0018	Snug
	1487	0.0012–0.0039	0.008–0.016	0.008–0.016	0.008–0.035	0.0008–0.0018	0.0008–0.0018	Snug
	1600	0.0012–0.0039	0.008–0.016	0.008–0.016	0.008–0.035	0.0008–0.0018	0.0008–0.0018	Snug
1977	1237	0.0012–0.0039	0.010–0.016	0.010–0.016	0.011–0.034	0.0008–0.0018	0.0008–0.0018	Snug
	1487	0.0012–0.0039	0.008–0.016	0.008–0.016	0.008–0.035	0.0008–0.0018	0.0008–0.0018	Snug
	1600	0.0012–0.0039	0.008–0.016	0.008–0.016	0.008–0.035	0.0008–0.0018	0.0008–0.0018	Snug
1978	1237	0.0012–0.0039	0.010–0.016	0.010–0.016	0.011–0.034	0.0008–0.0018	0.0008–0.0018	Snug
	1487	0.0012–0.0039	0.008–0.016	0.008–0.016	0.008–0.035	0.0008–0.0018	0.0008–0.0018	Snug
	1600	0.0012–0.0039	0.008–0.016	0.008–0.016	0.008–0.035	0.0008–0.0018	0.0008–0.0018	Snug
1979	1237	0.0012–0.0039	0.010–0.016	0.010–0.016	0.011–0.034	0.0008–0.0018	0.0008–0.0018	Snug
	1487	0.0012–0.0060	0.008–0.016	0.008–0.016	0.008–0.035	0.0008–0.0018	0.0008–0.0018	Snug
	1751	0.0008–0.0028	0.006–0.014	0.006–0.014	0.012–0.035	0.0008–0.0018	0.0008–0.0018	Snug
1980	1335	0.0004–0.0020	0.006–0.014	0.006–0.014	0.012–0.035	0.0008–0.0018	0.0008–0.0018	Snug
	1487	0.0004–0.0020	0.006–0.014	0.006–0.014	0.012–0.035	0.0008–0.0018	0.0008–0.0018	Snug
	1751	0.0008–0.0028	0.006–0.014	0.006–0.014	0.012–0.035	0.0008–0.0018	0.0008–0.0018	Snug
1981	1335	0.0004–0.0020	0.006–0.014	0.006–0.014	0.012–0.035	0.0008–0.0018	0.0008–0.0018	Snug
	1487	0.0004–0.0020	0.006–0.014	0.006–0.014	0.012–0.035	0.0008–0.0018	0.0008–0.0018	Snug
	1751	0.0008–0.0028	0.006–0.014	0.006–0.014	0.012–0.035	0.0008–0.0018	0.0008–0.0018	Snug

85913C05

PISTON AND RING SPECIFICATIONS

All measurements are given in inches.

Year	Engine Displacement (cc)	Piston Clearance	Ring Gap		Ring Side Clearance			Oil Control
			Top Compression	Bottom Compression	Oil Control	Top Compression	Bottom Compression	
1982	1335	0.0004–0.0020	0.006–0.014	0.006–0.014	0.012–0.035	0.0012–0.0024	0.0012–0.0024	Snug
	1487	0.0004–0.0020	0.006–0.014	0.006–0.014	0.012–0.035	0.0012–0.0020	0.0012–0.0020	Snug
	1751	0.0004–0.0024	0.006–0.014	0.006–0.014	0.012–0.035	0.0008–0.0018	0.0008–0.0018	Snug
1983	1335	0.0004–0.0020	0.006–0.014	0.006–0.014	0.012–0.035	0.0012–0.0024	0.0012–0.0024	Snug
	1487	0.0004–0.0020	0.006–0.014	0.006–0.014	0.012–0.035	0.0012–0.0020	0.0012–0.0020	Snug
	1751	0.0004–0.0024	0.006–0.014	0.006–0.014	0.012–0.035	0.0008–0.0018	0.0008–0.0018	Snug
	1829	0.0008–0.0016	0.008–0.014	0.008–0.014	0.008–0.035	0.0008–0.0018	0.0008–0.0018	Snug

85913Ca5

Engine

REMOVAL & INSTALLATION

✳✳WARNING

If any repair operation requires the removal of a component of the air conditioning system (on vehicles equipped), do not disconnect the refrigerant lines. If it is impossible to move the component out of the way with the lines attached, have the air conditioning system evacuated by a trained serviceman. The air conditioning system contains freon under pressure. This gas can be very dangerous. Therefore, under no circumstances should an untrained person attempt to disconnect the air conditioner refrigerant lines.

1170 and 1237cc Civic

▶ See Figures 20 and 21

1. Raise and support the front of the vehicle with safety stands.
2. Remove the front wheels.

✳✳CAUTION

The EPA warns that prolonged contact with used engine oil may cause a number of skin disorders, including cancer! You should make every effort to minimize your exposure to used engine oil. Protective gloves should be worn when changing the oil. Wash your hands and any other exposed skin areas as soon as possible after exposure to used engine oil. Soap and water, or waterless hand cleaner should be used.

3. Drain the oil from the engine and transaxle. Place a clean container under the radiator and drain the cooling system.
4. Remove the front turn signal lights and grille.

✳✳CAUTION

When draining the coolant, keep in mind that cats and dogs are attracted by the ethylene glycol antifreeze, and are quite likely to drink any that is left in an uncovered container or in puddles on the ground. This will prove fatal in sufficient quantity. Always drain the coolant into a sealable container. Coolant should be reused unless it is contaminated or several years old.

5. Remove the hood support bolts and the hood. Remove the fan shroud, if equipped.
6. Remove the air cleaner case and air intake pipe at the air cleaner.
7. Disconnect the battery and engine ground cables at the battery and the valve cover.
8. Disconnect the hose from the fuel vapor storage canister at the carburetor.
9. Disconnect the fuel line at the fuel pump.

➡Plug the line so that gas does not siphon from the tank.

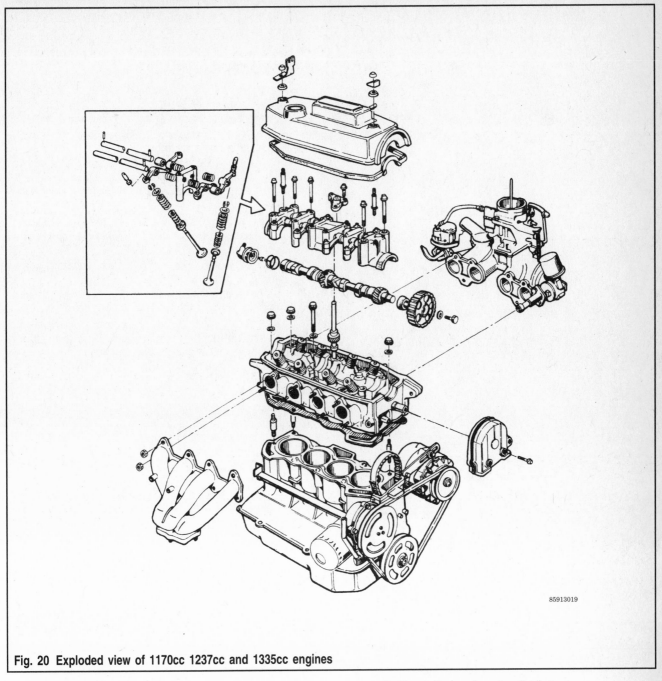

Fig. 20 Exploded view of 1170cc 1237cc and 1335cc engines

85913019

10. Disconnect the lower coolant hose from the water pump connecting tube and the upper hose from the thermostat cover.

11. Disconnect the following control cables and wires from the engine:

    a. Throttle and choke cables from the carburetor.

    b. Clutch cable from the release arm.

    c. Ignition coil wires from the distributor.

    d. Starter motor positive battery cable connection and solenoid wire.

    e. Back-up light switch and the TCS (Transmission Controlled Spark) switch wires from the transmission casing.

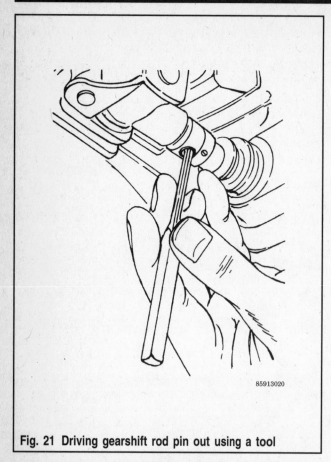

Fig. 21 Driving gearshift rod pin out using a tool

f. Speedometer and tachometer cables.

✳✳WARNING

When removing the speedometer cable from the transaxle, it is not necessary to remove the entire cable holder. Remove the end boot (gear holder seal) and the cable retaining clip, then, pull the cable out of the holder. In no way should you disturb the holder unless it is absolutely necessary! The holder consists of three pieces: the holder, collar and a dowel pin. The dowel pin indexes the holder and collar and is held in place by the bolt that retains the holder. If the bolt is removed and the holder rotated, the dowel pin can fall into the transmission case, necessitating transaxle disassembly to remove the pin. To insure that this does not happen when the holder must be removed, do not rotate the holder more than 30° in either direction when removing it. Once removed, make sure that the pin is still in place. Use the same precaution when installing the holder.

g. Alternator wire and wire harness connector.
h. The wires from both water temperature thermal switches on the intake manifold.
i. Cooling fan connector and radiator thermoswitch wires.
j. Oil pressure sensor.
k. On 1975-76 models, vacuum hose to throttle opener at opener and vacuum hose from carburetor insulator to throttle opener.

l. On 1976-77 models, bypass valve assemble and bracket.

➡ It would be a good idea to tag all of these wires to avoid confusion during installation.

12. Disconnect the heater hose by removing the **H** connector from the two hoses in the firewall.
13. Remove the engine torque rod from the engine and firewall.
14. Remove the starter motor.
15. Remove the radiator from the engine compartment.
16. Remove the exhaust pipe-to-manifold clamp.
17. Remove the exhaust pipe flange nuts and lower the exhaust pipe.
18. Using a Ball Joint Remover tool No. 07941-6340000 or equivalent, disconnect the left and right lower control arm ball joints from the steering knuckle.
19. Hold the brake disc, then, pull the both halfshafts from the differential case.
20. Depending on the transaxle used, perform the following procedures:
   a. Manual transaxle: Using a drift punch, drive out the gearshift rod pin (8mm) and disconnect the rod at the transaxle case.

➡ Do not disconnect the shift lever end of the gearshift rod and extension.

   b. Hondamatic only: Disconnect shift cable from the console and the cooler line from the transaxle.
21. If equipped with a manual transaxle, disconnect the gearshift extension from the engine.
22. Install two engine hanger bolts in the torque rod bolt hole and the bolt hole to the left of the distributor. Install a lift chain on the hanger bolts and lift the engine, slightly, to take the load off the engine mounts.
23. When the engine is properly supported, remove the two center mount bracket nuts.
24. On the 1973-74 models, remove the center beam.
25. Remove the left engine mount.
26. Lift the engine out slowly, taking care not to allow the engine to damage other parts of the vehicle.
27. To install, reverse the removal procedure. Pay special attention to the following points:
   a. Lower the engine into position and install the left mount. On 1973-74 models, install the center beam with the front end between the stabilizer bar and frame; DO NOT attach mounting bolts at this time.

➡ On 1973-74 models, be sure that the lower mount has the mount stop installed between the center beam and the rubber mount.

   b. Align the center mount studs with the beam, then, tighten the nuts several turns (just enough to support the beam). On 1973-74 models, attach the rear end of the center beam to the subframe.
   c. On 1973-74 models, attach the front end of the center beam. Torque the center beam bolts but do not tighten the lower mount nuts. Lower the engine so it rests on the lower mount. Torque the lower mount nuts.
   d. Use a new shift rod pin.

e. After installing the halfshafts, attempt to move the inner joint housing in and out of the transaxle housing. If it moves easily, the driveshaft end clips should be replaced.

f. Make sure that the control cables and wires are connected properly.

g. When connecting the heater hoses, the upper hose goes to the water pump connecting pipe and the lower hose to the intake manifold.

h. Refill the engine, transaxle and cooling system with their respective fluids to the proper levels.

i. On Hondamatic vehicles, check and/or adjust the shift cable.

1335cc and 1487cc Civic

▶ **See Figures 22 and 23**

1. Raise and support the front of the vehicle on jackstands. Remove both front wheels.

2. Remove the headlight rim screws and the rims. On 1980-82 models, remove the battery, tray and mount.

3. Open the hood and disconnect both parking light connectors. Remove the parking light bolts, backing plate and the parking lights.

4. Remove the lower grille molding, the grille-to-vehicle retaining bolts and the grille.

5. Disconnect and remove the windshield washer hose from the underside of the hood.

6. Disconnect the negative battery cable and the transaxle bracket-to-body ground cable.

7. Remove the upper torque (engine locating) arm.

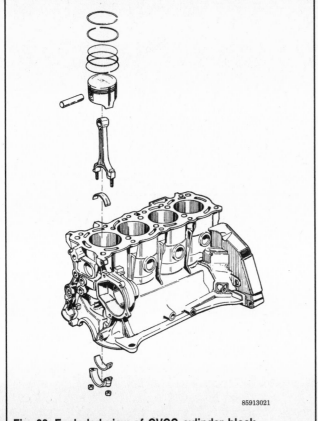

Fig. 22 Exploded view of CVCC cylinder block

85913021

8. Disconnect the vacuum hose from the power brake booster, thermosensors **A** and **B** at their wiring connectors and the coolant temperature gauge sending unit wire.

☀☀CAUTION

When draining the coolant, keep in mind that cats and dogs are attracted by the ethylene glycol antifreeze, and are quite likely to drink any that is left in an uncovered container or in puddles on the ground. This will prove fatal in sufficient quantity. Always drain the coolant into a sealable container. Coolant should be reused unless it is contaminated or several years old.

9. Drain the cooling system. After all coolant has drained, install the drain bolt fingertight.

10. Disconnect all four coolant hoses. Disconnect cooling fan motor connector and the temperature sensor. Remove the radiator hose to the overflow tank.

11. If equipped with a Hondamatic, remove both ATF cooler line bolts.

➡**Save the washers from the cooler line banjo connectors and replace if damaged.**

12. Remove the radiator.

13. Label and disconnect the starter motor wires. Remove the starter-to-engine bolts (one from each end of the starter) and the starter.

14. Label and disconnect the spark plug wires from the plugs. Remove the distributor cap and scribe the position of the rotor on the side of the distributor housing. Remove the top distributor swivel bolt and the distributor (the rotor will rotate 30° as the drive gear is beveled).

15. If equipped with a manual transaxle, remove the C-clip retaining the clutch cable at the firewall. To remove the end of the clutch cable from the clutch release arm and bracket: First, pull up on the cable, then, push it out to release it from the bracket. Remove the end from the release arm. •

16. Disconnect the backup light switch wires. Disconnect the control valve vacuum hose, the air intake hose and the preheat air intake hose. Disconnect the air bleed valve hose from the air cleaner. Label and disconnect all remaining vacuum hoses from the underside of the air cleaner. Remove the air cleaner.

17. Label and disconnect all remaining emission control vacuum hoses from the engine. Disconnect the emission box wiring connector and remove the black emission box from the firewall.

18. Remove the engine mount heat shield.

19. Disconnect the engine-to-body ground strap at the valve cover.

20. Disconnect the alternator wiring connector and oil pressure sensor leads.

21. Disconnect the vacuum hose from the start control and electrical leads to both cut-off solenoid valves.

22. Disconnect the vacuum hose from the charcoal canister and both fuel lines from the carburetor. Mark the adjustment, then, disconnect the choke and throttle cables from the carburetor.

23. If equipped with a Hondamatic, remove the center console and disconnect the gear selector control cable at the

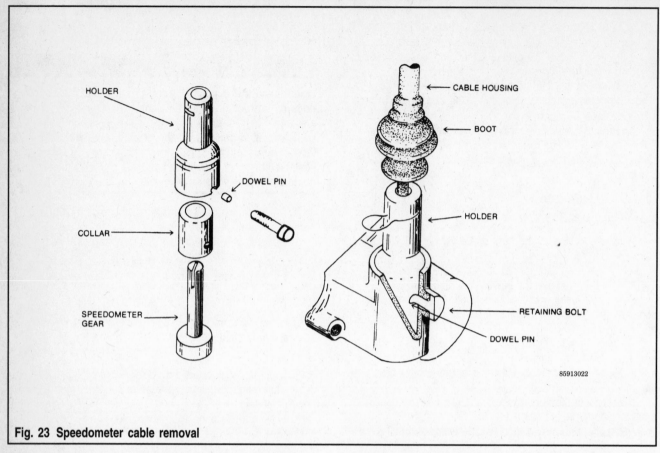

Fig. 23 Speedometer cable removal

console. This may be accomplished after removing the retaining clip and pin.

24. Drain the transaxle oil.

25. Remove the fender well shield under the right fender, exposing the speedometer drive cable. Remove the set screw securing the speedometer drive holder, then, slowly pull the cable assembly out of the transaxle, taking care not to drop the pin or drive gear. Finally, remove the pin, collar and drive gear from the cable assembly.

26. Disconnect the front suspension stabilizer bar from its mounts on both sides. Also, remove the bolt retaining the lower control arm to the sub-frame on both sides.

27. Remove the forward mounting nut on the radius rod from both sides. Pry the constant velocity joint out about ½ in. and pull the stub axle out of the transaxle case; repeat this procedure for the other side.

28. Remove the center beam-to-chassis bolts and the center beam.

29. If equipped with a manual transaxle, drive the retaining pin from the shift linkage.

30. Disconnect the lower torque arm from the transaxle.

31. If equipped with a Hondamatic, remove the control cable stay-to-transaxle bolt. Loosen the two U-bolt nuts and pull the cable out of its housing.

32. Disconnect the exhaust pipe from the manifold. Disconnect the retaining clamp also.

33. Remove the rear engine mount nut.

34. Attach a lifting hoist to the engine. Honda recommends using the threaded bolt holes at the extreme right and left ends of the cylinder head (with special hardened bolts) as lifting points, as opposed to wrapping a chain around the entire block and risk damaging some components such as the carburetor, etc.

35. Raise the engine to place a slight tension on the chain. Remove the front engine mount nut and bolts. Raise the engine and remove the mount.

36. Remove the three retaining bolts and push the left engine support into its shock mount bracket to the limit of its travel.

37. Slowly lift the engine from the vehicle.

38. To install, reverse the removal procedures. Refill the cooling system, the engine and the transaxle with the correct fluids. Start the engine, allow it to reach normal operating temperatures and check for leaks.

1600cc Accord and 1751cc Accord/Prelude

▶ See Figures 24, 25 and 26

1. Disconnect the negative battery terminal.

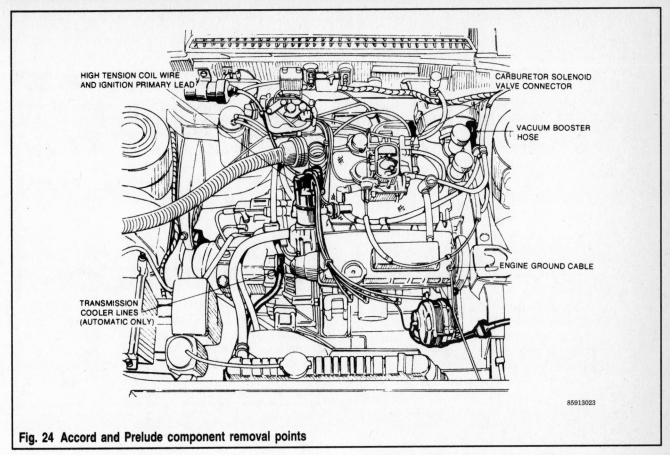

HIGH TENSION COIL WIRE
AND IGNITION PRIMARY LEAD

CARBURETOR SOLENOID
VALVE CONNECTOR

VACUUM BOOSTER
HOSE

ENGINE GROUND CABLE

TRANSMISSION
COOLER LINES
(AUTOMATIC ONLY)

85913023

Fig. 24 Accord and Prelude component removal points

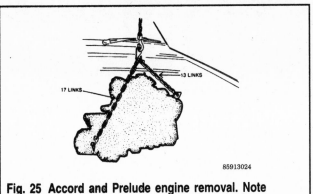

13 LINKS

17 LINKS

85913024

Fig. 25 Accord and Prelude engine removal. Note position of chain.

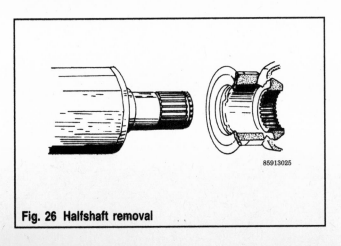

85913025

Fig. 26 Halfshaft removal

2. Drain the cooling system, the engine and transaxle of fluids.

✳✳CAUTION

When draining the coolant, keep in mind that cats and dogs are attracted by the ethylene glycol antifreeze, and are quite likely to drink any that is left in an uncovered container or in puddles on the ground. This will prove fatal in sufficient quantity. Always drain the coolant into a sealable container. Coolant should be reused unless it is contaminated or several years old. The EPA warns that prolonged contact with used engine oil may cause a number of skin disorders, including cancer! You should make every effort to minimize your exposure to used engine oil. Protective gloves should be worn when changing the oil. Wash your hands and any other exposed skin areas as soon as possible after exposure to used engine oil. Soap and water, or waterless hand cleaner should be used.

3. Raise and support the front of the vehicle, then, remove the front wheels.
4. Remove the air cleaner.
5. Remove the following wires and hoses:
   a. The coil wire and the ignition primary wire from the distributor.
   b. The engine subharness and the starter wires; mark the wires before removal to ease installation.
   c. The vacuum tube from the brake booster.
   d. On Hondamatic models, remove the ATF cooler hose from the transaxle.

e. The engine ground cable.

f. Alternator wiring harness.

g. Carburetor solenoid valve connector.

h. Carburetor fuel line.

i. On models with California and high altitude equipment, disconnect the hoses from the air controller.

6. Remove the choke and throttle cables.

7. Remove the radiator and heater hoses.

8. Remove the emission control 'black box'.

9. Remove the clutch slave cylinder with the hydraulic line attached.

10. Remove the speedometer cable. Pull the wire clip from the housing and the cable from the housing: DO NOT, under any circumstances, remove the housing from the transaxle.

11. Using an engine hoist, raise the engine slightly to remove the slack from the chain.

12. To disconnect the right or left lower ball joints and the tie rod ends, perform the following procedures:

a. Remove the cotter pin and nut from the ball joint(s) and the tie rod end(s).

b. Using a Ball Joint Remover tool or equivalent, separate the ball joint(s) and tie rod(s) from the steering knuckle.

c. An alternative method is to leave the ball joints connected, then, remove the lower control arm inner bolts and the radius rods from the lower control arms.

13. To remove the halfshafts from the transaxle, pry the snapring from the groove in the end of the shaft. While holding the steering knuckle, pull the halfshaft from the knuckle.

14. Remove the center engine mount.

15. Remove the shift rod positioner from the transaxle case.

16. Using a Pin Punch, drive the pin from the shift rod.

17. If equipped with a Hondamatic, remove the control cable from the transaxle.

18. Disconnect the exhaust pipe from the exhaust manifold.

19. Remove the three engine support bolts and push the left engine support into the shock mount bracket.

20. Remove the front and rear engine mounts.

21. Carefully, raise and remove the engine from the vehicle.

22. To install, reverse the removal procedures. Make sure the halfshaft clip seats in the transaxle groove; failure to do so could lead to the halfshaft disengaging from the transaxle while you are driving! Bleed the air from the cooling system. Adjust the throttle and choke cable tension. Check and/or adjust the clutch for the correct free play. Make sure that the transaxle shifts properly.

1829cc Prelude

▶ See Figure 27

1. Apply the parking brake and place blocks behind the rear wheels. Raise and support the front of the vehicle on jackstands.

2. Disconnect the negative, then, the positive battery terminals from the battery. Remove the battery and the battery tray from the engine compartment.

3. Remove the knob caps covering the headlight manual retracting knobs, then, turn the knobs to bring the headlights to the ON position. Remove the five grille screws and the grille.

4. From under the engine, remove the splash guard. Using a scratch awl, mark the hood hinge outline on the hood, then, remove the hood bolts and the hood.

5. Remove the oil filler cap and drain the engine oil.

➡When replacing the drain plug be sure to use a new washer.

✳✳CAUTION

The EPA warns that prolonged contact with used engine oil may cause a number of skin disorders, including cancer! You should make every effort to minimize your exposure to used engine oil. Protective gloves should be worn when changing the oil. Wash your hands and any other exposed skin areas as soon as possible after exposure to used engine oil. Soap and water, or waterless hand cleaner should be used.

6. Remove the radiator cap, then, open the radiator drain petcock and drain the coolant from the radiator.

✳✳CAUTION

When draining the coolant, keep in mind that cats and dogs are attracted by the ethylene glycol antifreeze, and are quite likely to drink any that is left in an uncovered container or in puddles on the ground. This will prove fatal in sufficient quantity. Always drain the coolant into a sealable container. Coolant should be reused unless it is contaminated or several years old.

7. Remove the transaxle filler plug, then, remove the drain plug and drain the transaxle.

8. Perform the following procedures:

a. Label and remove the coil wires and the engine secondary ground cable located on the valve cover.

b. Remove the air cleaner cover and filter.

c. Loosen the throttle cable locknut and adjusting nut, then, slip the cable end from the carburetor linkage.

➡Be careful not to bend or kink the throttle cable. Always replace a damaged cable.

d. Disconnect the No. 1 control box connector, then, remove the control box from its bracket and allow it hang next to the engine.

e. Disconnect the fuel line from the fuel filter and the solenoid vacuum hose from the charcoal canister.

f. For California and high altitude models, remove the air jet controller.

9. Label and disconnect the radiator and heater hoses from the engine.

10. If equipped with an automatic transaxle, disconnect the oil cooler hoses from the transaxle and drain the fluid, then, support the hoses near the radiator.

11. If equipped with a manual transaxle, loosen the clutch cable adjusting nut and remove the clutch cable from the release arm.

12. Disconnect the battery cable from the transaxle and the starter cable from the starter motor terminal.

13. Disconnect both electrical harness connectors from the engine.

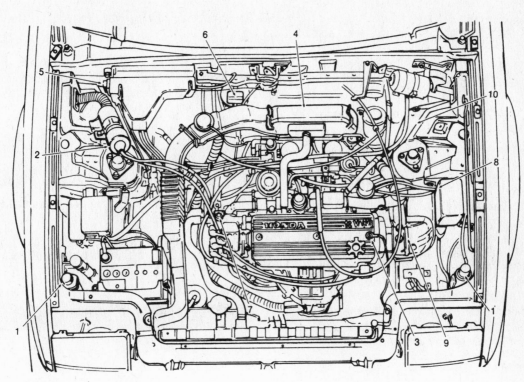

① Headlight retracting knobs
② Ignition coil wires
③ Secondary ground cable
④ Air cleaner assembly
⑤ No. 1 control box connector

⑥ Charcoal canister
⑦ Air bleed bolt for cooling system
⑧ No. 2 control box connector
⑨ Air chamber location (if so equipped)
⑩ Air jet controller location (if so equipped)

85913026

Fig. 27 Component removal points-1983 Prelude

14. Remove the speedometer cable clip, then, pull the cable from the holder.

➡**DO NOT remove the holder as the speedometer gear may drop into the transaxle.**

15. If equipped with power steering perform the following procedures:

   a. Remove the speed sensor-to-transaxle bolt and the sensor complete with the hoses.

➡**Do not disconnect the hoses from the speed sensor, for power steering fluid will flow from it.**

   b. Remove the power steering pump adjusting bolt, mounting bolt and the V-belt.

   c. Without disconnecting the hoses, pull the pump away from its mounting bracket and position it out of the way.

   d. Remove the power steering hose bracket from the cylinder head.

16. If equipped with air conditioning, perform the following procedures:

   a. Remove the compressor clutch lead wire.

   b. Loosen the belt adjusting bolt and the drive belt.

➡**DO NOT remove the air conditioner hoses. The air conditioner compressor can be moved without discharging the air conditioner system.**

   c. Remove the compressor mounting bolts, then, lift the compressor out of the bracket, with the hoses attached, and support it on the front bulkhead with a piece of wire.

17. If equipped with a manual transaxle, remove the shift rod yoke attaching bolt and disconnect the shift lever torque rod from the clutch housing.

18. If equipped with an automatic transaxle, perform the following procedures:

   a. Remove the center console.

   b. Place the shift lever in Reverse, then, remove the lock pin from the end of the shift cable.

   c. Remove the shift cable mounting bolts and the shift cable holder.

   d. Remove the throttle cable from the throttle lever. Loosen the lower locknut, then, remove the cable from the bracket.

➡**DO NOT loosen the upper locknut as it will change the transaxle shift points.**

19. Disconnect the right and left lower ball joints and the tie rod ends.

20. To remove the halfshafts, perform the following procedures:

   a. Remove the jackstands and lower the vehicle. Using a 32mm socket, loosen the spindle nuts. Raise and support the vehicle on jackstands.

   b. Remove the front wheel and the spindle nut.

   c. Remove the damper fork and damper pinch bolts.

   d. Remove the ball joint bolt and separate the ball joint from the lower control arm.

   e. Disconnect the tie rods from the steering knuckles.

   f. Pull the front hub outward and off the halfshafts.

   g. Using a small pry bar, pry out the inboard CV-joint approximately ½" to release the spring clip from the differential, then, pull the halfshaft from the transaxle case.

➡**When installing the halfshaft, insert the shaft until the spring clip clicks into the groove. Always use a new spring clip when installing halfshafts.**

21. Remove the exhaust header pipe.

22. Attach a chain hoist to the engine and raise it slightly to remove the slack.

23. Disconnect the No. 2 control box connector, lift the control box off of its bracket and allow it hang next to the engine.

24. If equipped with air conditioning, remove the idle control solenoid valve.

25. If equipped with an air chamber, remove it.

26. From under the air chamber, remove the three engine mount bolts, then, push the engine mount into the engine mount tower.

27. Remove the front and rear engine mount nuts.

28. Loosen the alternator bolts and remove the drive belt. Disconnect the alternator wire harness and remove the alternator.

29. At the engine, remove the bolt from the rear torque rod, then, loosen the bolt in the frame mount, swing the rod up and out of the way.

30. Carefully raise the engine from the vehicle, checking that all wires and hoses have been removed from the engine/transaxle, then, remove it from the vehicle.

31. To install the engine, reverse the removal procedures and make the following checks:

   a. Torque the engine mounting bolts in the proper sequence.

   b. Bleed the air from the cooling system.

   c. Adjust the clutch pedal free play.

   d. Adjust the throttle cable tension.

   e. Make sure the transaxle shifts properly.

Rocker Arm Cover

REMOVAL & INSTALLATION

1. Disconnect the negative battery cable. On some models, it will be necessary to remove the air cleaner assembly.

2. Remove the ground cable, the spark plug wires (if necessary) and the throttle cable (if necessary) from the rocker arm cover.

3. If equipped, remove the PCV hose from the rocker arm cover.

4. Remove the rocker arm cover-to-cylinder head nuts, the washer/grommet assemblies and the rocker arm cover.

➡**If the cover is difficult to remove, use a mallet to bump it loose.**

5. Using a putty knife, clean the gasket mounting surfaces.

6. To install, use a new gasket, sealant (if necessary) and reverse the removal procedures. Torque the rocker arm cover-to-cylinder head nuts, evenly to 7 ft. lbs.

Rocker Arms/Shafts

The rocker arms and shafts are an assembly; they must be removed from the engine as a unit.

REMOVAL & INSTALLATION

▶ **See Figures 28 and 29**

1. Disconnect the negative battery cable.

2. Remove the air cleaner housing.

3. Label and disconnect all vacuum hoses.

4. Remove the valve cover-to-cylinder head bolts and the valve cover.

5. Loosen the camshaft and rocker arm shaft holder bolts in a criss-cross pattern, beginning on the outside holder.

6. Remove the rocker arms, shafts and holders as an assembly.

7. Using a putty knife, clean the gasket mounting surfaces.

8. To install, reverse the removal procedures, being sure to install and tighten (in steps) the holder bolts in the reverse order of removal.

➡**Back off valve adjusting screws before installing rockers, then, adjust valves as outlined in Section 2.**

Thermostat

▶ **See Figures 30 and 31**

On 1170cc and 1237cc vehicles, the thermostat is located on the intake manifold, under the air cleaner nozzle, so you will first have to remove the air cleaner housing. On the CVCC and late model engines, it is located at the right rear of the distributor housing.

Fig. 28 View of the cylinder head with valve cover removed

Fig. 29 Removing the rocker arm shaft assembly

REMOVAL & INSTALLATION

1. Place a clean drain pan under the radiator, remove the drain plug from the radiator and drain the coolant into the pan.

✳✳CAUTION

When draining the coolant, keep in mind that cats and dogs are attracted by the ethylene glycol antifreeze, and are quite likely to drink any that is left in an uncovered container or in puddles on the ground. This will prove fatal in sufficient quantity. Always drain the coolant into a sealable container. Coolant should be reused unless it is contaminated or several years old.

2. Remove the thermostat cover-to-thermostat housing bolts, the cover, the gasket and the thermostat.
3. Using a putty knife, clean the gasket mounting surfaces.

➡**If the thermostat is equipped with a pin valve, be sure to install the thermostat with the pin facing upward.**

4. To install, use a new thermostat (if necessary), gasket, O-ring (if used), sealant (if necessary) and reverse the removal procedures. Always install the spring end of the thermostat facing the engine. Torque the thermostat cover-to-thermostat

housing bolts to 7 ft. lbs. (1973-78) or 9 ft. lbs. (1979-83). Bleed the cooling system.

Intake Manifold

REMOVAL & INSTALLATION

Carbureted Models

NON-CVCC ENGINES

◗ **See Figures 32, 33, 34 and 35**

1. Disconnect the negative battery cable. Place a clean pan under the radiator, remove the drain plug and drain the cooling system.

✳✳CAUTION

When draining the coolant, keep in mind that cats and dogs are attracted by the ethylene glycol antifreeze, and are quite likely to drink any that is left in an uncovered container or in puddles on the ground. This will prove fatal in sufficient quantity. Always drain the coolant into a sealable container. Coolant should be reused unless it is contaminated or several years old.

2. Remove the air cleaner and case.
3. Refer to the 'Carburetor, Removal & Installation' procedures in Section 5 and remove the carburetor from the intake manifold.
4. Remove the emission control hoses from the manifold T-joint; one hose leads to the condensation chamber and the other leads to the charcoal canister.
5. Remove the hose connected to the intake manifold directly above the T-joint and underneath the carburetor, leading to the air cleaner check valve (refer to diagrams of the various emission control hose connections, if necessary).
6. Remove the electrical connectors from the thermoswitches.
7. Remove the solenoid valve located next to the thermoswitch.
8. Remove the intake manifold-to-cylinder head nuts in a crisscross pattern, beginning from the center and moving out to both ends, then, remove the manifold.
9. Using a putty knife, clean the gasket mounting surfaces of the manifold and the cylinder head.
10. If the intake manifold is to be replaced, transfer all necessary components to the new manifold.
11. To install, use new gaskets, sealant (if necessary) and reverse the removal procedure, being sure to observe the following points:
   a. Apply a water-resistant sealer to the new intake manifold gasket before positioning it in place.
   b. Be sure all hoses are properly connected.
   c. Tighten the manifold attaching nuts in the reverse order of removal.

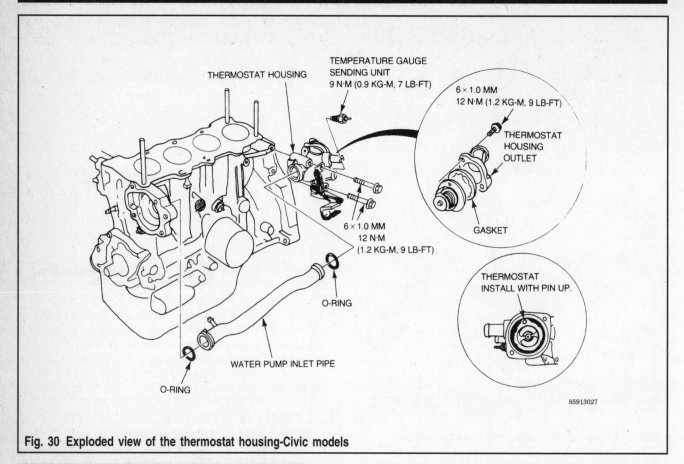

THERMOSTAT HOUSING

TEMPERATURE GAUGE
SENDING UNIT
9 N·M (0.9 KG-M, 7 LB-FT)

6 × 1.0 MM
12 N·M (1.2 KG-M, 9 LB-FT)

THERMOSTAT
HOUSING
OUTLET

GASKET

6 × 1.0 MM
12 N·M
(1.2 KG-M, 9 LB-FT)

THERMOSTAT
INSTALL WITH PIN UP.

O-RING

WATER PUMP INLET PIPE

O-RING

85913027

Fig. 30 Exploded view of the thermostat housing-Civic models

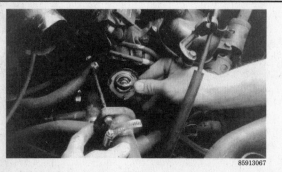

Fig. 31 View of removing the thermostat and housing-note radiator hose still connected to housing

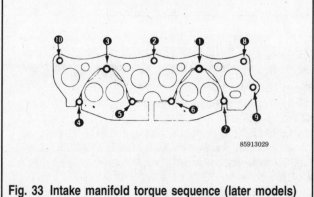

85913029

Fig. 33 Intake manifold torque sequence (later models)

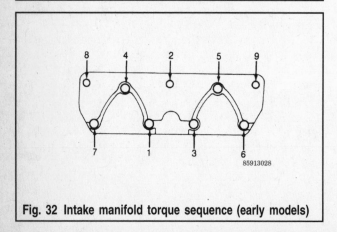

85913028

Fig. 32 Intake manifold torque sequence (early models)

85913068

Fig. 34 Removing the intake manifold retaining nuts

Fig. 35 Removing the intake manifold-note the shop towel in the carburetor mount opening

1829cc ENGINE

▶ **See Figures 36 and 37**

1. Disconnect the negative battery cable. Position a clean drain pan under the radiator, remove the drain plug and drain the cooling system.

✳✳CAUTION

When draining the coolant, keep in mind that cats and dogs are attracted by the ethylene glycol antifreeze, and are quite likely to drink any that is left in an uncovered container or in puddles on the ground. This will prove fatal in sufficient quantity. Always drain the coolant into a sealable container. Coolant should be reused unless it is contaminated or several years old.

2. Remove the air cleaner and housing from the carburetor(s).
3. Remove the air valve, the EGR valve, the air suction valve and the air chamber (if equipped).
4. Label and disconnect any electrical connectors from the carburetor(s) and intake manifold.
5. Disconnect the fuel line(s) from the carburetor. Disconnect the throttle cable from the carburetor.
6. Remove the carburetor(s) from the intake manifold.
7. Remove the intake manifold-to-cylinder head nuts (using a crisscross pattern), beginning from the center and moving out to both ends, then remove the manifold.
8. Using a putty knife, clean the gasket mounting surfaces.
9. If the intake manifold is to be replaced, transfer all the necessary components to the new manifold.
10. To install, use new gaskets, sealant (if necessary) and reverse the removal procedures. Tighten the nuts in a criss-cross pattern in 2-3 steps, starting with the inner nuts. Be sure all hoses and wires are correctly connected. Start the engine and check for leaks.

Exhaust Manifold

REMOVAL & INSTALLATION

Carbureted Engines

▶ **See Figure 38**

NON-CVCC MODELS

✳✳WARNING

Do not perform this operation on a warm or hot engine.

1. Disconnect the negative battery cable. Remove the front grille, as required.
2. Remove the three exhaust pipe-to-manifold nuts and disconnect the exhaust pipe from the manifold.
3. On 1975 and later models, disconnect the air injection tubes from the exhaust manifold, then, remove the air injection manifold.
4. Remove the hot air cover-to-exhaust manifold bolts and the cover.
5. Using a criss-cross pattern (starting from the center), remove the exhaust manifold-to-cylinder head nuts and the manifold.
6. Using a putty knife, clean the gasket mounting surfaces.
7. To install, use new gaskets and reverse the removal procedure. Torque the exhaust manifold-to-cylinder head nuts (in equal steps) in the reverse order of removal.

1829cc ENGINE

▶ **See Figure 39**

✳✳WARNING

Do not perform this operation on a warm or hot engine.

1. Disconnect the negative battery cable. Remove the header pipe or catalytic converter-to-exhaust manifold nuts and separate the pipe from the manifold.
2. Disconnect and remove the oxygen sensor (if equipped).
3. If equipped, remove the EGR and the air suction tubes from the exhaust manifold.
4. Remove the exhaust manifold shroud.
5. Remove the exhaust manifold bracket bolts.
6. Using a criss-cross pattern (starting from the center), remove the exhaust manifold-to-cylinder head nuts, the manifold and the gaskets (discard them).
7. Using a putty knife, clean the gasket mounting surfaces.
8. To install, use new gaskets and reverse the removal procedure. Torque the exhaust manifold-to-cylinder head nuts (using a criss-cross pattern, starting from the center) to 23 ft. lbs. and the header pipe-to-exhaust manifold nuts to 40 ft. lbs., the oxygen sensor-to-exhaust manifold to 33 ft. lbs. Start the engine and check for exhaust leaks.

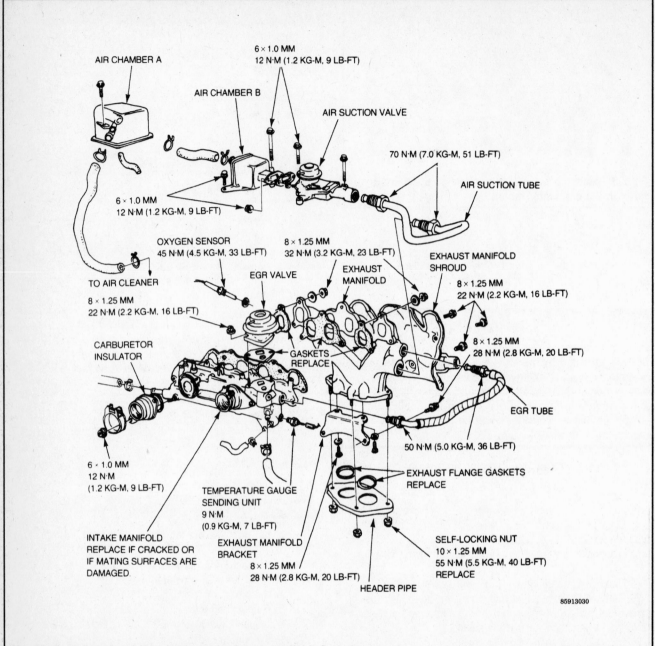

AIR CHAMBER A

6 × 1.0 MM
12 N·M (1.2 KG-M, 9 LB-FT)

AIR CHAMBER B

AIR SUCTION VALVE

70 N·M (7.0 KG-M, 51 LB-FT)

AIR SUCTION TUBE

6 × 1.0 MM
12 N·M (1.2 KG-M, 9 LB-FT)

OXYGEN SENSOR
45 N·M (4.5 KG-M, 33 LB-FT)

8 × 1.25 MM
32 N·M (3.2 KG-M, 23 LB-FT)

EXHAUST MANIFOLD
SHROUD

TO AIR CLEANER

EGR VALVE

EXHAUST
MANIFOLD

8 × 1.25 MM
22 N·M (2.2 KG-M, 16 LB-FT)

8 × 1.25 MM
22 N·M (2.2 KG-M. 16 LB-FT)

8 × 1.25 MM
28 N·M (2.8 KG-M, 20 LB-FT)

CARBURETOR
INSULATOR

GASKETS
REPLACE

EGR TUBE

50 N·M (5.0 KG-M, 36 LB-FT)

6 × 1.0 MM
12 N·M
(1.2 KG-M, 9 LB-FT)

TEMPERATURE GAUGE
SENDING UNIT
9 N·M
(0.9 KG-M, 7 LB-FT)

EXHAUST FLANGE GASKETS
REPLACE

INTAKE MANIFOLD
REPLACE IF CRACKED OR
IF MATING SURFACES ARE
DAMAGED.

EXHAUST MANIFOLD
BRACKET
8 × 1.25 MM
28 N·M (2.8 KG-M, 20 LB-FT)

HEADER PIPE

SELF-LOCKING NUT
10 × 1.25 MM
55 N·M (5.5 KG-M, 40 LB-FT)
REPLACE

85913030

Fig. 36 Exploded view of the intake and exhaust manifolds-Prelude

Combination Manifold — CVCC Models

REMOVAL & INSTALLATION

1335cc, 1487cc and 1751cc Engines
♦ See Figures 40, 41 and 42

1. Disconnect the negative battery cable. Place a clean drain pan under the radiator, remove the drain plug and drain the cooling system. Disconnect coolant hose(s) from the intake manifold coolant hoses.

❊❊CAUTION

When draining the coolant, keep in mind that cats and dogs are attracted by the ethylene glycol antifreeze, and are quite likely to drink any that is left in an uncovered container or in puddles on the ground. This will prove fatal in sufficient quantity. Always drain the coolant into a sealable container. Coolant should be reused unless it is contaminated or several years old.

2. Remove the air cleaner assembly.
3. Label and disconnect all vacuum hoses and electrical connectors from the carburetor.

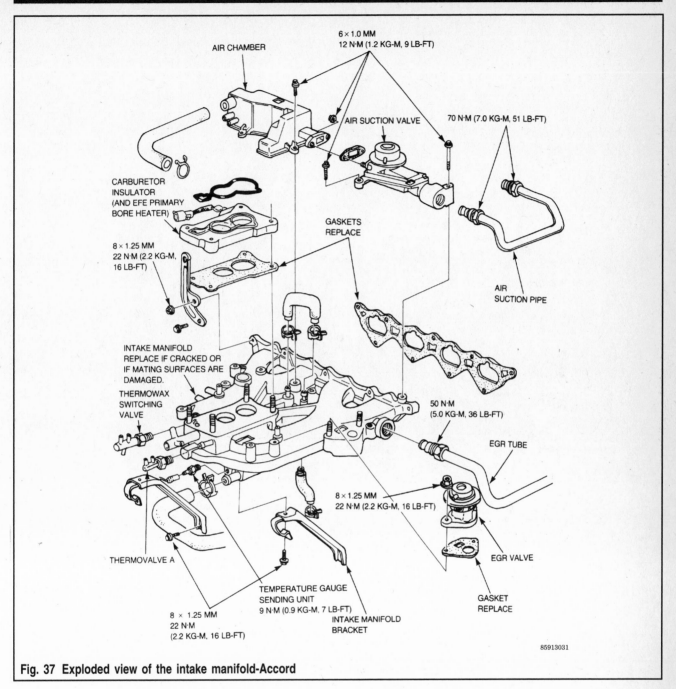

6 × 1.0 MM
12 N·M (1.2 KG-M, 9 LB-FT)

AIR CHAMBER

AIR SUCTION VALVE

70 N·M (7.0 KG-M, 51 LB-FT)

CARBURETOR
INSULATOR
(AND EFE PRIMARY
BORE HEATER)

GASKETS
REPLACE

8 × 1.25 MM
22 N·M (2.2 KG-M,
16 LB-FT)

AIR
SUCTION PIPE

INTAKE MANIFOLD
REPLACE IF CRACKED OR
IF MATING SURFACES ARE
DAMAGED.

THERMOWAX
SWITCHING
VALVE

50 N·M
(5.0 KG-M, 36 LB-FT)

EGR TUBE

8 × 1.25 MM
22 N·M (2.2 KG-M, 16 LB-FT)

EGR VALVE

THERMOVALVE A

TEMPERATURE GAUGE
SENDING UNIT
9 N·M (0.9 KG-M, 7 LB-FT)

INTAKE MANIFOLD
BRACKET

GASKET
REPLACE

8 × 1.25 MM
22 N·M
(2.2 KG-M, 16 LB-FT)

85913031

Fig. 37 Exploded view of the intake manifold-Accord

85913070

Fig. 38 Removing the exhaust manifold

4. Disconnect the fuel hose(s) and the throttle cable from the carburetor.

5. Remove the carburetor-to-intake manifold nuts and the carburetor.

6. Remove the upper heat shield. Loosen, but do not remove the four (1300cc) or two (1500cc) intake manifold-to-exhaust manifold bolts.

7. Remove the header pipe-to-exhaust manifold nuts (discard them), separate the header pipe from the exhaust manifold and discard the exhaust flange gasket.

8. Remove the combination manifold-to-cylinder head nuts/washers and the manifold assembly from the cylinder head.

9. Remove the intake manifold-to-exhaust manifold bolts and separate the manifolds.

10. Using a putty knife, clean the gasket mounting surfaces.

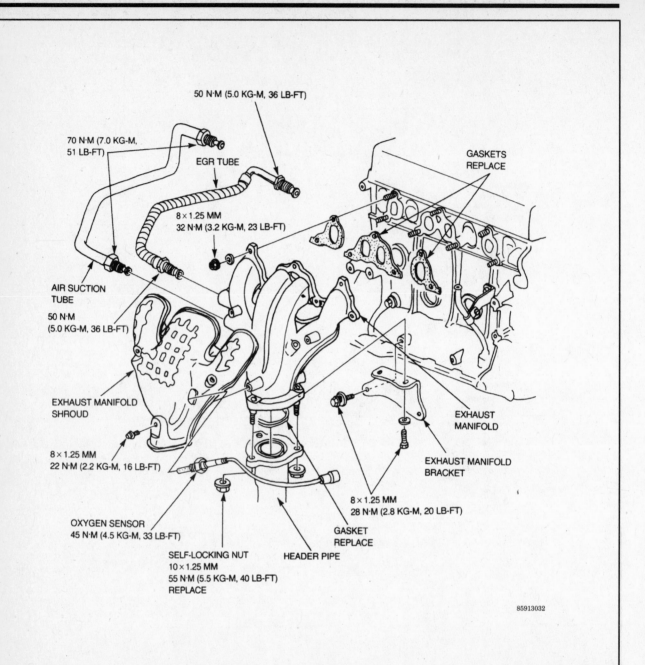

50 N·M (5.0 KG-M, 36 LB-FT)

70 N·M (7.0 KG-M, 51 LB-FT)

EGR TUBE

GASKETS REPLACE

8 × 1.25 MM
32 N·M (3.2 KG-M, 23 LB-FT)

AIR SUCTION TUBE

50 N·M (5.0 KG-M, 36 LB-FT)

EXHAUST MANIFOLD SHROUD

8 × 1.25 MM
22 N·M (2.2 KG-M, 16 LB-FT)

EXHAUST MANIFOLD

EXHAUST MANIFOLD BRACKET

8 × 1.25 MM
28 N·M (2.8 KG-M, 20 LB-FT)

OXYGEN SENSOR
45 N·M (4.5 KG-M, 33 LB-FT)

SELF-LOCKING NUT
10 × 1.25 MM
55 N·M (5.5 KG-M, 40 LB-FT)
REPLACE

GASKET REPLACE

HEADER PIPE

85913032

Fig. 39 Exploded view exhaust manifold assembly-Accord and Prelude

11. To install, use new gaskets and reverse the removal procedures. The thick washers used beneath the cylinder head-to-manifold retaining nuts must be installed with the dished (concave), side toward the engine. Torque the combination manifold-to-cylinder head nuts (in a circular pattern from the center to the ends) to 16 ft. lbs., the intake manifold-to-exhaust manifold bolts to 16 ft. lbs. and the header pipe-to-exhaust manifold nuts to 36 ft. lbs. Check and/or adjust the choke and throttle linkage. Bleed the cooling system.

Air Conditioning Compressor

REMOVAL & INSTALLATION

1. Operate the engine at idle speed and turn ON the air conditioning system for a few minutes.
2. Turn OFF the air conditioning system and the engine. Disconnect the negative battery terminal from the battery and the clutch wire from the air conditioning compressor.
3. Discharge the air conditioning system using the appropriate equipment, as described in Section 1 of this manual.

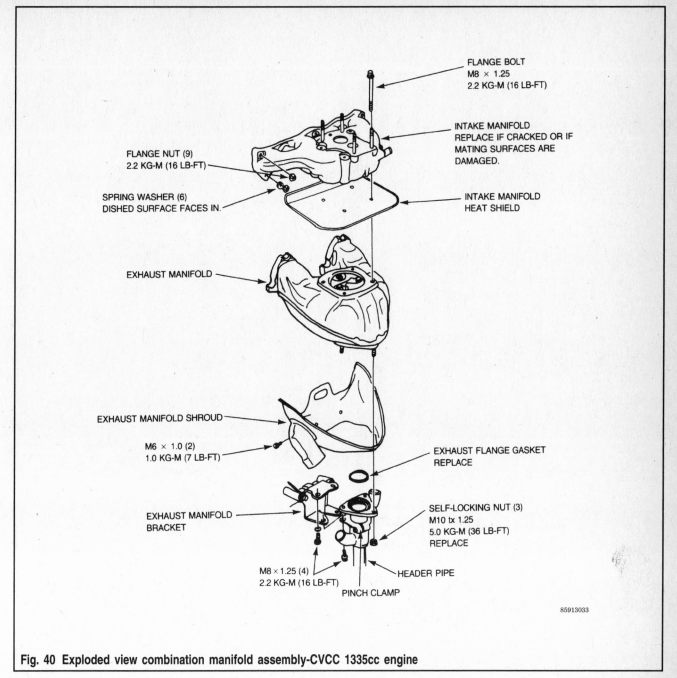

FLANGE BOLT
M8 × 1.25
2.2 KG-M (16 LB-FT)

INTAKE MANIFOLD
REPLACE IF CRACKED OR IF
MATING SURFACES ARE
DAMAGED.

FLANGE NUT (9)
2.2 KG-M (16 LB-FT)

SPRING WASHER (6)
DISHED SURFACE FACES IN.

INTAKE MANIFOLD
HEAT SHIELD

EXHAUST MANIFOLD

EXHAUST MANIFOLD SHROUD

M6 × 1.0 (2)
1.0 KG-M (7 LB-FT)

EXHAUST FLANGE GASKET
REPLACE

EXHAUST MANIFOLD
BRACKET

SELF-LOCKING NUT (3)
M10 tx 1.25
5.0 KG-M (36 LB-FT)
REPLACE

M8 × 1.25 (4)
2.2 KG-M (16 LB-FT)

HEADER PIPE

PINCH CLAMP

85913033

Fig. 40 Exploded view combination manifold assembly-CVCC 1335cc engine

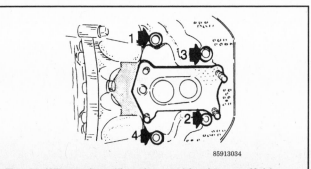

85913034

Fig. 41 When reinstalling the combination manifold on CVCC models, tighten these 4 bolts after the manifolds have been installed to the engine

4. On the Civic models, remove the left front under cover and the engine lower grille cowling, then, remove the receiver from the connecting lines.

5. On the Accord and Prelude equipped with power steering, perform the following procedures:

a. Loosen the power steering pump adjusting and mounting bolts.

b. Remove the drive belt from the pump's pulley.

c. Remove the power steering pump and support it out of the way; DO NOT disconnect the hoses from the pump.

6. From the air conditioning compressor, disconnect the suction and discharge hoses.

➡When disconnecting the hoses from the compressor, be sure to plug the openings to keep dirt and moisture out of the system.

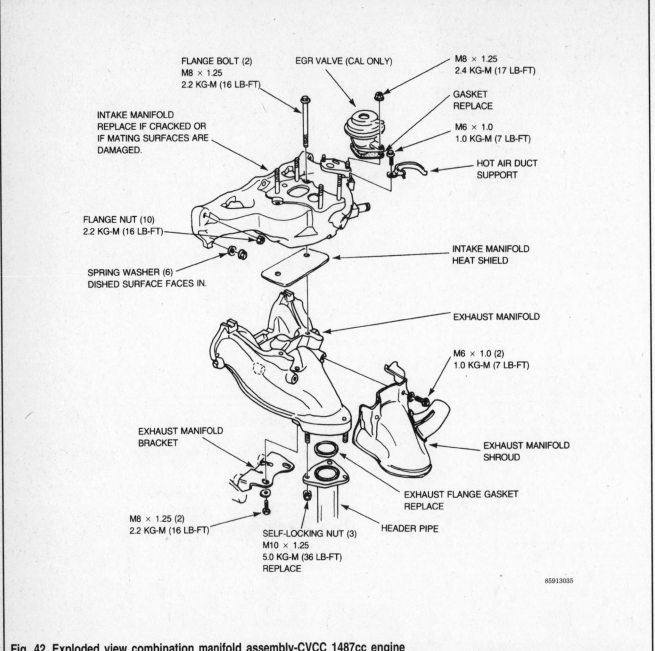

FLANGE BOLT (2)
M8 × 1.25
2.2 KG-M (16 LB-FT)

EGR VALVE (CAL ONLY)

M8 × 1.25
2.4 KG-M (17 LB-FT)

GASKET
REPLACE

INTAKE MANIFOLD
REPLACE IF CRACKED OR
IF MATING SURFACES ARE
DAMAGED.

M6 × 1.0
1.0 KG-M (7 LB-FT)

HOT AIR DUCT
SUPPORT

FLANGE NUT (10)
2.2 KG-M (16 LB-FT)

INTAKE MANIFOLD
HEAT SHIELD

SPRING WASHER (6)
DISHED SURFACE FACES IN.

EXHAUST MANIFOLD

M6 × 1.0 (2)
1.0 KG-M (7 LB-FT)

EXHAUST MANIFOLD
BRACKET

EXHAUST MANIFOLD
SHROUD

EXHAUST FLANGE GASKET
REPLACE

M8 × 1.25 (2)
2.2 KG-M (16 LB-FT)

HEADER PIPE

SELF-LOCKING NUT (3)
M10 × 1.25
5.0 KG-M (36 LB-FT)
REPLACE

85913035

Fig. 42 Exploded view combination manifold assembly-CVCC 1487cc engine

7. Loosen the air conditioning compressor-to-bracket adjusting and mounting bolts/nut(s), then, remove the drive belt from the compressor.

☛**On the Accord and Prelude, it may be necessary to remove the air conditioning cooling fan shroud and fan with the mounting frame.**

8. Remove the air conditioning compressor-to-bracket bolts and set the compressor on the engine support beam.

9. Remove the compressor bracket-to-engine bolts, the bracket and the compressor.

☛**If installing a new compressor, install 1 oz. of refrigerant oil through the suction fitting of the compressor.**

10. To install, reverse the removal procedures. Torque the bracket-to-engine bolts to 34 ft. lbs., the air conditioning compressor-to-bracket bolts to 35 ft. lbs. or nut(s) to 32 ft. lbs. Adjust the drive belt tension to 5/16" deflection. Charge the air conditioning system and test its performance.

Radiator

The Honda employs water-cooling for engine heat dissipation. Air is forced through the radiator by an electric fan which is, in turn, activated by a water temperature sensor screwed into the base of the radiator.

✳✳CAUTION

DO NOT attempt to open the cooling system when the engine is Hot; the system will be under high pressure and scalding may occur.

REMOVAL & INSTALLATION

▶ **See Figures 43, 44, 45, 46 and 47**

➡**When removing the radiator, take care not to damage the core and fins.**

1. Position a clean drain pan under the radiator, open the drain plug, remove the radiator cap and drain the cooling system.

✳✳CAUTION

When draining the coolant, keep in mind that cats and dogs are attracted by the ethylene glycol antifreeze, and are quite likely to drink any that is left in an uncovered container or in puddles on the ground. This will prove fatal in sufficient quantity. Always drain the coolant into a sealable container. Coolant should be reused unless it is contaminated or several years old.

2. Disconnect the electrical connectors from the thermo-switch and the cooling fan motor.
3. Disconnect the upper coolant hose at the upper radiator tank and the lower hose at the water pump connecting pipe. Disconnect the overflow hose from the coolant tank.
4. Remove the turn signals (Civic 1973-77) and front grille.
5. Remove the radiator-to-chassis bolts and the radiator with the fan attached. The fan can be easily unbolted from the back of the radiator.
6. Inspect the hoses for damage, leaks and/or deterioration; if necessary, replace them. If the radiator fins are clogged, wash off any insects or dirt with low pressure water.
7. To install, use new O-rings (if used) and reverse the removal procedure. Torque the radiator-to-chassis bolts to 7 ft. lbs. Refill and bleed the cooling system; if equipped with a coolant reservoir, be sure to fill it to proper level. Start the

Fig. 44 Removing the radiator upper hose

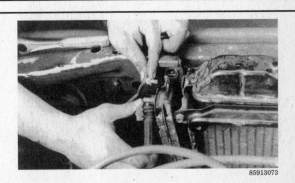
Fig. 45 Removing the transaxle oil cooler from the radiator

Fig. 46 Removing the radiator with cooling fan attached

engine, allow it to reach normal operating temperatures and check for leaks.

Air Conditioning Condenser

REMOVAL & INSTALLATION

1. Disconnect the negative battery terminal from the battery.
2. Discharge the air conditioning system using the appropriate equipment, as described in Section 1 of this manual.
3. On the Prelude models, remove the front grille and the upper radiator frame bolts, then, slightly move the frame to obtain access to the condenser.

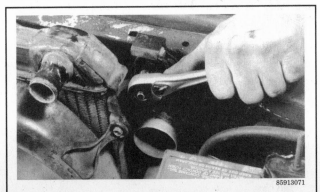
Fig. 43 Removing the radiator mounting bolts

85913075

Fig. 47 View of the electrical connectors for the radiator thermo-switch

4. On the Accord models, remove the hood lock brace bolts and position the brace on the engine; DO NOT disconnect the hood opener cable from the hood lock.

5. On the Civic models, perform the following procedures:

    a. Remove the front bumper.

    b. Disconnect the aluminum receiver line from the copper receiver line and the sight glass.

    c. Remove the discharge hose clamp (from the base of the condenser) and the discharge hose from the condenser.

    d. Disconnect the electrical connector from the condenser fan.

6. Disconnect and plug the refrigerant lines from the condenser.

➡**Be careful not to damage the condenser fins and tubes.**

7. Remove the condenser from the vehicle.

8. On the Civic models, remove the condenser fan from the condenser (if necessary).

➡**If installing a new condenser, pour 10ml of refrigerant oil in it.**

9. To install, reverse the removal procedures. Torque the condenser mounting bolts to 12 ft. lbs. Charge the air conditioning system as described in Section 1 of this manual. Test the performance of the air conditioning system.

Water Pump

REMOVAL & INSTALLATION

All Engines
▶ **See Figures 48, 49, 50, 51, 52, 53 and 54**

1. Place a clean drain pan under the radiator. Remove the drain plug from the front side of the engine block and the drain the cooling system to a level below the water pump.

❄❄CAUTION

When draining the coolant, keep in mind that cats and dogs are attracted by the ethylene glycol antifreeze, and are quite likely to drink any that is left in an uncovered container or in puddles on the ground. This will prove

fatal in sufficient quantity. Always drain the coolant into a sealable container. Coolant should be reused unless it is contaminated or several years old.

2. If the water pump and alternator operate from the same drive belt, loosen the alternator bolts, move the alternator toward the cylinder block and remove the drive belt.

3. Remove the pulley-to-water pump bolts and the pulley.

4. Remove the water pump-to-engine bolts and the pump together with the pulley and the O-ring seal.

5. Using a putty knife, clean the gasket mounting surfaces.

6. To install, use a new O-ring (or gasket) and reverse the removal procedures. Torque the water pump-to-engine bolts to 9 ft. lbs. and the pulley-to-water pump bolts to 9 ft. lbs. Adjust the drive belt tension. Refill and bleed the cooling system. Operate the engine to normal operating temperatures and check for leaks.

Cylinder Head

➡**You will need a 12 point socket to remove and install the head bolts on the CVCC engine.**

PRECAUTIONS

- To prevent warping, the cylinder head should be removed when the engine is Cold.
- Remove oil, scale or carbon deposits accumulated from each part. When decarbonizing take care not to score or scratch the mating surfaces.
- After washing the oil holes or orifices in each part, make sure they are not restricted by blowing out with compressed air.
- If the parts will not be reinstalled immediately after washing, spray the parts with a rust preventive to protect from corrosion.

REMOVAL & INSTALLATION

1170cc, 1237cc, 1335cc, 1487cc and 1600cc Engines
▶ **See Figures 55, 56 and 57**

1. Disconnect the negative battery cable. On the Civic (1973-77) models, remove the turn signals, grille and hood.

2. Place a clean drain pan under the radiator, remove radiator cap, the drain plug (from the front side of the engine block, if equipped) and drain the cooling system.

❄❄CAUTION

When draining the coolant, keep in mind that cats and dogs are attracted by the ethylene glycol antifreeze, and are quite likely to drink any that is left in an uncovered container or in puddles on the ground. This will prove fatal in sufficient quantity. Always drain the coolant into a sealable container. Coolant should be reused unless it is contaminated or several years old.

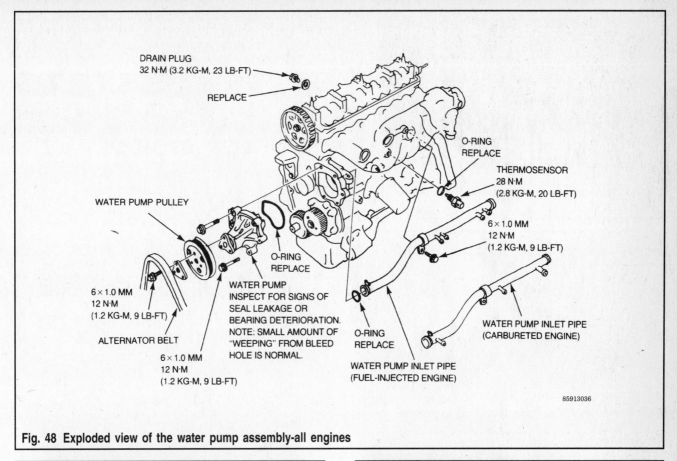

Fig. 48 Exploded view of the water pump assembly-all engines

Fig. 49 Removing the drive belt for water pump assembly

Fig. 51 Removing the water pump pulley

Fig. 50 Removing the water pump pulley bolts

Fig. 52 Removing the water pump

85913080

Fig. 53 Removing the water pump from the engine block

85913081

Fig. 54 Removing the water pump from the engine compartment

3. Disconnect the upper radiator hose from the thermostat housing.

4. On CVCC models, remove distributor cap, ignition wires (mark for correct installation) and primary wire. Loosen the alternator bracket and remove the upper mounting bolt from the cylinder head.

5. Remove the air cleaner housing.

6. Disconnect the charcoal canister-to-carburetor tube from the canister.

7. Disconnect the throttle and choke control cables. Label and disconnect all vacuum hoses.

8. Disconnect the heater hose from the intake manifold.

9. Disconnect the electrical connectors from both thermoswitches.

10. Disconnect the fuel line from the carburetor.

11. On the CVCC models, disconnect the temperature gauge sending unit wire, idle cut-off solenoid valve and the primary/main cut-off solenoid valve.

12. Remove the engine torque rod from the engine. Disconnect the exhaust pipe from the exhaust manifold.

13. Remove the valve cover-to-cylinder head bolts and the valve cover.

14. Remove the upper timing belt cover-to-engine bolts and the cover.

15. Rotate the crankshaft to position the No. 1 piston to the TDC of its compression stroke; to do this, align the notch next to the red notch used for setting ignition timing, with the index mark on the timing belt cover (1170cc and 1237cc) or the rear of engine block (CVCC).

16. Loosen, but do not remove, the timing belt adjusting bolt and pivot bolt.

17. On 1170cc and 1237cc models, remove the camshaft pulley bolt. Do not let the woodruff key fall inside the timing cover. Using the Pulley Removal tool No. 07935-6110000 or equivalent, remove the pulley.

✳✳WARNING

Use care when handling the timing belt. Do not use sharp instruments to remove the belt. Do not get oil or grease on the belt. Do not bend or twist the belt more than 90°.

18. If equipped with a 1170cc or 1237cc engine, perform the following procedures:

    a. Remove the fuel pump and distributor.

    b. Remove the oil pump gear holder, then, the pump gear and shaft.

19. Remove the cylinder head bolts in the reverse order of the torquing sequence; the No. 1 cylinder head bolt is hidden under the oil pump.

20. Remove the cylinder head with the carburetor and manifolds attached.

21. If necessary, remove the intake and exhaust manifolds from the cylinder head.

➡After removing the cylinder head, cover the engine with a clean cloth to prevent materials from getting into the cylinders.

To install:

22. Using a putty knife, clean the gasket mounting surfaces.

23. Use new gaskets and reverse the removal procedures, being sure to pay attention to the following points.

    a. Be sure that No. 1 cylinder is at TDC of its compression stroke.

    b. Use a new head gasket and make sure the head, engine block and gasket are clean.

    c. The cylinder head aligning dowel pins should be in their proper place in the block before installing the cylinder head.

    d. Using the torquing sequence, torque the head bolts according to the diagram. On the 1335cc and 1487cc engines, torque the cylinder head-to-engine bolts in two steps: to 22 ft. lbs., then, to 43 ft. lbs., in sequence each time.

    e. After the head bolts have been tightened, install the woodruff key and camshaft pulley (if removed) and torque the pulley bolt according to specification. On the non-CVCC engines, align the marks on the camshaft pulley so they are parallel with the top of the head and the woodruff key is facing upwards; on the CVCC engines, the word **UP** should be facing upward and the mark on the cam gear should be aligned with the arrow on the cylinder head.

    f. After installing the pulley (if removed), install the timing belt. Be careful not to disturb the timing position already set when installing the belt.

1751cc and 1829cc Engines

▶ See Figures 58, 59, 60, 61, 62, 63, 64, 65, 66, 67 and 68

✳✳WARNING

The cylinder head temperature must be below 100°F.

1. Disconnect the negative battery terminal from the battery.

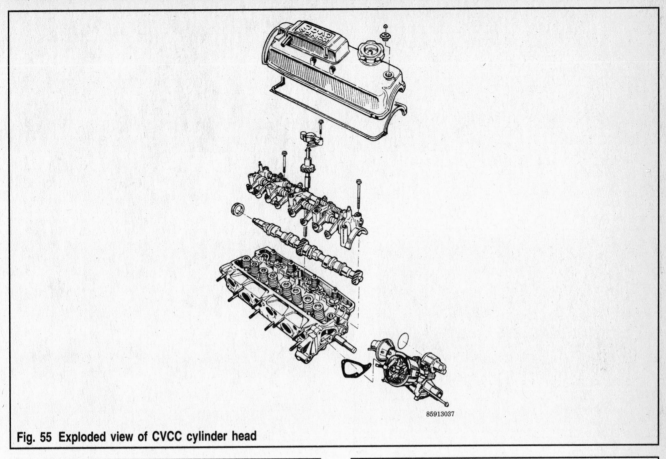

Fig. 55 Exploded view of CVCC cylinder head

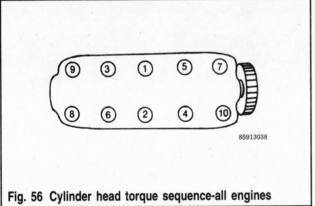

Fig. 56 Cylinder head torque sequence-all engines

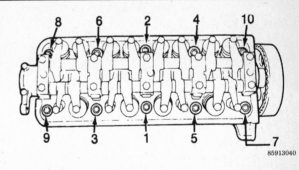

Fig. 58 Cylinder head bolt torque sequence-1751cc and 1829cc engines

2. Place a clean drain pan under the radiator, remove the drain plug and the radiator cap, then, drain the cooling system.

❋❋CAUTION

When draining the coolant, keep in mind that cats and dogs are attracted by the ethylene glycol antifreeze, and are quite likely to drink any that is left in an uncovered container or in puddles on the ground. This will prove fatal in sufficient quantity. Always drain the coolant into a sealable container. Coolant should be reused unless it is contaminated or several years old.

3. Label and disconnect the vacuum hoses from the air cleaner.

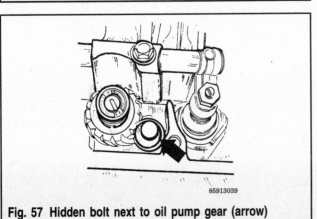

Fig. 57 Hidden bolt next to oil pump gear (arrow)

4. Disconnect the electrical connectors from the thermosensor temperature gauge sending unit, idle cut-off solenoid valve, primary/main cut-off solenoid valve and the automatic choke.

5. Disconnect the fuel lines and throttle cable from the carburetor(s).

6. Label and disconnect all emission hoses from the carburetor, then, remove the carburetor.

7. Label and disconnect the electrical connectors wires and hoses from the distributor, then, remove the distributor.

8. Remove the coolant hoses from the cylinder head.

9. Loosen the exhaust manifold-to-engine bracket bolts to ease assembly, then, disconnect the hot air ducts and head pipe from the cylinder head.

10. If equipped with power steering, loosen the adjustment bolt and remove the belt. Disconnect and plug the

Fig. 59 View of the cylinder head, camshaft and timing belt assembly-note rocker shaft assembly removed

Fig. 60 Removing the camshaft sprocket and woodruff key

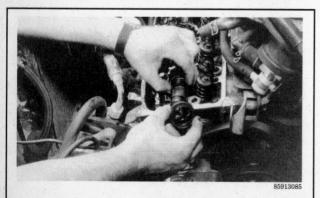

Fig. 61 Removing the camshaft oil seal

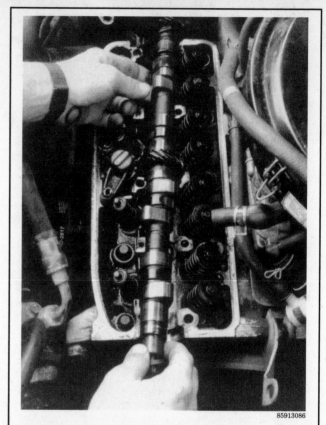

Fig. 62 Removing the camshaft

Fig. 63 Removing the cylinder head retaining bolts

hoses/fittings to prevent contamination. Remove the pump-to-engine bolts and swing the pump to the right side of the engine.

11. If not equipped with air conditioning, remove the alternator bracket-to-cylinder head bolt and loosen the adjusting bolt.

12. If equipped with air conditioning, remove the alternator and bracket from the engine.

13. Disconnect the brake booster vacuum hose from the one-way valve.

14. Remove the valve cover and upper timing belt cover.

15. Loosen the timing belt pivot and adjusting bolts, then, slide the belt from the pulley.

16. Remove the oil pump gear cover and pull the oil pump shaft out of the cylinder head.

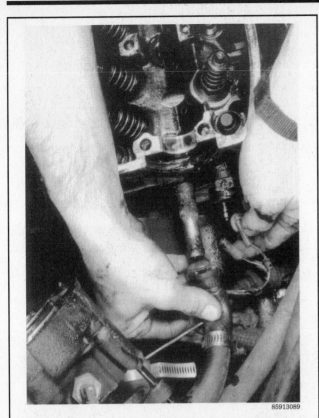

Fig. 64 Removing all necessary connections from the cylinder head assembly before removal

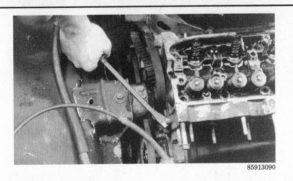

Fig. 65 Removing the cylinder head assembly-note location of pry bar

Fig. 66 Removing the cylinder head assembly from the engine block

Fig. 67 Removing the cylinder head gasket

Fig. 68 Installing the cylinder head gasket. Make sure gasket is installed correctly.

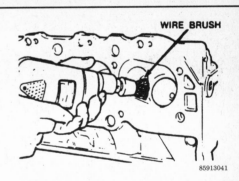

Fig. 69 Remove the carbon from the cylinder head with a wire brush and drill

17. Remove the head bolts in sequence working from the outer ends, toward the center; this is the reverse of the torquing sequence. To prevent warpage, loosen the bolts 1/3 turn (in sequence) until they are loose.

18. Carefully lift the cylinder head from the engine block.

To install:

19. Using a putty knife, clean the gasket mounting surfaces.

20. Use new gaskets, seals and reverse the removal procedures. Make sure the head dowel pins are aligned. Make sure that the **UP** mark on the timing belt pulley is at the top.

21. Torque the cylinder head bolts in two equal steps to 43 ft. lbs. (1751cc engine) or 49 ft. lbs. (1829cc engine). Road test the vehicle for proper operation.

CLEANING AND INSPECTION

▶ **See Figures 69, 70 and 71**

1. Refer to the 'Valves, Removal & Installation' in this section and remove the valve assemblies from the cylinder head.

2. Using a small wire power brush, clean the carbon from the combustion chambers and the valve ports.

3. Inspect the cylinder head for cracks in the exhaust ports, combustion chambers or external cracks in the water chamber.

4. Thoroughly clean the valve guides using a suitable wire bore brush.

➡**Excessive valve stem-to-bore clearance will cause excessive oil consumption and may cause valve breakage. Insufficient clearance will result in noisy and sticky functioning of the valve and disturb engine smoothness.**

5. Measure the valve stem clearance as follows:

a. Clamp a dial indicator on one side of the cylinder head rocker arm cover gasket rail.

b. Locate the indicator so movement of the valve stem from side-to-side (crosswise to the head) will cause a direct movement of the indicator stem. The indicator stem must contact the side of the valve stem just above the valve guide.

c. Prop the valve head about 1/16″ off the valve seat.

d. Move the stem of the valve from side-to-side using light pressure to obtain a clearance reading. If the clearance exceeds specifications, it will be necessary to ream (for original valves) the valve guides.

Fig. 70 Using a dial indicator to measure the valve stem clearances

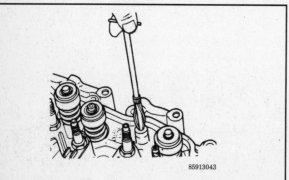

Fig. 71 Using an expandable wire type cleaner to clean the valve guides

6. Inspect the rocker arm studs for wear or damage.

7. Install a dial micrometer into the valve guide and check the valve seat for concentricity.

RESURFACING

▶ **See Figure 72**

1. Using a straightedge, check the cylinder for warpage.

2. If the warpage exceeds 0.076mm in a 152mm span or 0.152mm over the total length, the cylinder head must be resurfaced. Resurfacing can be performed at most machine shops.

Valves

REMOVAL & INSTALLATION

▶ **See Figures 73, 74, 75, 76, 77, 78 and 79**

1. Refer to the 'Cylinder Head, Removal & Installation' and the 'Camshaft, Removal & Installation' procedures in this section, then, remove the cylinder head from the engine and the camshaft from the cylinder head.

2. Using a plastic mallet, tap each valve stem to loosen the valve keepers.

3. Using a Valve Spring Compressor tool, compress the valve springs, then, remove the valve keepers, retainers and springs. Remove the valves from the opposite side of the cylinder head.

➡**When removing the valves and components, keep them in order for reinstallation purposes.**

4. To replace the valve seals, simply pull the seal from the valve guide. If the valve seals are being reused, it is good idea to replace the springs around the seal's neck.

➡**The exhaust valve seal uses a black spring, while the intake valve seal uses a white spring.**

5. Inspect the valves for wear, damage and/or cracks. If necessary, reface the valves on a valve grinding machine.

➡**When replacing the valve springs, place the closely wound end toward the cylinder head.**

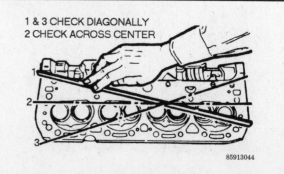

Fig. 72 Using a straight-edge to inspect the cylinder head for warpage

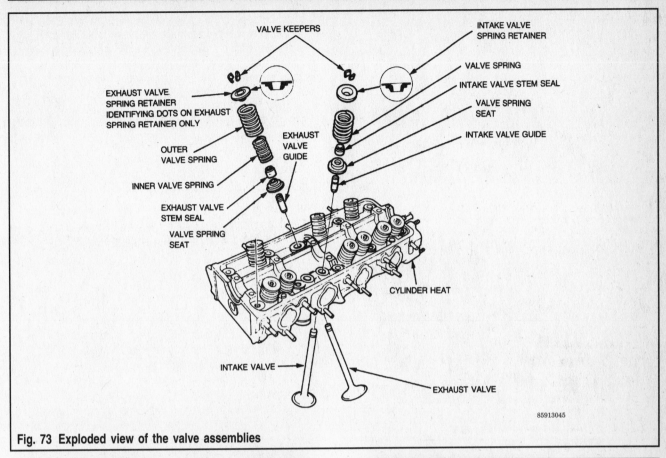

Fig. 73 Exploded view of the valve assemblies

Fig. 74 Installing special tool on valve spring

Fig. 76 Use a magnet to remove valve spring keepers

Fig. 75 Installing special tool on valve spring-note position of tool

Fig. 77 Removing special tool on valve spring

Fig. 78 Removing the valve stem seal

Fig. 79 Removing the valve spring seat

6. To assemble the cylinder head, use new valve seals, lubricate the valve parts with clean engine oil and reverse the disassembly procedures. After removing the valve spring compressor, tap the valve stems 2-3 times to make sure the valve keepers and valves are fully seated.

✳✳CAUTION

When removing the valve spring compressor tool, remove it slowly and make sure the valve keepers are fully seated; otherwise, the springs may be launched like a missile.

7. To complete the installation, use new gaskets and reverse the removal procedures.

INSPECTION

Inspect the valve faces and seats (in the head) for pits, burned spots and other evidence of poor seating. If a valve face is in such bad shape that the head of the valve must be ground, in order to true the face, discard the valve, because the sharp edge will run too hot. The correct angle for valve faces is 45°. We recommend the refacing be performed by a reputable machine shop.

Check the valve stem for scoring and burned spots. If not noticeably scored or damaged, clean the valve stem with solvent to remove all gum and varnish. Clean the valve guides using and an expanding wire-type valve guide cleaner. If you have access to a dial indicator for measuring valve stem-to-guide clearance, mount it so the stem of the indicator is at 90°

to the valve stem and as closer to the valve guide as possible. Move the valve off its seat, then, measure the valve guide-to-stem clearance by rocking the stem back and for the actuate the dial indicator. Measure the valve stem diameter using a micrometer and compare it to specifications to determine whether the stem or guide wear is responsible for the excess clearance. If a dial indicator and micrometer are not available, take the cylinder head and valves to a reputable machine shop for inspection.

REFACING

➡**All valve grinding operations should be performed by a qualified machine shop; ONLY the valve lapping operation is recommended to be performed by the inexperienced mechanic.**

Valve Lapping
◆ **See Figure 80**

When valve faces and seats have been refaced and/or recut, or if they are determined to be in good condition, the valves MUST BE lapped in to ensure efficient sealing when the valve closes against the seat.

1. Invert the cylinder head so the combustion chambers are facing upward.
2. Lightly lubricate the valve stems with clean engine oil and coat the valve seats with valve grinding compound. Install the valves in the cylinder head as numbered.
3. Using a valve lapping tool, attach the suction cup to a valve head. *You will probably have to moisten the suction cup to securely attach the tool to the valve.*
4. Rotate the tool between the palms, changing position and lifting the tool often to prevent grooving. Lap the valve until a smooth polished seat is evident (you may have to add a bit more compound after some lapping is done).
5. Remove the valve and tool, then, remove all traces of the grinding compound with a solvent-soaked rag or rinse the head with solvent.

➡**Valve lapping can also be done by fastening a suction to a piece of drill rod in a hang egg-beater type drill. Proceed as above, using the drill as a lapping tool. Due to the higher speeds involved when using the hand drill, care must be exercised to avoid grooving the seat. Lift the tool and change direction of rotation often.**

Fig. 80 Lapping the valves by hand

Valve Springs

If the cylinder head is removed from the engine, refer to the 'Valves, Removal & Installation' procedures in this section and remove the valve springs.

REMOVAL & INSTALLATION

▶ **See Figures 81, 82 and 83**

1. Refer to the 'Rocker Arm, Removal & Installation' procedures in this section and remove the rocker arm assembly.
2. Using an old set of rocker arm shafts, install them in place of the rocker arm assembly; this will prevent bending or scratching the original set of shafts.
3. Remove the spark plug(s) from the cylinder head.
4. Rotate the crankshaft to position the cylinder (being worked on) to the TDC of its compression stroke.
5. Using a Spark Plug Air Hold tool, install it into the spark plug hole and inject compressed air into the cylinder to hold the valves in place.

➡ **Be advised that if air pressure in the cylinder is lost while the valve keepers are removed, the valve will fall into the cylinder. It will then be necessary to remove the cylinder head to extract the valve.**

6. Using the Spring Compressor tool, compress the spring(s) and remove the valve keepers. Relax the spring compressor tool, then, remove the valve retainer, the spring(s) and the valve seal; keep the parts in the order for reinstallation purposes. Work on one valve at a time.

➡ **If reusing the valve seals, it is recommended to replace the neck springs of the seal; the black spring is used on the exhaust valve seal and the white spring is used on the intake valve seal. The seals are not interchangeable between the intake and the exhaust valves.**

7. Inspect the springs for fatigue, cracks and/or uniformity; if necessary, replace them. Using a putty knife, clean the gasket mounting surfaces.
8. To assemble, use new seals (if necessary) and reverse the disassembly procedures. Using a plastic mallet, tap the

valve a few times to make sure the valve keepers are seated correctly.

➡ **When installing the springs, be sure to position the closely wound coils ends or painted part toward the cylinder head.**

9. To install, use new gaskets, seals and reverse the removal procedures. Start the engine and check for leaks.

INSPECTION

▶ **See Figure 84**

1. Position the valve spring on a flat, clean surface next to a square.
2. Rotate the spring against the square to measure the distortion (out-of-roundness). If the spring height varies (between similar springs) by more than $1/16''$, replace the spring.

Valve Seats

▶ **See Figure 85**

The valve seats can be machined during a valve job to provide optimum sealing between the valve and the seat.

The seating services should be performed by a professional machine shop which has the specialized knowledge and tools necessary to perform the service.

Valve Guides

If replacement valve guides are not available or you determine the replacement procedure is too involved, the guides can be reconditioned using a procedure known as knurling (machining the inner surface).

REMOVAL & INSTALLATION

1. Refer to the 'Valve, Removal & Installation' procedures in this section and remove the valves.
2. Place the cylinder head in an oven and heat it to 300°F; this procedure will loosen the valve guides enough to drive them out.
3. Place the new valve guides in the freezer section of a refrigerator for about an hour; this contraction procedure will make them easier to install.
4. Using a hammer and the Valve Guide Driver tool No. 07942-SA50000, 07942-8230000 or equivalent (exhaust) or 07942-6570100, 07942-6110000 or equivalent (intake), drive the valve guide(s) toward the camshaft side of the cylinder head.
5. Using a hammer and the Valve Guide Driver tool No. 07942-SA50000, 07942-8230000 or equivalent (exhaust) or 07942-6570100, 07942-6110000 or equivalent (intake), remove the new guide from the freezer and drive it into the cylinder head from the camshaft side until the guide projects 15.5mm above the cylinder head surface.
6. Using the Valve Guide Reamer tool No. 07984-SA50000, 07984-689010A or equivalent (exhaust) or 07984-6110000, 07984-657010A or equivalent, coat the reamer with cutting oil

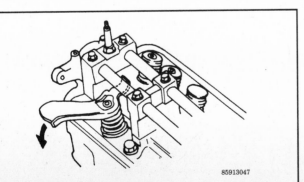

85913047

Fig. 81 Using a spring compressor tool to remove the valve springs from the cylinder head

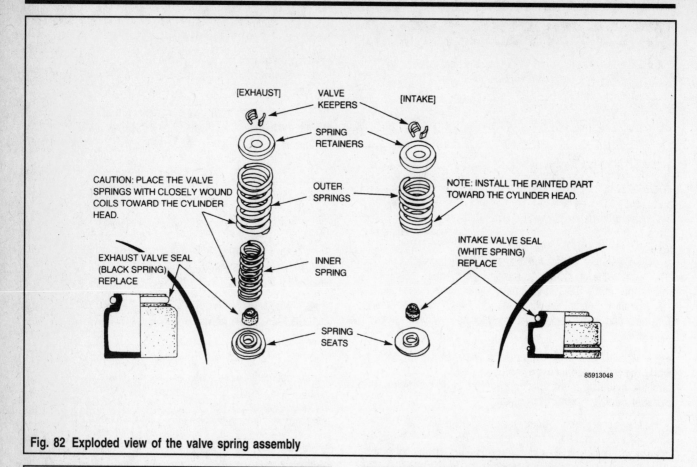

Fig. 82 Exploded view of the valve spring assembly

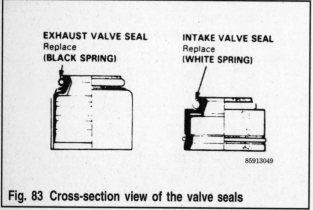

Fig. 83 Cross-section view of the valve seals

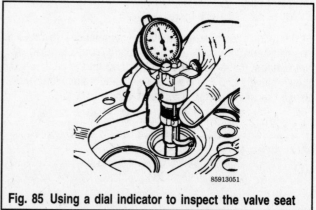

Fig. 85 Using a dial indicator to inspect the valve seat

and ream the valve guides to the proper valve stem fit. Use the reamer with an in-out motion while rotating it. For the finished dimension of the valve guide, check the 'Valve Specifications' chart.

➡**Do not forget to install the valve guide seals.**

7. To assemble, reverse the disassembly procedures.

8. To complete the installation, use new gaskets and reverse the removal procedures. Refill the cooling system. Start the engine and check for leaks.

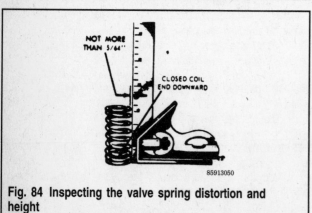

Fig. 84 Inspecting the valve spring distortion and height

KNURLING

▶ **See Figure 86**

Knurling is a process in which the metal on the valve guide bore is displaced and raised, thereby reducing the clearance. It also provides excellent oil control. The option of knurling rather than reaming valve guides should be discussed with a reputable machinist or engine specialist.

Oil Pan

REMOVAL & INSTALLATION

All Engines
▶ **See Figures 87, 88 and 89**

1. Firmly apply the parking brake and block the rear wheels.
2. Raise and support the front of the vehicle on jackstands.

➡**On some vehicles, it may be necessary to attach a chain to the clutch cable bracket on the transaxle case and raise just enough to take the load off the center mount; do not remove the left engine mount.**

3. Position a clean drain pan under the engine, remove the drain plug and drain the engine oil.

✳✳CAUTION

The EPA warns that prolonged contact with used engine oil may cause a number of skin disorders, including cancer! You should make every effort to minimize your exposure to used engine oil. Protective gloves should be worn when changing the oil. Wash your hands and any other exposed skin areas as soon as possible after exposure to used engine oil. Soap and water, or waterless hand cleaner should be used.

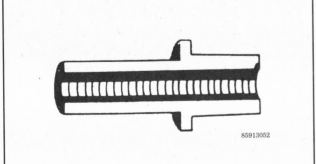

Fig. 86 Cross-section view of a knurled valve guide

4. If equipped, it may be necessary to remove the center beam and the engine lower mount.
5. If equipped with flywheel dust shield, it may be necessary to remove it.
6. Remove the oil pan-to-engine nuts/bolts (in a criss-cross pattern) and the oil pan; if necessary, use a mallet to tap the corners of the oil pan.
7. To install, use new gasket(s), sealant and reverse the removal procedures. Torque the oil pan-to-engine nuts/bolts to 9 ft. lbs. Refill the crankcase with clean engine oil.

Fig. 87 Support the engine/ transmission assembly with a suitable jack and block of wood

Fig. 88 Support the engine/ transmission assembly then remove the crossmember

Fig. 89 Removing the oil pan and gasket

Oil Pump

REMOVAL & INSTALLATION

Except 1829cc Engine

1. Refer to the 'Oil Pan, Removal & Installation' procedures in this section and remove the oil pan.
2. Remove the oil pump-to-engine bolts and the pump.
3. Using a putty knife, clean the gasket mounting surfaces.

➡**If removing the oil pump screen, remove the screen-to-pump bolt and the screen.**

4. To install, use new gaskets, sealant and reverse the removal procedures. Torque the oil pump-to-engine bolts to 8 ft. lbs. Refill the crankcase with clean engine oil. Start the engine and check for leaks.

1829cc Engine

1. Refer to the 'Timing Belt, Removal & Installation' procedures in this section and remove the timing belt.
2. Remove the oil pump-to-engine bolts and the oil pump from the engine.

To install:

3. Using a putty knife, clean the gasket mounting surfaces.

➡**If removing the oil pump pick-up screen, follow the procedure to remove the oil pan.**

4. Remove the pump cover-to-pump housing bolts and the cover.
5. Inspect the pump for wear and/or damage; replace the parts, if necessary.
6. Using petroleum jelly, pack the pump assembly. Reassemble the pump assembly and torque the pump cover-to-pump housing bolts to 5 ft. lbs.
7. To install, use a new O-rings and reverse the removal procedures. Torque the oil pump-to-engine nut/bolts to 9 ft. lbs. Check and/or adjust the timing. Start the engine and check for leaks.

OIL PUMP OVERHAUL

➡**These procedures are performed with the oil pump removed from the engine.**

Except 1829cc Engine

1. Check the rotor radial clearance on both the inner and outer rotors. Clearance is 0.05-0.15mm.
2. Using a wire gauge, check body-to-rotor clearance of both rotors. Clearance is 0.10-0.18mm new, with 0.20mm as the service limit.
3. Using a feeler gauge and a straight edge, check the rotor end-play between the rotor face and the gasket surface, gasket installed. End-play should be 0.025-0.100mm new, with a service limit of 0.152mm.
4. If the rotors should require replacement, inner and outer rotors on both upper and lower halves are installed with the punch marks aligned adjacent to one another.

5. To install, reverse the removal procedures.

1829cc Engine

1. Check the rotor radial clearance on both the inner and outer rotors. Clearance is 0.152-0.203mm.
2. Using a feeler gauge, check body-to-rotor clearance of both rotors. Clearance is 0.10-0.18mm new, with 0.200mm as the service limit.
3. Using a feeler gauge and a straight edge, check the rotor end-play between the rotor face and the gasket surface, gasket installed. End play should be 0.025-0.100mm new, with a service limit of 0.152mm.
4. If the rotors should require replacement, inner and outer rotors on both upper and lower halves are installed with the punch marks aligned adjacent to one another.
5. Using petroleum jelly, pack the pump cavity and reassemble it.
6. To install, reverse the removal procedures.

Timing Belt Cover and Seal

REMOVAL & INSTALLATION

All Engines

1. Rotate the crankshaft to align the crankshaft pulley (1170cc and 1237cc) or flywheel pointer (CVCC) to Top Dead Center (TDC) of the No. 1 cylinder's compression stroke.
2. Remove the upper timing belt cover bolts and the cover.
3. Loosen the alternator and air pump (if equipped), then, remove the pulley belt(s).
4. On all vehicles, remove the water pump pulley-to-water pump bolts and the pulley.
5. Remove the crankshaft pulley-to-crankshaft bolt. Using a Wheel Puller tool, remove the crankshaft pulley.
6. Remove the timing gear cover retaining bolts and the timing gear cover.
7. To install, reverse the removal procedure. Make sure that the timing guide plates, pulleys and front oil seal are properly installed on the crankshaft end before replacing the cover.

✳✳CAUTION

Be sure not to upset the timing position already set (TDC).

Timing Belt and Tensioner

REMOVAL & INSTALLATION

▶ **See Figures 90, 91, 92 and 93**

All Engines

1. Disconnect the negative battery cable. Turn the crankshaft pulley until it is at Top Dead Center.
2. Remove the pulley belt, water pump pulley, crankshaft pulley, and timing gear cover. Mark the direction of timing belt rotation.

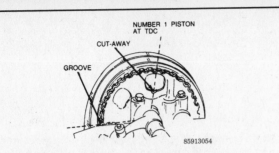

Fig. 90 On the 1980-83 Civic and the 1983 Accord, when the No. 1 piston is set at TDC, the cut-away in the pulley is at the top and the groove on the pulley is aligned with top of the cylinder head

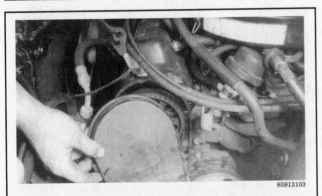

Fig. 91 Removing the upper timing case cover

Fig. 92 View of the camshaft gear and timing belt assembly

3. Loosen, but do not remove, the tensioner adjusting bolt and pivot bolt.

4. Slide the timing belt off of the camshaft timing gear and the crankshaft pulley gear and remove it from the engine.

5. To remove the camshaft timing gear pulley, first remove the center bolt and then remove the pulley with a pulley remover or a brass hammer. This can be accomplished by simply removing the timing belt upper cover, loosening the tensioner bolts, and sliding the timing belt off of the gear to expose the gear for removal.

➡️**If you remove the timing gear with the timing belt cover in place, be sure not to let the woodruff key fall when removing the gear from the camshaft.**

Fig. 93 View of the crankshaft gear and key

Inspect the timing belt. Replace if over 10,000 miles old, if oil soaked (find source of oil leak also), or if worn on leading edges of belt teeth.

To install:

6. Reverse the removal procedure. Be sure to install the crankshaft pulley and the camshaft timing gear pulley in the top dead center position. (See 'Cylinder Head Removal' for further details). On the non-CVCC engine, align the marks on the camshaft timing gear so they are parallel with the top of the cylinder head and the woodruff key is facing up.

➡️**When installing the timing belt, do not allow oil to come in contact with the belt. Oil will cause the rubber to swell. Be careful not to bend or twist the belt unnecessarily, since it is made of fiberglass; nor should you use tools having sharp edges when installing or removing the belt. Be sure to install the belt with the arrow facing in the same direction it was facing during removal.**

7. After installing the belt, adjust the belt tension by first rotating the crankshaft counterclockwise ¼ turn. Then, retighten the adjusting bolt and finally the tensioner pivot bolt.

✳️✳️WARNING

Do not remove the adjusting or pivot bolts, only loosen them. When adjusting, do not use any force other than the adjuster spring. If the belt is too tight, it will result in a shortened belt life.

Camshaft Sprockets

REMOVAL & INSTALLATION

1. Turn the crankshaft pulley until No. 1 is at Top Dead Center of the compression stroke. This can be determined by observing the valves (all closed) or by feeling for pressure in the spark plug hole (with your thumb or a compression gauge) as the engine is turned.

2. Remove the pulley belt, water pump pulley (if so equipped), crankshaft pulley, and timing gear cover. Mark the direction of timing belt rotation.

3. Loosen, but do not remove, the tensioner adjusting bolt and pivot bolt.

4. Slide the timing belt off the camshaft sprocket, crankshaft sprocket, then remove it from the engine.

5. To remove the either camshaft or crankshaft timing sprocket, first remove the center bolt and then remove the sprocket with a pulley remover or a brass hammer.

To install:

6. Reverse the removal procedure. Be sure to position the crankshaft and camshaft timing sprockets in the Top Dead Center position. Torque the camshaft sprocket bolt to 30 ft. lbs.

7. When installing the timing belt, do not allow oil to come in contact with the belt. Oil will cause the rubber to swell. Be careful not to bend or twist the belt unnecessarily, since it is made of fiberglass; nor should you use tools having sharp edges when installing or removing the belt. Be sure to install the belt with the arrow facing in the same direction it was facing during removal.

After installing the timing belt, adjust the belt tension by first rotating the crankshaft counterclockwise ¼ turn or 3 teeth on the camshaft pulley. Then, retighten the adjusting bolt and finally the tensioner pivot bolt.

➡ **Do not remove the adjusting or pivot bolts, only loosen them. When adjusting, do not use any force other than the adjuster spring. If the belt is too tight, it will result in a shortened belt life.**

Camshaft

Most engines utilize an oil pump drive gear incorporated on the camshaft.

REMOVAL & INSTALLATION

All Engines

➡ **To facilitate the installation, make sure that No. 1 piston is at Top Dead Center before removing the camshaft.**

1. Follow the 'Cylinder Head, Removal & Installation' procedures before attempting to remove the camshaft.
2. Loosen the camshaft and rocker arm shaft holder bolts in a criss-cross pattern, beginning on the outside holder.
3. Remove the rocker arms, shafts and holders as an assembly.
4. Lift out the camshaft and right head seal.
5. Using a putty knife, clean the gasket mounting surfaces.
6. To install, reverse the removal procedures, being sure to install and tighten (in steps) the holder bolts in the reverse order of removal.

➡ **Back off valve adjusting screws before installing rockers, then, adjust valves as outlined in Section 2.**

INSPECTION

Degrease the camshaft using safe solvent, clean all oil grooves. Visually inspect the cam lobes and bearing journals for excessive wear. If a lobe is questionable, check all lobes and journals with a micrometer.

Measure the lobes from nose to base and again at 90°. The lift is determined by subtracting the second measurement from the first. If all exhaust lobes and all intake lobes are not

identical, the camshaft must be reground or replaced. Measure the bearing journals and compare to specifications. If a journal is worn there is a good chance that the cam bearings are worn too, requiring replacement.

If the lobes and journals appear intact, place the front and rear cam journals in V-blocks and rest a dial indicator on the center journal. Rotate the camshaft to check for straightness, if deviation exceeds 0.025mm, replace the camshaft.

Pistons and Connecting Rods

REMOVAL & INSTALLATION

➡ **For removal with the engine out of the vehicle, begin with Step 8.**

1. Remove the turn signals (Civic 1973-77), grille and engine hood.
2. Drain the radiator.

❋❋CAUTION

When draining the coolant, keep in mind that cats and dogs are attracted by the ethylene glycol antifreeze, and are quite likely to drink any that is left in an uncovered container or in puddles on the ground. This will prove fatal in sufficient quantity. Always drain the coolant into a sealable container. Coolant should be reused unless it is contaminated or several years old.

3. Drain the engine oil.

❋❋CAUTION

The EPA warns that prolonged contact with used engine oil may cause a number of skin disorders, including cancer! You should make every effort to minimize your exposure to used engine oil. Protective gloves should be worn when changing the oil. Wash your hands and any other exposed skin areas as soon as possible after exposure to used engine oil. Soap and water, or waterless hand cleaner should be used.

4. Raise the front of the vehicle and support it with safety stands.
5. Attach a chain to the clutch cable bracket on the transaxle case or equivalent loacation and raise just enough to take the load off of the center mount.

➡ **Do not remove the left engine mount.**

6. Remove the center beam and engine lower mount.
7. Remove the cylinder head (see 'Cylinder Head, Removal & Installation').
8. Loosen the oil pan bolts and remove the oil pan and flywheel dust shield. Loosen the oil pan bolts in a criss-cross pattern beginning with the outside bolt. To remove the oil pan, lightly tap the corners of the oil pan with a mallet.

❋❋WARNING

Do not pry the oil pan off with the tip of a screwdriver.

9. Remove the oil passage block and the oil pump assembly.

✳✳WARNING

As soon as the oil passage block bolts are loosened, the oil in the oil line may flow out.

10. Working from the underside of the vehicle, remove the connecting rod bearing caps. Using the wooden handle of a hammer, push the pistons and connecting rods out of the cylinders.

➡**Before removing the pistons, check the top of the cylinder bore for carbon build-up or a ridge. Remove the carbon or use a ridge reamer to remove the ridge before removing the pistons. Bearing caps, bearings, and pistons should be marked to indicate their location for reassembly.**

11. When removing the piston rings, be sure not to apply excessive force as the rings are made of cast iron and can be easily broken.

➡**A hydraulic press is necessary for removing the piston pin. This is a job best left to the professional, if you need to go this far.**

To install:

12. Observe the following points when installing the piston rings:

a. When installing the three-piece oil ring, first place the spacer and then the rails in position. The spacer and rail gaps must be staggered 20-30mm.

b. Install the second and top rings on the piston with their markings facing upward.

c. After installing all rings on the piston, rotate them to be sure they move smoothly without signs of binding.

d. The ring gaps must be staggered 120° and must NOT be in the direction of the piston pin boss or at right angles to the pin. The gap of the three-piece oil ring refers to that of the middle spacer.

➡**Pistons and rings are also available in four oversizes, 0.25mm, 0.50mm, 0.75mm, and 1.00mm.**

13. Using a ring compressor, install the piston into the cylinder with the skirt protruding about ⅓ of the piston height below the ring compressor. Prior to installation, apply a thin coat of oil to the rings and to the cylinder wall.

➡**When installing the piston, the connecting rod oil jet hole or the mark on the piston crown faces the intake manifold.**

14. Using the wooden handle of a hammer, slowly press the piston into the cylinder. Guide the connecting rod so it does not damage the crankshaft journals.

15. Reassemble the remaining components in the reverse order of removal. Install the connecting rod bearing caps so that the recess in the cap and the recess in the rod are on the same side. After tightening the cap bolts (in steps), move the rod back and forth on the journal to check for binding.

CLEANING AND INSPECTION

1. Use a piston ring expander and remove the rings from the piston.

2. Clean the ring grooves using an appropriate cleaning tool, exercise care to avoid cutting too deeply.

3. Clean all varnish and carbon from the piston with a safe solvent. Do not use a wire brush or caustic solution on the pistons.

4. Inspect the pistons for scuffing, scoring, cracks, pitting or excessive ring groove wear. If wear is evident, the piston must be replaced.

5. Have the piston and connecting rod assembly checked by a machine shop for correct alignment, piston pin wear and piston diameter. If the piston has collapsed it will have to be replace or knurled to restore original diameter. Connecting rod bushing replacement, piston pin fitting and piston changing can be handled by the machine shop.

CYLINDER BORE

Check the cylinder bore for wear using a telescope gauge and a micrometer, measure the cylinder bore diameter perpendicular to the piston pin at a point 63.5mm below the top of the engine block. Measure the piston skirt perpendicular to the piston pin. The difference between the two measurements is the piston clearance. If the clearance is within specifications, finish honing or glaze breaking is all that is required. If clearance is excessive a slightly oversize piston may be required. If greatly oversize, the engine will have to be bored and 0.25mm or larger oversized pistons installed.

FITTING AND POSITIONING PISTON RINGS

1. Take the new piston rings and compress them, one at a time into the cylinder that they will be used in. Press the ring about 25mm below the top of the cylinder block using an inverted piston.

2. Use a feeler gauge and measure the distance between the ends of the ring. This is called measuring the ring end gap. Compare the reading to the one called for in the specifications table. File the ends of the ring with a fine file to obtain necessary clearance.

➡**If inadequate ring end gap is utilized, ring breakage will result.**

3. Inspect the ring grooves on the piston for excessive wear or taper. If necessary have the grooves recut for use with a standard ring and spacer. The machine shop can handle the job for you.

4. Check the ring grooves by rolling the new piston ring around the groove to check for burrs or carbon deposits. If any are found, remove with a fine file. Hold the ring in the groove and measure side clearance with a feeler gauge. If clearance is excessive, spacer(s) will have to be added.

➡**Always add spacers above the piston ring.**

5. Install the ring on the piston, lower oil ring first. Use a ring installing tool on the compression rings. Consult the instruction sheet that comes with the rings to be sure they are installed with the correct side up. A mark on the ring usually faces upward.

6. When installing oil rings, first, install the expanding ring in the groove. Hold the ends of the ring butted together (they must not overlap) and install the bottom rail (scraper) with the end about 25mm away from the butted end of the control ring. Install the top rail about 25mm away from the butted end of the control but on the opposite side from the lower rail.

7. Install the two compression rings.

8. Install a ring compressor and insert the piston and rod assembly into the engine.

Rear Main Seal

REMOVAL & INSTALLATION

The rear oil seal is installed in the rear main bearing cap. Replacement of the seal requires the removal of the transaxle, flexplate or flywheel and clutch housing, as well as the oil pan. Refer to the appropriate sections for the removal and installation of the above components. Both the front and rear main seal are installed after the crankshaft has been torqued, in the event it was removed. Special drivers are used.

Crankshaft and Main Bearings

REMOVAL & INSTALLATION

1. Remove the engine from the vehicle and place it on a work stand.

2. Remove the crankshaft pulley attaching bolts and washer.

3. Remove the front cover and the air conditioning idler pulley assembly, if so equipped. Remove cover assembly.

4. Check the timing belt deflection. Remove the timing belt and sprockets.

5. Invert the engine on work stand. Remove the flywheel and the rear seal cover. Remove the oil pan and gasket. Remove the oil pump inlet and the oil pump assembly.

6. Ensure all bearing caps (main and connecting rod) are marked so they can be installed in their original positions. Turn the crankshaft until the connecting rod from which cap is being removed is up. Remove the connecting rod cap. Push the connecting rod and piston assembly up in the cylinder. Repeat the procedure for the remaining connecting rod assemblies.

7. Remove the main bearing caps.

8. Carefully lift crankshaft out of block so upper thrust bearing surfaces are not damaged.

❉❉WARNING

Handle the crankshaft with care to avoid possible fracture or damage to the finished surfaces.

➡**If the bearings are to be reused they should be identified to ensure that they are installed in their original position.**

9. Remove the main bearing inserts from the block and bearing caps.

10. Remove the connecting rod bearing inserts from connecting rods and caps.

To install:

11. Install a new rear oil seal in rear seal cover.

12. Apply a thin coat of Polyethylene Grease to the rear crankshaft surface. Do not apply sealer to the area forward of oil sealer groove. Inspect all the machined surfaces on the crankshaft for nicks, scratches or scores which could cause premature bearing wear.

13. If the crankshaft main bearing journals have been refinished to a definite undersize, install the correct undersize bearings. Ensure the bearing inserts and bearing bores are clean. Foreign material under the inserts will distort the bearing and cause a failure.

14. Place the upper main bearing inserts in position in the bores with the tang fitted in the slot provided.

15. Install the lower main bearings inserts in the bearing caps.

16. Carefully lower the crankshaft into place.

17. Check the clearance of each main bearing. Select fit the bearings for proper clearance.

18. After the bearings have been fitted, apply a light coat of heavy engine oil, SAE 50 weight to journals and bearings. Install all the bearing caps.

➡**The main bearing cap must be installed in their original positions.**

19. Align the upper thrust bearing.

20. Check the crankshaft end-play.

21. If the end-play exceeds specification, replace the upper thrust bearing. If the end-play is less than the specification, inspect the thrust bearing faces for damage, dirt or improper alignment. Install the thrust bearing and align the faces. Check the end-play.

22. Install the new bearing inserts in the connecting rods and caps. Check the clearance of each bearing.

23. If the bearing clearances are to specification, apply a light coat of heavy engine oil, SAE 50 weight to the journals and bearings.

24. Turn the crankshaft throw to the bottom of the stroke. Push the piston all the way down until the rod bearings seat on the crankshaft journal.

25. Install the connecting rod cap.

26. After the piston and connecting rod assemblies have been installed, check the connecting rod crankshaft journal.

27. Turn the engine on the work stand so the front end is up. Install the timing belt, sprockets, front cover, oil seal and the crankshaft pulley.

28. Clean the oil pan, oil pump and the oil pump screen assembly.

29. Prime the oil pump by filling the inlet opening with oil and rotating the pump shaft until oil emerges from the outlet opening. Install the oil pump.

30. Position the flywheel or flexplate on the crankshaft. Install the attaching bolts. Tighten to specification.

➡**On the flywheel (manual transaxle only) locate clutch disc and install pressure plate.**

31. Turn the engine on the work stand so the engine is in the normal upright position. Install the oil level dipstick. Install the accessory drive pulley, if so equipped. Install and adjust the drive belt and the accessory belts to specification.

32. Install either the clutch assembly or the torque converter.

33. Install the oil pan.

34. Remove the engine from work stand. Install the engine in the vehicle.

BEARING OIL CLEARANCE INSPECTION

◆ **See Figures 94, 95 and 96**

Remove cap from the bearing to be checked. Using a clean, dry rag, thoroughly clean all oil from crankshaft journal and bearing insert.

➡**Plastigage® is soluble in oil, therefore, oil on the journal or bearing could result in erroneous readings.**

Place a pieced of Plastigage® along the full width of the bearing insert, reinstall cap, and torque to specifications.

➡**Specifications are given in the engine specifications earlier in this section.**

Remove bearing cap, and determine bearing clearance by comparing width of Plastigage® to the scale on Plastigage® envelope. Journal taper is determined by comparing width of the bearing insert, reinstall cap, and torque to specifications.

➡**Do not rotate crankshaft with Plastigage® installed. If bearing insert and journal appear intact, and are within tolerances, no further main bearing service is required. If bearing or journal appear defective, cause of failure should be determined before replacement.**

CRANKSHAFT ENDPLAY/CONNECTING ROD SIDE PLAY

◆ **See Figures 97 and 98**

Place a pry bar between a main bearing cap and crankshaft casting taking care not to damage any journals. Pry backward and forward, measure the distance between the thrust bearing and crankshaft with a feeler gauge. Compare reading with specifications. If too great a clearance is determined, a main bearing with a larger thrust surface or crank machining may be required. Check with an automotive machine shop for their advice.

Connecting rod clearance between the rod and crankthrow casting can be checked with a feeler gauge. Pry the rod carefully on one side as far as possible and measure the distance on the other side of the rod.

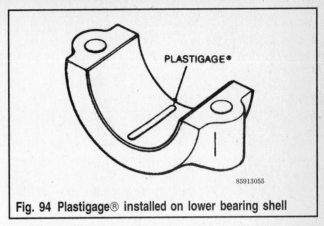

Fig. 94 Plastigage® installed on lower bearing shell

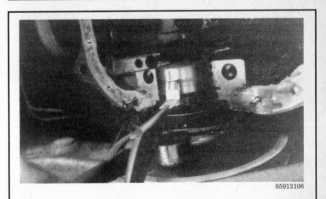

Fig. 95 Measure Plastigage® to determine bearing clearance

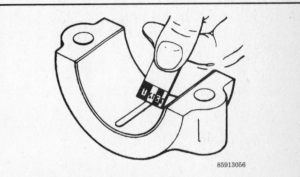

Fig. 96 View of Plastigage® on crankshaft

CRANKSHAFT REPAIRS

If a journal is damaged on the crankshaft, repair is possible by having the crankshaft machined to a standard undersize.

In most cases, however, since the engine must be removed from the car and disassembled, some thought should be given to replacing the damaged crankshaft with a reground shaft kit. A reground crankshaft kit contains the necessary main and rod bearings for installation. The shaft has been ground and polished to undersize specifications and will usually hold up well if installed correctly.

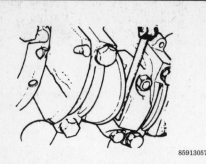

Fig. 97 Check the connecting rod side clearance with feeler gauge

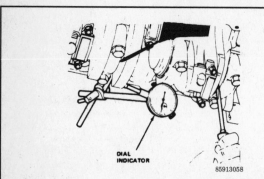

Fig. 98 Check the crankshaft end-play with a dial indicator

Flywheel/Flex Plate

REMOVAL & INSTALLATION

1. Remove the transmission.
2. Remove the flywheel/flex plate attaching bolts and the flywheel.
3. The rear cover plate can be removed (manual transmission only).

To install:

All major rotating components including the flex plate/flywheel are individually balance to zero. Engine assembly balancing is not required. Balance weights should NOT be installed on new flywheels.

4. Install the rear cover plate, if removed.
5. Position the flywheel on the crankshaft and install the attaching bolts. Tighten the attaching bolts to specification shown in the Torque specification chart using the standard cross-tightening sequence.

EXHAUST SYSTEM

Safety Precautions

Exhaust system work can be the most dangerous type of work you can do on your car. Always observe the following precautions:

• Support the car extra securely. Not only will you often be working directly under it, but you'll frequently be using a lot of force, say, heavy hammer blows, to dislodge rusted parts. This can cause a car that's improperly supported to shift and possibly fall.

• Wear goggles. Exhaust system parts are always rusty. Metal chips can be dislodged, even when you're only turning rusted bolts. Attempting to pry pipes apart with a chisel makes the chips fly even more frequently.

• If you're using a cutting torch, keep it a great distance from either the fuel tank or lines. Stop what you're doing and feel the temperature of the fuel bearing pipes on the tank frequently. Even slight heat can expand and/or vaporize fuel, resulting in accumulated vapor, or even a liquid leak, near your torch.

• Watch where your hammer blows fall and make sure you hit squarely. You could easily tap a brake or fuel line when you hit an exhaust system part with a glancing blow. Inspect all lines and hoses in the area where you've been working.

✳✳CAUTION

Be very careful when working on or near the catalytic converter! External temperatures can reach 1,500°F (816°C) and more, causing severe burns. Removal or installation should be performed only on a cold exhaust system.

Special Tools

A number of special exhaust system tools can be rented from auto supply houses or local stores that rent special equipment. A common one is a tail pipe expander, designed to enable you to join pipes of identical diameter.

It may also be quite helpful to use solvents designed to loosen rusted bolts or flanges. Soaking rusted parts the night before you do the job can speed the work of freeing rusted parts considerably. Remember that these solvents are often flammable. Apply only to parts after they are cool!

INSPECTION

Once or twice a year, check the muffler(s) and pipes for signs of corrosion and damage. Check the hangers for wear, cracks or hardening. Check the heat shields for corrosion or damage. Replace components as necessary.

All vehicles are equipped with a catalytic converter, which is attached to the front exhaust pipe. The exhaust system is bolted together. Replacement parts are usually the same as the original system, with the exception of some mufflers.

Use only the proper size sockets or wrenches when unbolting system components. Do not tighten completely until all components are attached, aligned, and suspended. Check the system for leaks after the installation is completed.

Muffler Assembly

REMOVAL & INSTALLATION

1. Raise the vehicle and support on jackstands.
2. Remove the U-bolt assembly and the rubber insulators from the hanger brackets and remove the muffler assembly. Slide the muffler assembly toward the rear of the car to disconnect it from the converter.
3. Replace parts as needed.

To install:

4. Position the muffler assembly under the car and slide it forward onto the converter outlet pipe. Check that the slot in the muffler and the tab on the converter are fully engaged.
5. Install the rubber insulators on the hanger assemblies. Install the U-bolt and tighten
6. Check the system for leaks. Lower the vehicle.

Catalytic Converter and/or Pipe Assembly

REMOVAL & INSTALLATION

▶ **See Figure 99**

1. Raise the vehicle and support on jackstands.
2. Remove the front catalytic converter flange fasteners at the flex joint and discard the flex joint gasket, remove the rear U-bolt connection.
3. Separate the catalytic converter inlet and outlet connections. Remove the converter.

To install:

4. Install the converter to the muffler. Install a new flex joint gasket.
5. Install the converter and muffler assembly to the inlet pipe/flex joint. Connect the air hoses and position the U-bolt.
6. Align the exhaust system into position and, starting at the front of the system, tighten all the nuts and bolts.
7. Check the system for leaks. Lower the vehicle.

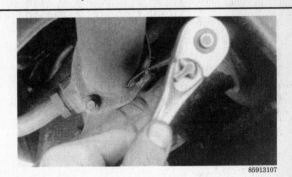

85913107

Fig. 99 Removing the front exhaust pipe-to-manifold nuts

TORQUE SPECIFICATIONS

Component	U.S.	Metric
Oil pan drain plug	33 ft. lbs.	45 Nm
Transmission drain plug	29 ft. lbs.	40 Nm
A/C compressor bracket	42 ft. lbs.	58 Nm
Tie-rod end locknut	32 ft. lbs.	44 Nm
Exhaust pipe-to-manifold	36 ft. lbs.	50 Nm
Engine mount bolts	54 ft. lbs.	75 Nm
Valve cover crown nut	7 ft. lbs.	10 Nm
Cylinder head bolts	43 ft. lbs.	60 Nm
Timing belt cover bolts	7 ft. lbs.	10 Nm
Timing belt—Pivot or adjusting bolt	32 ft. lbs.	43 Nm
Camshaft pulley	22 ft. lbs.	30 Nm
Thermostat housing	9 ft. lbs.	12 Nm
Rocker shaft (6x1.0mm) bolts	7 ft. lbs.	10 Nm
Rocker shaft (8x1.25mm) bolts	16 ft. lbs.	22 Nm
Distributor holder	9 ft. lbs.	12 Nm
Engine torque rods	54 ft. lbs.	75 Nm
Intake and exhaust manifolds	16 ft. lbs.	22 Nm
Crankshaft pulley	80 ft. lbs.	110 Nm
Flywheel (manual transmission)	50 ft. lbs.	70 Nm
Drive plate (automatic transmission)	36 ft. lbs.	50 Nm
Oil pressure switch	13 ft. lbs.	18 Nm
Oil pump assembly	7 ft. lbs.	10 Nm
Oil pan bolts	7 ft. lbs.	10 Nm
Carburetor mounting	15 ft. lbs.	20 Nm

85913C09

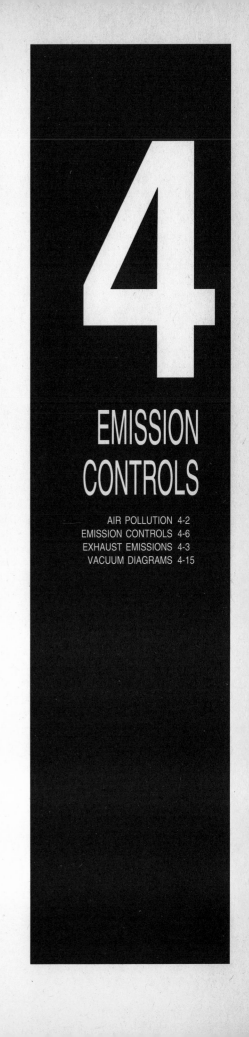

4

EMISSION CONTROLS

AIR POLLUTION

The earth's atmosphere, at or near sea level, consists approximately of 78% nitrogen, 21% oxygen and 1% other gases. If it were possible to remain in this state, 100% clean air would result. However, many varied causes allow other gases and particulates to mix with the clean air, causing the air to become unclean or polluted.

Certain of these pollutants are visible while others are invisible, with each having the capability of causing distress to the eyes, ears, throat, skin and respiratory system. Should these pollutants become concentrated in a specific area and under certain conditions, death could result due to the displacement or chemical change of the oxygen content in the air. These pollutants can also cause great damage to the environment and to the many man made objects that are exposed to the elements.

To better understand the causes of air pollution, the pollutants can be categorized into 3 separate types, natural, industrial and automotive.

Natural Pollutants

Natural pollution has been present on earth since before man appeared and continues to be a factor when discussing air pollution, although it causes only a small percentage of the overall pollution problem existing in our country today. It is the direct result of decaying organic matter, wind born smoke and particulates from such natural events as plain and forest fires (ignited by heat or lightning), volcanic ash, sand and dust which can spread over a large area of the countryside.

Such a phenomenon of natural pollution has been recently seen in the form of volcanic eruptions, with the resulting plume of smoke, steam and volcanic ash blotting out the sun's rays as it spreads and rises higher into the atmosphere. As it travels into the atmosphere the upper air currents catch and carry the smoke and ash, while condensing the steam back into water vapor. As the water vapor, smoke and ash traveled on their journey, the smoke dissipates into the atmosphere while the ash and moisture settle back to earth in a trail hundred of miles long. In some cases, lives are lost and millions of dollars of property damage result. Ironically, man can only stand by and watch it happen.

Industrial Pollution

Industrial pollution is caused primarily by industrial processes, the burning of coal, oil and natural gas, which in turn produce smoke and fumes. Because the burning fuels contain large amounts of sulfur, the principal ingredients of smoke and fumes are sulfur dioxide and particulate matter. This type of pollutant occurs most severely during still, damp and cool weather, such as at night. Even in its less severe form, this pollutant is not confined to just cities. Because of air movements, the pollutants move for miles over the surrounding countryside, leaving in its path a barren and unhealthy environment for all living things.

Working with Federal, State and Local mandated regulations and by carefully monitoring the emissions, big business has greatly reduced the amount of pollutant emitted from its industrial sources, striving to obtain an acceptable level. Because of the mandated industrial emission clean up, many land areas and streams in and around the cities that were formerly barren of vegetation and life, have now begun to move back in the direction of nature's intended balance.

Automotive Pollutants

The third major source of air pollution is automotive emissions. The emissions from the internal combustion engine were not an appreciable problem years ago because of the small number of registered vehicles and the nation's small highway system. However, during the early 1950's, the trend of the American people was to move from the cities to the surrounding suburbs. This caused an immediate problem in transportation because the majority of suburbs were not afforded mass transit conveniences. This lack of transportation created an attractive market for the automobile manufacturers, which resulted in a dramatic increase in the number of vehicles produced and sold, along with a marked increase in highway construction between cities and the suburbs. Multi-vehicle families emerged with a growing emphasis placed on an individual vehicle per family member. As the increase in vehicle ownership and usage occurred, so did pollutant levels in and around the cities, as suburbanites drove daily to their businesses and employment, returning at the end of the day to their homes in the suburbs.

It was noted that a fog and smoke type haze was being formed and at times, remained in suspension over the cities, taking time to dissipate. At first this "smog", derived from the words "smoke" and "fog", was thought to result from industrial pollution but it was determined that automobile emissions shared the blame. It was discovered that when normal automobile emissions were exposed to sunlight for a period of time, complex chemical reactions would take place.

It is now known that smog is a photo chemical layer which develops when certain oxides of nitrogen (NO_x) and unburned hydrocarbons (HC) from automobile emissions are exposed to sunlight. Pollution was more severe when smog would become stagnant over an area in which a warm layer of air settled over the top of the cooler air mass, trapping and holding the cooler mass at ground level. The trapped cooler air would keep the emissions from being dispersed and diluted through normal air flows. This type of air stagnation was given the name "Temperature Inversion".

Temperature Inversion

In normal weather situations, the surface air is warmed by heat radiating from the earth's surface and the sun's rays and will rise upward, into the atmosphere. Upon rising it will cool through a convection type heat exchange with the cooler upper air. As warm air rises, the surface pollutants are carried upward and dissipated into the atmosphere.

When a temperature inversion occurs, we find the higher air is no longer cooler but warmer than the surface air, causing the cooler surface air to become trapped. This warm air blanket can extend from above ground level to a few hundred or even a few thousand feet into the air. As the surface air is trapped, so are the pollutants, causing a severe smog condition. Should this stagnant air mass extend to a few thousand feet high, enough air movement with the inversion takes place to allow the smog layer to rise above ground level but the pollutants still cannot dissipate. This inversion can remain for days over an area, with the smog level only rising or lowering from ground level to a few hundred feet high. Meanwhile, the pollutant levels increase, causing eye irritation, respiratory problems, reduced visibility, plant damage and in some cases, disease.

This inversion phenomenon was first noted in the Los Angeles, California area. The city lies terrain resembling a basin and with certain weather conditions, a cold air mass is held in the basin while a warmer air mass covers it like a lid.

Because this type of condition was first documented as prevalent in the Los Angeles area, this type of trapped pollution was named Los Angeles Smog, although it occurs in other areas where a large concentration of automobiles are used and the air remains stagnant for any length of time.

Internal Combustion Engine Pollutants

Consider the internal combustion engine as a machine in which raw materials must be placed so a finished product comes out. As in any machine operation, a certain amount of wasted material is formed. When we relate this to the internal combustion engine, we find that through the input of air and fuel, we obtain power during the combustion process to drive the vehicle. The by-product or waste of this power is, in part, heat and exhaust gases with which we must dispose.

EXHAUST EMISSIONS

Composition Of The Exhaust Gases

The exhaust gases emitted into the atmosphere are a combination of burned and unburned fuel. To understand the exhaust emission and its composition, we must review some basic chemistry.

When the air/fuel mixture is introduced into the engine, we are mixing air, composed of nitrogen (78%), oxygen (21%) and other gases (1%) with the fuel, which is 100% hydrocarbons (HC), in a semi-controlled ratio. As the combustion process is accomplished, power is produced to move the vehicle while the heat of combustion is transferred to the cooling system. The exhaust gases are then composed of nitrogen, a diatomic gas (N_2), the same as was introduced in the engine, carbon dioxide (CO_2), the same gas that is used in beverage carbonation and water vapor (H_2O). The nitrogen (N_2), for the most part passes through the engine unchanged, while the oxygen (O_2) reacts (burns) with the hydrocarbons (HC) and produces the carbon dioxide (CO_2) and the water vapors (H_2O). If this chemical process would be the only process to take place, the exhaust emissions would be harmless. However, during the combustion process, other compounds are formed which are considered dangerous. These pollutants are carbon monoxide (CO), hydrocarbons (HC), oxides of nitrogen (NOx) oxides of sulfur (SOx) and engine particulates.

Heat Transfer

The heat from the combustion process can rise to over 4000°F (2204°C). The dissipation of this heat is controlled by a ram air effect, the use of cooling fans to cause air flow and having a liquid coolant solution surrounding the combustion area to transfer the heat of combustion through the cylinder walls and into the coolant. The coolant is then directed to a thin-finned, multi-tubed radiator, from which the excess heat is transferred to the atmosphere by 1 of the 3 heat transfer methods, conduction, convection or radiation.

The cooling of the combustion area is an important part in the control of exhaust emissions. To understand the behavior of the combustion and transfer of its heat, consider the air/fuel charge. It is ignited and the flame front burns progressively across the combustion chamber until the burning charge reaches the cylinder walls. Some of the fuel in contact with the walls is not hot enough to burn, thereby snuffing out or quenching the combustion process. This leaves unburned fuel in the combustion chamber. This unburned fuel is then forced out of the cylinder and into the exhaust system, along with the exhaust gases.

Many attempts have been made to minimize the amount of unburned fuel in the combustion chambers due to the snuffing out or quenching, by increasing the coolant temperature and lessening the contact area of the coolant around the combustion area. Design limitations within the combustion chambers prevent the complete burning of the air/fuel charge, so a certain amount of the unburned fuel is still expelled into the exhaust system, regardless of modifications to the engine.

HYDROCARBONS

Hydrocarbons (HC) are essentially fuel which was not burned during the combustion process or which has escaped into the atmosphere through fuel evaporation. The main sources of incomplete combustion are rich air/fuel mixtures, low engine temperatures and improper spark timing. The main sources of hydrocarbon emission through fuel evaporation on most cars used to be the vehicle's fuel tank and carburetor bowl.

To reduce combustion hydrocarbon emission, engine modifications were made to minimize dead space and surface area in the combustion chamber. In addition the air/fuel mixture was made more lean through the improved control which feedback carburetion and fuel injection offers and by the addition of external controls to aid in further combustion of the hydrocarbons outside the engine. Two such methods were the addition of an air injection system, to inject fresh air into the exhaust manifolds and the installation of a catalytic converter, a unit that is able to burn traces of hydrocarbons without affecting the internal combustion process or fuel economy. The vehicles covered in this manual may utilize either, both or none of these methods, depending on the year and model.

To control hydrocarbon emissions through fuel evaporation, modifications were made to the fuel tank to allow storage of the fuel vapors during periods of engine shut-down.

Modifications were also made to the air intake system so that at specific times during engine operation, these vapors may be purged and burned by blending them with the air/fuel mixture.

CARBON MONOXIDE

Carbon monoxide is formed when not enough oxygen is present during the combustion process to convert carbon (C) to carbon dioxide (CO_2). An increase in the carbon monoxide (CO) emission is normally accompanied by an increase in the hydrocarbon (HC) emission because of the lack of oxygen to completely burn all of the fuel mixture.

Carbon monoxide (CO) also increases the rate at which the photo chemical smog is formed by speeding up the conversion of nitric oxide (NO) to nitrogen dioxide (NO_2). To accomplish this, carbon monoxide (CO) combines with oxygen (O_2) and nitric oxide (NO) to produce carbon dioxide (CO_2) and nitrogen dioxide (NO_2). ($CO + O_2 + NO = CO_2 + NO_2$).

The dangers of carbon monoxide, which is an odorless and colorless toxic gas are many. When carbon monoxide is inhaled into the lungs and passed into the blood stream, oxygen is replaced by the carbon monoxide in the red blood cells, causing a reduction in the amount of oxygen being supplied to the many parts of the body. This lack of oxygen causes headaches, lack of coordination, reduced mental alertness and should the carbon monoxide concentration be high enough, death could result.

NITROGEN

Normally, nitrogen is an inert gas. When heated to approximately 2500°F (1371°C) through the combustion process, this gas becomes active and causes an increase in the nitric oxide (NOx) emission.

Oxides of nitrogen (NOx) are composed of approximately 97-98% nitric oxide (NO). Nitric oxide is a colorless gas but when it is passed into the atmosphere, it combines with oxygen and forms nitrogen dioxide (NO2). The nitrogen dioxide then combines with chemically active hydrocarbons (HC) and when in the presence of sunlight, causes the formation of photo chemical smog.

OZONE

To further complicate matters, some of the nitrogen dioxide (NO2) is broken apart by the sunlight to form nitric oxide and oxygen. (NO2 + sunlight = NO + O). This single atom of oxygen then combines with diatomic (meaning 2 atoms) oxygen (O2) to form ozone (O3). Ozone is 1 of the smells associated with smog. It has a pungent and offensive odor, irritates the eyes and lung tissues, affects the growth of plant life and causes rapid deterioration of rubber products. Ozone can be formed by sunlight as well as electrical discharge into the air.

The most common discharge area on the automobile engine is the secondary ignition electrical system, especially when inferior quality spark plug cables are used. As the surge of high voltage is routed through the secondary cable, the circuit builds up an electrical field around the wire, acting upon the oxygen in the surrounding air to form the ozone. The faint glow along the cable with the engine running that may be visible on a dark night, is called the "corona discharge." It is the result of the electrical field passing from a high along the cable, to a low in the surrounding air, which forms the ozone gas. The combination of corona and ozone has been a major cause of cable deterioration. Recently, different and better quality insulating materials have lengthened the life of the electrical cables.

Although ozone at ground level can be harmful, ozone is beneficial to the earth's inhabitants. By having a concentrated ozone layer called the "ozonosphere", between 10 and 20 miles (16-32km) up in the atmosphere much of the ultra violet radiation from the sun's rays are absorbed and screened. If this ozone layer were not present, much of the earth's surface would be burned, dried and unfit for human life.

There is much discussion concerning the ozone layer and its density. A feeling exists that this protective layer of ozone is slowly diminishing and corrective action must be directed to this problem. Much experimentation is presently being conducted to determine if a problem exists and if so, the short and long term effects of the problem and how it can be remedied.

OXIDES OF SULFUR

Oxides of sulfur (SOx) were initially ignored in the exhaust system emissions, since the sulfur content of gasoline as a fuel is less than 1/10 of 1%. Because of this small amount, it was felt that it contributed very little to the overall pollution problem. However, because of the difficulty in solving the sulfur emissions in industrial pollutions and the introduction of catalytic converter to the automobile exhaust systems, a change was mandated. The automobile exhaust system, when equipped with a catalytic converter, changes the sulfur dioxide (SO2) into the sulfur trioxide (SO3).

When this combines with water vapors (H2O), a sulfuric acid mist (H2SO4) is formed and is a very difficult pollutant to handle since it is extremely corrosive. This sulfuric acid mist that is formed, is the same mist that rises from the vents of an automobile battery when an active chemical reaction takes place within the battery cells.

When a large concentration of vehicles equipped with catalytic converters are operating in an area, this acid mist will rise and be distributed over a large ground area causing land, plant, crop, paints and building damage.

PARTICULATE MATTER

A certain amount of particulate matter is present in the burning of any fuel, with carbon constituting the largest percentage of the particulates. In gasoline, the remaining particulates are the burned remains of the various other compounds used in its manufacture. When a gasoline engine is in good internal condition, the particulate emissions are low but as the engine wears internally, the particulate emissions increase. By visually inspecting the tail pipe emissions, a determination can be made as to where an engine defect may exist. An engine with light gray smoke emitting from the tail pipe normally indicates an increase in the oil consumption through burning due to internal engine wear. Black smoke would indicate a defective fuel delivery system, causing the engine to operate in a rich mode. Regardless of the color of the smoke, the internal part of the engine or the fuel delivery system should be repaired to a "like new" condition to prevent excess particulate emissions.

Diesel and turbine engines emit a darkened plume of smoke from the exhaust system because of the type of fuel used. Emission control regulations are mandated for this type of emission and more stringent measures are being used to prevent excess emission of the particulate matter. Electronic components are being introduced to control the injection of the fuel at precisely the proper time of piston travel, to achieve the optimum in fuel ignition and fuel usage. Other particulate after-burning components are being tested to achieve a cleaner emission.

Good grades of engine lubricating oils should be used, which meet the manufacturers specification. "Cut-rate" oils can contribute to the particulate emission problem because of their low "flash" or ignition temperature point. Such oils burn prematurely during the combustion process causing emissions of particulate matter.

The cooling system is an important factor in the reduction of particulate matter. With the cooling system operating at a temperature specified by the manufacturer, the optimum of combustion will occur. The cooling system must be maintained in the same manner as the engine oiling system, as each system is required to perform properly in order for the engine to operate efficiently for a long time.

Other Automobile Emission Sources

Before emission controls were mandated on the internal combustion engines, other sources of engine pollutants were discovered, along with the exhaust emission. It was determined the engine combustion exhaust produced 60% of the total emission pollutants, fuel evaporation from the fuel tank and carburetor vents produced 20%, with the another 20% being produced through the crankcase as a by-product of the combustion process.

CRANKCASE EMISSIONS

Crankcase emissions are made up of water, acids, unburned fuel, oil fumes and particulates. The emissions are classified as hydrocarbons (HC) and are formed by the small amount of unburned, compressed air/fuel mixture entering the crankcase from the combustion area during the compression and power strokes, between the cylinder walls and piston rings. The head of the compression and combustion help to form the remaining crankcase emissions.

Since the first engines, crankcase emissions were allowed into the atmosphere through a road draft tube, mounted on the lower side of the engine block. Fresh air came in through an open oil filler cap or breather. The air passed through the crankcase mixing with blow-by gases. The motion of the vehicle and the air blowing past the open end of the road draft tube caused a low pressure area at the end of the tube.

Crankcase emissions were simply drawn out of the road draft tube into the air.

To control the crankcase emission, the road draft tube was deleted. A hose and/or tubing was routed from the crankcase to the intake manifold so the blow-by emission could be burned with the air/fuel mixture. However, it was found that intake manifold vacuum, used to draw the crankcase emissions into the manifold, would vary in strength at the wrong time and not allow the proper emission flow. A regulating type valve was needed to control the flow of air through the crankcase.

Testing, showed the removal of the blow-by gases from the crankcase as quickly as possible, was most important to the longevity of the engine. Should large accumulations of blow-by gases remain and condense, dilution of the engine oil would occur to form water, soots, resins, acids and lead salts, resulting in the formation of sludge and varnishes. This condensation of the blow-by gases occur more frequently on vehicles used in numerous starting and stopping conditions, excessive idling and when the engine is not allowed to attain normal operating temperature through short runs.

FUEL EVAPORATIVE EMISSIONS

Gasoline fuel is a major source of pollution, before and after it is burned in the automobile engine. From the time the fuel is refined, stored, pumped and transported, again stored until it is pumped into the fuel tank of the vehicle, the gasoline gives off unburned hydrocarbons (HC) into the atmosphere. Through redesigning of the storage areas and venting systems, the pollution factor was diminished, but not eliminated, from the refinery standpoint. However, the automobile still remained the primary source of vaporized, unburned hydrocarbon (HC) emissions.

Fuel pumped from an underground storage tank is cool but when exposed to a warmer ambient temperature, will expand. Before controls were mandated, an owner would fill the fuel tank with fuel from an underground storage tank and park the vehicle for some time in warm area, such as a parking lot. As the fuel would warm, it would expand and should no provisions or area be provided for the expansion, the fuel would spill out the filler neck and onto the ground, causing hydrocarbon (HC) pollution and creating a severe fire hazard. To correct this condition, the vehicle manufacturers added overflow plumbing and/or gasoline tanks with built in expansion areas or domes.

However, this did not control the fuel vapor emission from the fuel tank. It was determined that most of the fuel evaporation occurred when the vehicle was stationary and the engine not operating. Most vehicles carry 5-25 gallons (19-95 liters) of gasoline. Should a large concentration of vehicles be parked in one area, such as a large parking lot, excessive fuel vapor emissions would take place, increasing as the temperature increases.

To prevent the vapor emission from escaping into the atmosphere, the fuel system is designed to trap the fuel vapors while the vehicle is stationary, by sealing the fuel system from the atmosphere. A storage system is used to collect and hold the fuel vapors from the carburetor and the fuel tank when the engine is not operating. When the engine is started, the storage system is then purged of the fuel vapors, which are drawn into the engine and burned with the air/fuel mixture.

EMISSION CONTROLS

▶ **See Figures 1 and 2**

Emission controls on the Honda fall into one of three basic systems:
- I. Crankcase Emission Control System.
- II. Exhaust Emission Control System.
- III. Evaporative Emission Control System.

Crankcase Emission Control System

OPERATION

▶ **See Figure 3**

The Honda's engine is equipped with a Dual Return System to prevent crankcase vapor emissions. Blow-by gas is returned to the combustion chamber through the intake manifold and carburetor air cleaner. When the throttle is partially opened, blow-by gas is returned to the intake manifold through breather tubes leading into the tee orifice located on the outside of the intake manifold. When the throttle is opened wide and vacuum in the air cleaner rises, blow-by gas is returned to the intake manifold through an additional passage in the air cleaner case.

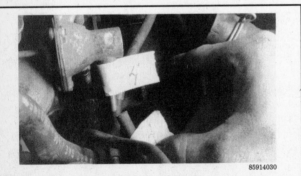

85914030

Fig. 1 Whem removing vacuum hoses or lines always mark both ends for correct installation

85914031

Fig. 2 View of control box (upper left corner) under hood

SERVICE

1. Squeeze the lower end of the drain tube and drain any oil or water which may have collected.

2. Make sure that the intake manifold T-joint is clear by passing the shank end of a No. 65 (0.035″ diameter) drill through both ends (orifices) of the joint.

3. Check for any loose, disconnected or deteriorated tubes and replace (if necessary).

Exhaust Emission Control System

OPERATIONS

1973-74 Models

Control of exhaust emissions, hydrocarbon (HC), carbon monoxide (CO) and Oxides of nitrogen (NOx), is achieved by a combination of engine modifications and special control devices. Improvements to the combustion chamber, intake manifold, valve timing, carburetor and distributor comprise the engine modifications. These modifications, in conjunction with the special control devices, enable the engine to produce low emission with leaner air/fuel mixtures while maintaining good driveability. The special control devices consist of the following:

Intake air temperature control.

Throttle opener.

Ignition timing retard unit (1973 models only).

Transmission and temperature controlled spark advance (TCS) for the 4-speed transmission.

Temperature controlled spark advance for Hondamatic automatic transmission (1974 models only).

INTAKE AIR TEMPERATURE CONTROL

Intake air temperature control is designed to provide the most uniform carburetion possible under various ambient air temperature conditions by maintaining the intake air temperature within a narrow range. When the temperature in the air cleaner is below 100°F (38°C), the air bleed valve, which consists of a bimetal strip and a rubber seal, remains closed. Intake manifold vacuum is then led to a vacuum motor, located on the snorkel of the air cleaner case, which moves the air control valve door, allowing only preheated air to enter the air cleaner.

When the temperature in the air cleaner becomes higher than approximately 100°F (38°C), the air bleed valve opens and the air control valve door returns to the open position allowing only unheated air through the snorkel.

THROTTLE OPENER

When the throttle is closed suddenly at high engine speed, hydrocarbon (HC) emissions increase due to engine misfire caused by an incombustible mixture. The throttle opener is designed to prevent misfiring during deceleration by causing the throttle valve to remain slightly open, allowing better mixture control. The control valve is set to allow the passage of

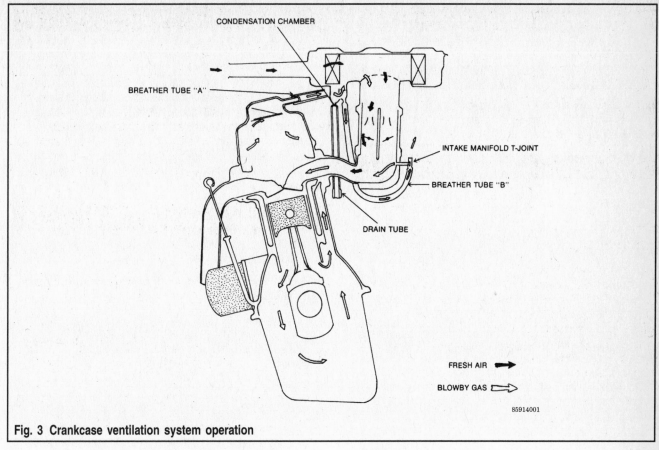

Fig. 3 Crankcase ventilation system operation

vacuum to the throttle opener diaphragm when the engine vacuum is equal to or greater than the control valve preset vacuum (20-23 in. Hg) during acceleration.

Under running conditions, other than fully closed throttle deceleration, the intake manifold vacuum is less than the control valve set vacuum; therefore the control valve is not actuated. The vacuum remaining in the throttle opener and control valve is returned to atmospheric pressure by the air passage at the valve center.

IGNITION TIMING RETARD UNIT

On 1973 models, when the engine is idling, the vacuum produced in the carburetor retarder port is communicated to the spark retard unit and the ignition timing, at idle, is retarded.

TCS SYSTEM

The transmission and temperature controlled spark advance for 4-speed transmissions is designed to reduce NOx emissions during normal vehicle operation.

On 1973 models, when the coolant temperature is approximately 120°F (49°C) or higher, and the transmission is in 1st, 2nd or 3rd gear, the solenoid valve cuts off the vacuum to the spark advance unit, resulting in lower NOx levels.

On 1974 models, the vacuum is cut off to the spark advance unit regardless of temperature when 1st, 2nd or 3rd gear is selected. Vacuum advance is restored when 4th gear is selected.

SERVICE

Intake Air Temperature Control System (Engine Cold)

1973-74 MODELS

1. Inspect for loose, disconnected, or deteriorated vacuum hoses and replace as necessary.

2. Remove the air cleaner cover and element.

3. With the transmission in Neutral and the blue distributor hose disconnected, engage the starter motor for approximately two (2) seconds. Manifold vacuum to the vacuum motor should completely raise the air control valve door. Once opened, the valve door should stay open unless there is a leak in the system.

4. If the valve door does not open, check the intake manifold port by passing a No. 78 (0.016″ diameter) drill or compressed air through the orifice in the manifold.

5. If the valve door still does not open, proceed to the following steps:

   a. Vacuum Motor Test: Disconnect the vacuum line from the vacuum motor inlet pipe. Fully open the air control valve door; block the vacuum motor inlet pipe, then release the door. If the door does not remain open, the vacuum motor is defective. Replace as necessary and repeat Steps 1-3.

   b. Air Bleed Valve Test: Unblock the inlet pipe and make sure that the valve door fully closes without sticking or binding. Reconnect the vacuum line to the vacuum motor inlet pipe. Connect a vacuum source (e.g. hand vacuum pump) to the manifold vacuum line (disconnect at the intake manifold fixed orifice) and draw enough vacuum to fully open the

valve door. If the valve door closes with the manifold vacuum line plugged (by the vacuum pump), then vacuum is
leaking through the air bleed valve. Replace as necessary
and repeat Steps 1-3.

✳✳WARNING

**Never force the air bleed valve (bi-metal strip) on or off
its valve seat. The bimetallic strip and the valve seat may
be damaged.**

c. Check Valve Test: Again draw a vacuum (at the manifold vacuum line) until the valve door opens. Unplug the line
by disconnecting the pump from the manifold vacuum line. If
the valve door closes, vacuum is leaking past the check
valve. Replace as necessary and repeat Steps 1-3.

6. After completing the above steps, replace the air cleaner
element and cover and fit a vacuum gauge into the line leading to the vacuum motor.

7. Start the engine and raise the idle to 1500-2000 rpm. As
the engine warms, the vacuum gauge reading should drop to
zero.

➡**Allow sufficient time for the engine to reach normal operating temperature — when the cooling fan cycles on
and off.**

If the reading does not drop to zero before the engine
reaches normal operating temperature, the air bleed valve is
defective and must be replaced. Repeat Step 3 as a final
check.

**Temperature and Transaxle Controlled Spark Advance (En-
gine Cold)**

All Models

1. Check for loose, disconnected or deteriorated vacuum
hoses and replace (if necessary).

2. Check the coolant temperature sensor switch for proper
operation with an ohmmeter or 12V light. The switch should
normally be open (no continuity across the switch terminals)
when the coolant temperature is below approximately 120°F
(49°C). If the switch is closed (continuity across the terminals),
replace the switch and repeat the check.

3. On manual transaxle models, check the transmission
sensor switch. The switch should be open (no continuity
across the connections) when Fourth gear is selected, and
closed (continuity across the connections) in all other gear
positions. Replace if necessary and repeat the check.

4. Remove the spark control vacuum tube, leading between
the spark advance/retard unit and the solenoid valve, and connect a vacuum gauge to the now vacant hole in the solenoid
valve, according to the diagram.

5. Start the engine and raise the idle to 2000 rpm. With a
cold engine, the vacuum gauge should read approximately 3
in. Hg or more. As the coolant temperature reaches 120°F
(49°C), the vacuum reading should drop to 0. On manual
transaxle models, vacuum should return when 4th gear is selected (transmission switch is opened). If this is not the case,
proceed to the following steps:

➡**If the engine is warm from the previous test, disconnect
the coolant temperature switch wires when making the following tests.**

6. If vacuum is not initially available, disconnect the vacuum signal line from the charcoal canister and plug the open
end, which will block a possible vacuum leak from the idle cut-
off valve of the canister. With the line plugged, again check for
vacuum at 2000 rpm. If vacuum is now available, reconnect
the vacuum signal line and check the canister for vacuum
leaks. (Refer to the Evaporative Emission Control System
check.) If vacuum is still not available, stop the engine and
disconnect the vacuum line from the solenoid valve (the line
between the solenoid valve and the manifold T-joint) and insert
a vacuum gauge in the line. If vacuum is not available, the
vacuum port is blocked. Clear the port with compressed air
and repeat the test sequence beginning with Step 3.

7. If vacuum is available in Step 5 after the engine is warm
and in all ranges of the automatic transaxle and in 1st, 2nd
and 3rd of the manual transaxle, stop the engine and check
for electrical continuity between the terminals of the coolant
temperature sensor:

➡**After completing the following steps, repeat test procedure beginning with Step 4.**

a. If there is no continuity (engine is warm), replace the
temperature sensor switch and recheck for continuity.

b. If there is continuity, check the battery voltage to the
vacuum solenoid. If no voltage is available (ignition switch
ON), check the wiring, fuses and connections.

c. If there is battery voltage and the temperature sensor
is operating correctly, check connections and/or replace the
solenoid valve.

Feedback Control System
▶ **See Figures 4 and 5**

➡**These tests require the use of two hand held vacuum
pumps.**

1. Disconnect the air suction hose at the vacuum hose
manifold. Tee in a vacuum pump as shown in the illustration.
Hook up the pump so as to apply pressure. Then, use the
vacuum pump to attempt to force air pressure into the system.
If air does not flow, proceed to step 2. If it does, proceed to 3.

2. If air flows into the system, remove the air box cover
and then pinch off the vacuum hose leading to frequency solenoid valve **A**. Then, blow air through the hose. If air flows,
replace air control valve **B** and then recheck that air does not
flow. If air does not flow, replace the frequency solenoid valve
A and retest as in Step 1.

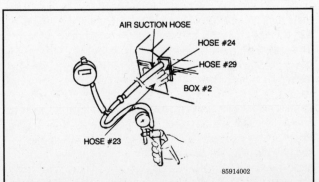

AIR SUCTION HOSE

HOSE #24

HOSE #29

BOX #2

HOSE #23

85914002

**Fig. 4 Tee in the vacuum pump to force air into the
feedback control system as shown**

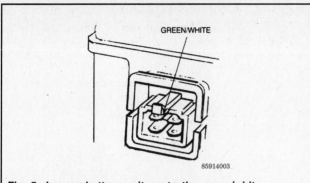

GREEN/WHITE

85914003

Fig. 5 Jumper battery voltage to the green/white connector of connector box 2

3. Disconnect vacuum hose #24 at surge tank **B**. Connect the vacuum pump to the end of this hose so as to apply pressure. Then, disconnect the hose leading from Air Control Valve **B** and frequency solenoid valve **A**. Connect the hand pump so as to apply pressure. Apply vacuum at hose #24 and blow air into the other hose (the B-valve side of the Air Control Valve). Air should flow. If it does, proceed to Step 4. If not, proceed to 5.

4. Replace air control valve **B** and then retest the system to make sure air does flow.

5. Jumper battery voltage (from the + terminal) to the green/white connector of connector box #2 (see illustration). Blow air into the vacuum hose going to frequency valve **A**. If air flows, the valve is okay and you should proceed to Step 7. If not, proceed to Step 6.

6. If air does not flow, disconnect the hose leading from frequency solenoid valve A to air control valve A and check for air flow with the pump in operation. If air flows, replace control valve A and then retest to make sure the system now works. If air does not flow, replace frequency solenoid valve A and retest to make sure the system now works.

7. Disconnect vacuum hose #29 at the vacuum hose manifold and connect the vacuum pump to the open end. Apply vacuum to the open end and blow air into the air suction hose leading to Control Valve **A**. When there is vacuum applied via the pump, air should flow without resistance. When vacuum is released, air should flow into the system only with significant resistance; that is, pressure should build up on the gauge of the pump supplying pressure and then be released only gradually. If this occurs, reconnect the air suction hose and hose #29 and then go on to Step 6. If there is no such change in resistance, replace air control valve A and then repeat the test.

8. Jumper battery voltage from the battery (+) terminal to the frequency solenoid valve **B**. Disconnect the vacuum hose #23 from surge tank **B** and connect a vacuum pump to it. Then, apply vacuum. Vacuum should build up on the pressure gauge. If there is vacuum, go to Step 7. If not, pinch the hose leading from the frequency solenoid valve **B** to the constant vacuum valve. Then, repeat the test. If there is now vacuum, replace the constant vacuum valve and then retest to make sure the system is repaired. If there is still no vacuum, replace the frequency solenoid valve **B** and repeat the test to make sure the system is repaired.

9. Leaving the vacuum pump hooked up, disconnect the jumper wire leading to frequency solenoid valve **B**. Make sure there is still vacuum in the system. Vacuum should disappear when the wire is disconnected. If it does disappear, reconnect vacuum hose #23 and go on to Step 8. If it does not disappear, replace solenoid valve **B** and retest to make sure it now disappears.

10. Remove the cover of control box #2 and disconnect the hose connecting the constant vacuum valve and frequency solenoid valve **B** from its connection within the box. Then, connect a vacuum pump to the open end of the hose. Now, start the engine, allow it to idle, and measure the vacuum with a gauge. It should stabilize in the range 6-11 in. Hg (manual transaxle) vehicles and 2-7 in. Hg (automatic transaxle). If vacuum stabilizes in this range, the constant vacuum valve is okay, and you should reconnect the hose. If not, replace the constant vacuum valve, and then retest to make sure you have corrected the malfunction.

Temperature Controlled Spark Advance

OPERATION

Temperature controlled spark advance on vehicles equipped with Hondamatic transmission is designed to reduce NOx emissions by disconnecting the vacuum to the spark advance unit during normal vehicle operation. When the coolant temperature is approximately 120°F (49°C) or higher, the solenoid valve is energized, cutting off vacuum to the advance unit.

1975-79 1237cc Air Models

INTAKE AIR TEMPERATURE CONTROLS

Same as 1973-74 models.

THROTTLE OPENER

Same as 1973-74 models.

TRANSMISSION CONTROLLED SPARK ADVANCE

Same as 1974 models, with no coolant control override.

IGNITION TIMING RETARD UNIT

Same as 1973 models, but is used only on Hondamatic models and has no vacuum advance mechanism.

Air Injection System

OPERATION

▶ **See Figures 6, 7, 8, 9, 10 and 11**

Beginning with the 1975 model year, an air injection system is used to control hydrocarbon and carbon monoxide emissions. With this system, a belt driven air pump delivers filtered air under pressure to injection nozzles located at each exhaust port. Here, the additional oxygen supplied by the vane type pump reacts with any unburned fuel mixture, promoting an afterburning effect in the hot exhaust manifold. To prevent a reverse flow in the air injection manifold when exhaust gas pressure exceeds air supply pressure, a non-return check valve is used. To prevent exhaust afterburning or backfiring during deceleration, an anti-afterburn valve delivers air to the intake manifold instead. When manifold vacuum rises above the preset vacuum of the air control valve and/or below that of the air bypass valve, air pump air is returned to the air cleaner.

1975-82 1487cc, 1600cc and 1751cc Models

INTAKE AIR TEMPERATURE CONTROL

Same as 1973-74 models.

Throttle Controls

OPERATION

This system controls the closing of the throttle during periods of gear shifting, deceleration, or any time the gas pedal is released. In preventing the sudden closing of the throttle during these conditions, an overly rich mixture is prevented which controls excessive emissions of hydrocarbons and carbon monoxide. This system has two main parts; a dashpot system and a throttle positioner system. The dashpot diaphragm and solenoid valve act to dampen or slow down the throttle return time to 1-4 seconds. The throttle positioner part consists of a speed sensor, a solenoid valve, a control valve and an opener diaphragm which will keep the throttle open and predetermined minimum amount any time the gas pedal is released when the vehicle is traveling 15 mph or faster, and closes it when the vehicle slows to 10 mph.

Ignition Timing Controls

OPERATION

This system uses a coolant temperature sensor to switch distributor vacuum ignition timing controls on or off to reduce hydrocarbon and oxides of nitrogen emissions. The coolant switch is calibrated at 149°F (49°C) for 1487cc and 1600cc engines, or 167°F (75°C) for 1751cc engine.

Hot Start Controls

OPERATION

This system is designed to prevent an overly rich mixture condition in the intake manifold due to vaporization of residual fuel when starting a hot engine. This reduces hydrocarbon and carbon monoxide emissions.

Anti-Afterburn Valve

OPERATION

1979-82 1751cc engines have an anti-afterburn valve. This unit is used only on models with manual transmission. The

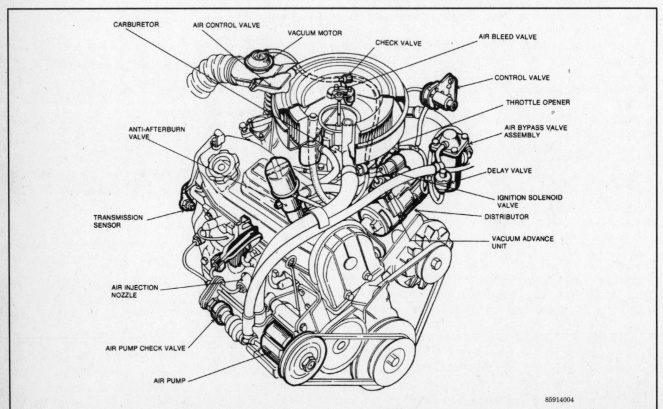

85914004

Fig. 6 Location of emission control system components-1975 1237cc AIR models with manual transmission; other years similar

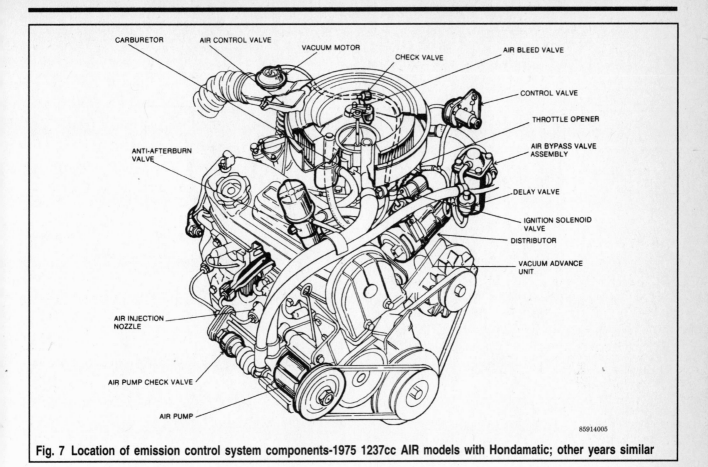

Fig. 7 Location of emission control system components-1975 1237cc AIR models with Hondamatic; other years similar

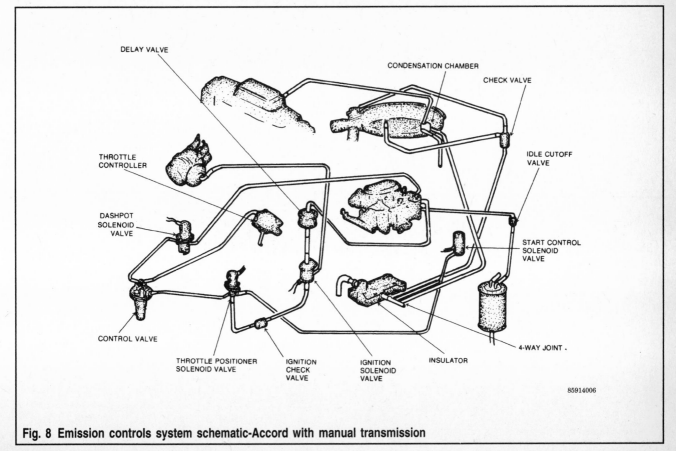

Fig. 8 Emission controls system schematic-Accord with manual transmission

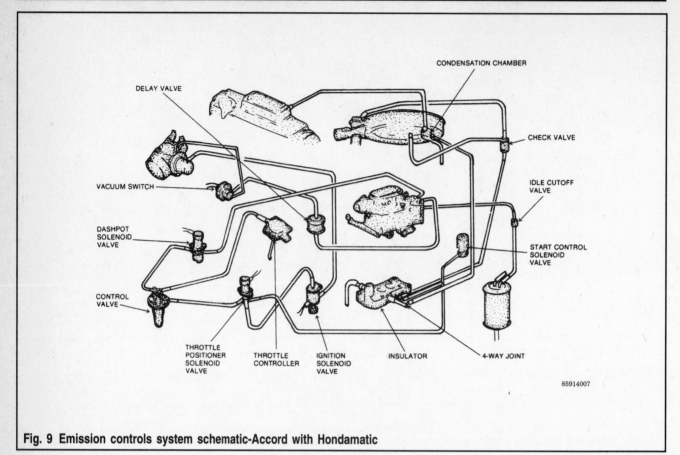

Fig. 9 Emission controls system schematic-Accord with Hondamatic

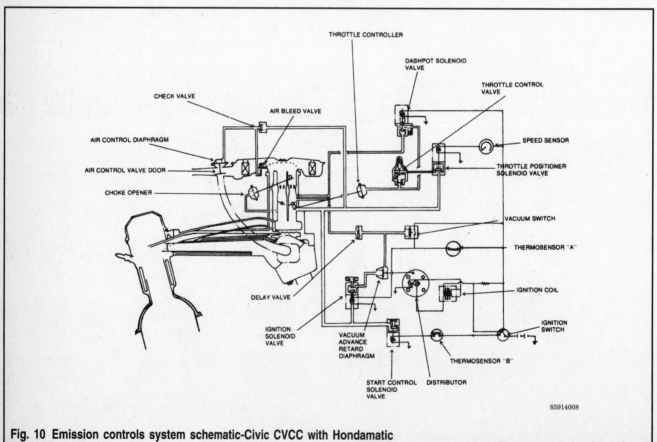

Fig. 10 Emission controls system schematic-Civic CVCC with Hondamatic

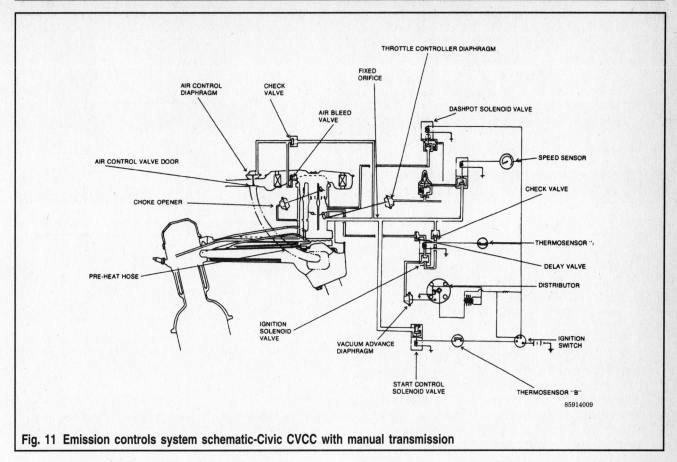

Fig. 11 Emission controls system schematic-Civic CVCC with manual transmission

valve lets fresh air into the intake manifold when it senses sudden increases in manifold vacuum. The valve responds only to sudden increases in vacuum and the amount of time it stays open is determined by an internal diaphragm which is acted on by the vacuum level.

CVCC Engine Modifications

OPERATION

By far, the most important part of the CVCC engine emission control system is the Compound Vortex Controlled Combustion (CVCC) cylinder head itself. Each cylinder has three valves: a conventional intake and conventional exhaust valve, and a smaller auxiliary intake valve. There are actually two combustion chambers per cylinder: a pre-combustion or auxiliary chamber, and the main chamber. During the intake stroke, an extremely lean mixture is drawn into the main combustion chamber. Simultaneously, a very rich mixture is drawn into the smaller precombustion chamber via the auxiliary intake valve. The spark plug, located in the precombustion chamber, easily ignites the rich pre-mixture, and this combustion spreads out into the main combustion chamber where the lean mixture is ignited. Due to the fact that the volume of the auxiliary chamber is much smaller than the main chamber, the overall mixture is very lean (about 18 parts air to one part fuel). The result is low hydrocarbon emissions due to the slow, stable combustion of the lean mixture in the main chamber; low carbon monoxide emissions due to the excess oxygen available; and low oxides of nitrogen emissions due to the lowered peak combustion temperatures. An added benefit of burning the lean mixture is the excellent gas mileage.

Air Jet Controller

OPERATION

Used on 1981 and later California and High Altitude models, this system senses atmospheric pressure and regulates carburetor air flow accordingly.

Oxygen Sensor

OPERATION

The oxygen sensor (if so equipped) is mounted in the exhaust manifold. It is used to sense oxygen concentration in the exhaust gas. If the fuel ratio is leaner than the stoichiometric ratio in the mixture (i.e. excessive amount of air), the exhaust gas contains more oxygen. On the other hand, if the fuel ratio is richer than the stoichiometric ratio, the exhaust gas hardly contains any oxygen.

REMOVAL & INSTALLATION

1. Disconnect the negative battery cable.
2. Disconnect the electrical connector from sensor.
3. Remove the sensor from the manifold (spark plug removal is similar procedure).
4. Installation is the reverse of the removal procedure. Do not handle or allow dirt on sensor tip. Torque sensor to about 30 ft. lbs. and reconnect the electrical connector.

Evaporative Emission Control System

OPERATION

This system prevents gasoline vapors from escaping into the atmosphere from the fuel tank and carburetor and consists of the components listed in the illustration.

Fuel vapor is stored in the expansion chamber, in the fuel tank and in the vapor line. When the vapor pressure becomes higher than the set pressure of the one-way valve, the valve opens and allows vapor into the charcoal canister. While the engine is stopped or idling, the idle cut-off valve in the canister is closed and the vapor is absorbed by the charcoal.

At partially opened throttle, the idle cut-off valve is opened by manifold vacuum. The vapor that was stored in the charcoal canister and in the vapor line is purged into the intake manifold. Any excessive pressure or vacuum which might build up in the fuel tank is relieved by the two-way valve in the filler cap.

SERVICE

▶ **See Figures 12, 13, 14 and 15**

Purge Control/Unloader Solenoid Valve

CARBURETED-ENGINE COLD

➡**The coolant temperature must be below the thermosensor(s) set temperature; the thermosensor(s) must have continuity.**

1. Using a Vacuum Pump/Gauge tool No. H/C 058369 or equivalent, disconnect the upper hose (purge control diaphragm valve) from the evaporative canister and connect the hose to the gauge.
2. Start the engine and allow it to idle; there should be no vacuum.
3. If there is vacuum and the vehicle is equipped with a purge control/unloader solenoid valve, perform the following procedures:

    a. Disconnect the purge control/unloader solenoid valve electrical connector.

    b. Using an ohmmeter, check for voltage at the connector.

    c. If there is voltage, replace the purge control/unloader solenoid valve, then, retest.

    d. If there is no voltage, for the 49ST/HI ALT models, inspect the wiring, the fuse and the Thermosensor A, then,

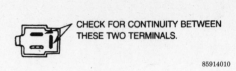

CHECK FOR CONTINUITY BETWEEN THESE TWO TERMINALS.

85914010

Fig. 12 Purge control/unloader solenoid valve electrical connector

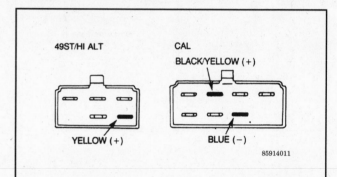

49ST/HI ALT

CAL

BLACK/YELLOW (+)

YELLOW (+)

BLUE (−)

85914011

Fig. 13 Purge control/unloader solenoid valve electrical connector

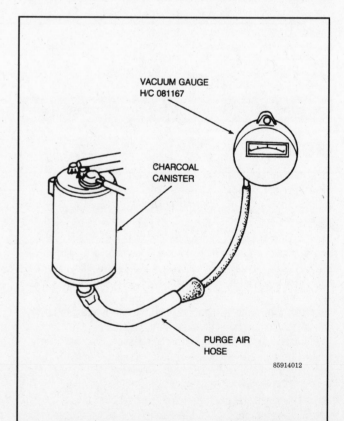

VACUUM GAUGE
H/C 081167

CHARCOAL
CANISTER

PURGE AIR
HOSE

85914012

Fig. 14 Testing charcoal canister with vacuum gauge tool

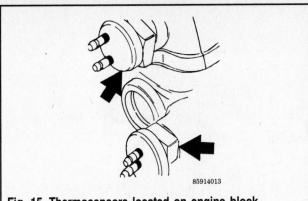

Fig. 15 Thermosensors located on engine block

retest. If there is no voltage, for the CAL models, inspect the wiring, the fuse and the Thermosensor B, then, retest.

4. If there is vacuum and the vehicle is not equipped with a purge control/unloader solenoid valve, replace the thermosensor and retest.

5. To install, reverse the removal procedures.

CARBURETED-ENGINE HOT

1. Using a Vacuum Pump/Gauge tool No. H/C 058369 or equivalent, disconnect the upper hose (purge control diaphragm valve) from the evaporative canister and connect the hose to the gauge.

2. Start the engine and allow it to warm up; there should be vacuum at idle.

3. If there is no vacuum and the vehicle is equipped with a purge control/unloader solenoid valve, perform the following procedures:

   a. Disconnect the purge control/unloader solenoid valve electrical connector.

   b. Using an ohmmeter, check for voltage at the connector.

   c. If there is voltage, replace the thermosensor, then, retest.

   d. If there is no voltage, replace the purge control/unloader solenoid valve, then, retest.

4. If there is no vacuum and the vehicle is not equipped with a purge control/unloader solenoid valve, perform the following procedures:

   a. Pinch off the thermosensor-to-air filter hose; there should be vacuum.

   b. If no vacuum is present, check the hoses for blockage or leaks.

5. To install, reverse the removal procedures.

Charcoal Canister

➡**This procedure is to be performed with the engine Hot.**

1. Using a tachometer, connect it to the engine. Start the engine and allow it to reach normal operating temperatures; until the cooling fan turns on.

2. Remove the fuel filler cap.

3. Using a Vacuum Gauge tool No. H/C 081167 or equivalent, disconnect the charcoal canister from the frame and connect the gauge to it.

4. Raise the engine speed to 3,500 rpm; vacuum should appear on the gauge in 1 minute. If vacuum appears, the canister is OK; end of test.

5. If no vacuum appears, perform the following procedures:

   a. Disconnect the vacuum gauge and reinstall the fuel filler cap.

   b. Remove the charcoal canister and check for signs of damage or defects.

   c. If necessary, replace the canister.

6. Stop the engine and disconnect the PVC hose from the charcoal canister.

7. Using a Vacuum Gauge tool No. H/C058369 or equivalent, install it to the purge control solenoid valve (on top of the canister) and perform the following procedures:

   a. Hand pump the vacuum gauge to create vacuum.

   b. If the vacuum remains steady, proceed with the next step; if the vacuum drops, replace the canister and retest.

8. Reconnect the PCV hose and start the engine; the Purge side vacuum should drop to zero. If the vacuum does not drop to zero, perform the following procedures:

   a. Disconnect the hose from the PCV fitting and check for vacuum at the hose.

   b. If vacuum exists, replace the canister and retest.

   c. If no vacuum exists, recheck the thermosensor valve operation.

   d. If the purge side vacuum drops to zero, connect the vacuum gauge to the purge hose and check for vacuum with the engine speed at 3,500 rpm. If vacuum exists, replace the canister and retest; if no vacuum, inspect the hose and carburetor for blockage.

9. Connect the vacuum gauge to the fuel tank hose and check for vacuum. If no vacuum exists, replace the fuel filler cap — test complete. If vacuum exists, replace the canister and retest.

VACUUM DIAGRAMS

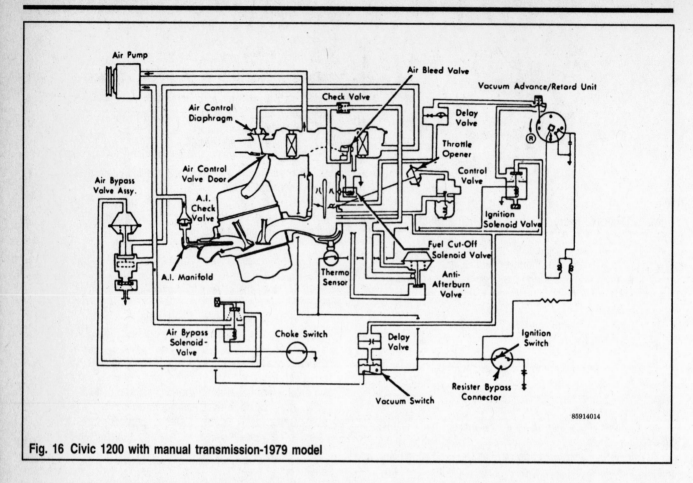

Fig. 16 Civic 1200 with manual transmission-1979 model

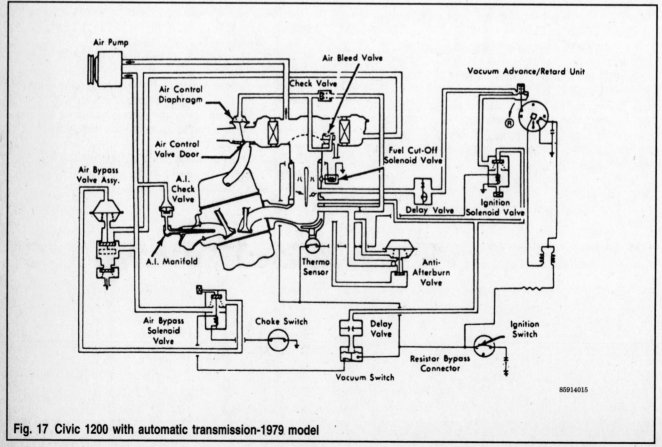

Fig. 17 Civic 1200 with automatic transmission-1979 model

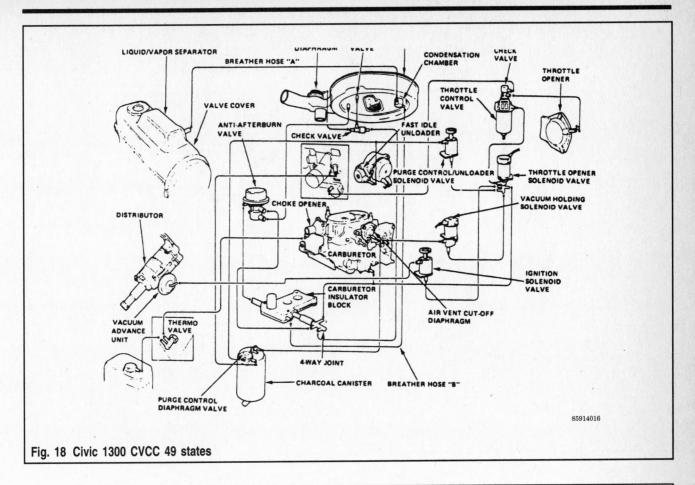

Fig. 18 Civic 1300 CVCC 49 states

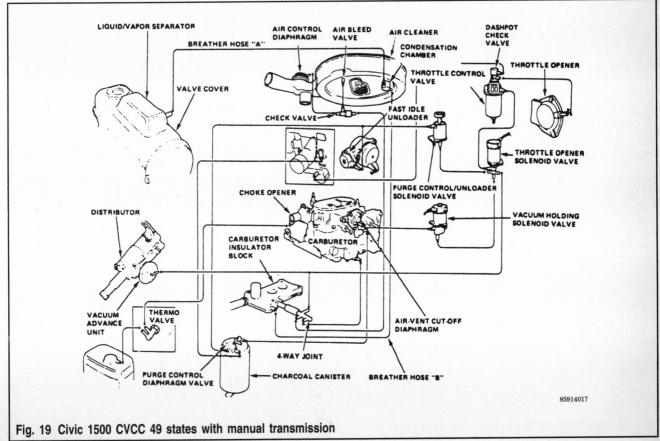

Fig. 19 Civic 1500 CVCC 49 states with manual transmission

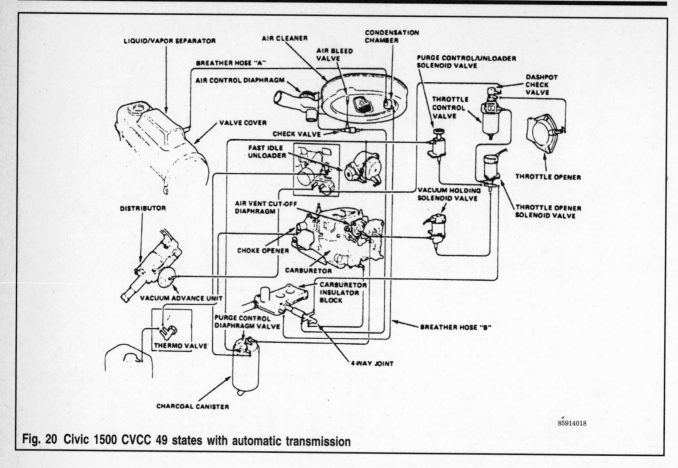

Fig. 20 Civic 1500 CVCC 49 states with automatic transmission

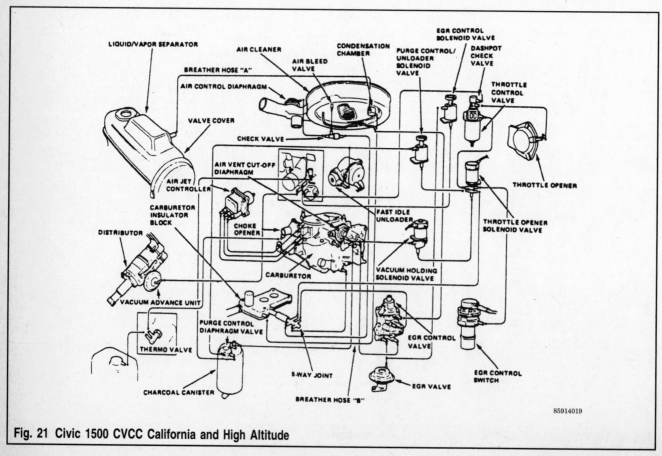

Fig. 21 Civic 1500 CVCC California and High Altitude

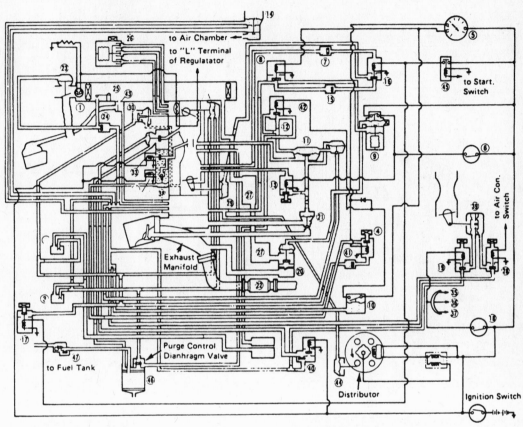

to Air Chamber
to "L" Terminal of Regulatator
to Start. Switch
to Air Con. Switch
Exhaust Manifold
Purge Control Dianhragm Valve
to Fuel Tank
Distributor
Ignition Switch

① INTAKE AIR TEMP. SENSOR
② THERMOVALVE A
③ THERMOVALVE B
④ PJ CUT SOLENOID VALVE
⑤ SPEED SENSOR
⑥ THERMOSENSOR A
⑦ DASHPOT CHECK VALVE
   (EXCEPT 1300 49 ST 5-SPEED)
⑧ CONTROL SWITCH SOLENOID VALVE
⑨ CONTROL SWITCH
⑩ VACUUM SWITCH
⑪ EGR CONTROL VALVE A AND B
⑫ EGR CONTROL SOLENOID VALVE B
⑬ EGR CONTROL SOLENOID VALVE A
⑭ ANTI-AFTERBURN VALVE
⑮ THROTTLE CONTROLLER CHECK VALVE
⑯ CRANKING SOLENOID VALVE
⑰ CRANKING LEAK SOLENOID VALVE
⑱ THERMOSENSOR B
   (MANUAL TRANSMISSION ONLY)
⑲ IDLE CONTROL SOLENOID VALVE A
   (MANUAL TRANSMISSION ONLY)
⑳ AIR SUCTION VALVE AND AIR SUCTION
   CUT-OFF DIAPHRAGM VALVE
㉑ EGR VALVE
㉒ CATALYTIC CONVERTER
㉓ INTAKE AIR CONTROL DIAPHRAGM
㉔ CHECK VALVE FOR INTAKE AIR TEMPERATURE
   CONTROL

㉕ AIR BLEED VALVE
㉖ AIR JET CONTROLLER (CAL AND HI ALT ONLY)
㉗ AIR CHAMBERS A AND B
㉘ IDLE CONTROL SOLENOID VALVE B
   (CAR WITH AIR CONDITIONER ONLY)
㉙ THROTTLE CONTROLLER
㉚ CHOKE OPENER
㉛ FAST IDLE UNLOADER
㉜ AIR VENT CUT-OFF DIAPHRAGM
㉝ PRIMARY MAIN FUEL CUT-OFF SOLENOID VALVE
㉞ PRIMARY SLOW MIXTURE CUT-OFF SOLENOID
   VALVE
㉟ REAR WINDOW DEFROSTER SWITCH
   (MANUAL TRANSMISSION ONLY)
㊱ HEATER BLOWER SWITCH
   (MANUAL TRANSMISSION ONLY)
㊲ HEADLIGHT SWITCH (MANUAL TRANSMISSION
   ONLY)
㊳ POWER VALVE
㊴ IDLE CONTROLLER
㊵ VACUUM HOLDING SOLENOID VALVE
㊶ POWER VALVE CHECK VALVE
㊷ EGR AIR FILTER
㊸ CONDENSATION CHAMBER
㊹ DISTRIBUTOR VACUUM ADVANCE
㊺ STARTER RELAY
㊻ CANISTER
㊼ TWO-WAY VALVE

85914020

Fig. 22 1982 Civic-all models

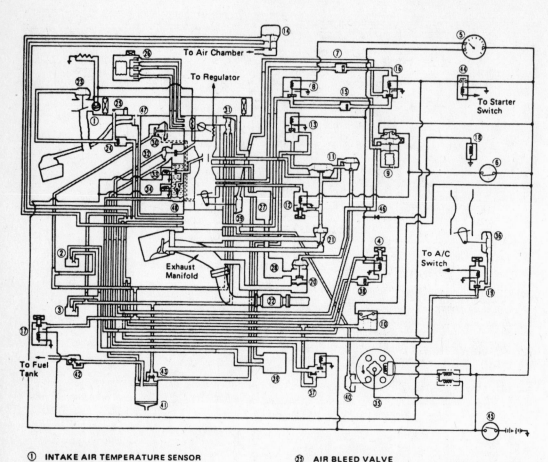

To Air Chamber →

To Regulator

To Starter Switch

To A/C Switch

Exhaust Manifold

To Fuel Tank

① INTAKE AIR TEMPERATURE SENSOR
② THERMOVALVE A
③ THERMOVALVE B
④ POWER VALVE CONTROL SOLENOID VALVE
⑤ SPEED SENSOR
⑥ THERMOSENSOR
⑦ DASHPOT CHECK VALVE
⑧ CONTROL SWITCH SOLENOID VALVE
⑨ CONTROL SWITCH
⑩ VACUUM SWITCH
⑪ EGR CONTROL VALVE A AND B
⑫ EGR CONTROL SOLENOID VALVE A
⑬ EGR CONTROL SOLENOID VALVE B
⑭ ANTI-AFTERBURN VALVE
⑮ THROTTLE CONTROLLER CHECK VALVE
⑯ CRANKING SOLENOID VALVE
⑰ CRANKING LEAK SOLENOID VALVE
⑱ AUXILIARY COIL
⑲ IDLE CONTROL SOLENOID VALVE (A/C)
⑳ AIR SUCTION VALVE AND AIR SUCTION
   CUT-OFF DIAPHRAGM VALVE
㉑ EGR VALVE
㉒ CATALYTIC CONVERTER
㉓ INTAKE AIR CONTROL DIAPHRAGM
㉔ CHECK VALVE FOR INTAKE AIR TEMPERATURE
   CONTROL

㉕ AIR BLEED VALVE
㉖ AIR JET CONTROLLER (CAL AND HI ALT ONLY)
㉗ AIR CHAMBERS A
㉘ AIR CHAMBER B
㉙ THROTTLE CONTROLLER
㉚ CHOKE OPENER
㉛ FAST IDLE UNLOADER
㉜ AIR VENT CUT-OFF DIAPHRAGM
㉝ PRIMARY MAIN FUEL CUT-OFF SOLENOID VALVE
㉞ PRIMARY SLOW MIXTURE CUT-OFF SOLENOID
   VALVE
㉟ DISTRIBUTER
㊱ IDLE CONTROLLER (A/C)
㊲ VACUUM HOLDING SOLENOID VALVE
㊳ POWER VALVE CHECK VALVE
㊴ AIR FILTER
㊵ DISTRIBUTOR VACUUM ADVANCE
㊶ CANISTER
㊷ TWO-WAY VALVE
㊸ PURGE CONTROL DIAPHRAGM VALVE
㊹ STARTER RELAY
㊺ IGNITION SWITCH
㊻ DIODE
㊼ CONDENSATION CHAMBER
㊽ POWER VALVE

85914021

Fig. 23 1982 Accord and Prelude

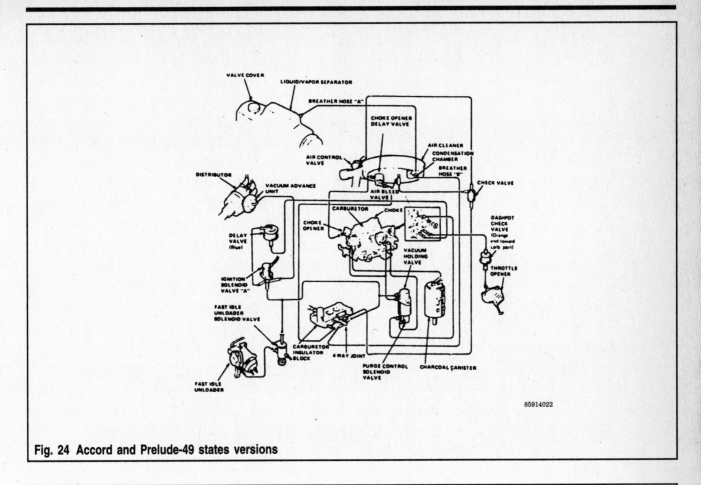

Fig. 24 Accord and Prelude-49 states versions

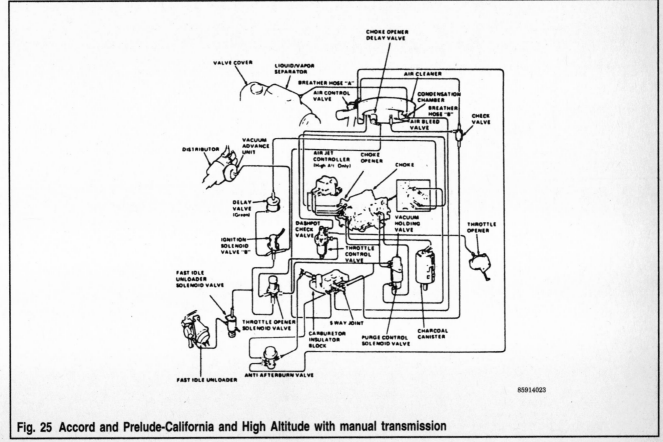

Fig. 25 Accord and Prelude-California and High Altitude with manual transmission

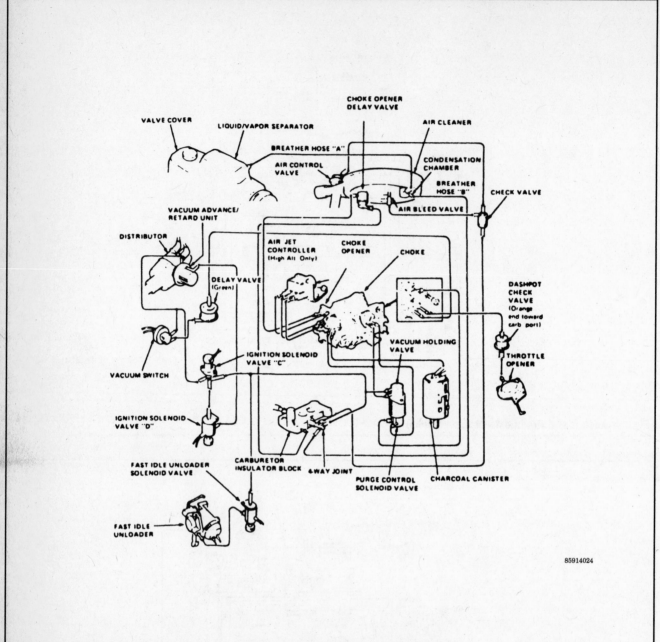

Fig. 26 Accord and Prelude-California and High Altitude with automatic transmission

85914024

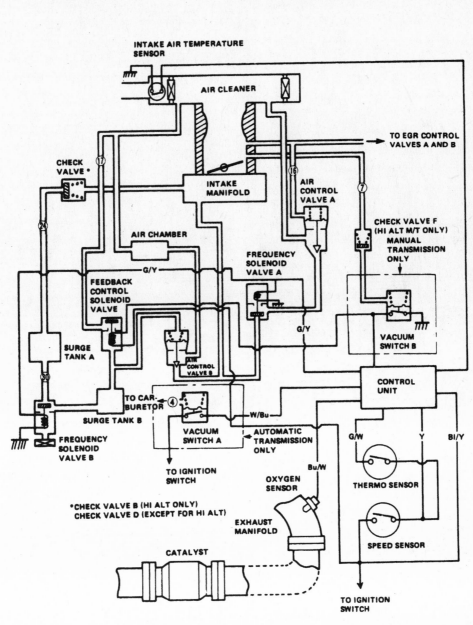

Fig. 27 Feedback control system schematic

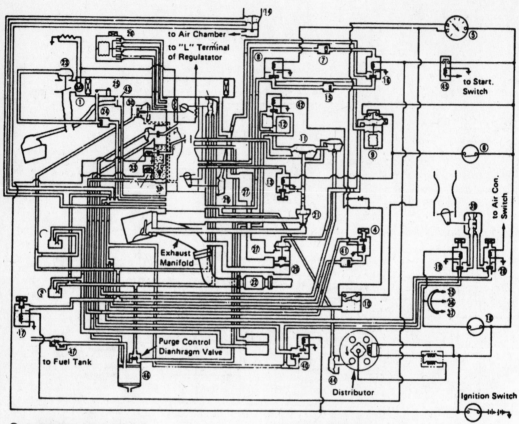

<table>
<tr><td>①</td><td>INTAKE AIR TEMP. SENSOR</td><td>㉕</td><td>AIR BLEED VALVE</td></tr>
<tr><td>②</td><td>THERMOVALVE A</td><td>㉖</td><td>AIR JET CONTROLLER (CAL AND HI ALT ONLY)</td></tr>
<tr><td>③</td><td>THERMOVALVE B</td><td>㉗</td><td>AIR CHAMBERS A AND B</td></tr>
<tr><td>④</td><td>PJ CUT SOLENOID VALVE</td><td>㉘</td><td>IDLE CONTROL SOLENOID VALVE B</td></tr>
<tr><td>⑤</td><td>SPEED SENSOR</td><td></td><td>(CAR WITH AIR CONDITIONER ONLY)</td></tr>
<tr><td>⑥</td><td>THERMOSENSOR A</td><td>㉙</td><td>THROTTLE CONTROLLER</td></tr>
<tr><td>⑦</td><td>DASHPOT CHECK VALVE</td><td>㉚</td><td>CHOKE OPENER</td></tr>
<tr><td></td><td>(EXCEPT 1300 49 ST 5-SPEED)</td><td>㉛</td><td>FAST IDLE UNLOADER</td></tr>
<tr><td>⑧</td><td>CONTROL SWITCH SOLENOID VALVE</td><td>㉜</td><td>AIR VENT CUT-OFF DIAPHRAGM</td></tr>
<tr><td>⑨</td><td>CONTROL SWITCH</td><td>㉝</td><td>PRIMARY MAIN FUEL CUT-OFF SOLENOID VALVE</td></tr>
<tr><td>⑩</td><td>VACUUM SWITCH</td><td>㉞</td><td>PRIMARY SLOW MIXTURE CUT-OFF SOLENOID</td></tr>
<tr><td>⑪</td><td>EGR CONTROL VALVE A AND B</td><td></td><td>VALVE</td></tr>
<tr><td>⑫</td><td>EGR CONTROL SOLENOID VALVE B</td><td>㉟</td><td>REAR WINDOW DEFROSTER SWITCH</td></tr>
<tr><td>⑬</td><td>EGR CONTROL SOLENOID VALVE A</td><td></td><td>(MANUAL TRANSMISSION ONLY)</td></tr>
<tr><td>⑭</td><td>ANTI-AFTERBURN VALVE</td><td>㊱</td><td>HEATER BLOWER SWITCH</td></tr>
<tr><td>⑮</td><td>THROTTLE CONTROLLER CHECK VALVE</td><td></td><td>(MANUAL TRANSMISSION ONLY)</td></tr>
<tr><td>⑯</td><td>CRANKING SOLENOID VALVE</td><td>㊲</td><td>HEADLIGHT SWITCH (MANUAL TRANSMISSION</td></tr>
<tr><td>⑰</td><td>CRANKING LEAK SOLENOID VALVE</td><td></td><td>ONLY)</td></tr>
<tr><td>⑱</td><td>THERMOSENSOR B</td><td>㊳</td><td>POWER VALVE</td></tr>
<tr><td></td><td>(MANUAL TRANSMISSION ONLY)</td><td>㊴</td><td>IDLE CONTROLLER</td></tr>
<tr><td>⑲</td><td>IDLE CONTROL SOLENOID VALVE A</td><td>㊵</td><td>VACUUM HOLDING SOLENOID VALVE</td></tr>
<tr><td></td><td>(MANUAL TRANSMISSION ONLY)</td><td>㊶</td><td>POWER VALVE CHECK VALVE</td></tr>
<tr><td>⑳</td><td>AIR SUCTION VALVE AND AIR SUCTION</td><td>㊷</td><td>EGR AIR FILTER</td></tr>
<tr><td></td><td>CUT-OFF DIAPHRAGM VALVE</td><td>㊸</td><td>CONDENSATION CHAMBER</td></tr>
<tr><td>㉑</td><td>EGR VALVE</td><td>㊹</td><td>DISTRIBUTOR VACUUM ADVANCE</td></tr>
<tr><td>㉒</td><td>CATALYTIC CONVERTER</td><td>㊺</td><td>STARTER RELAY</td></tr>
<tr><td>㉓</td><td>INTAKE AIR CONTROL DIAPHRAGM</td><td>㊻</td><td>CANISTER</td></tr>
<tr><td>㉔</td><td>CHECK VALVE FOR INTAKE AIR TEMPERATURE</td><td>㊼</td><td>TWO-WAY VALVE</td></tr>
<tr><td></td><td>CONTROL</td><td></td><td></td></tr>
</table>

85914026

Fig. 28 1982 Civic

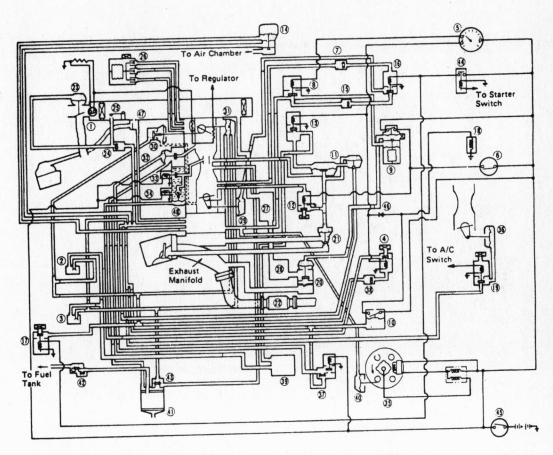

To Air Chamber →

To Regulator

To Starter Switch

To A/C Switch

Exhaust Manifold

To Fuel Tank

① INTAKE AIR TEMPERATURE SENSOR
② THERMOVALVE A
③ THERMOVALVE B
④ POWER VALVE CONTROL SOLENOID VALVE
⑤ SPEED SENSOR
⑥ THERMOSENSOR
⑦ DASHPOT CHECK VALVE
⑧ CONTROL SWITCH SOLENOID VALVE
⑨ CONTROL SWITCH
⑩ VACUUM SWITCH
⑪ EGR CONTROL VALVE A AND B
⑫ EGR CONTROL SOLENOID VALVE A
⑬ EGR CONTROL SOLENOID VALVE B
⑭ ANTI-AFTERBURN VALVE
⑮ THROTTLE CONTROLLER CHECK VALVE
⑯ CRANKING SOLENOID VALVE
⑰ CRANKING LEAK SOLENOID VALVE
⑱ AUXILIARY COIL
⑲ IDLE CONTROL SOLENOID VALVE (A/C)
⑳ AIR SUCTION VALVE AND AIR SUCTION
CUT-OFF DIAPHRAGM VALVE
㉑ EGR VALVE
㉒ CATALYTIC CONVERTER
㉓ INTAKE AIR CONTROL DIAPHRAGM
㉔ CHECK VALVE FOR INTAKE AIR TEMPERATURE
CONTROL

㉕ AIR BLEED VALVE
㉖ AIR JET CONTROLLER (CAL AND HI ALT ONLY)
㉗ AIR CHAMBERS A
㉘ AIR CHAMBER B
㉙ THROTTLE CONTROLLER
㉚ CHOKE OPENER
㉛ FAST IDLE UNLOADER
㉜ AIR VENT CUT-OFF DIAPHRAGM
㉝ PRIMARY MAIN FUEL CUT-OFF SOLENOID VALVE
㉞ PRIMARY SLOW MIXTURE CUT-OFF SOLENOID
VALVE
㉟ DISTRIBUTER
㊱ IDLE CONTROLLER (A/C)
㊲ VACUUM HOLDING SOLENOID VALVE
㊳ POWER VALVE CHECK VALVE
㊴ AIR FILTER
㊵ DISTRIBUTOR VACUUM ADVANCE
㊶ CANISTER
㊷ TWO-WAY VALVE
㊸ PURGE CONTROL DIAPHRAGM VALVE
㊹ STARTER RELAY
㊺ IGNITION SWITCH
㊻ DIODE
㊼ CONDENSATION CHAMBER
㊽ POWER VALVE

85914027

Fig. 29 1983 Accord

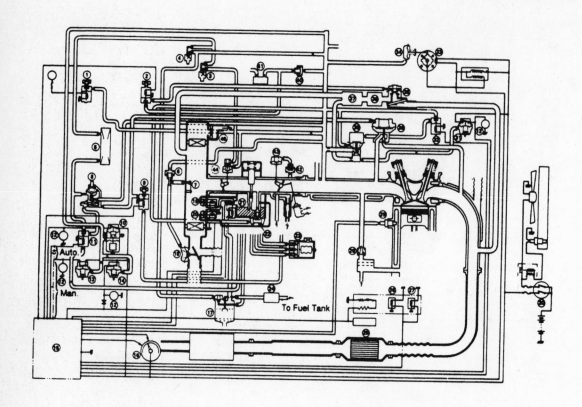

1. Cranking Leak Solenoid Valve
2. Air Suction Control Solenoid Valve
3. Thermovalve A
4. Thermovalve B
5. Air Filter
6. Check Valve
   (Intake Air Control)
7. Air Bleed Valve
8. EGR Control Valves A & B
9. EGR Control Solenoid Valve A
10. Control Switch
11. EGR Control Solenoid Valve B
12. Auxiliary Coil
13. Vacuum Switch A
   (Manual: Main Air Jet)
   (Automatic: EGR)
14. Vacuum Switch B (Main Air Jet)
   (Federal & High Altitude)
15. Control Unit
16. Speed Sensor
17. Canister
18. Intake Air Control Diaphragm
19. Inner Vent Solenoid Valve
20. Main Air Jet Solenoid Valve
21. Air Vent Cut-Off Solenoid Valve
22. Power Valve
23. Air Jet Controller
   (Calif. & High Altitude)

24. 2-Way Valve
25. Catalytic Converter
26. Auxiliary Slow Mixture
   Cut-Off Solenoid Valve
27. Primary Slow Mixture
   Cut-Off Solenoid Valve
28. PCV Valve
29. Thermister
30. Ignition Switch
31. Vacuum Switch (Air Suction)
32. Anti-Afterburn Control
   Solenoid Valve
33. Distributor
34. Distributor Vacuum Advance
35. Air Suction Valve & Air
   Suction Cut-Off Diaphragm Valve
36. Air Chamber "A"
37. Air Chamber "B"
38. EGR Valve
39. Anti-Afterburn Valve
40. Check Valve
41. Vacuum Tank
42. Dashpot Check Valve
43. Throttle Opener
44. Choke Opener
45. Blow-By Filter

Fig. 30 1983 Prelude

5

FUEL SYSTEM

CARBURETED FUEL SYSTEM

On the 1170cc and 1237cc models, a 2-bbl downdraft Hitachi carburetor is used. Fuel pressure is provided by a camshaft driven mechanical fuel pump. A replaceable fuel filter is located in the engine compartment inline between the fuel pump and carburetor.

On the 1335cc, 1487cc and 1600cc Civic, Accord, 1751cc Accord and Prelude, a Keihin 3-bbl carburetor is used. On this carburetor, the primary and second venturi's deliver a lean air/fuel mixture to the main combustion chamber. Simultaneously, the third or auxiliary venturi which has a complete separate fuel metering circuit, delivers a small (in volume) but very rich air/fuel mixture to the precombustion chamber. Fuel pressure is provided by an electric fuel pump which is actuated when the ignition switch is turned to the **ON** position. The electric pump is located under the rear seat beneath a special access plate on sedan and hatchback models, and located under the rear of the vehicle adjacent to the fuel tank on station wagon and Accord models. A replaceable inline fuel filter located on the inlet side of the electric fuel pump is used on all later models.

On the 1829cc Prelude model twin Keihin 2-bbl sidedraft carburetors are used. Fuel pressure is supplied from an electric pump mounted near the left rear tire.

Mechanical Fuel Pump

REMOVAL & INSTALLATION

1170cc and 1237cc Engines

The fuel pump in the Civic is located in back of the engine, underneath the air cleaner snorkel.

1. Remove the air cleaner and cover assembly.
2. Remove the inlet and outlet fuel lines at the pump.
3. Loosen the pump nuts and remove the pump.

➡**Do not disassemble the pump. Disassembly may cause fuel or oil leakage. If the pump is defective, replace it as an assembly.**

4. To install the fuel pump, reverse the removal procedure.

TESTING

1. Check the following items.
   a. Looseness of the pump connector.
   b. Looseness of the upper and lower body and cover screws.
   c. Looseness of the rocker arm pin.
   d. Contamination or clogging of the air hole.
   e. Improper operation of the pump.
2. Check to see if there are signs of oil or fuel around the air hole. If so, the diaphragm is damaged and you must replace the pump.
3. To inspect the pump for operation, first disconnect the fuel line at the carburetor. Connect a fuel pressure gauge to

the delivery side of the pump. Start the engine and measure the pump delivery pressure.

4. After measuring, stop the engine and check to see if the gauge drops suddenly. If the gauge drops suddenly and/or the delivery pressure is incorrect, check for a fuel or oil leak from the diaphragm or from the valves.

5. To test for volume, disconnect the fuel line from the carburetor and inset it into a one quart container. Crank the engine for 60 seconds at 600 rpm, or 40 seconds at 3,000 rpm. The bottle should be half full (1 pint).

Electric Fuel Pump

▶ **See Figures 1, 2, 3 and 4**

REMOVAL & INSTALLATION

All Engines

1. Remove the gas filler cap to relieve any excess pressure in the system.
2. Obtain a pair of suitable clamps to pinch shut the fuel lines to the pump.
3. Disconnect the negative battery cable.
4. Locate the fuel pump. On Civic sedan and hatchback models (1982 only), you will first have to remove the rear seat by removing the bolt at the rear center of the bottom cushion and pivoting the seat forward from the rear. The pump and filter are located on the driver's side of the rear seat floor section beneath an access plate retained by four Phillips head screws.

On station wagon and 1983 sedan & hatchback models and the Accord and Prelude, you will probably have to raise the rear of the car to obtain access to the pump. On Accord and Prelude models, remove the left rear wheel. In all cases, make sure, if you are crawling under the car, that the car is securely supported.

5. Pinch the inlet and outlet fuel lines shut. Loosen the hose clamps. On station wagon and Accord models, remove the filter mounting clip on the left hand side of the bracket.

6. Disconnect the positive lead wire and ground wire from the pump at their quick disconnect.

7. Remove the two fuel pump retaining bolts, taking care not to lose the two spacers and bolt collars.

8. Remove the fuel lines and fuel pump.

9. Reverse the above procedure to install. The pump cannot be disassembled and must be replaced if defective. Operating fuel pump pressure is 2-3 psi.

PRESSURE TESTING

1. Relieve the fuel pressure from the system as previously outline in this section.
2. Disconnect the fuel line at the fuel filter and attach the pressure gauge to it.
3. Remove the fuel cut off relay from the fuse box and connect a jumper wire in its place. Turn the ignition switch to

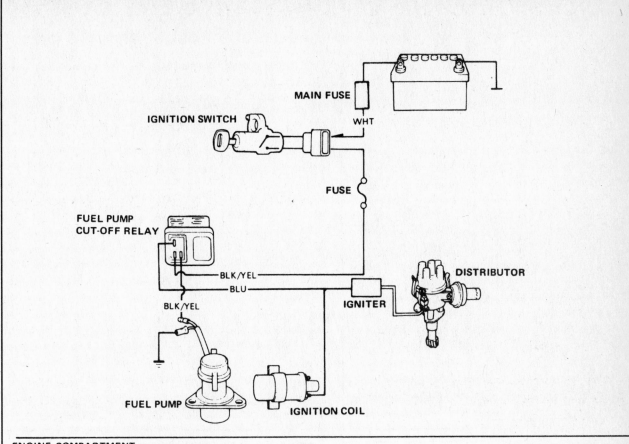

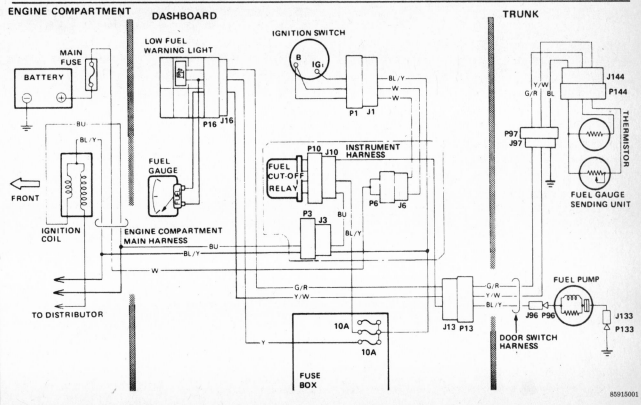

Fig. 1 Electrical fuel pump wiring-1982 Prelude

85915001

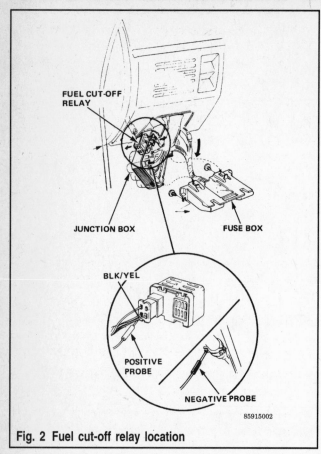

Fig. 2 Fuel cut-off relay location

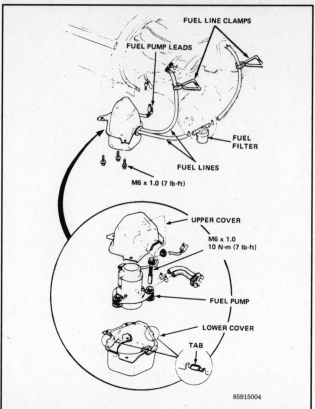

Fig. 4 Electrical fuel pump removal and installation-1982 Prelude

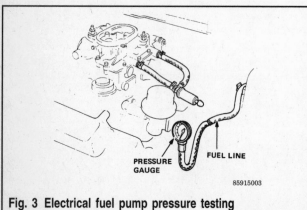

Fig. 3 Electrical fuel pump pressure testing

ON until the pressure stabilizes and then turn it **OFF**. The pressure should be 2.6-3.3 psi.

4. If the fuel pressure is not as specified, first check the fuel pump. If the fuel pump is good, check the following:

a. If the pressure is higher than specified, inspect for a pinched or clogged fuel return hose or piping.

b. If the pressure is lower than specified, inspect for a clogged fuel filter, pinched or clogged fuel hose from the fuel tank to the fuel pump or leakage in the fuel line.

Carburetor

TROUBLESHOOTING

Carburetor problems are among the most difficult internal combustion engine malfunctions to diagnose. The most reliable way for a nonprofessional to diagnose a bad carburetor is to eliminate all other possible sources of the problem. If you suspect the carburetor is the problem, perform the adjustments given in this section. Check the ignition system to ensure that the spark plugs, contact points, and condenser are in good shape and adjusted properly. Check the emission control equipment. Check the ignition timing adjustment. Check all vacuum hoses on the engine for loose connections or splits or breaks. Make sure the carburetor and intake manifold attaching bolts are tightened to the proper torque.

If you do determine that the carburetor is malfunctioning, and the adjustments in this section don't help, you have three alternatives: you can take it to a professional mechanic and let him fix it, you can buy a new or rebuilt carburetor to replace the one now on your vehicle, or you can buy a carburetor rebuilding kit and overhaul your carburetor.

ADJUSTMENTS

Fast Idle

During cold engine starting and the engine warm-up period, a specially enriched fuel mixture is required. If the engine fails to run properly or if the engine over-revs with the choke knob (if so equipped) pulled out in cold weather, the fast idle system should be checked and adjusted. This is accomplished with the carburetor installed.

1973 1170cc AND 1237cc MODELS

1. Run the engine until it reaches normal operating temperature.
2. With the engine still running, pull the choke knob out to the first detent. The idle speed should rise to 1,500-2,000 rpm.
3. If the idle speed is not within this range, adjust by bending the choke rod. (See 'Choke Adjustment' section below for further details.)

1974-79 1170cc AND 1237cc MODELS

1. Open the primary throttle plate and insert an 0.8mm diameter drill bit between the plate and the bore.
2. With the throttle plate opened 0.8mm, bend the reference tab so it is midway between the two scribed lines on the throttle control lever.

1975-79 1487cc AND 1600cc MODELS

1. Run the engine until it reaches normal operating temperature.
2. Place the choke control knob in its second detent position (two clicks out from the dash). With the choke knob in this position, run the engine for 30 seconds and check that the fast idle speed is 2,500-3,500 rpm.
3. To adjust, bend the slot in the fast idle adjusting link. Narrow the slot to lower the fast idle, and widen the slot to increase. Make all adjustments in small increments.

1335cc, 1487cc (1980-83) AND 1751cc MODELS

1. Run the engine to normal operating temperature.
2. Connect a tachometer according to the manufacturer's specifications.
3. Disconnect and plug the hose from the fast idle unloader.
4. Shut the engine off, hold the choke valve closed, and open and close the throttle to engage the fast idle cam.
5. Start the engine, run it for one minute. Fast idle speed should be 2,300-3,300 rpm (manual transaxle) or 2,200-3,200 rpm (automatic transaxle).
6. Adjust the idle by turning the fast idle screw.

1829cc PRELUDE

1. Start the engine and bring it to normal operating temperature. Turn the engine **OFF**.
2. Remove the E-clip and flat washer from the thermo-wax valve linkage, then, slide the linkage past the fast idle cam.

➡**Be careful not to bend the linkage or the fast idle speed will be changed.**

3. While holding open the throttle, turn the fast idle cam counterclockwise until the fast idle lever is on the 3rd step.

4. Without touching the throttle, start the engine and check the idle speed. The idle speed should be 2,000 rpm. Adjustment of the idle speed can be made by turning the fast idle adjusting screw.
5. Stop the engine and reconnect the thermo-wax valve linkage.
6. Start the engine and check that as the engine warms up, the idle speed decreases.

➡**If the idle speed doesn't drop, clean the linkage along with the carburetor. If the speed still doesn't drop, check for damaged or stuck linkage.**

Float and Fuel Level

Poor fuel combustion, black sooty exhaust, and fuel overflow are indications of improper float level. Lean running may also be a symptom, although you should also check for such causes as jets blocked by dirt and vacuum leaks.

1170cc AND 1237cc MODELS

1. Check the float level by looking at the sight glass on the right of the carburetor. Fuel level should align with the dot on the sight glass. If the level is above or below the dot, the carburetor must be disassembled and the float level set.

➡**Try to check float level with the dot at eye level.**

2. Remove the carburetor from the engine and disconnect the air horn assembly from the carburetor body.
3. Invert the air horn and raise the float.
4. Now lower the float carefully until the float tang just touches the needle valve stem. The valve stem is spring loaded, so do not allow the float to compress the spring during measurement. Measure the distance between the float and the air horn flange (without gasket). The distance should be 11mm. Adjust by bending the tang.
5. Raise the float until the float stop contacts the air horn body. Measure the distance between the float tang and the needle valve stem. The distance should be 1.3-1.77mm. Adjust by bending the float stop tang.
6. When the carburetor is installed, recheck the float level by looking into the carburetor float sight glass. Fuel level should be within the range of the dot on the glass.

1335cc, 1487cc, 1600cc AND 1751cc MODELS THROUGH 1981

◆ **See Figures 5, 6 and 7**

Due to the rather unconventional manner in which the Keihin 3-bbl carburetor float level is checked and adjusted, this is one job best left to the dealer, or someone with Honda tool No. 07501-6570000 (1487 and 1600cc engines) or 07501-6950100 (1751cc engines); which is a special float level gauge/fuel catch tray/drain bottle assembly not generally available to the public. This carburetor is adjusted while mounted on a running engine. After the auxiliary and the primary/secondary main jet covers are removed, the special float gauge apparatus is installed over the jet apertures. With the engine running, the float level is checked against a red index line on the gauge. If adjustment proves necessary, there are adjusting screws provided for both the auxiliary and the primary/secondary circuits atop the carburetor.

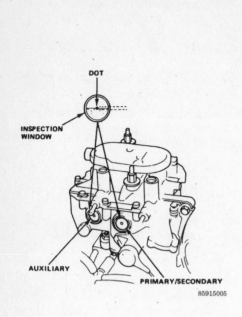

Fig. 5 Inspection window showing the fuel level on the 1982 and later models, except 1829cc Prelude

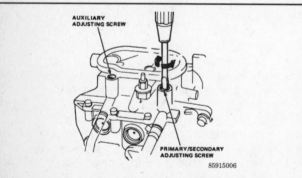

Fig. 6 Float level adjustment screw-1982 and later models, except 1829cc Prelude

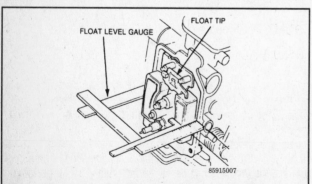

Fig. 7 Float level measurement on the dual Keihin sidedraft carburetors-1829cc Prelude

Fig. 8 Loosen the throttle cable adjustment retaining nut

Fig. 9 Throttle cable adjustment

1982 AND LATER, EXCEPT 1829cc PRELUDE

With the vehicle on level ground and at normal operating temperature, check the primary and secondary fuel level inspection windows. If the fuel level is not touching the dot, adjust it by turning the adjusting screws which are located in recessed bosses above the inspection windows.

➡ Do not turn the adjusting screws more than 1 turn every 15 seconds.

1982 AND LATER 1829cc PRELUDE

1. Remove the side draft carburetors from the engine and remove the float chambers from the carburetors.

2. Using a float level gauge, measure the float level with the float tip lightly touching the float valve and the float chamber surface tilted about 30° from vertical. The float level should be 16mm.

3. To adjust the float level on the sub carburetor, remove the float chamber. Using a float level gauge, measure the float level as described above.

➡ The float level of the sub carburetor cannot be adjusted. If the float level is incorrect the float must be replaced.

Throttle Linkage

▶ See Figures 8 and 9

1170cc AND 1237cc MODELS

1. Check the gas pedal free-play (the amount of free movement before the throttle cable starts to pull the throttle valve).

Adjust the free-play at the throttle cable adjusting nut (near the carburetor) so the pedal has 1.0-3.0mm free-play.

2. Make sure that when the accelerator pedal is fully depressed, the primary and secondary throttle valves are opened fully (contact the stops). If the secondary valve does not open fully, adjust by bending the secondary throttle valve connecting rod.

1335cc, 1487cc, 1600cc AND 1751cc MODELS

1. Remove the air cleaner assembly to provide access.
2. Check that the cable free-play (deflection) is 4.0-10.0mm (1335, 1487 and 1600cc engines) or 4.5-9.5mm (1751cc engines). This is measured right before the cable enters the throttle shaft bellcrank.
3. If deflection is not to specifications, rotate the cable adjusting nuts in the required direction.
4. As a final check, have a friend press the gas pedal all the way to the floor, while you look down inside the throttle bore checking that the throttle plates reach the wide open throttle (WOT) vertical position.
5. Install the air cleaner.

Choke

1170cc AND 1237cc MODELS

The choke valve should be **FULLY OPEN** when the choke knob is pushed **IN** and/or **FULLY CLOSED** with the choke knob pulled **OUT**. The choke valve is held in the fully closed position by spring action. Pull the choke knob to the fully closed position, then, open and close the choke valve by rotating the choke valve shaft. The movement should be free and unrestricted.

If adjustment is required, adjust the cable length by loosening the cable clamp bolt.

Precision Adjustment

1170cc AND 1237cc MODELS

▶ See Figure 10

1. Using a wire gauge, check the primary throttle valve opening, dimension when the choke valve is fully closed. The opening should be 1.28-1.68mm.
2. If the opening is out of specification, adjust it by bending the choke rod. After installing make sure that the highest fast idle speed is 2,500-2,800 rpm while the engine is warm.

➡**When adjusting the fast idle speed, be sure the throttle adjusting screw does not contact the stop.**

1487cc (1975-79) AND 1600cc MODELS

1. Push the choke actuator rod towards its diaphragm, so it does not contact the choke valve linkage.
2. Pull the choke knob out to the 1st detent (click) position from the dash. With the knob in this position, check the distance between the choke butterfly valve and the venturi opening with a ³⁄₁₆ drill (shank end).
3. Adjust as necessary by bending the relief lever adjusting tang with needle nose pliers.
4. Now, pull out the choke knob to its 2nd detent position from the dash. Again, make sure the choke actuator rod does not contact the choke valve linkage.

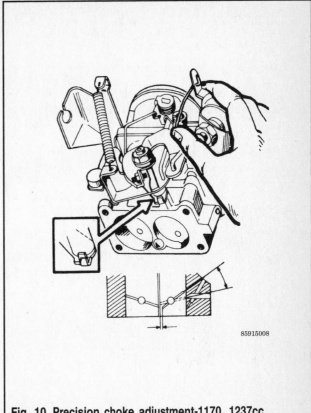

85915008

Fig. 10 Precision choke adjustment-1170, 1237cc models

5. With the choke knob in this position, check that the clearance between the butterfly valve and venturi opening is ⅛ using the shank end of a ⅛ drill.
6. Adjust as necessary by bending the stop tab for the choke butterfly linkage.

1335cc, 1487cc (1980-83) AND 1751cc MODELS

1. With the engine **COLD**, remove the air cleaner.
2. Open and close the throttle all the way to engage the fast idle cam.
3. The choke plate should close to within ⅛ of the air horn wall.
4. If not, remove the choke cover and inspect the linkage for free movement. Repair or replace parts if necessary.
5. Install the cover and adjust so that the index marks align. Recheck the choke for proper closing clearance. If the clearance is not correct, replace the cap and retest.

Choke Cable

1974-79 1237cc MODELS

▶ See Figure 11

➡**Perform the adjustment only after the throttle plate opening has been set and referenced.**

1. Make sure that the choke cable is correctly adjusted.
   a. With the choke knob in, the choke butterfly should be completely **OPEN**.
   b. Slowly pull out the choke knob and check for slack in the cable. Remove any excessive free-play and recheck for **FULL OPEN** when the knob is pushed **IN**.

2. Check the link rod adjustment by pulling the choke knob out to the 1st detent. The two scribed lines on the throttle control lever should align on either side of the reference tab. If not, adjust by bending the choke link rod.

1487cc AND 1600cc MODELS

1. Remove the air cleaner assembly.

2. Push the choke knob all the way in at the dash. Check that the choke butterfly valve (choke plate) is **FULLY OPEN** (vertical).

3. Next, have a friend pull out the choke knob while you observe the action of the butterfly valve. When the choke knob is pulled out to the 2nd detent position, the butterfly valve should just close. Then, when the choke knob is pulled all the way out, the butterfly valve should remain in the **CLOSED** position.

4. To adjust, loosen the choke cable locknut and rotate the adjusting nut so that with the choke knob pushed flush against the dash (open position), the butterfly valve just rests against its positioning stop tab. Tighten the locknut.

5. If the choke butterfly valve is sticky in operation or if it does not close properly, check the butterfly valve and shaft for binding. Check also the operation of the return spring.

Throttle Valve Operation

1170cc AND 1237cc MODELS

1. Check to see if the throttle valve opens fully when the throttle lever is moved to the fully open position. See if the valve closes fully when the lever is released.

2. Measure the clearance between the primary throttle valve and the chamber wall where the connecting rod begins to open the secondary throttle valve. The clearance should be 5.6-6.0mm.

3. If the clearance is out of specification, adjust by bending the connecting rod.

➡ **After adjusting, operate the throttle lever and check for any sign of binding.**

Accelerator Pump

1170cc AND 1237cc MODELS

Check the pump for smooth operation. See if fuel squirts out of the pump nozzle by operating the pump lever or the throttle

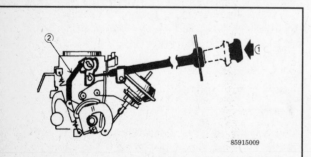

85915009

Fig. 11 Choke cable adjustment-1974 and later 1237cc models. Number one is the detent position and number two is the link adjustment location

lever. When the pump is operated slowly, fuel must squirt out until the pump comes to the end of its travel. If the pump is defective, check for clogging or a defective piston. Adjust the pump by either repositioning the end of the connecting rod arm in the pump lever or the arm itself.

1975-79 1487cc AND 1600cc MODELS

1. Remove the air cleaner assembly.

2. Check that the distance between the tang at the end of the accelerator pump lever and the lever stop at the edge of the throttle body the distance is 0.80-0.85mm (1975-77) or 14.5-15.0mm (1978-79). This corresponds to effective pump lever travel.

3. To adjust, bend the pump lever tang in the required direction.

4. Install the air cleaner.

1980-83 1487cc AND 1751cc MODELS

1. Remove the air cleaner.

2. Make sure that the pump shaft is moving freely throughout the pump stroke.

3. Check that the pump lever is in contact with the pump shaft.

4. Measure between the bottom end of the pump lever and the lever stop tang. The gap should be 14-15mm through 1980 or 11.5-12.0mm (1981-83). If not, bend the tang to adjust.

REMOVAL & INSTALLATION

▶ **See Figures 12, 13, 14, 15, 16, 17, 18, 19 and 20**

1. Disconnect the negative battery cable. Disconnect (mark for correct installation) the following:
   a. Hot air tube.
   b. Vacuum hose between the one-way valve and the manifold at the manifold.
   c. Breather chamber (on air cleaner case) to intake manifold at the breather chamber.
   d. Hose from the air cleaner case to the valve cover.
   e. Hose from the carbon canister to the carburetor, at the carburetor.
   f. Throttle opener hose at the throttle opener.

2. Disconnect the fuel line at the carburetor. Plug the end of the fuel line to prevent dust entry.

3. Disconnect the choke and throttle control cables.

4. Disconnect the fuel shut-off solenoid wires.

5. Remove the carburetor retaining bolts and the carburetor (do not turn assembly upside down). Leave the insulator on the manifold.

➡ **After removing the carburetor, cover the intake manifold parts to keep out foreign materials.**

6. Installation is the reverse of the removal procedure (replace mounting gasket). Torque the mounting bolts evenly. Adjust the carburetor. Road test the vehicle for proper operation.

Fig. 12 Removing the air cleaner for carburetor removal

Fig. 13 Mark all vacuum hoses and lines for carburetor removal

Fig. 14 Removing the carburetor mounting bolts

Fig. 15 Removing the carburetor mounting nuts

Fig. 16 Removing the carburetor assembly

Fig. 17 View of the carburetor mounting area

OVERHAUL

All Types

▶ See Figure 21

Efficient carburetion depends greatly on careful cleaning and inspection during overhaul since dirt, gum, water or varnish in or on the carburetor parts are often responsible for poor performance.

Overhaul your carburetor in a clean, dust-free area. Carefully disassemble the carburetor, referring often to the exploded views. Keep all similar and look-alike parts segregated during disassembly and cleaning to avoid accidental interchange during assembly. Make a note of all jet sizes.

Fig. 18 View of the carburetor adaptor plate

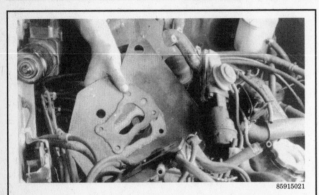

Fig. 19 View of the carburetor mounting gaskets

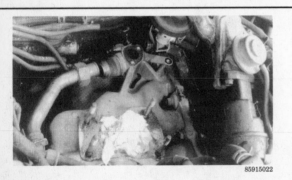

Fig. 20 Close off the carburetor mounting hole with a shop towel

When the carburetor is disassembled, wash all parts (except diaphragms, electric choke units, pump plunger and any other plastic, leather, fiber or rubber parts) in clean carburetor solvent. Do not leave parts in the solvent any longer than is necessary to sufficiently loosen the deposits. Excessive cleaning may remove the special finish from the float bowl and choke valve bodies, leaving these parts unfit for service. Rinse all parts in clean solvent and blow them dry with compressed air or allow them to air dry. Wipe clean all cork, plastic, leather and fiber parts with a clean, lint-free cloth.

Blow out all passages and jets with compressed air and be sure that there are no restrictions or blockages. Never use wire or similar tools to clean jets, fuel passages or air bleeds. Clean all jets and valves separately to avoid accidental interchange.

Check all parts for wear or damage. If wear or damage is found, replace the defective parts. Especially check the following:

1. Check the float needle and seat for wear. If wear is found, replace the complete assembly.

2. Check the float hinge pin for wear and the float(s) for dents or distortion. Replace the float if fuel has leaked into it.

3. Check the throttle and choke shaft bores for wear or an out-of-round condition. Damage or wear to the throttle arm, shaft or shaft bore will often require replacement of the throttle body. These parts require a close tolerance of fit; wear may allow air leakage, which could affect starting and idling.

➡Throttle shafts and bushings are not included in overhaul kits. They can be purchased separately.

4. Inspect the idle mixture adjusting needles for burrs or grooves. Any such condition requires replacement of the needle, since you will not be able to obtain a satisfactory idle.

5. Test the accelerator pump check valves. They should pass air one way but not the other. Test for proper seating by blowing and sucking on the valve. Replace the valve if necessary. If the valve is satisfactory, wash the valve again to remove breath moisture.

6. Check the bowl cover for warped surfaces with a straightedge.

7. Closely inspect the valves and seats for wear and damage, replacing as necessary.

8. After the carburetor is assembled, check the choke valve for freedom of operation.

Carburetor overhaul kits are recommended for each overhaul. These kits contain all gaskets and new parts to replace those that deteriorate most rapidly. Failure to replace all parts supplied with the kit (especially gaskets) can result in poor performance later.

Some carburetor manufacturers supply overhaul kits of three basic types: minor repair; major repair; and gasket kits. Basically, they contain the following:

Minor Repair Kits:
- All gaskets
- Float needle valve
- Volume control screw
- All diaphragms
- Spring for the pump diaphragm

Major Repair Kits:
- All jets and gaskets
- All diaphragms
- Float needle valve
- Volume control screw
- Pump ball valve
- Main jet carrier
- Float
- Complete intermediate rod
- Intermediate pump lever
- Complete injector tube
- Some cover holddown screws and washers

Gasket Kits:
- All gaskets

After cleaning and checking all components, reassemble the carburetor, using new parts and referring to the exploded view. When reassembling, make sure that all screws and jets are tight in their seats, but do not overtighten, as the tips will be distorted. Tighten all screws gradually, in rotation. Do not tighten needle valves into their seats; uneven jetting will result.

Always use new gaskets. Be sure to adjust the float level when reassembling.

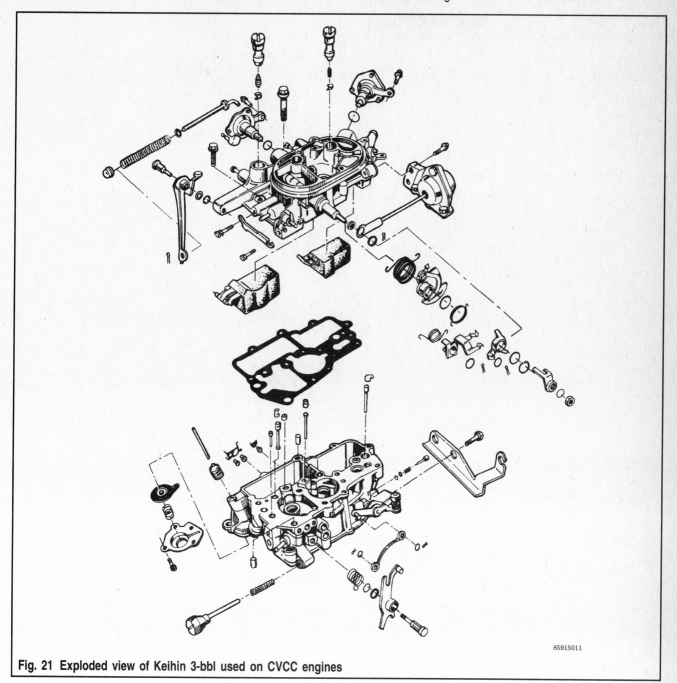

85915011

Fig. 21 Exploded view of Keihin 3-bbl used on CVCC engines

FUEL TANK

Tank Assembly

REMOVAL & INSTALLATION

▶ **See Figures 22 and 23**

All Models

1. Drain the tank by loosening the tank drain bolt.

➡**Catch the fuel in a clean, safe container.**

2. Disconnect the fuel tubes, filler neck connecting tube and the clear vinyl tube.

➡**Disconnect the fuel tubes by removing the clips, taking care not to damage the tubes.**

3. Disconnect the fuel meter unit wire at its connection.
4. Remove the fuel tank by removing its attaching bolts.
5. To install, reverse the removal procedures. Be sure that all tubes and fuel lines are securely fastened by the clips.

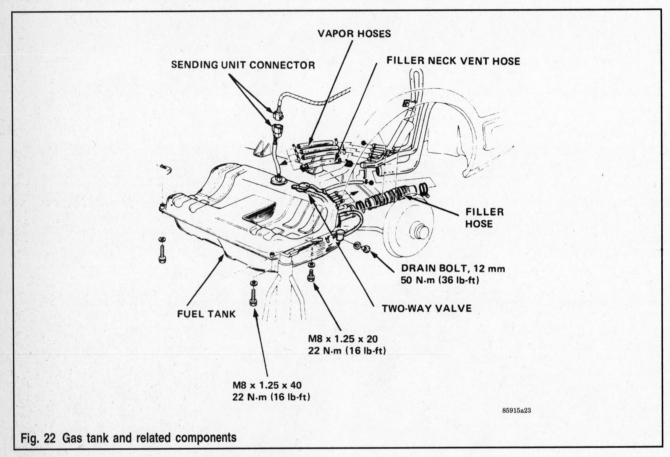

VAPOR HOSES

SENDING UNIT CONNECTOR

FILLER NECK VENT HOSE

FILLER HOSE

DRAIN BOLT, 12 mm 50 N·m (36 lb-ft)

TWO-WAY VALVE

FUEL TANK

M8 x 1.25 x 20 22 N·m (16 lb-ft)

M8 x 1.25 x 40 22 N·m (16 lb-ft)

85915a23

Fig. 22 Gas tank and related components

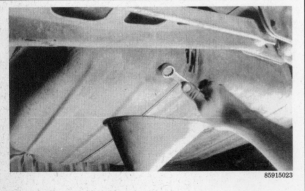

85915023

Fig. 23 Gas tank drain plug

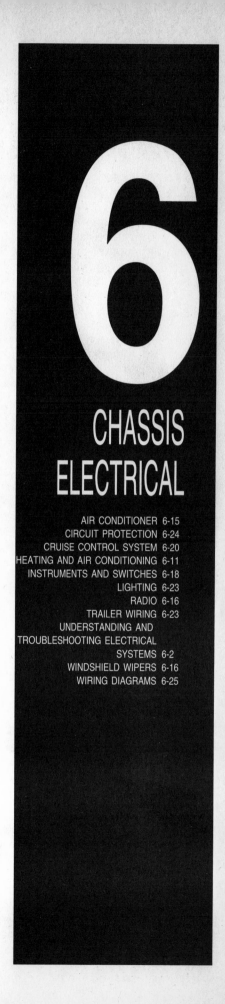

6

CHASSIS
ELECTRICAL

UNDERSTANDING AND TROUBLESHOOTING ELECTRICAL SYSTEMS

At the rate which both import and domestic manufacturers are incorporating electronic control systems into their production lines, it won't be long before every new vehicle is equipped with one or more on-board computer. These electronic components (with no moving parts) should theoretically last the life of the vehicle, provided nothing external happens to damage the circuits or memory chips.

While it is true that electronic components should never wear out, in the real world malfunctions do occur. It is also true that any computer-based system is extremely sensitive to electrical voltages and cannot tolerate careless or haphazard testing or service procedures. An inexperienced individual can literally do major damage looking for a minor problem by using the wrong kind of test equipment or connecting test leads or connectors with the ignition switch ON. When selecting test equipment, make sure the manufacturers instructions state that the tester is compatible with whatever type of electronic control system is being serviced. Read all instructions carefully and double check all test points before installing probes or making any test connections.

The following section outlines basic diagnosis techniques for dealing with computerized automotive control systems. Along with a general explanation of the various types of test equipment available to aid in servicing modern electronic automotive systems, basic repair techniques for wiring harnesses and connectors is given. Read the basic information before attempting any repairs or testing on any computerized system, to provide the background of information necessary to avoid the most common and obvious mistakes that can cost both time and money. Although the replacement and testing procedures are simple in themselves, the systems are not, and unless one has a thorough understanding of all components and their function within a particular computerized control system, the logical test sequence these systems demand cannot be followed. Minor malfunctions can make a big difference, so it is important to know how each component affects the operation of the overall electronic system to find the ultimat e cause of a problem without replacing good components unnecessarily. It is not enough to use the correct test equipment; the test equipment must be used correctly.

Safety Precautions

✳✳CAUTION

Whenever working on or around any computer based microprocessor control system, always observe these general precautions to prevent the possibility of personal injury or damage to electronic components.

- Never install or remove battery cables with the key ON or the engine running. Jumper cables should be connected with the key OFF to avoid power surges that can damage electronic control units. Engines equipped with computer controlled systems should avoid both giving and getting jump starts due to the possibility of serious damage to components from arcing in the engine compartment when connections are made with the ignition ON.

- Always remove the battery cables before charging the battery. Never use a high output charger on an installed battery or attempt to use any type of 'hot shot' (24 volt) starting aid.

- Exercise care when inserting test probes into connectors to insure good connections without damaging the connector or spreading the pins. Always probe connectors from the rear (wire) side, NOT the pin side, to avoid accidental shorting of terminals during test procedures.

- Never remove or attach wiring harness connectors with the ignition switch ON, especially to an electronic control unit.

- Do not drop any components during service procedures and never apply 12 volts directly to any component (like a solenoid or relay) unless instructed specifically to do so. Some component electrical windings are designed to safely handle only 4 or 5 volts and can be destroyed in seconds if 12 volts are applied directly to the connector.

- Remove the electronic control unit if the vehicle is to be placed in an environment where temperatures exceed approximately 176°F (80°C), such as a paint spray booth or when arc or gas welding near the control unit location in the car.

ORGANIZED TROUBLESHOOTING

When diagnosing a specific problem, organized troubleshooting is a must. The complexity of a modern automobile demands that you approach any problem in a logical, organized manner. There are certain troubleshooting techniques that are standard:

1. Establish when the problem occurs. Does the problem appear only under certain conditions? Were there any noises, odors, or other unusual symptoms?

2. Isolate the problem area. To do this, make some simple tests and observations; then eliminate the systems that are working properly. Check for obvious problems such as broken wires, dirty connections or split or disconnected vacuum hoses. Always check the obvious before assuming something complicated is the cause.

3. Test for problems systematically to determine the cause once the problem area is isolated. Are all the components functioning properly? Is there power going to electrical switches and motors? Is there vacuum at vacuum switches and/or actuators? Is there a mechanical problem such as bent linkage or loose mounting screws? Doing careful, systematic checks will often turn up most causes on the first inspection without wasting time checking components that have little or no relationship to the problem.

4. Test all repairs after the work is done to make sure that the problem is fixed. Some causes can be traced to more than one component, so a careful verification of repair work is important to pick up additional malfunctions that may cause a problem to reappear or a different problem to arise. A blown fuse, for example, is a simple problem that may require more than another fuse to repair. If you don't look for a problem that caused a fuse to blow, for example, a shorted wire may go undetected.

Experience has shown that most problems tend to be the result of a fairly simple and obvious cause, such as loose or corroded connectors or air leaks in the intake system; making careful inspection of components during testing essential to quick and accurate troubleshooting. Special, hand held computerized testers designed specifically for diagnosing the system are available from a variety of aftermarket sources, as well as from the vehicle manufacturer, but care should be taken that any test equipment being used is designed to diagnose that particular computer controlled system accurately without damaging the control unit (ECU) or components being tested.

➡️**Pinpointing the exact cause of trouble in an electrical system can sometimes only be accomplished by the use of special test equipment. The following describes commonly used test equipment and explains how to put it to best use in diagnosis. In addition to the information covered below, the manufacturer's instructions booklet provided with the tester should be read and clearly understood before attempting any test procedures.**

TEST EQUIPMENT

Jumper Wires

Jumper wires are simple, yet extremely valuable, pieces of test equipment. Jumper wires are merely wires that are used to bypass sections of a circuit. The simplest type of jumper wire is merely a length of multistrand wire with an alligator clip at each end. Jumper wires are usually fabricated from lengths of standard automotive wire and whatever type of connector (alligator clip, spade connector or pin connector) that is required for the particular vehicle being tested. The well equipped tool box will have several different styles of jumper wires in several different lengths. Some jumper wires are made with three or more terminals coming from a common splice for special purpose testing. In cramped, hard-to-reach areas it is advisable to have insulated boots over the jumper wire terminals in order to prevent accidental grounding, sparks, and possible fire, especially when testing fuel system components.

Jumper wires are used primarily to locate open electrical circuits, on either the ground (-) side of the circuit or on the hot (+) side. If an electrical component fails to operate, connect the jumper wire between the component and a good ground. If the component operates only with the jumper installed, the ground circuit is open. If the ground circuit is good, but the component does not operate, the circuit between the power feed and component is open. You can sometimes connect the jumper wire directly from the battery to the hot terminal of the component, but first make sure the component uses 12 volts in operation. Some electrical components, such as fuel injectors, are designed to operate on about 4 volts and running 12 volts directly to the injector terminals can burn out the wiring. By inserting an inline fuseholder between a set of test leads, a fused jumper wire can be used for bypassing open circuits. Use a 5 amp fuse to provide protection against voltage spikes. When in doubt, use a voltmeter to check the voltage input to the component and measure how much voltage is being applied normally. By moving the jumper wire

successively back from the lamp toward the power source, you can isolate the area of the circuit where the open is located. When the component stops functioning, or the power is cut off, the open is in the segment of wire between the jumper and the point previously tested.

✳️✳️CAUTION

Never use jumpers made from wire that is of lighter gauge than used in the circuit under test. If the jumper wire is of too small gauge, it may overheat and possibly melt. Never use jumpers to bypass high resistance loads (such as motors) in a circuit. Bypassing resistances, in effect, creates a short circuit which may, in turn, cause damage and fire. Never use a jumper for anything other than temporary bypassing of components in a circuit.

12 Volt Test Light
▶ See Figure 1

The 12 volt test light is used to check circuits and components while electrical current is flowing through them. It is used for voltage and ground tests. Twelve volt test lights come in different styles but all have three main parts; a ground clip, a probe, and a light. The most commonly used 12 volt test lights have pick-type probes. To use a 12 volt test light, connect the ground clip to a good ground and probe wherever necessary with the pick. The pick should be sharp so that it can penetrate wire insulation to make contact with the wire, without making a large hole in the insulation. The wrap-around light is handy in hard to reach areas or where it is difficult to support a wire to push a probe pick into it. To use the wrap around light, hook the wire to probed with the hook and pull the trigger. A small pick will be forced through the wire insulation into the wire core.

✳️✳️CAUTION

Do not use a test light to probe electronic ignition spark plug or coil wires. Never use a pick-type test light to probe wiring on computer controlled systems unless specifically instructed to do so. Any wire insulation that is pierced by the test light probe should be taped and sealed with silicone after testing.

Like the jumper wire, the 12 volt test light is used to isolate opens in circuits. But, whereas the jumper wire is used to bypass the open to operate the load, the 12 volt test light is used to locate the presence of voltage in a circuit. If the test light glows, you know that there is power up to that point; if the 12 volt test light does not glow when its probe is inserted into the wire or connector, you know that there is an open circuit (no power). Move the test light in successive steps back toward the power source until the light in the handle does glow. When it does glow, the open is between the probe and point previously probed.

➡️**The test light does not detect that 12 volts (or any particular amount of voltage) is present; it only detects that some voltage is present. It is advisable before using the test light to touch its terminals across the battery posts to make sure the light is operating properly.**

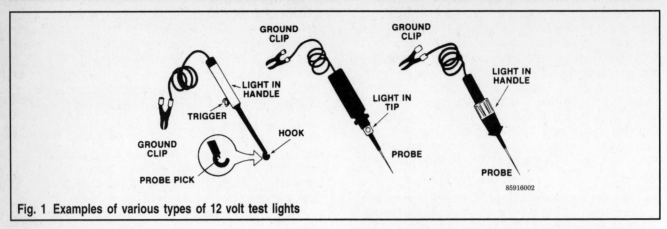

Fig. 1 Examples of various types of 12 volt test lights

Self-Powered Test Light

▶ See Figure 2

The self-powered test light usually contains a 1.5 volt pen-light battery. One type of self-powered test light is similar in design to the 12 volt test light. This type has both the battery and the light in the handle and pick-type probe tip. The second type has the light toward the open tip, so that the light illuminates the contact point. The self-powered test light is dual purpose piece of test equipment. It can be used to test for either open or short circuits when power is isolated from the circuit (continuity test). A powered test light should not be used on any computer controlled system or component unless specifically instructed to do so. Many engine sensors can be destroyed by even this small amount of voltage applied directly to the terminals.

Open Circuit Testing

To use the self-powered test light to check for open circuits, first isolate the circuit from the vehicle's 12 volt power source by disconnecting the battery or wiring harness connector. Connect the test light ground clip to a good ground and probe sections of the circuit sequentially with the test light. (start from either end of the circuit). If the light is out, the open is between the probe and the circuit ground. If the light is on, the open is between the probe and end of the circuit toward the power source.

Short Circuit Testing

By isolating the circuit both from power and from ground, and using a self-powered test light, you can check for shorts

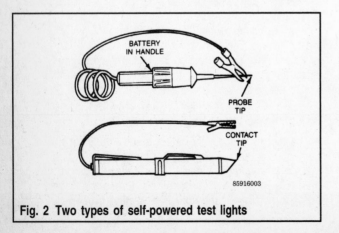

Fig. 2 Two types of self-powered test lights

to ground in the circuit. Isolate the circuit from power and ground. Connect the test light ground clip to a good ground and probe any easy-to-reach test point in the circuit. If the light comes on, there is a short somewhere in the circuit. To isolate the short, probe a test point at either end of the isolated circuit (the light should be on). Leave the test light probe connected and open connectors, switches, remove parts, etc., sequentially, until the light goes out. When the light goes out, the short is between the last circuit component opened and the previous circuit opened.

➡ **The 1.5 volt battery in the test light does not provide much current. A weak battery may not provide enough power to illuminate the test light even when a complete circuit is made (especially if there are high resistances in the circuit). Always make sure that the test battery is strong. To check the battery, briefly touch the ground clip to the probe; if the light glows brightly the battery is strong enough for testing. Never use a self-powered test light to perform checks for opens or shorts when power is applied to the electrical system under test. The 12 volt vehicle power will quickly burn out the 1.5 volt light bulb in the test light.**

Voltmeter

A voltmeter is used to measure voltage at any point in a circuit, or to measure the voltage drop across any part of a circuit. It can also be used to check continuity in a wire or circuit by indicating current flow from one end to the other. Voltmeters usually have various scales on the meter dial and a selector switch to allow the selection of different voltages. The voltmeter has a positive and a negative lead. To avoid damage to the meter, always connect the negative lead to the negative (-) side of circuit (to ground or nearest the ground side of the circuit) and connect the positive lead to the positive (+) side of the circuit (to the power source or the nearest power source). Note that the negative voltmeter lead will always be black and that the positive voltmeter will always be some color other than black (usually red). Depending on how the voltmeter is connected into the circuit, it has several uses.

A voltmeter can be connected either in parallel or in series with a circuit and it has a very high resistance to current flow. When connected in parallel, only a small amount of current will flow through the voltmeter current path; the rest will flow through the normal circuit current path and the circuit will work normally. When the voltmeter is connected in series with a circuit, only a small amount of current can flow through the circuit. The circuit will not work properly, but the voltmeter reading will show if the circuit is complete or not.

Available Voltage Measurement
♦ See Figure 3

Set the voltmeter selector switch to the 20V position and connect the meter negative lead to the negative post of the battery. Connect the positive meter lead to the positive post of the battery and turn the ignition switch ON to provide a load. Read the voltage on the meter or digital display. A well charged battery should register over 12 volts. If the meter reads below 11.5 volts, the battery power may be insufficient to operate the electrical system properly. This test determines voltage available from the battery and should be the first step in any electrical trouble diagnosis procedure. Many electrical problems, especially on computer controlled systems, can be caused by a low state of charge in the battery. Excessive corrosion at the battery cable terminals can cause a poor contact that will prevent proper charging and full battery current flow.

Normal battery voltage is 12 volts when fully charged. When the battery is supplying current to one or more circuits it is said to be 'under load'. When everything is off the electrical system is under a 'no-load' condition. A fully charged battery may show about 12.5 volts at no load; will drop to 12 volts under medium load; and will drop even lower under heavy load. If the battery is partially discharged the voltage decrease under heavy load may be excessive, even though the battery shows 12 volts or more at no load. When allowed to discharge further, the battery's available voltage under load will decrease more severely. For this reason, it is important that the battery be fully charged during all testing procedures to avoid errors in diagnosis and incorrect test results.

Voltage Drop
♦ See Figure 4

When current flows through a resistance, the voltage beyond the resistance is reduced (the larger the current, the greater the reduction in voltage). When no current is flowing, there is no voltage drop because there is no current flow. All points in the circuit which are connected to the power source are at the same voltage as the power source. The total voltage drop always equals the total source voltage. In a long circuit with many connectors, a series of small, unwanted voltage drops due to corrosion at the connectors can add up to a total loss

of voltage which impairs the operation of the normal loads in the circuit.

INDIRECT COMPUTATION OF VOLTAGE DROPS

1. Set the voltmeter selector switch to the 20 volt position.
2. Connect the meter negative lead to a good ground.
3. Probe all resistances in the circuit with the positive meter lead.
4. Operate the circuit in all modes and observe the voltage readings.

DIRECT MEASUREMENT OF VOLTAGE DROPS

1. Set the voltmeter switch to the 20 volt position.
2. Connect the voltmeter negative lead to the ground side of the resistance load to be measured.
3. Connect the positive lead to the positive side of the resistance or load to be measured.
4. Read the voltage drop directly on the 20 volt scale.

Too high a voltage indicates too high a resistance. If, for example, a blower motor runs too slowly, you can determine if there is too high a resistance in the resistor pack. By taking voltage drop readings in all parts of the circuit, you can isolate the problem. Too low a voltage drop indicates too low a resistance. If, for example, a blower motor runs too fast in the MED and/or LOW position, the problem can be isolated in the resistor pack by taking voltage drop readings in all parts of the circuit to locate a possibly shorted resistor. The maximum allowable voltage drop under load is critical, especially if there is more than one high resistance problem in a circuit because all voltage drops are cumulative. A small drop is normal due to the resistance of the conductors.

HIGH RESISTANCE TESTING

1. Set the voltmeter selector switch to the 4 volt position.
2. Connect the voltmeter positive lead to the positive post of the battery.
3. Turn on the headlights and heater blower to provide a load.
4. Probe various points in the circuit with the negative voltmeter lead.
5. Read the voltage drop on the 4 volt scale. Some average maximum allowable voltage drops are:
   FUSE PANEL — 7 volts
   IGNITION SWITCH — 5 volts
   HEADLIGHT SWITCH — 7 volts
   IGNITION COIL (+) — 5 volts
   ANY OTHER LOAD — 1.3 volts

➡**Voltage drops are all measured while a load is operating; without current flow, there will be no voltage drop.**

Ohmmeter
♦ See Figure 5

The ohmmeter is designed to read resistance (ohms) in a circuit or component. Although there are several different styles of ohmmeters, all will usually have a selector switch which permits the measurement of different ranges of resistance (usually the selector switch allows the multiplication of the meter reading by 10, 100, 1,000, and 10,000). A calibration knob allows the meter to be set at zero for accurate measurement. Since all ohmmeters are powered by an internal battery

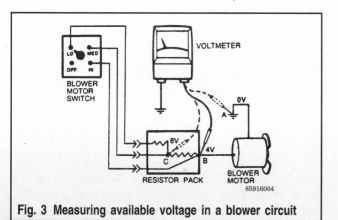

Fig. 3 Measuring available voltage in a blower circuit

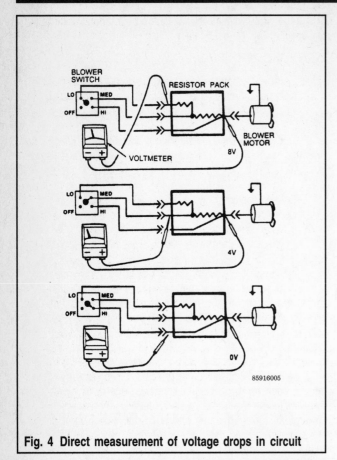

Fig. 4 Direct measurement of voltage drops in circuit

(usually 9 volts), the ohmmeter can be used as a self-powered test light. When the ohmmeter is connected, current from the ohmmeter flows through the circuit or component being tested. Since the ohmmeter's internal resistance and voltage are known values, the amount of current flow through the meter depends on the resistance of the circuit or component being tested.

The ohmmeter can be used to perform continuity test for opens or shorts (either by observation of the meter needle or as a self-powered test light), and to read actual resistance in a circuit. It should be noted that the ohmmeter is used to check the resistance of a component or wire while there is no voltage applied to the circuit. Current flow from an outside voltage source (such as the vehicle battery) can damage the ohmmeter, so the circuit or component should be isolated from the vehicle electrical system before any testing is done. Since the

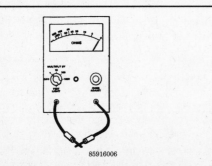

Fig. 5 Analog voltmeters must be calibrated before use by touching the probes together and turning adjusting knobs

ohmmeter uses its own voltage source, either lead can be connected to any test point.

➡**When checking diodes or other solid state components, the ohmmeter leads can only be connected one way in order to measure current flow in a single direction. Make sure the positive (+) and negative (-) terminal connections are as described in the test procedures to verify the one-way diode operation.**

In using the meter for making continuity checks, do not be concerned with the actual resistance readings. Zero resistance, or any resistance readings, indicate continuity in the circuit. Infinite resistance indicates an open in the circuit. A high resistance reading where there should be none indicates a problem in the circuit. Checks for short circuits are made in the same manner as checks for open circuits except that the circuit must be isolated from both power and normal ground. Infinite resistance indicates no continuity to ground, while zero resistance indicates a dead short to ground.

RESISTANCE MEASUREMENT

The batteries in an ohmmeter will weaken with age and temperature, so the ohmmeter must be calibrated or 'zeroed' before taking measurements. To zero the meter, place the selector switch in its lowest range and touch the two ohmmeter leads together. Turn the calibration knob until the meter needle is exactly on zero.

➡**All analog (needle) type ohmmeters must be zeroed before use, but some digital ohmmeter models are automatically calibrated when the switch is turned on. Self-calibrating digital ohmmeters do not have an adjusting knob, but its a good idea to check for a zero readout before use by touching the leads together. All computer controlled systems require the use of a digital ohmmeter with at least 10 megohms impedance for testing. Before any test procedures are attempted, make sure the ohmmeter used is compatible with the electrical system or damage to the on-board computer could result.**

To measure resistance, first isolate the circuit from the vehicle power source by disconnecting the battery cables or the harness connector. Make sure the key is OFF when disconnecting any components or the battery. Where necessary, also isolate at least one side of the circuit to be checked to avoid reading parallel resistances. Parallel circuit resistances will always give a lower reading than the actual resistance of either of the branches. When measuring the resistance of parallel circuits, the total resistance will always be lower than the smallest resistance in the circuit. Connect the meter leads to both sides of the circuit (wire or component) and read the actual measured ohms on the meter scale. Make sure the selector switch is set to the proper ohm scale for the circuit being tested to avoid misreading the ohmmeter test value.

✳✳WARNING

Never use an ohmmeter with power applied to the circuit. Like the self-powered test light, the ohmmeter is designed to operate on its own power supply. The normal 12 volt automotive electrical system current could damage the meter!

Ammeters

▶ **See Figures 6 and 7**

An ammeter measures the amount of current flowing through a circuit in units called amperes or amps. Amperes are units of electron flow which indicate how fast the electrons are flowing through the circuit. Since Ohms Law dictates that current flow in a circuit is equal to the circuit voltage divided by the total circuit resistance, increasing voltage also increases the current level (amps). Likewise, any decrease in resistance will increase the amount of amps in a circuit. At normal operating voltage, most circuits have a characteristic amount of amperes, called 'current draw' which can be measured using an ammeter. By referring to a specified current draw rating, measuring the amperes, and comparing the two values, one can determine what is happening within the circuit to aid in diagnosis. An open circuit, for example, will not allow any current to flow so the ammeter reading will be zero. More current flows through a heavily loaded circuit or when the charging system is operating.

An ammeter is always connected in series with the circuit being tested. All of the current that normally flows through the circuit must also flow through the ammeter; if there is any other path for the current to follow, the ammeter reading will not be accurate. The ammeter itself has very little resistance to current flow and therefore will not affect the circuit, but it will measure current draw only when the circuit is closed and electricity is flowing. Excessive current draw can blow fuses and drain the battery, while a reduced current draw can cause motors to run slowly, lights to dim and other components to

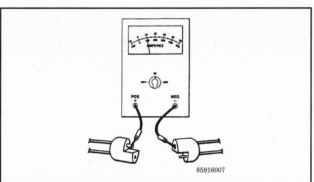

85916007

Fig. 6 An ammeter must be connected in series with the circuit being tested

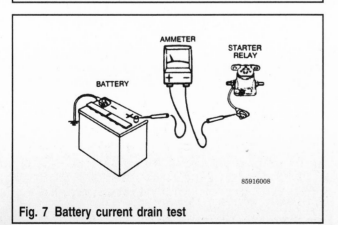

85916008

Fig. 7 Battery current drain test

not operate properly. The ammeter can help diagnose these conditions by locating the cause of the high or low reading.

Multimeters

Different combinations of test meters can be built into a single unit designed for specific tests. Some of the more common combination test devices are known as Volt/Amp testers, Tach/Dwell meters, or Digital Multimeters. The Volt/Amp tester is used for charging system, starting system or battery tests and consists of a voltmeter, an ammeter and a variable resistance carbon pile. The voltmeter will usually have at least two ranges for use with 6, 12 and 24 volt systems. The ammeter also has more than one range for testing various levels of battery loads and starter current draw and the carbon pile can be adjusted to offer different amounts of resistance. The Volt/Amp tester has heavy leads to carry large amounts of current and many later models have an inductive ammeter pickup that clamps around the wire to simplify test connections. On some models, the ammeter also has a zero-center scale to allow testing of charging and starting systems without switching leads or polarity. A digital multimeter is a voltmeter, ammeter and ohmmeter combined in an instrument which gives a digital readout. These are often used when testing solid state circuits because of their high input impedance (usually 10 megohms or more).

The tach/dwell meter combines a tachometer and a dwell (cam angle) meter and is a specialized kind of voltmeter. The tachometer scale is marked to show engine speed in rpm and the dwell scale is marked to show degrees of distributor shaft rotation. In most electronic ignition systems, dwell is determined by the control unit, but the dwell meter can also be used to check the duty cycle (operation) of some electronic engine control systems. Some tach/dwell meters are powered by an internal battery, while others take their power from the car battery in use. The battery powered testers usually require calibration much like an ohmmeter before testing.

Special Test Equipment

A variety of diagnostic tools are available to help troubleshoot and repair computerized engine control systems. The most sophisticated of these devices are the console type engine analyzers that usually occupy a garage service bay, but there are several types of aftermarket electronic testers available that will allow quick circuit tests of the engine control system by plugging directly into a special connector located in the engine compartment or under the dashboard. Several tool and equipment manufacturers offer simple, hand held testers that measure various circuit voltage levels on command to check all system components for proper operation. Although these testers usually cost about $300-500, consider that the average computer control unit (or ECM) can cost just as much and the money saved by not replacing perfectly good sensors or components in an attempt to correct a problem could justify the purchase price of a special diagnostic tester the first time it's used.

These computerized testers can allow quick and easy test measurements while the engine is operating or while the car is being driven. In addition, the on-board computer memory can be read to access any stored trouble codes; in effect allowing the computer to tell you where it hurts and aid trouble diagnosis by pinpointing exactly which circuit or component is malfunctioning. In the same manner, repairs can be tested to make sure the problem has been corrected. The biggest advantage these special testers have is their relatively easy hookups that minimize or eliminate the chances of making the wrong connections and getting false voltage readings or damaging the computer accidentally.

➡ **It should be remembered that these testers check voltage levels in circuits; they don't detect mechanical problems or failed components if the circuit voltage falls within the preprogrammed limits stored in the tester PROM unit. Also, most of the hand held testers are designed to work only on one or two systems made by a specific manufacturer.**

A variety of aftermarket testers are available to help diagnose different computerized control systems. Owatonna Tool Company (OTC), for example, markets a device called the OTC Monitor which plugs directly into the assembly line diagnostic link (ALDL). The OTC tester makes diagnosis a simple matter of pressing the correct buttons and, by changing the internal PROM or inserting a different diagnosis cartridge, it will work on any model from full size to subcompact, over a wide range of years. An adapter is supplied with the tester to allow connection to all types of ALDL links, regardless of the number of pin terminals used. By inserting an updated PROM into the OTC tester, it can be easily updated to diagnose any new modifications of computerized control systems.

Wiring Harnesses

The average automobile contains about ½ mile of wiring, with hundreds of individual connections. To protect the many wires from damage and to keep them from becoming a confusing tangle, they are organized into bundles, enclosed in plastic or taped together and called wire harnesses. Different wiring harnesses serve different parts of the vehicle. Individual wires are color coded to help trace them through a harness where sections are hidden from view.

A loose or corroded connection or a replacement wire that is too small for the circuit will add extra resistance and an additional voltage drop to the circuit. A ten percent voltage drop can result in slow or erratic motor operation, for example, even though the circuit is complete. Automotive wiring or circuit conductors can be in any one of three forms:

1. Single strand wire
2. Multistrand wire
3. Printed circuitry

Single strand wire has a solid metal core and is usually used inside such components as alternators, motors, relays and other devices. Multistrand wire has a core made of many small strands of wire twisted together into a single conductor. Most of the wiring in an automotive electrical system is made up of multistrand wire, either as a single conductor or grouped together in a harness. All wiring is color coded on the insulator, either as a solid color or as a colored wire with an identification stripe. A printed circuit is a thin film of copper or other conductor that is printed on an insulator backing. Occasionally, a printed circuit is sandwiched between two sheets of plastic for more protection and flexibility. A complete printed circuit,

consisting of conductors, insulating material and connectors for lamps or other components is called a printed circuit board. Printed circuitry is used in place of individual wires or harnesses in places where space is limited, such as behind instrument panels.

WIRE GAUGE

Since computer controlled automotive electrical systems are very sensitive to changes in resistance, the selection of properly sized wires is critical when systems are repaired. The wire gauge number is an expression of the cross section area of the conductor. The most common system for expressing wire size is the American Wire Gauge (AWG) system.

Wire cross section area is measured in circular mils. A mil is 1/1000″ (0.001″); a circular mil is the area of a circle one mil in diameter. For example, a conductor ¼″ in diameter is 0.250″ or 250 mils. The circular mil cross section area of the wire is 250 squared (250″)or 62,500 circular mils. Imported car models usually use metric wire gauge designations, which is simply the cross section area of the conductor in square millimeters.

Gauge numbers are assigned to conductors of various cross section areas. As gauge number increases, area decreases and the conductor becomes smaller. A 5 gauge conductor is smaller than a 1 gauge conductor and a 10 gauge is smaller than a 5 gauge. As the cross section area of a conductor decreases, resistance increases and so does the gauge number. A conductor with a higher gauge number will carry less current than a conductor with a lower gauge number.

➡ **Gauge wire size refers to the size of the conductor, not the size of the complete wire. It is possible to have two wires of the same gauge with different diameters because one may have thicker insulation than the other.**

12 volt automotive electrical systems generally use 10, 12, 14, 16 and 18 gauge wire. Main power distribution circuits and larger accessories usually use 10 and 12 gauge wire. Battery cables are usually 4 or 6 gauge, although 1 and 2 gauge wires are occasionally used. Wire length must also be considered when making repairs to a circuit. As conductor length increases, so does resistance. An 18 gauge wire, for example, can carry a 10 amp load for 10 feet without excessive voltage drop; however if a 15 foot wire is required for the same 10 amp load, it must be a 16 gauge wire.

An electrical schematic shows the electrical current paths when a circuit is operating properly. It is essential to understand how a circuit works before trying to figure out why it doesn't. Schematics break the entire electrical system down into individual circuits and show only one particular circuit. In a schematic, no attempt is made to represent wiring and components as they physically appear on the vehicle; switches and other components are shown as simply as possible. Face views of harness connectors show the cavity or terminal locations in all multi-pin connectors to help locate test points.

If you need to backprobe a connector while it is on the component, the order of the terminals must be mentally reversed. The wire color code can help in this situation, as well as a keyway, lock tab or other reference mark.

WIRING REPAIR

Soldering is a quick, efficient method of joining metals permanently. Everyone who has the occasion to make wiring repairs should know how to solder. Electrical connections that are soldered are far less likely to come apart and will conduct electricity much better than connections that are only 'pigtailed' together. The most popular (and preferred) method of soldering is with an electrical soldering gun. Soldering irons are available in many sizes and wattage ratings. Irons with higher wattage ratings deliver higher temperatures and recover lost heat faster. A small soldering iron rated for no more than 50 watts is recommended, especially on electrical systems where excess heat can damage the components being soldered.

There are three ingredients necessary for successful soldering; proper flux, good solder and sufficient heat. A soldering flux is necessary to clean the metal of tarnish, prepare it for soldering and to enable the solder to spread into tiny crevices. When soldering, always use a resin flux or resin core solder which is non-corrosive and will not attract moisture once the job is finished. Other types of flux (acid core) will leave a residue that will attract moisture and cause the wires to corrode. Tin is a unique metal with a low melting point. In a molten state, it dissolves and alloys easily with many metals. Solder is made by mixing tin with lead. The most common proportions are 40/60, 50/50 and 60/40, with the percentage of tin listed first. Low priced solders usually contain less tin, making them very difficult for a beginner to use because more heat is required to melt the solder. A common solder is 40/60 which is well suited for all-around general use, but 60/40 melts easier, has more tin for a better joint and is preferred for electrical work.

Soldering Techniques

Successful soldering requires that the metals to be joined be heated to a temperature that will melt the solder — usually 360-460°F (182-238°C). Contrary to popular belief, the purpose of the soldering iron is not to melt the solder itself, but to heat the parts being soldered to a temperature high enough to melt the solder when it is touched to the work. Melting flux-cored solder on the soldering iron will usually destroy the effectiveness of the flux.

➡**Soldering tips are made of copper for good heat conductivity, but must be 'tinned' regularly for quick transference of heat to the project and to prevent the solder from sticking to the iron. To 'tin' the iron, simply heat it and touch the flux-cored solder to the tip; the solder will flow over the hot tip. Wipe the excess off with a clean rag, but be careful as the iron will be hot.**

After some use, the tip may become pitted. If so, simply dress the tip smooth with a smooth file and 'tin' the tip again. An old saying holds that 'metals well cleaned are half soldered.' Flux-cored solder will remove oxides but rust, bits of insulation and oil or grease must be removed with a wire brush or emery cloth. For maximum strength in soldered parts, the joint must start off clean and tight. Weak joints will result in gaps too wide for the solder to bridge.

If a separate soldering flux is used, it should be brushed or swabbed on only those areas that are to be soldered. Most solders contain a core of flux and separate fluxing is unnecessary. Hold the work to be soldered firmly. It is best to solder on a wooden board, because a metal vise will only rob the piece to be soldered of heat and make it difficult to melt the solder. Hold the soldering tip with the broadest face against the work to be soldered. Apply solder under the tip close to the work, using enough solder to give a heavy film between the iron and the piece being soldered, while moving slowly and making sure the solder melts properly. Keep the work level or the solder will run to the lowest part and favor the thicker parts, because these require more heat to melt the solder. If the soldering tip overheats (the solder coating on the face of the tip burns up), it should be retinned. Once the soldering is completed, let the soldered joint stand until cool. Tape and seal all soldered wire splices after the repair has cooled.

Wire Harness and Connectors
▶ See Figures 8 and 9

The on-board computer (ECM) wire harness electrically connects the control unit to the various solenoids, switches and sensors used by the control system. Most connectors in the engine compartment or otherwise exposed to the elements are protected against moisture and dirt which could create oxidation and deposits on the terminals. This protection is important because of the very low voltage and current levels used by the computer and sensors. All connectors have a lock which secures the male and female terminals together, with a secondary lock holding the seal and terminal into the connector. Both terminal locks must be released when disconnecting ECM connectors.

These special connectors are weather-proof and all repairs require the use of a special terminal and the tool required to service it. This tool is used to remove the pin and sleeve terminals. If removal is attempted with an ordinary pick, there is a good chance that the terminal will be bent or deformed. Unlike standard blade type terminals, these terminals cannot be straightened once they are bent. Make certain that the connectors are properly seated and all of the sealing rings in place when connecting leads. On some models, a hinge-type flap provides a backup or secondary locking feature for the terminals. Most secondary locks are used to improve the connector reliability by retaining the terminals if the small terminal lock tangs are not positioned properly.

Molded-on connectors require complete replacement of the connection. This means splicing a new connector assembly into the harness. All splices in on-board computer systems should be soldered to insure proper contact. Use care when probing the connections or replacing terminals in them as it is possible to short between opposite terminals. If this happens to the wrong terminal pair, it is possible to damage certain components. Always use jumper wires between connectors for circuit checking and never probe through weatherproof seals.

Open circuits are often difficult to locate by sight because corrosion or terminal misalignment are hidden by the connectors. Merely wiggling a connector on a sensor or in the wiring harness may correct the open circuit condition. This should always be considered when an open circuit or a failed sensor is indicated. Intermittent problems may also be caused by oxidized or loose connections. When using a circuit tester for

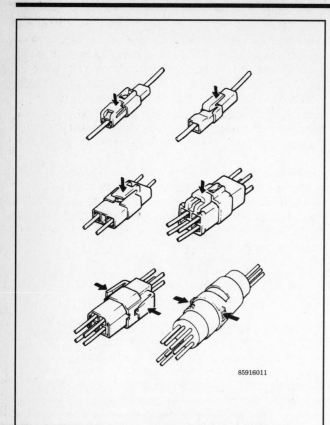

85916011

Fig. 8 Various types of locking harness connectors-depress locks at the arrows to separate connectors

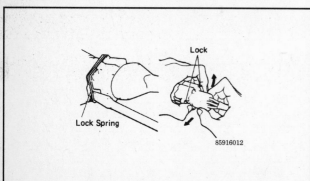

Lock

Lock Spring

85916012

Fig. 9 Some connectors use a lock spring instead of the molded locking tabs

diagnosis, always probe connections from the wire side. Be careful not to damage sealed connectors with test probes.

All wiring harnesses should be replaced with identical parts, using the same gauge wire and connectors. When signal wires are spliced into a harness, use wire with high temperature insulation only. With the low voltage and current levels found in the system, it is important that the best possible connection at all wire splices be made by soldering the splices together. It is seldom necessary to replace a complete harness. If replacement is necessary, pay close attention to insure proper harness routing. Secure the harness with suitable plastic wire clamps to prevent vibrations from causing the harness to wear in spots or contact any hot components.

➡**Weatherproof connectors cannot be replaced with standard connectors. Instructions are provided with replacement connector and terminal packages. Some wire harnesses have mounting indicators (usually pieces of colored tape) to mark where the harness is to be secured.**

In making wiring repairs, it's important that you always replace damaged wires with wires that are the same gauge as the wire being replaced. The heavier the wire, the smaller the gauge number. Wires are color-coded to aid in identification and whenever possible the same color coded wire should be used for replacement. A wire stripping and crimping tool is necessary to install solderless terminal connectors. Test all crimps by pulling on the wires; it should not be possible to pull the wires out of a good crimp.

Wires which are open, exposed or otherwise damaged are repaired by simple splicing. Where possible, if the wiring harness is accessible and the damaged place in the wire can be located, it is best to open the harness and check for all possible damage. In an inaccessible harness, the wire must be bypassed with a new insert, usually taped to the outside of the old harness.

When replacing fusible links, be sure to use fusible link wire, NOT ordinary automotive wire. Make sure the fusible segment is of the same gauge and construction as the one being replaced and double the stripped end when crimping the terminal connector for a good contact. The melted (open) fusible link segment of the wiring harness should be cut off as close to the harness as possible, then a new segment spliced in as described. In the case of a damaged fusible link that feeds two harness wires, the harness connections should be replaced with two fusible link wires so that each circuit will have its own separate protection.

➡**Most of the problems caused in the wiring harness are due to bad ground connections. Always check all vehicle ground connections for corrosion or looseness before performing any power feed checks to eliminate the chance of a bad ground affecting the circuit.**

Repairing Hard Shell Connectors

Unlike molded connectors, the terminal contacts in hard shell connectors can be replaced. Weatherproof hard-shell connectors with the leads molded into the shell have non-replaceable terminal ends. Replacement usually involves the use of a special terminal removal tool that depress the locking tangs (barbs) on the connector terminal and allow the connector to be removed from the rear of the shell. The connector shell should be replaced if it shows any evidence of burning, melting, cracks, or breaks. Replace individual terminals that are burnt, corroded, distorted or loose.

➡**The insulation crimp must be tight to prevent the insulation from sliding back on the wire when the wire is pulled. The insulation must be visibly compressed under the crimp tabs, and the ends of the crimp should be turned in for a firm grip on the insulation.**

The wire crimp must be made with all wire strands inside the crimp. The terminal must be fully compressed on the wire strands with the ends of the crimp tabs turned in to make a firm grip on the wire. Check all connections with an ohmmeter to insure a good contact. There should be no measurable resistance between the wire and the terminal when connected.

Mechanical Test Equipment

VACUUM GAUGE

Most gauges are graduated in inches of mercury (in. Hg), although a device called a manometer reads vacuum in inches of water (in. H2O). The normal vacuum reading usually varies between 18 and 22 in. Hg at sea level. To test engine vacuum, the vacuum gauge must be connected to a source of manifold vacuum. Many engines have a plug in the intake manifold which can be removed and replaced with an adapter fitting. Connect the vacuum gauge to the fitting with a suitable rubber hose or, if no manifold plug is available, connect the vacuum gauge to any device using manifold vacuum, such as EGR valves, etc. The vacuum gauge can be used to determine if enough vacuum is reaching a component to allow its actuation.

HAND VACUUM PUMP

▶ **See Figure 10**

Small, hand-held vacuum pumps come in a variety of designs. Most have a built-in vacuum gauge and allow the com-

ponent to be tested without removing it from the vehicle. Operate the pump lever or plunger to apply the correct amount of vacuum required for the test specified in the diagnosis routines. The level of vacuum in inches of Mercury (in. Hg) is indicated on the pump gauge. For some testing, an additional vacuum gauge may be necessary.

Intake manifold vacuum is used to operate various systems and devices on late model vehicles. To correctly diagnose and solve problems in vacuum control systems, a vacuum source is necessary for testing. In some cases, vacuum can be taken from the intake manifold when the engine is running, but vacuum is normally provided by a hand vacuum pump. These hand vacuum pumps have a built-in vacuum gauge that allow testing while the device is still attached to the component. For some tests, an additional vacuum gauge may be necessary.

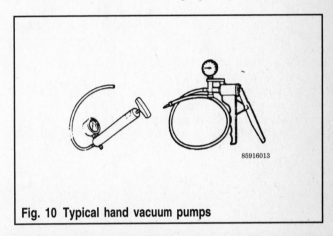

85916013

Fig. 10 Typical hand vacuum pumps

HEATING AND AIR CONDITIONING

Blower Motor

REMOVAL & INSTALLATION

All Models

1. Disconnect the negative battery cable. Remove the glove box assembly.
2. Pry the retainer clip out of each end of the heater duct and compress and remove the duct.
3. Remove the 3 blower mounting bolts, then turn the blower over on its right side and let it rest on the floor.
4. Disconnect the control cable and the harness connectors. Remove the blower motor.
5. Install in the reverse of removal. Make sure both ends of the heater duct fit over the blower and heater flanges all the the way around.

Heater Assembly

REMOVAL & INSTALLATION

▶ **See Figures 11, 12, 13, 14, 15, 16, 17, 18, 19 and 20**

Civic (1973-79)

➡**This procedure does not apply to vehicles equipped with air conditioning. On vehicles equipped with air conditioning, removal may differ from the procedures listed below. Only a trained air conditioning specialist should disassemble air conditioning equipped units. Air conditioning units contain pressurized freon which can be extremely dangerous (e.g. frostbite burns and/or blindness) to the untrained.**

1. Drain the radiator.

✳✳CAUTION

When draining the coolant, keep in mind that cats and dogs are attracted by the ethylene glycol antifreeze, and are quite likely to drink any that is left in an uncovered container or in puddles on the ground. This will prove fatal in sufficient quantity. Always drain the coolant into a sealable container. Coolant should be reused unless it is contaminated or several years old.

2. Disconnect the right and left defroster hoses.
3. Disconnect the inlet and outlet water hoses at the heater assembly.

➡There will be a coolant leakage when disconnecting the hoses. Catch the coolant in a container to prevent damage to the interior.

4. Disconnect the following items:
   a. Fre/Rec control cable.
   b. Temperature control rod.
   c. Room/Def. control cable.
   d. Fan motor switch connector.
   e. Upper attaching bolts.
   f. Lower attaching bolts.
   g. Lower bracket.
5. Remove the heater assembly through the passenger side.
   To install:
6. Install the heater assembly by reversing the removal procedure. Pay attention to the following points:
   a. When installing the heater assembly, do not forget to connect the motor ground wire to the right side of the upper bracket.
   b. Connect the inlet and outlet water hoses SECURELY.

➡The inlet hose is a straight type, and the outlet hose is an L-type.

   c. Install the defroster nozzles in the correct position.
   d. Connect the control cables securely. Operate the control valve and lever to check for proper operation.
   e. Be sure to bleed the cooling system (see Section 1).

Fig. 11 Typical view of blower motor assembly

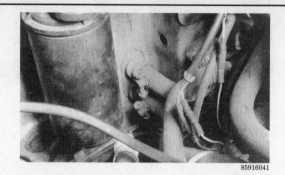
Fig. 12 View of heater hoses-note heater hose clamp positioning

Fig. 13 Removing the heater hoses

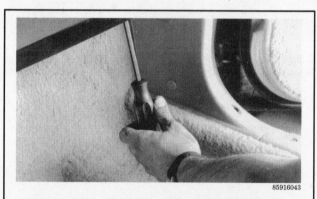
Fig. 14 Removing the lower trim panel retaining screws

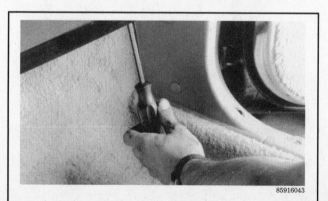
Fig. 15 Removing the lower trim panel

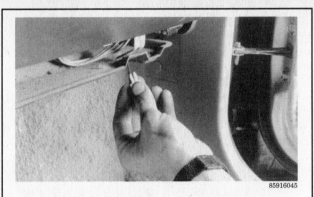

Fig. 16 Removing the cover panel retaining clips

Fig. 17 Removing the cover panel

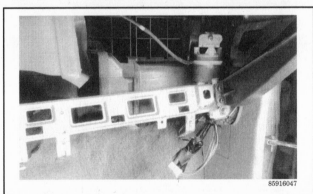

Fig. 18 View of the heater ducts

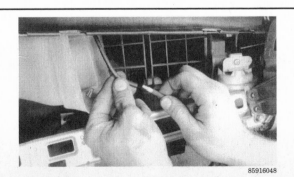

Fig. 19 Mark and disconnect all vacuum hoses for the heater assembly

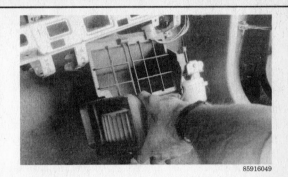

Fig. 20 Removing the blower motor assembly for the heater assembly

Civic (1980-83)

➡This procedure does not apply to vehicles equipped with air conditioning. On vehicles equipped with air conditioning, removal may differ from the procedures listed below. Only a trained air conditioning specialist should disassemble air conditioning equipped units. Air conditioning units contain pressurized freon which can be extremely dangerous (e.g. frostbite burns and/or blindness) to the untrained.

1. Drain the radiator.

✳✳CAUTION

When draining the coolant, keep in mind that cats and dogs are attracted by the ethylene glycol antifreeze, and are quite likely to drink any that is left in an uncovered container or in puddles on the ground. This will prove fatal in sufficient quantity. Always drain the coolant into a sealable container. Coolant should be reused unless it is contaminated or several years old.

2. Remove the dashboard.
3. Disconnect both heater hoses at the firewall and drain the coolant into a container.
4. Remove the heater lower mounting nut on the firewall.
5. Remove the two heater duct retaining clips.
6. Disconnect the control cables from the heater.
7. Remove the heater valve cable cover. Remove the heater assembly.
   To install:
8. Reverse the removal procedures. Bleed cooling system and make sure cables are properly adjusted. Apply a sealant to the grommets and make sure inlet and outlet hoses are connected to the right connections and are secure.

Accord (1976-83)
▶ See Figure 21

➡This procedure does not apply to vehicles equipped with air conditioning. On vehicles equipped with air conditioning, removal may differ from the procedures listed below. Only a trained air conditioning specialist should disassemble air conditioning equipped units. Air conditioning units contain pressurized freon which can be extremely dangerous (e.g. frostbite burns and/or blindness) to the untrained.

1. The heater blower assembly can be removed by disconnecting the battery cable, removing the glove box, the fresh air control cable, and the three bolts that hold the blower.

2. Drain the radiator. Remove the heater hose connections.

✴✴CAUTION

When draining the coolant, keep in mind that cats and dogs are attracted by the ethylene glycol antifreeze, and are quite likely to drink any that is left in an uncovered container or in puddles on the ground. This will prove fatal in sufficient quantity. Always drain the coolant into a sealable container. Coolant should be reused unless it is contaminated or several years old.

3. Remove the instrument panel.

4. Once the instrument panel is removed, remove the heater assembly mounting bolts.

5. Remove the control cables from their clips. Remove all necessary hoses. Remove the heater assembly.

6. Remove the left and right upper bolts for heater assembly.

7. Remove the lower bolts from the heater assembly and remove the heater core.

To install:

8. Reverse the removal procedures. Keep the following points in mind:

   a. Don't interchange the inlet and outlet water hoses.

   b. Make sure all the cables operate correctly.

   c. Bleed the air from the cooling system (see Section 1).

Prelude 1979-82

➡This procedure does not apply to vehicles equipped with air conditioning. On vehicles equipped with air conditioning, removal may differ from the procedures listed below. Only a trained air conditioning specialist should disassemble air conditioning equipped units. Air conditioning units contain pressurized freon which can be extremely dangerous (e.g. frostbite burns and/or blindness) to the untrained.

1. Disconnect the negative battery cable.

2. Remove the glove box.

3. Remove the blower-to-heater case bolts and the blower.

4. Drain the coolant.

✴✴CAUTION

When draining the coolant, keep in mind that cats and dogs are attracted by the ethylene glycol antifreeze, and are quite likely to drink any that is left in an uncovered container or in puddles on the ground. This will prove fatal in sufficient quantity. Always drain the coolant into a sealable container. Coolant should be reused unless it is contaminated or several years old.

5. Remove the lower dash panel.

6. Place a drain pan under the case and disconnect both heater hoses from the core tubes.

7. Remove the lower heater-to-firewall nut.

8. Disconnect the cable at the water valve.

9. Remove the control cables from the heater case.

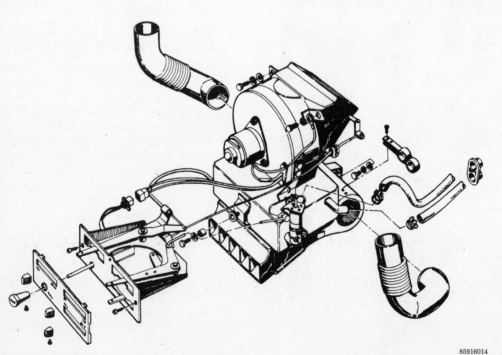

85916014

Fig. 21 Typical heater assembly

10. Remove the upper heater mount bolts and the heater assembly.

To install:

11. Reverse the removal procedures. Keep the following points in mind:

    a. Don't interchange the inlet and outlet water hoses.

    b. Make sure all the cables operate correctly.

    c. Bleed the air from the cooling system (see Section 1).

➡**Only the Prelude (1983) model may have the heater core replaced without removing the heater assembly. On all other models remove the heater assembly then remove the heater core from the heater assembly.**

Prelude (1983)

1. Drain the cooling system. Remove the heater pipe cover and heater pipe clamps.

❊❊CAUTION

When draining the coolant, keep in mind that cats and dogs are attracted by the ethylene glycol antifreeze, and are quite likely to drink any that is left in an uncovered container or in puddles on the ground. This will prove fatal in sufficient quantity. Always drain the coolant into a sealable container. Coolant should be reused unless it is contaminated or several years old.

2. Remove the heater core retaining plate.

3. Pull the cotter pin out of the hose clamp joint and separate the heater pipes.

➡**Engine coolant will drain from the heater pipes when they are disconnected. Place a drip pan under the pipes to catch the coolant.**

4. When all the coolant has drained from the heater core, remove it from the heater housing.

To install:

5. Reverse the removal procedures noting the following points:

    a. Replace the hose clamps with new ones.

    b. Turn the cotter pin in the hose clamps tightly to prevent leaking coolant.

    c. Refill the cooling system with coolant and open the bleed bolt until coolant begins to flow from it. Tighten the bolt when all the air has escaped from the system.

Heater Core

REMOVAL & INSTALLATION

➡**Only the 1983 Prelude model may have the heater core replaced without removing the heater assembly. On all other models, remove the heater assembly (refer to the necessary service procedures) then disassemble the heater box and remove the heater core. Install the heater core in the the heater box (seal heater box with a gasket or sealant before installation) and then install the heater box assembly in the vehicle. Check the system for proper operation.**

1983 Prelude

1. Disconnect the negative battery cable. Drain the cooling system. Remove the heater pipe cover and heater pipe clamps.

❊❊CAUTION

When draining the coolant, keep in mind that cats and dogs are attracted by the ethylene glycol antifreeze, and are quite likely to drink any that is left in an uncovered container or in puddles on the ground. This will prove fatal in sufficient quantity. Always drain the coolant into a sealable container. Coolant should be reused unless it is contaminated or several years old.

2. Remove the heater core retaining plate.

3. Pull the cotter pin out of the hose clamp joint and separate the heater pipes.

➡**Engine coolant will drain from the heater pipes when they are disconnected. Place a drip pan under the pipes to catch the coolant.**

4. When all the coolant has drained from the heater core, remove it from the heater housing.

5. Installation is the reverse of the removal procedure, please note the following:

    a. Replace the hose clamps with new ones.

    b. Turn the cotter pin in the hose clamps tightly to prevent leaking coolant.

    c. Fill the cooling system with coolant and open the bleed bolt until coolant begins to flow from it. Tighten the bolt when all the air has escaped from the system.

AIR CONDITIONER

Compressor

REMOVAL & INSTALLATION

For service procedures refer to Section 3

Condenser

REMOVAL & INSTALLATION

For service procedures refer to Section 3

RADIO

✳✳WARNING

Never operate the radio without a speaker; severe damage to the output transistors will result. If the speaker must be replaced, use a speaker of the correct impedance (ohms) or else the output transistors will be damaged and require replacement.

Radio Assembly

REMOVAL & INSTALLATION

Civic

1. Disconnect the negative battery cable. From under the dash, remove the rear radio bracket-to-back tray screw. Remove the radio-to-bracket wing nut and the bracket.
2. Remove the control knobs, hex nuts and trim plate from the radio control shafts.
3. Disconnect the antenna and speaker leads, the bullet type radio fuse and the white lead connected directly over the radio opening.

4. Drop the radio out, bottom first, through the package tray.
5. To install, reverse the removal procedures. Check radio for proper operation.

➡When inserting the radio through the package tray, be sure the bottom side is up and the control shafts are facing toward the engine. Otherwise, you will not be able to position the radio properly through its opening in the dash.

Accord And Prelude

1. Disconnect the negative battery cable. Remove the center lower lid screws and the lid.
2. From under the lid, remove the radio mounting screws.
3. Remove the radio knobs and the faceplate.
4. Remove the heater fan switch knob and the heater lever knobs.
5. Remove the heater control bezel and the center panel. To do this, remove the three center panel screws and the ash tray. Slide the panel to the left to remove it. Disconnect the cigarette lighter leads.
6. Remove the radio electrical leads and the radio.
7. To install, reverse the removal procedures. Check radio for proper operation.

WINDSHIELD WIPERS

Windshield Wiper Motor

REMOVAL & INSTALLATION

◗ **See Figures 22, 23, 24, 25, 26, 27, 28 and 29**

All Models

The wiper motor is connected to the engine compartment wall, below the front windshield.
1. Remove the negative (-) terminal from the battery.
2. Disconnect the motor leads from the connector.

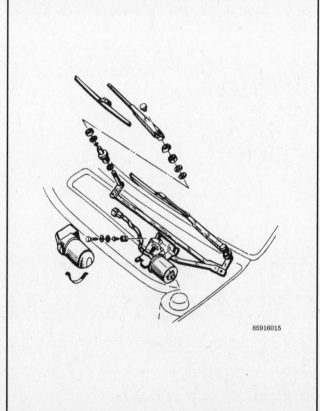

85916015

Fig. 22 Windshield wiper motor and linkage

Fig. 23 Removing the wiper motor cover

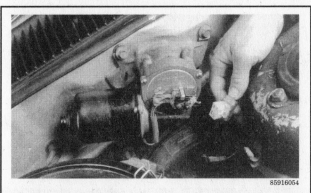

Fig. 24 Removing the wiper motor electrical connection

Fig. 25 Removing the wiper motor retaining bolts

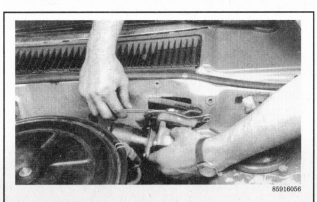

Fig. 26 Removing the wiper motor crank arm

Fig. 27 Removing the wiper arm hold down nut

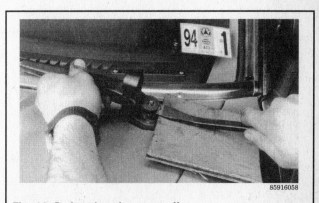

Fig. 28 Prying the wiper arm off

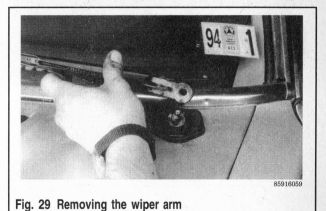

Fig. 29 Removing the wiper arm

3. Remove the motor water seal cover clamp and the seal from the motor.

4. Remove the wiper arm-to-pivot shaft nuts and the arms.

5. Remove the pivot nuts from both sides and push the pivots downward.

6. Remove the wiper motor mounting bolts and the wiper/linkage assembly from the engine compartment.

7. Pull out the motor arm cotter pin and separate the linkage from the motor.

8. Remove the motor bracket bolts and the motor.

To install:

9. Reverse the removal procedures. Be sure to inspect the linkage and pivots for wear and looseness. When installing the motor, be sure it is in the **automatic stop** position.

10. Check system for proper operation.

INSTRUMENTS AND SWITCHES

Instrument Cluster

REMOVAL & INSTALLATION

Meter Case Assembly

1. Disconnect the negative battery cable. From the rear of the instrument panel, remove the meter case mounting wing nuts.
2. Disconnect the speedometer and tachometer drive cables from the engine.
3. Pull the meter case away from the panel. Disconnect the meter wires from the connectors.

➡**Be sure to label the wires to avoid confusion during reassembly.**

4. Disconnect the speedometer and tachometer cables from the meter case and remove the case from the vehicle.
5. To install, reverse the removal procedures.

Switch Panel
▶ **See Figures 30 and 31**

1. Disconnect the negative battery cable. Loosen the steering wheel column cover screws, then, remove the upper and lower covers.

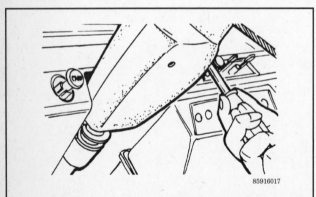

Fig. 30 Removing the steering column cover

2. Remove the steering column bolts (remove the upper bolts 1st) and rest the steering assembly on the floor.
3. From the rear of the instrument panel, remove the switch panel screws.
4. To release the switch panel, remove the switches in the following manner:
    a. Remove the light switch by prying the cover off the front of the knob. Pinch the retaining tabs and pull off the knob.
    b. Remove the wiper switch by pushing the knob in and turning counterclockwise, then, remove the retaining nut.
    c. Remove the choke knob by loosening the set screw, then, remove the retaining nut.
5. To install, reverse the removal procedures. Check all systems for proper operation.

Windshield Wiper Switch

REMOVAL & INSTALLATION

1. Disconnect the negative battery cable. Mark and remove the steering wheel.
2. Disconnect the column wiring harness and coupler.

✳✳CAUTION

Be careful not to damage the steering column or shaft.

3. Remove the upper and lower column covers.
4. On models so equipped, remove the cruise control slip ring.
5. Remove the turn signal canceling sleeve.
6. On later models, remove the switch retaining screws, then remove the switch.
7. Loosen the screw on the turn signal switch cam nut and lightly tap its head to permit the cam nut to loosen. Then remove the turn signal switch assembly and the steering shaft upper bushing.
  To install:
8. Assemble and install by reversing the above procedure. When installing the turn signal switch assembly, engage the locating tab on the switch with the notch in the steering col-

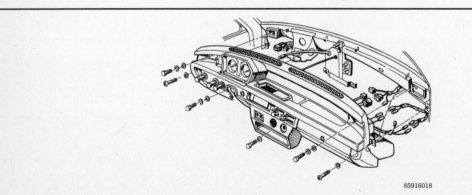

Fig. 31 Instrument panel removal

umn. The steering shaft upper bushing should be installed with the flat side facing the upper side of the column. The alignment notch for the turn signal switch will be centered on the flat side of the bushing.

➡ **On earlier models, if the cam nut has been removed, be sure to install it with the small end up.**

Headlight Switch

REMOVAL & INSTALLATION

1. Disconnect the negative battery cable. Mark and remove the steering wheel.
2. Disconnect the column wiring harness and coupler.

✳✳CAUTION

Be careful not to damage the steering column or shaft.

3. Remove the upper and lower column covers.
4. On models so equipped, remove the cruise control slip ring.
5. Remove the turn signal canceling sleeve.
6. On later models, remove the switch retaining screws, then remove the switch.
7. Loosen the screw on the turn signal switch cam nut and lightly tap its head to permit the cam nut to loosen. Then remove the turn signal switch assembly and the steering shaft upper bushing.
   To install:
8. Assemble and install, reversing the above procedure. When installing the turn signal switch assembly, engage the locating tab on the switch with the notch in the steering column. The steering shaft upper bushing should be installed with the flat side facing the upper side of the column. The alignment notch for the turn signal switch will be centered on the flat side of the bushing.

➡ **On earlier models, if the cam nut has been removed, be sure to install it with the small end up.**

Rear Window Defogger System

The rear window defogger system consists of a rear window with 2 vertical bus bars and a series of electrically connected grid lines baked on the inside surface. A control switch and a relay are also used in this system.

➡ **Since the grid lines can be damaged or scraped off with sharp instruments, caution should be used when cleaning the glass or removing foreign materials, decals or stickers. Normal glass cleaning solvents or hot water used with rags or toweling is recommended.**

REMOVAL & INSTALLATION

Rear Window Defogger Switch

ACCORD

1. Disconnect the negative battery cable. Remove the combination meter housing.
2. Pull out the combination meter housing far enough to gain access to the rear defroster switch retaining screws.
3. Disconnect the switch electrical connector. Remove the switch retaining screws and remove the switch from the rear of the meter housing.
4. Installation is the reverse order of the removal procedure. Check system for proper operation.

CIVIC

1. Disconnect the negative battery cable and remove the lower dashboard panel.
2. Disconnect the wire harness from behind the console. Depress the switch locking pawls and remove the switch from the front of the dash panel.
3. Installation is the reverse order of the removal procedure. Check system for proper operation.

PRELUDE

1. Disconnect the negative battery cable. Lower the steering column and remove the lower dashboard panel.
2. Remove the 4 instrument panel retaining screws. Pull the instrument panel out and disconnect the wire connectors.
3. Remove the instrument panel. Remove the rear defroster switch retaining screws and pull the switch out of the instrument panel.
4. Installation is the reverse order of the removal procedure. Check system for proper operation.

COMPONENT TESTING

Rear Defroster Relay
▶ **See Figure 32**

1. Check for continuity between top left A terminal and the bottom left B terminal, when applying battery voltage to upper right C terminal and grounding the lower right D terminals.
2. Once the voltage is removed from the C and D terminals, there should be no continuity in the relay. If the relay fails this test, replace it. The relays are located under the dash on the left side.

Rear Window Defogger Grid
▶ **See Figure 33**

1. Turn **ON** the rear window defroster switch. Connect the positive lead of a voltmeter to the center of each filament and connect the negative lead to the body of the vehicle.
2. The standard voltage at the center of the filament is 6 volts. If the meter is higher than 6 volts, the problem exists in the ground side of the filament.
3. If the meter indication is low or 0, the problem is between the center and the power side. Isolate the problem grid line and mark the break in the grid wire.

CRUISE CONTROL SYSTEM

The cruise control system maintains the vehicle speed at a setting selected by the driver by mean of mechanical, electrical, and vacuum operated devices.

The cruise control unit receives command signals from the cruise control main switch and the cruise control set/resume switch. The control unit also receives information about operating conditions from the brake switch, the distributor, speed sensor, the clutch switch (with manual transaxle), or the shift lever position switch (with automatic transaxle). The cruise control unit, in turn, sends operational signals to the devices that regulate the throttle position. The throttle position maintains the selected vehicle speed. The cruise control compares the actual speed of the vehicle to the selected speed. Then, the control unit uses the result of that comparison to open or close the throttle.

The control unit will disengage the instant the driver depresses the brake pedal. The brake switch sends an electronic signal to the control unit when the brake pedal is depressed; the control unit responds by allowing the throttle to close. The shift lever position switch (automatic transaxle) or the clutch switch (manual transaxle) sends a disengage signal input to the control unit that also allows the throttle to close.

➡**The use of the speed control is not recommended when driving conditions do not permit maintaining a constant speed, such as in heavy traffic or on roads that are winding, icy, snow covered or slippery.**

SYSTEM OPERATION

The cruise control system will set and automatically maintain any speed above 30 mph (45 kph). To set the system, make sure that the main switch is in the **ON** position. After reaching the desired speed, press the set switch. The cruise control unit will receive a set signal input and, in turn, will actuate the cruise control actuator. When the set switch is depressed and the cruise control system is on, the cruise control on indicator on the warning display will light up.

To cancel the cruise control system, press the main switch to **OFF**. This removes power to the control unit and erases the set speed from memory. If the system is disengaged temporarily by the brake switch, clutch switch, or gear selector switch and vehicle speed is still above 30 mph, press the resume switch. With the resume switch depressed and the set memory retained, the vehicle automatically returns to the previous set speed.

For a gradual acceleration without depressing the accelerator pedal, push the resume switch down and hold it there until the desired speed is reached. This will send an acceleration signal input to the control unit. When the switch is released, the system will be reprogrammed for the new speed. To slow the vehicle down, depress the set switch. This will send a deceleration signal input to the control unit causing the vehicle to coast until the desired speed is reached. When the desired speed is reached, release the set switch. This will reprogram the system for the new speed.

ADJUSTMENT

Actuator Cable
▶ See Figure 34

1. Check that actuator cable operates smoothly with no binding or sticking.
2. Start engine.
3. Measure amount of movement of actuator rod until cable pulls on accelerator lever (engine speed starts to increase). Free-play should be 11mm ± 1.5mm.
4. If free play is not within specifications, loosen locknut and turn adjusting nut as required.

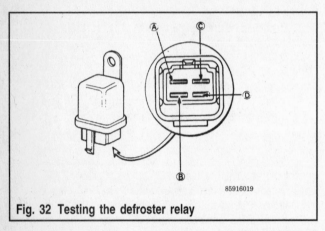

Fig. 32 Testing the defroster relay

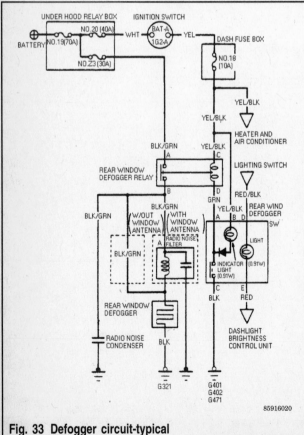

Fig. 33 Defogger circuit-typical

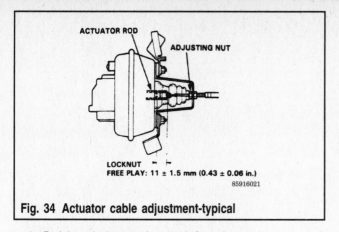

Fig. 34 Actuator cable adjustment-typical

5. Retighten locknut and recheck free-play.
6. Test car under drive to make sure that overshoot and undershoot are held within ± 2 mph of set speed.

➡**If necessary, check throttle cable free-play, then recheck actuator rod free-play.**

REMOVAL AND REPLACEMENT

Main Switch

▶ **See Figure 35**

1. Remove fuse panel door.
2. Push out switch from behind dashboard panel.
3. Disconnect electrical connector from switch.
4. To install, reverse removal procedure.

Set/Resume Switch

▶ **See Figure 36**

1. Remove steering wheel.
2. Separate horn cover and body cover by removing 4 screws.
3. Remove 3 screws and set/resume switch from steering wheel.
4. To install, reverse removal procedure.

Slip Ring

▶ **See Figure 37**

1. Remove steering wheel.

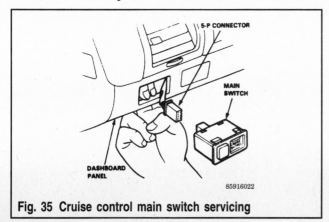

Fig. 35 Cruise control main switch servicing

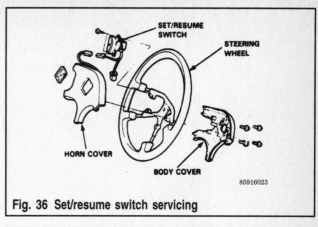

Fig. 36 Set/resume switch servicing

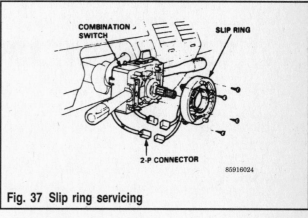

Fig. 37 Slip ring servicing

2. Remove upper and lower steering column covers.
3. Remove 4 screws and remove slip ring assembly.
4. To install, reverse removal procedure.

Actuator/Cable

▶ **See Figures 38 and 39**

1. Pull back boot and loosen locknut, then disconnect cable from bracket.
2. Disconnect cable end from actuator rod.
3. Disconnect 4 pin connector.
4. Pull ventilation hose from grommet.
5. Disconnect vacuum hose from check valve.
6. Remove 2 mount bolts and actuator with bracket.
7. If necessary, disconnect cable end from linkage over accelerator pedal.

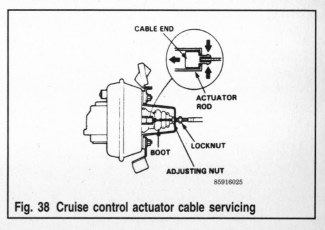

Fig. 38 Cruise control actuator cable servicing

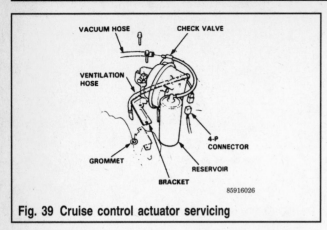

Fig. 39 Cruise control actuator servicing

8. To install, reverse removal procedure and adjust free-play at actuator rod after connecting cable.

Diagnosis and Testing

COMPONENT TESTING

Slip Ring

1. Remove column cover, then disconnect 3 pin connector.
2. Check continuity between connector terminal with blue/red wire and terminal **A**.
3. Check continuity between connector terminal with light green/red and terminal **B**.
4. Check continuity between connector terminal with light green/black and terminal **C**.
5. Replace slip ring assembly if 1 or more do not have continuity.

Actuator Solenoid

▶ See Figure 40

1. Disconnect 4 pin connector from actuator solenoid.
2. Connect ohmmeter between connector terminal with brown/white wire and brown/black wire (vacuum solenoid) and measure resistance. Resistance should be 30-50Ω.

➡**Resistance will vary slightly with temperature. Resistance values given are at 70°F (21°C).**

3. Connect ohmmeter between connector terminal with brown/white wire and brown wire (vent solenoid) and measure resistance. Resistance should be 40-60Ω.
4. Connect ohmmeter between connector terminal with brown/white wire and black wire (safety solenoid) and measure resistance. Resistance should be 40-60Ω.
5. If any resistance values are not as specified, check/replace actuator solenoid.

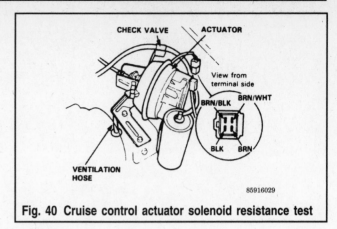

Fig. 40 Cruise control actuator solenoid resistance test

Actuator

▶ See Figures 41, 42, 43, 44 and 45

1. Disconnect actuator cable from actuator rod.
2. Disconnect 4 pin connector.
3. Connect battery positive wire to brown/white terminal and negative to brown/black, brown and black terminals.
4. Connect a vacuum pump to check valve. Then apply vacuum to actuator.
5. Actuator rod should pull in completely. If rod pulls in only part way or not at all for a leaking vacuum line or defective solenoid.
6. With voltage and vacuum still applied, try to pull actuator rod out by hand. Actuator rod should not pull out. If it does, replace actuator.
7. Disconnect battery negative wire from brown terminal. Actuator rod should return. If it does not return and ventilation hose and filter are free, replace actuator.
8. Repeat Steps 3-7, but disconnect battery negative wire from black terminal. Actuator rod should return. If not and ventilation hose and filter are free, replace solenoid valve assembly.

➡**If solenoid valve assembly is replaced, be sure to use new O-rings at each solenoid.**

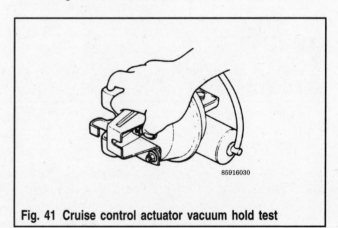

Fig. 41 Cruise control actuator vacuum hold test

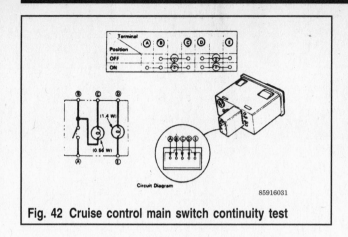

Fig. 42 Cruise control main switch continuity test

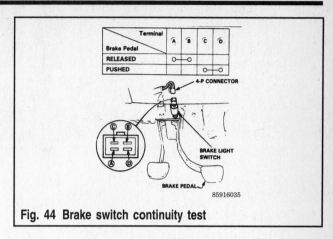

Fig. 44 Brake switch continuity test

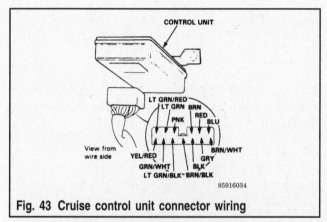

Fig. 43 Cruise control unit connector wiring

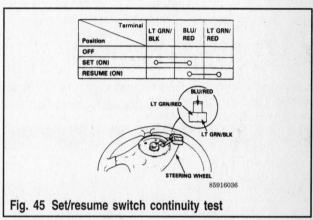

Fig. 45 Set/resume switch continuity test

LIGHTING

Headlights

REMOVAL & INSTALLATION

◆ See Figure 46

1. If equipped with retractable headlights, turn the retractor switch **ON**. If equipped with a garnish panel, remove it by removing the screws and slide it upward. Remove the retaining ring screws and the ring. DO NOT touch the headlight adjustment screws.

2. While holding the connector plug by the rear of the bulb, pull the headlight out of the housing; it may be necessary to work the bulb back and forth a few times to break it loose from the connector.

3. Insert the replacement bulb into the connector, then, install the retaining ring and screws.

TRAILER WIRING

Wiring the car for towing is fairly easy. There are a number of good wiring kits available and these should be used, rather than trying to design your own. All trailers will need brake lights and turn signals as well as tail lights and side marker lights. Most states require extra marker lights for overly wide trailers. Also, most states have recently required back-up lights for trailers, and most trailer manufacturers have been building trailers with back-up lights for several years.

Additionally, some Class I, most Class II and just about all Class III trailers will have electric brakes.

Add to this number an accessories wire, to operate trailer internal equipment or to charge the trailer's battery, and you can have as many as seven wires in the harness.

Determine the equipment on your trailer and buy the wiring kit necessary. The kit will contain all the wires needed, plus a plug adapter set which included the female plug, mounted on the bumper or hitch, and the male plug, wired into, or plugged into the trailer harness.

When installing the kit, follow the manufacturer's instructions. The color coding of the wires is standard throughout the industry.

One point to note: some domestic vehicles, and most imported vehicles, have separate turn signals. On most domestic vehicles, the brake lights and rear turn signals operate with the same bulb. For those vehicles with separate turn signals, you can purchase an isolation unit so that the brake lights won't blink whenever the turn signals are operated, or, you can go to your local electronics supply house and buy four diodes to wire in series with the brake and turn signal bulbs. Diodes will isolate the brake and turn signals. The choice is yours. The

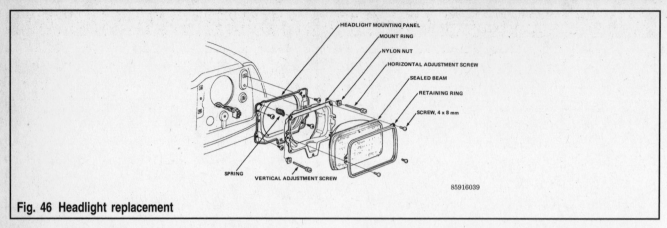

Fig. 46 Headlight replacement

isolation units are simple and quick to install, but far more expensive than the diodes. The diodes, however, require more work to install properly, since they require the cutting of each bulb's wire and soldering in place of the diode.

One final point, the best kits are those with a spring loaded cover on the vehicle mounted socket. This cover prevents dirt and moisture from corroding the terminals. Never let the vehicle socket hang loosely; always mount it securely to the bumper or hitch.

CIRCUIT PROTECTION

Fuses

LOCATIONS

▶ **See Figures 47 and 48**

The fuse box is located below the glove compartment, on the right bulkhead on Civic models. The Accord and Prelude are equipped with a fuse tray which swings down from the instrument panel (left side below steering wheel). Some vehicles also are equipped with junction/relay box which contains various relays or circuit breakers, located near the main fuse box. Most fuse boxes contain 8 fuses, some of which are rated at 10 amps and others at 15 amps. The rating and function of each fuse is posted inside the fuse box cap for quick reference.

REMOVAL & INSTALLATION

Fuses can be replaced or removed simply by pulling them out of their retaining clips. Since each fuse protects more than one circuit, detection of a fuse blowout is an easy task of elimination.

➡The turn signal relay and hazzard flasher relay are located in a junction/relay panel under the dash area on the left side near kick panel area, on all models. To replace the relay just pull it out from fuse panel/relay box. To install just push-in the fuse panel/relay box.

Fig. 47 Remove the cover on the emission box located under hood

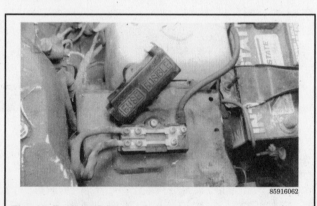

Fig. 48 Fusible link near battery

WIRING DIAGRAMS

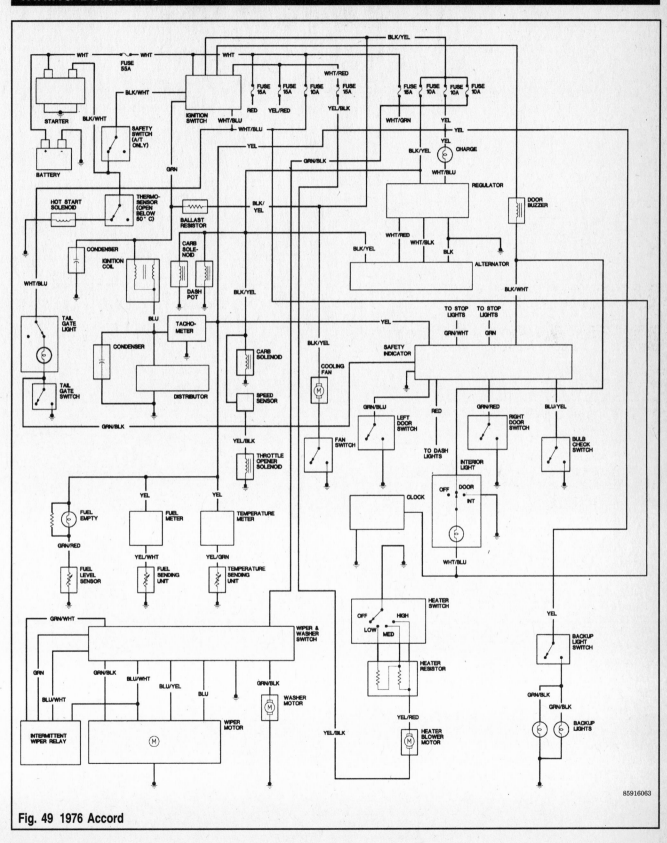

Fig. 49 1976 Accord

85916063

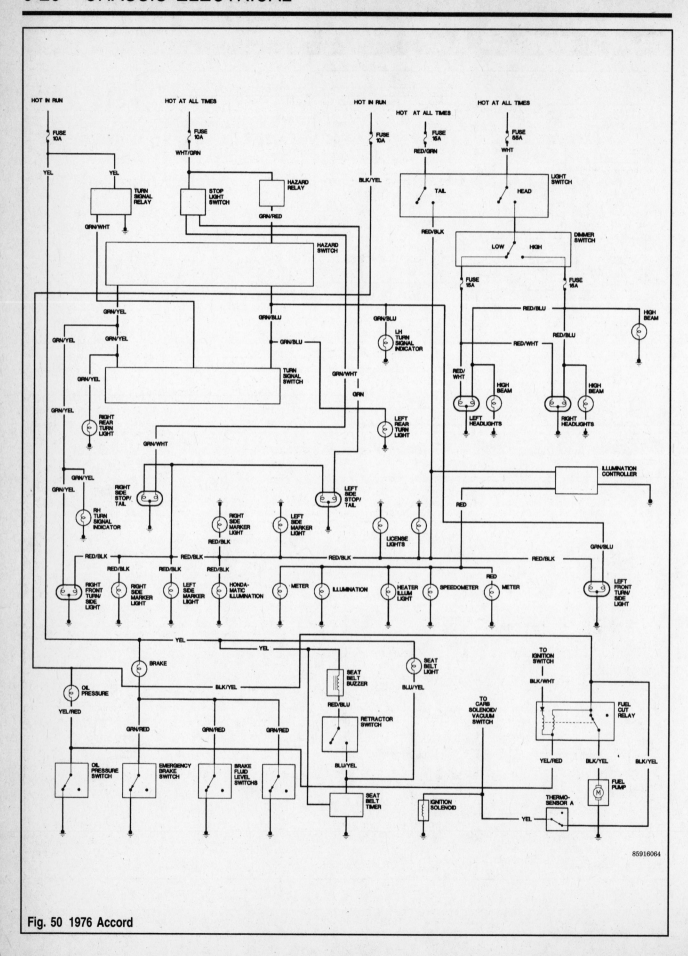

Fig. 50 1976 Accord

85916064

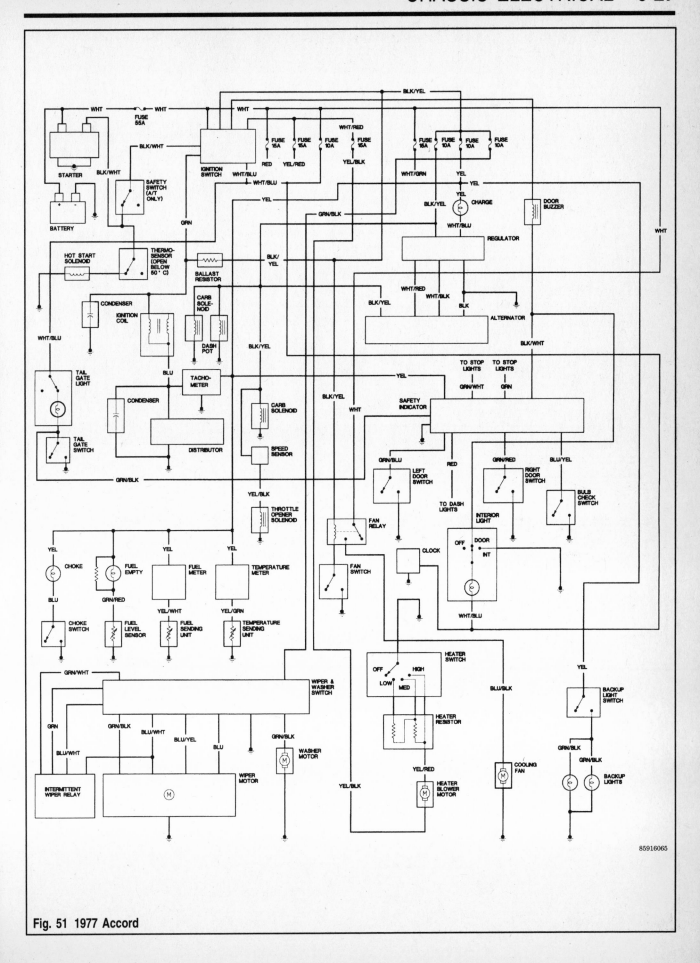

Fig. 51 1977 Accord

85916065

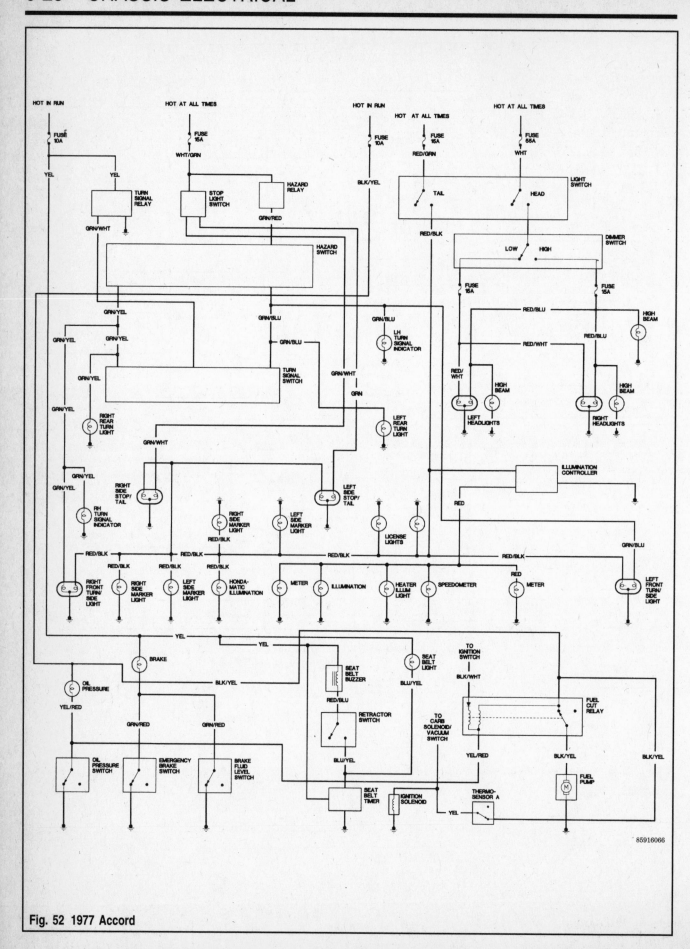

Fig. 52 1977 Accord

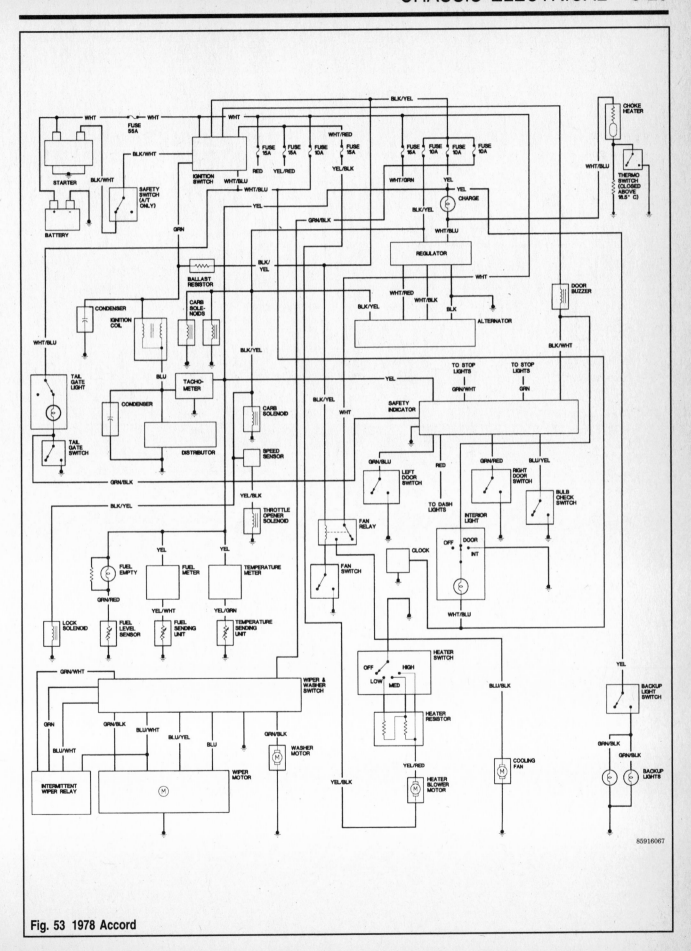

Fig. 53 1978 Accord

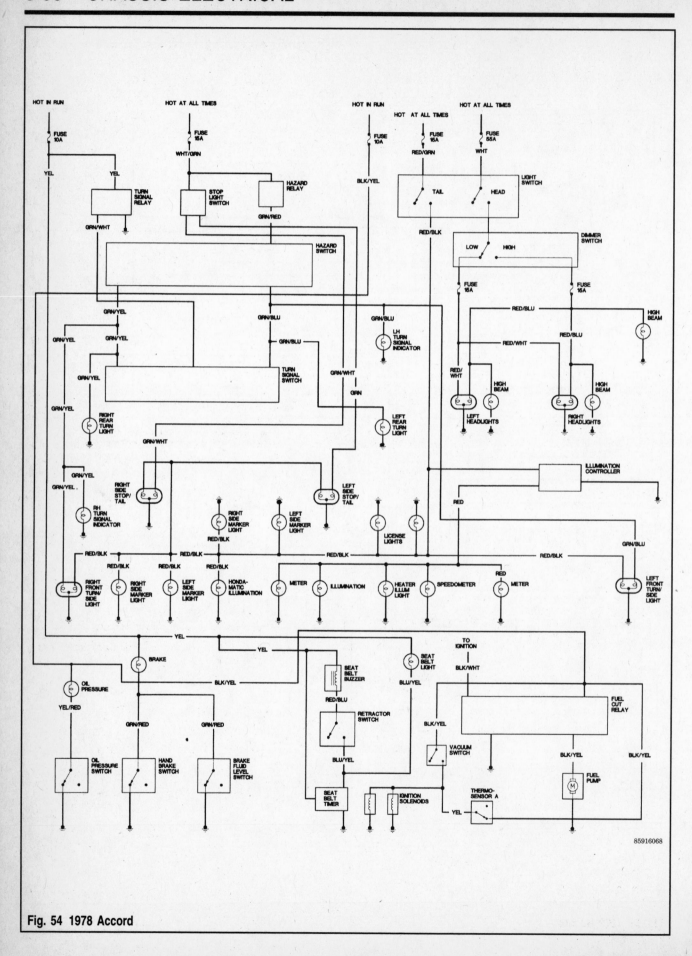

Fig. 54 1978 Accord

85916068

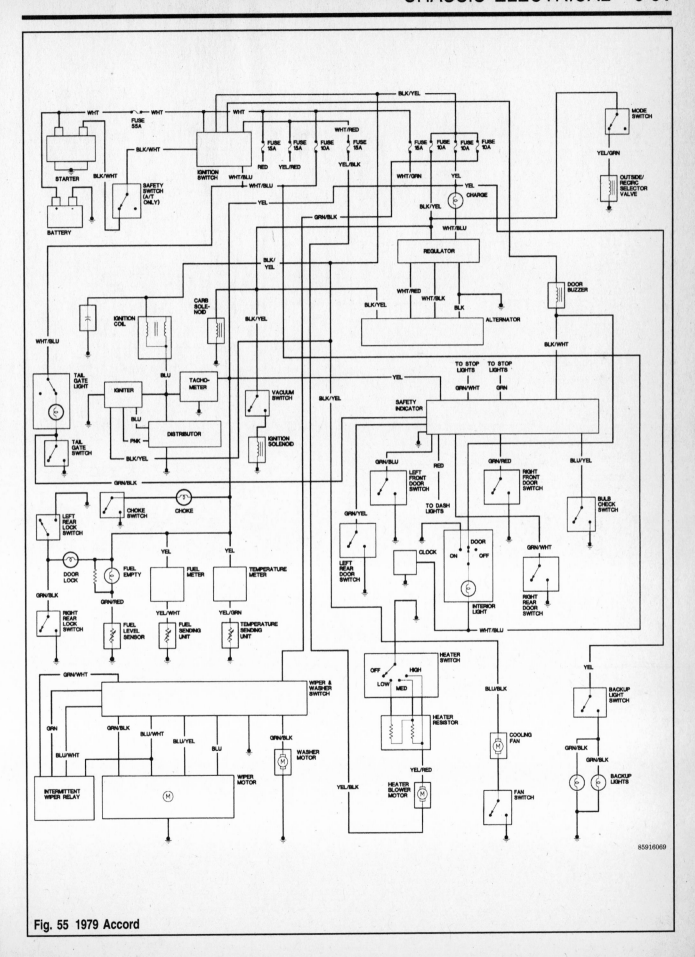

Fig. 55 1979 Accord

85916069

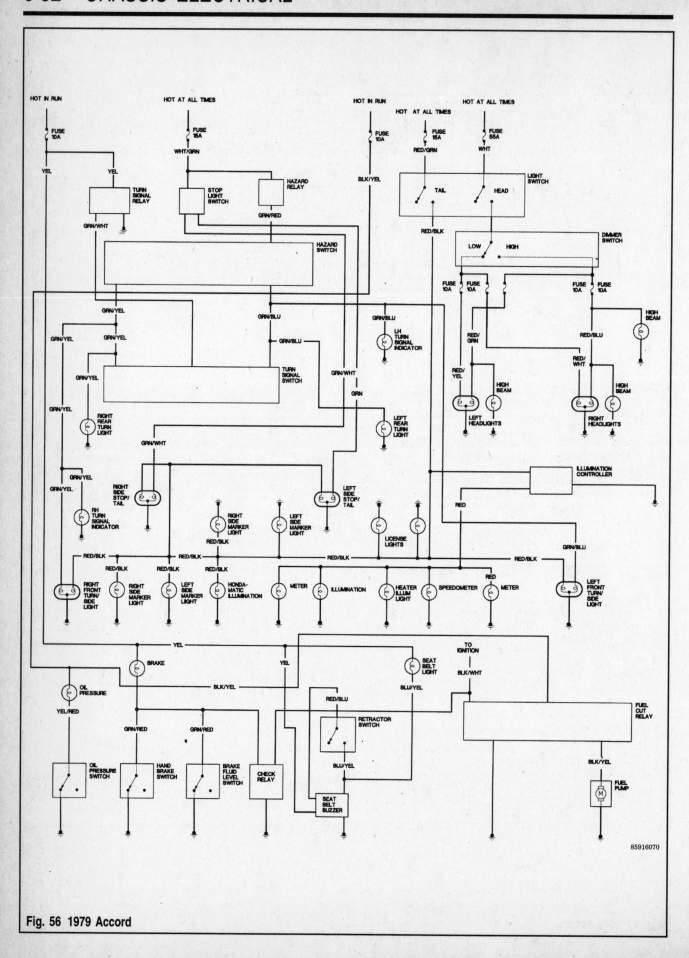

Fig. 56 1979 Accord

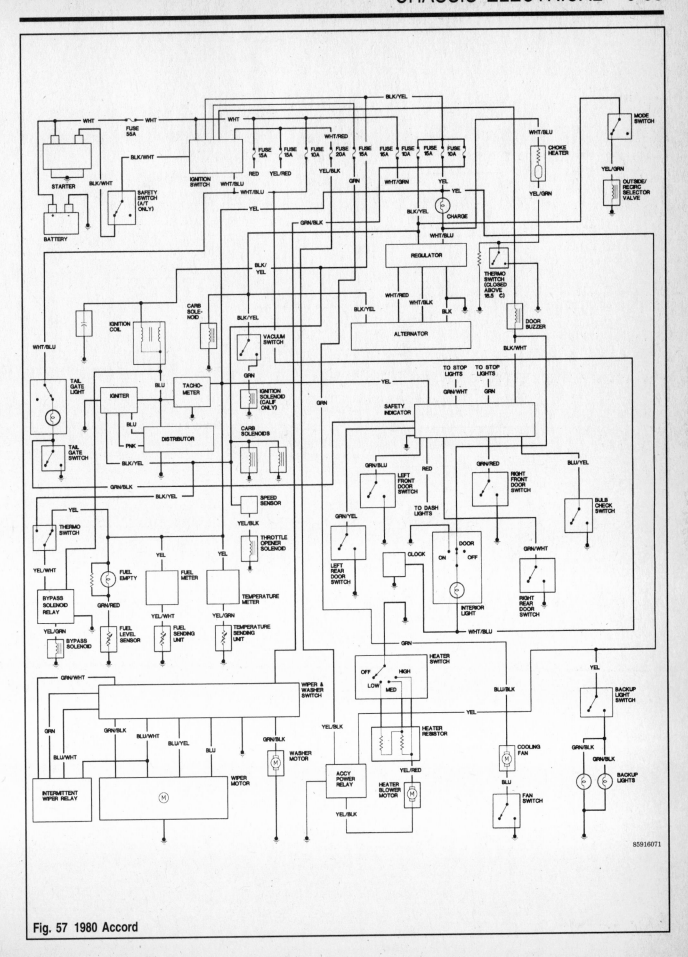

Fig. 57 1980 Accord

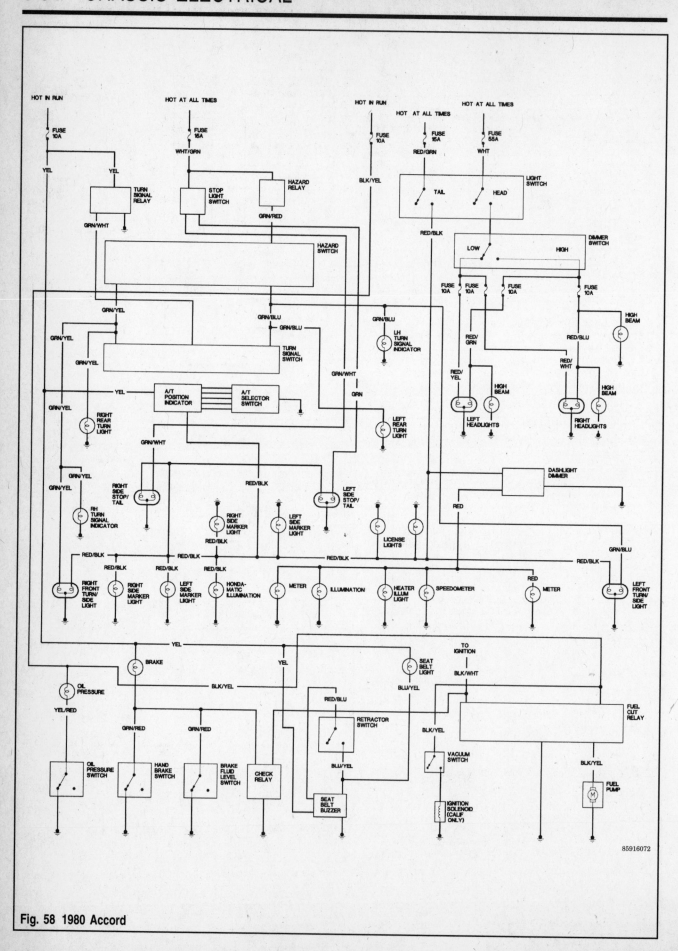

Fig. 58 1980 Accord

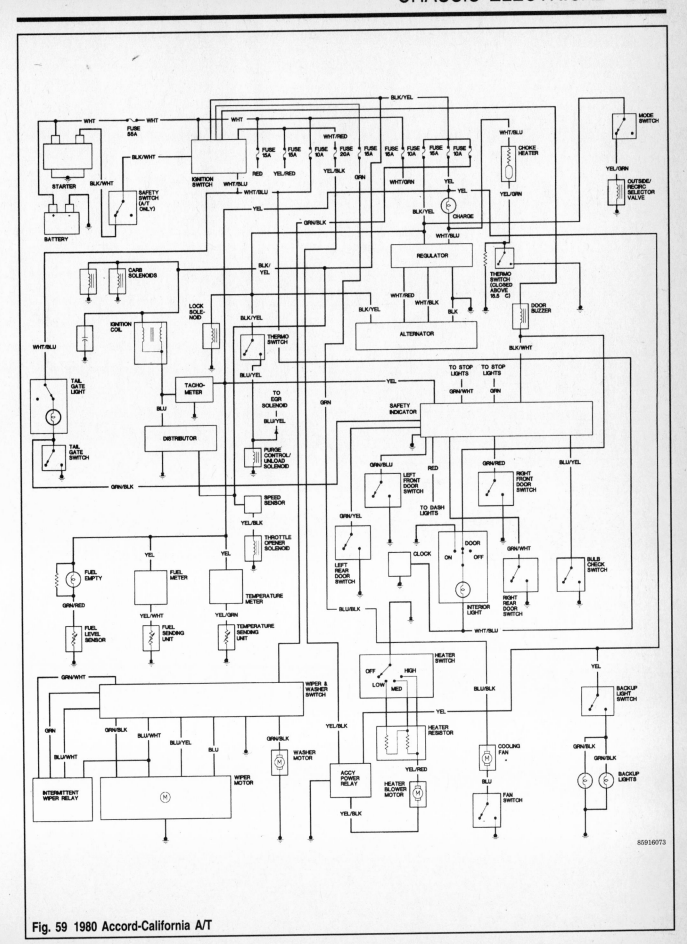

Fig. 59 1980 Accord-California A/T

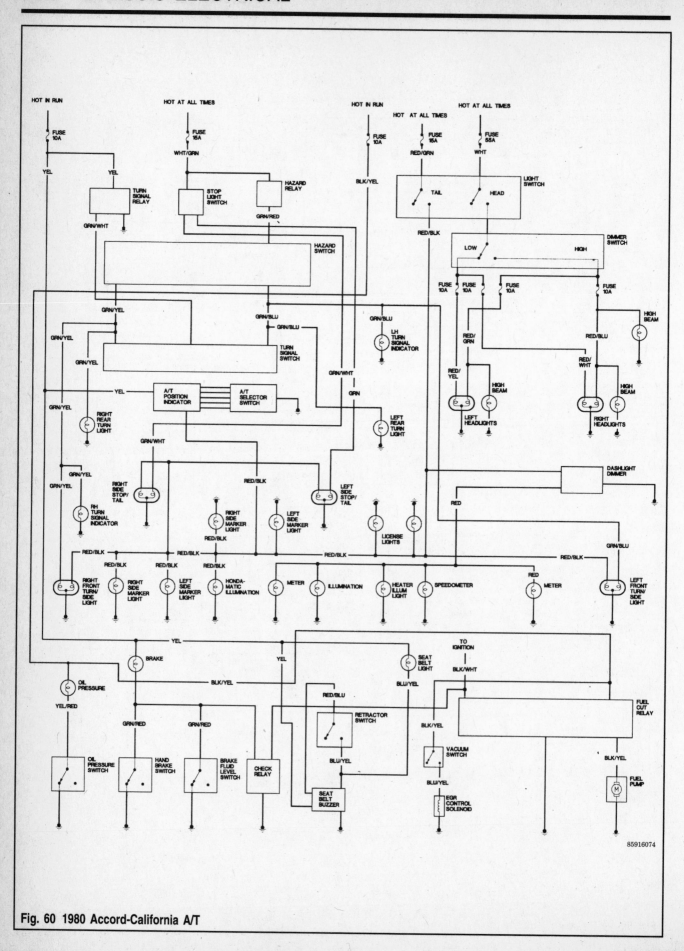

Fig. 60 1980 Accord-California A/T

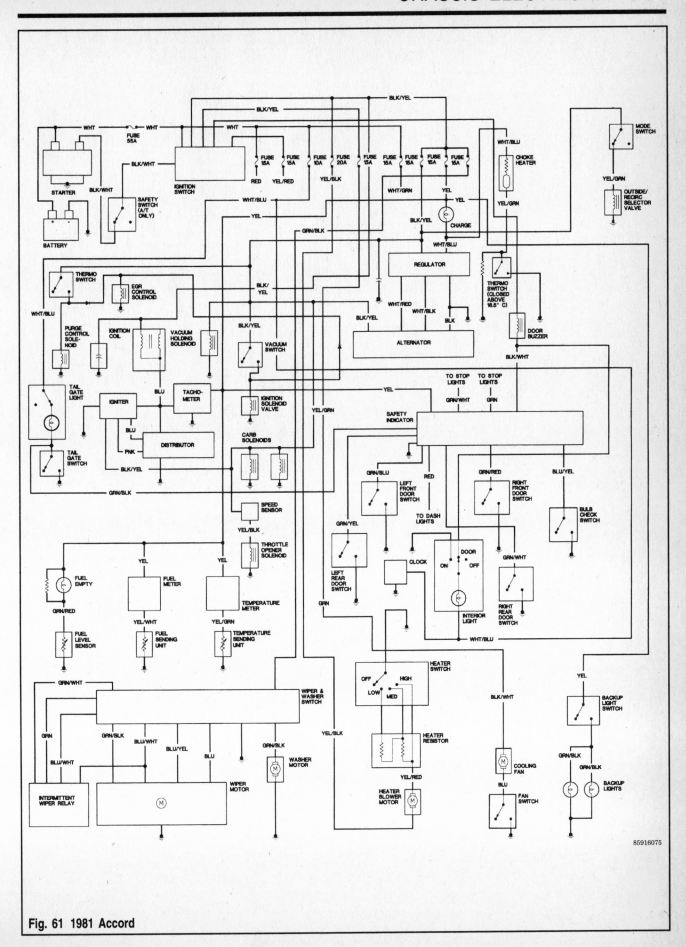

Fig. 61 1981 Accord

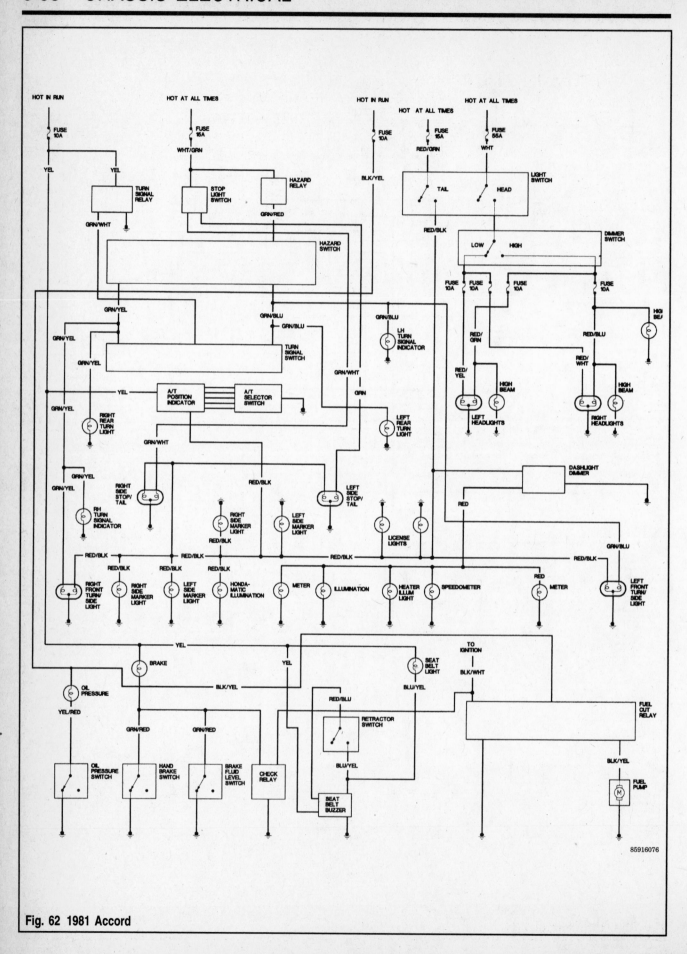

Fig. 62 1981 Accord

85916076

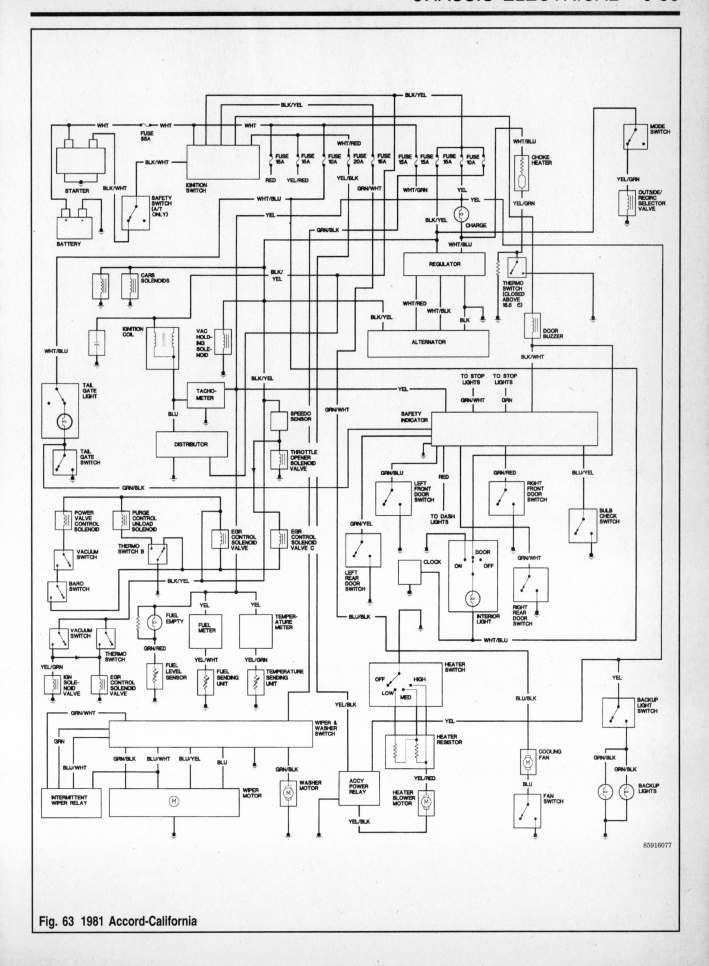

Fig. 63 1981 Accord-California

85916077

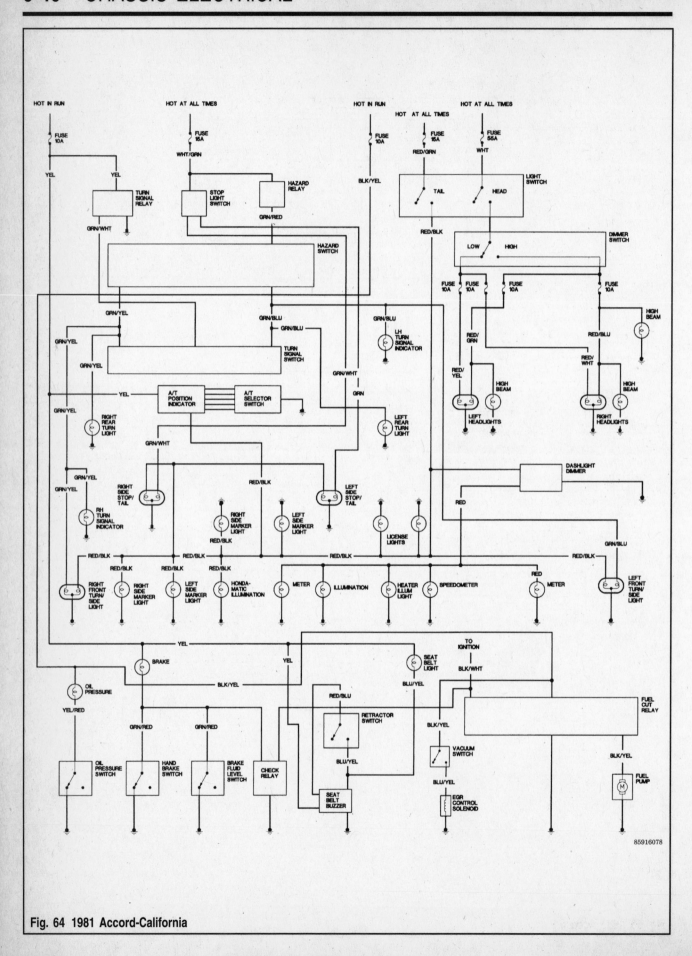

Fig. 64 1981 Accord-California

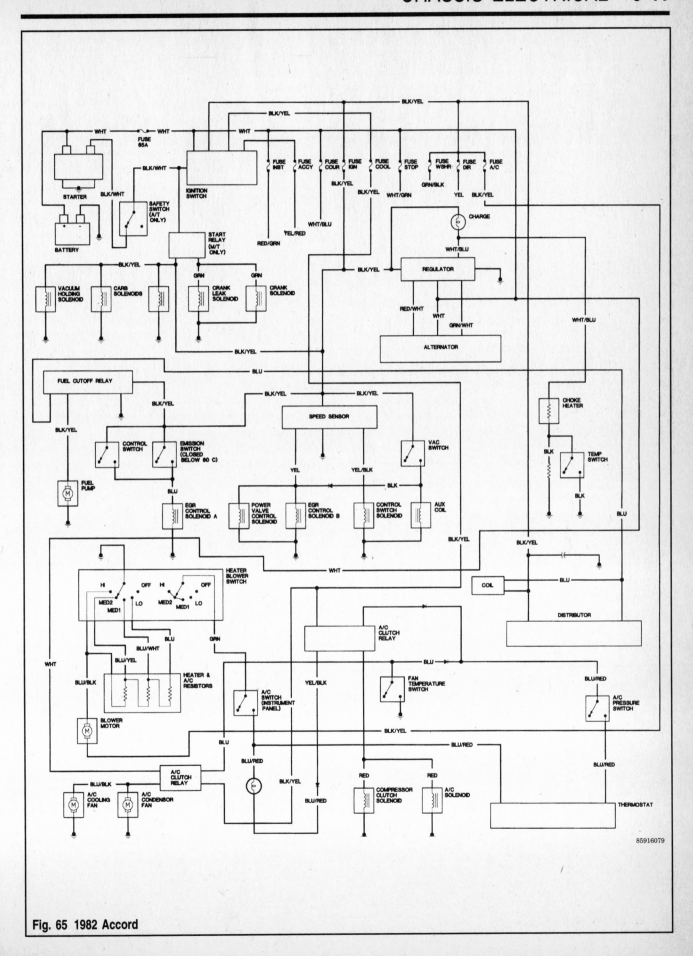

Fig. 65 1982 Accord

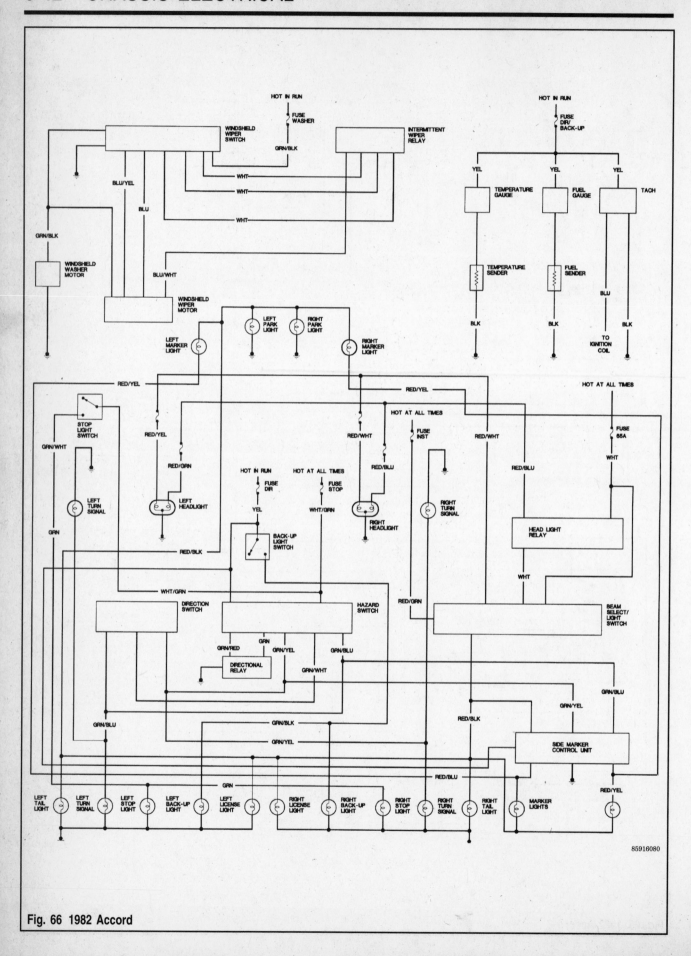

Fig. 66 1982 Accord

85916080

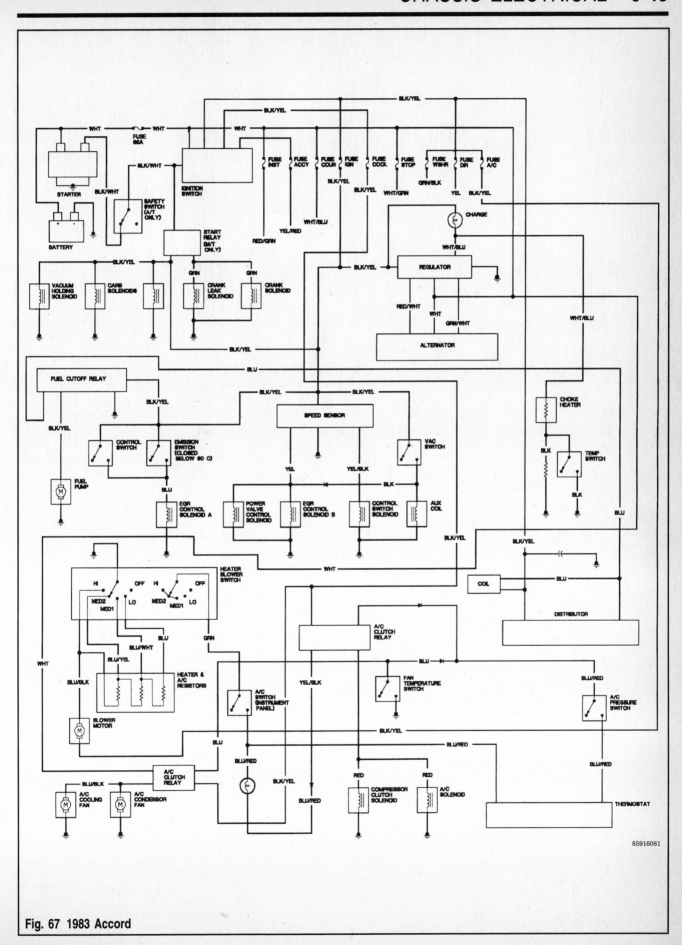

Fig. 67 1983 Accord

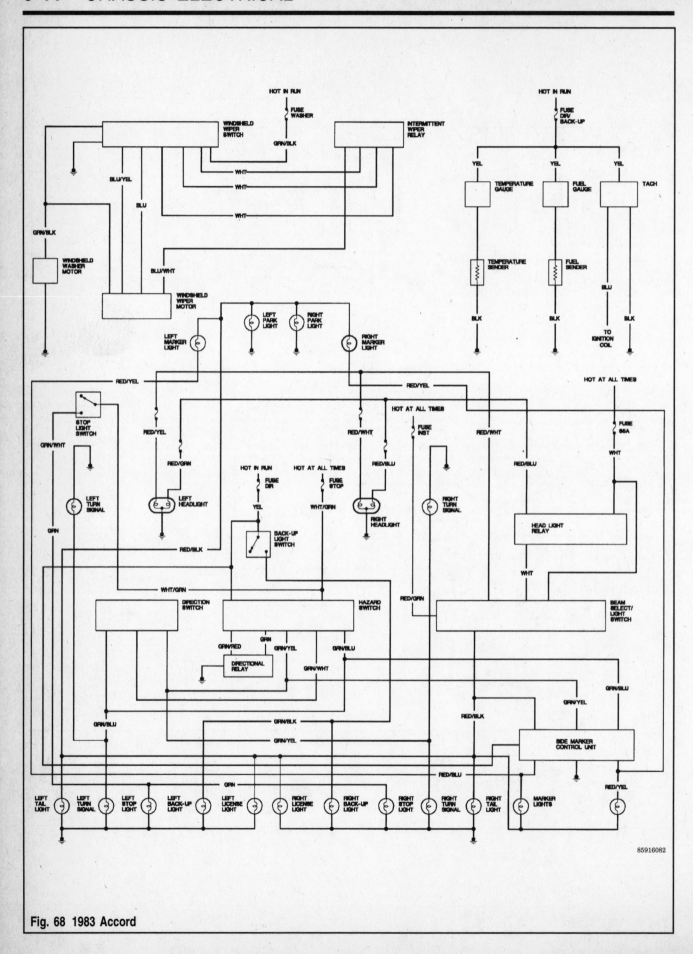

Fig. 68 1983 Accord

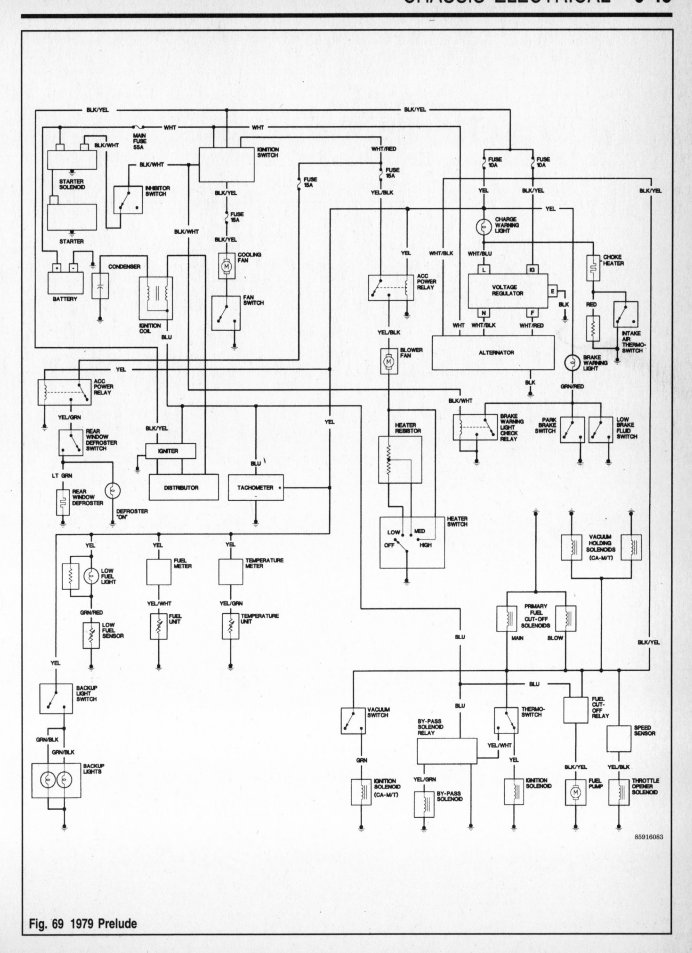

Fig. 69 1979 Prelude

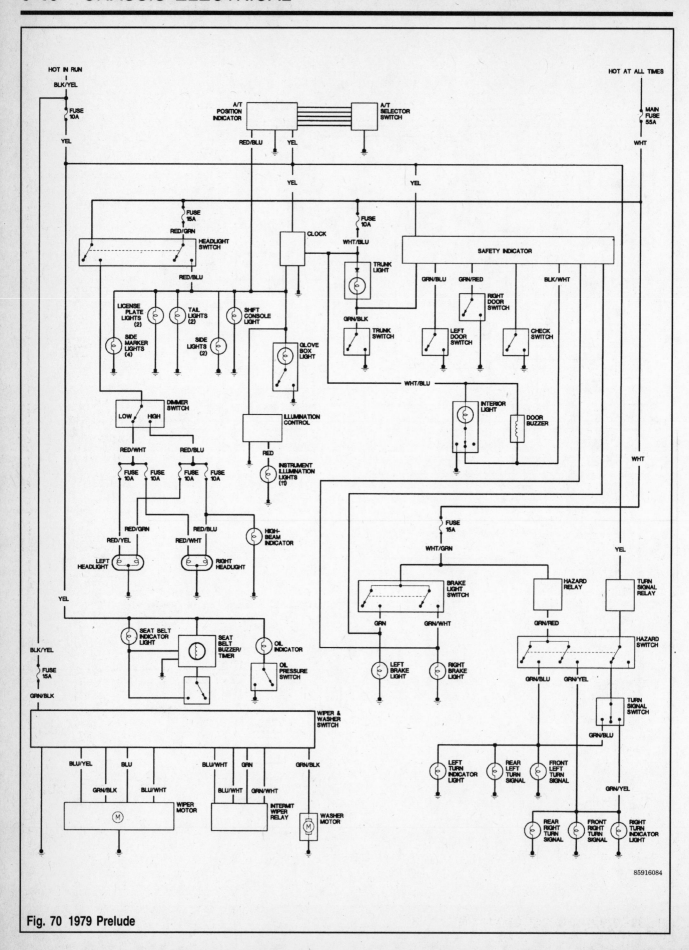

Fig. 70 1979 Prelude

85916084

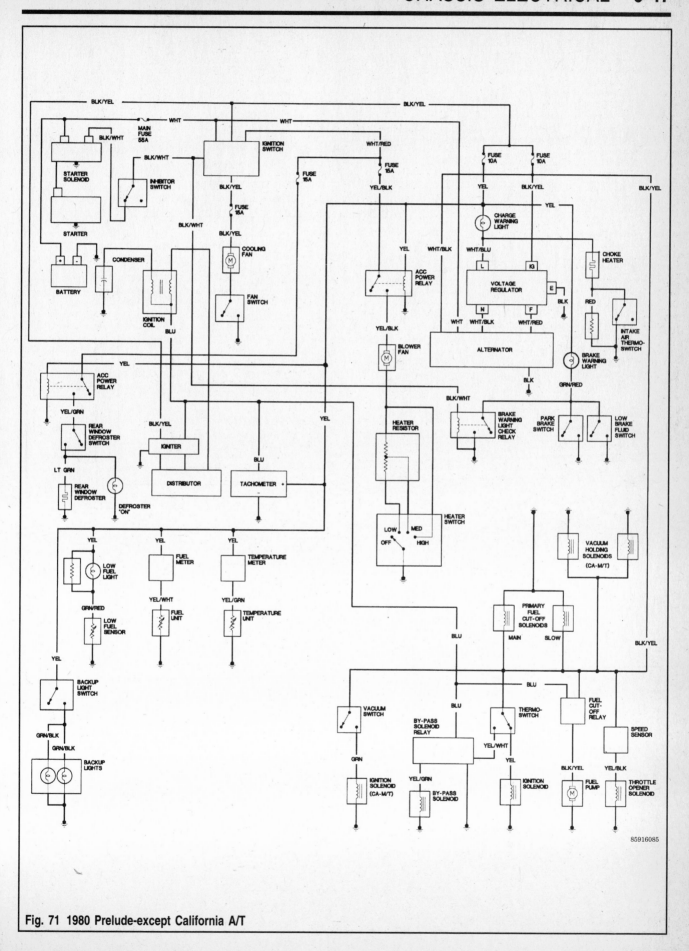

Fig. 71 1980 Prelude-except California A/T

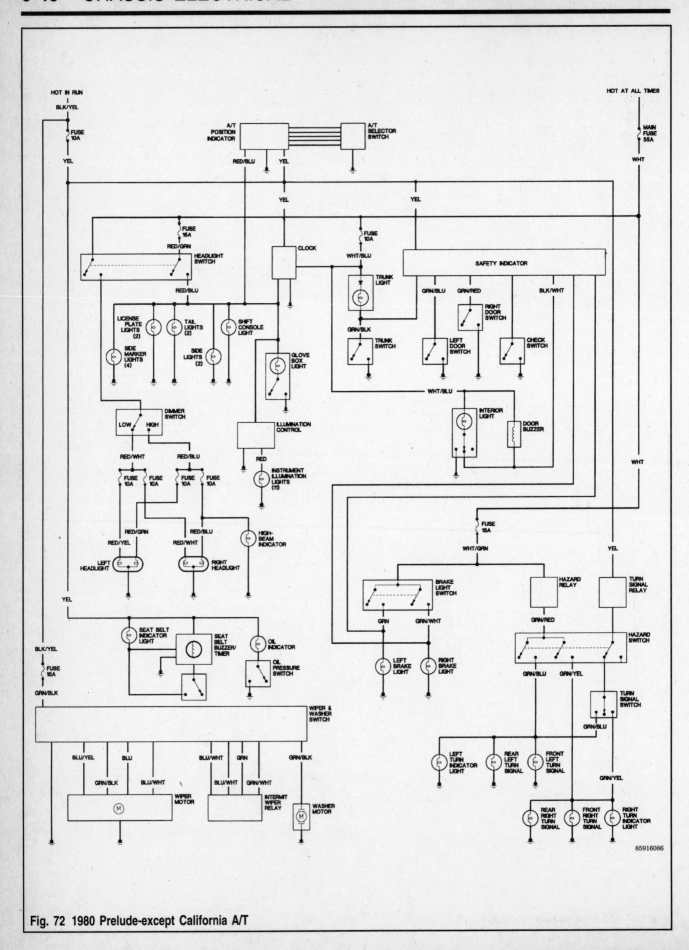

Fig. 72 1980 Prelude-except California A/T

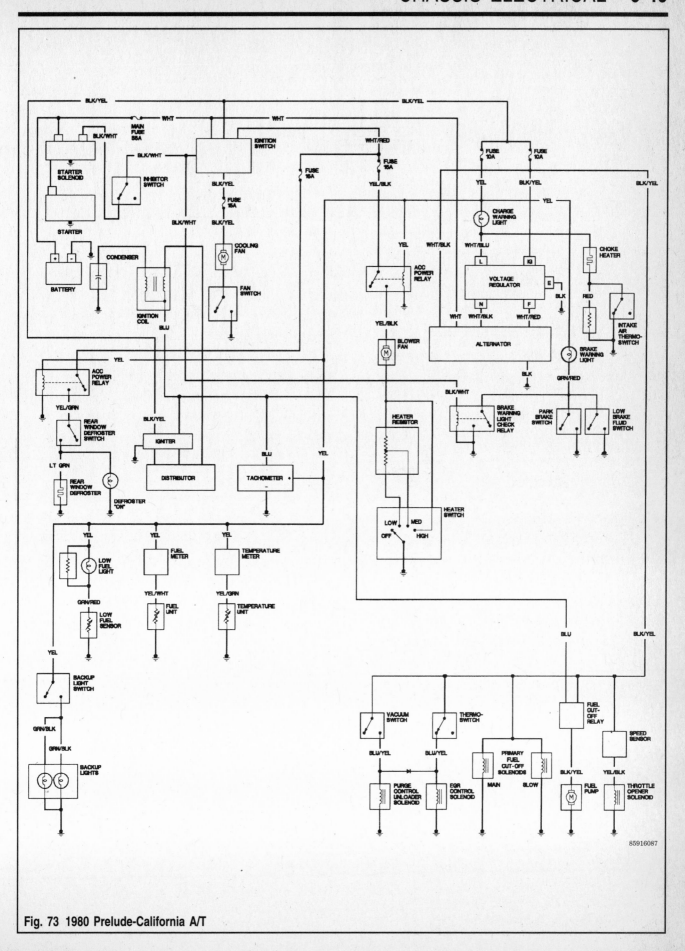

Fig. 73 1980 Prelude-California A/T

85916087

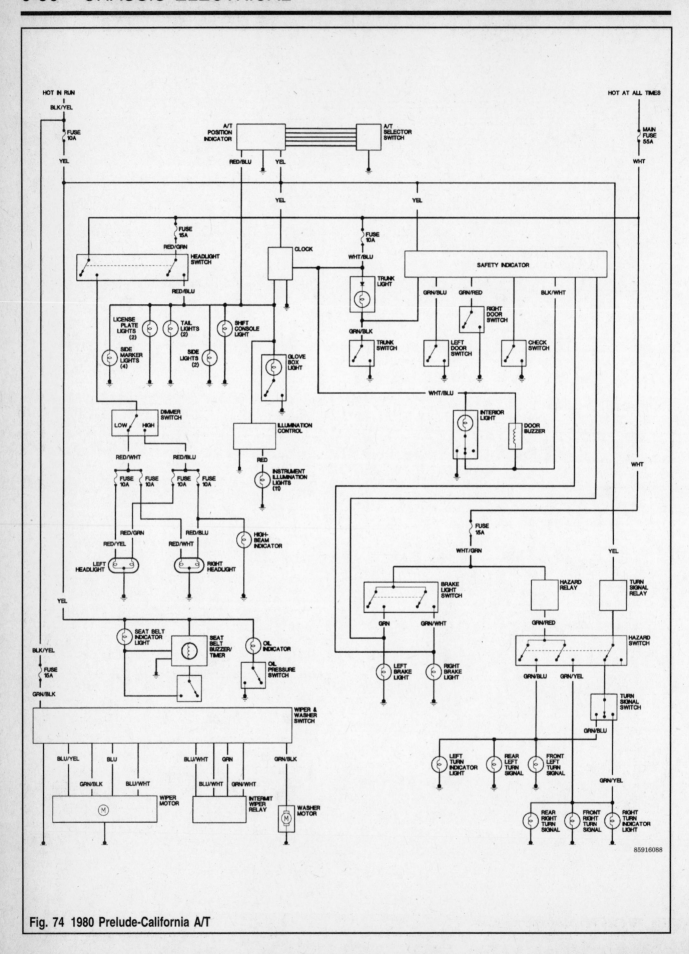

Fig. 74 1980 Prelude-California A/T

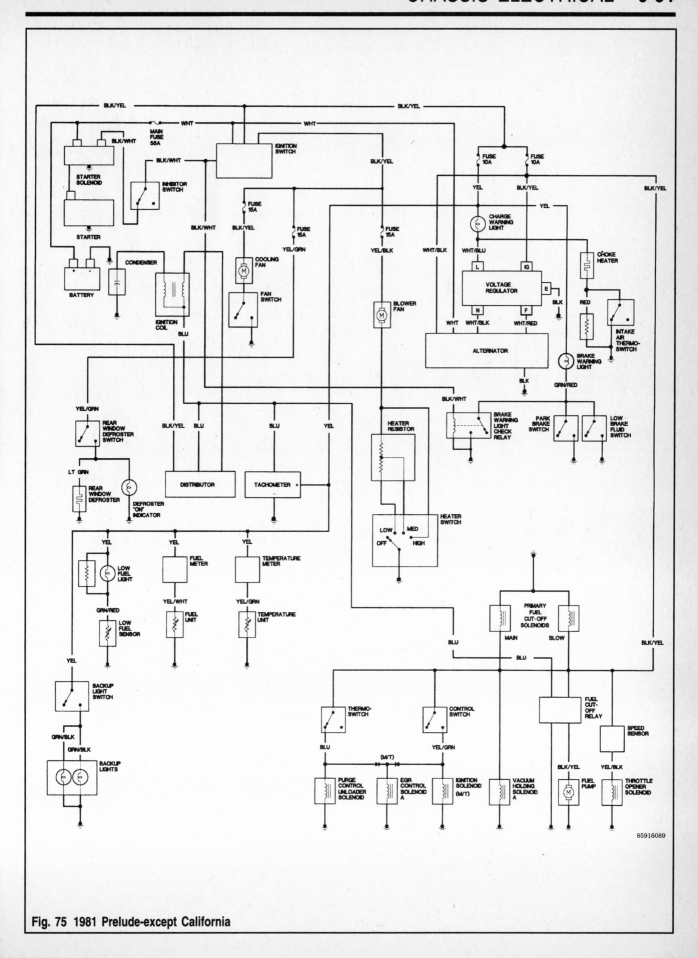

Fig. 75 1981 Prelude-except California

85916089

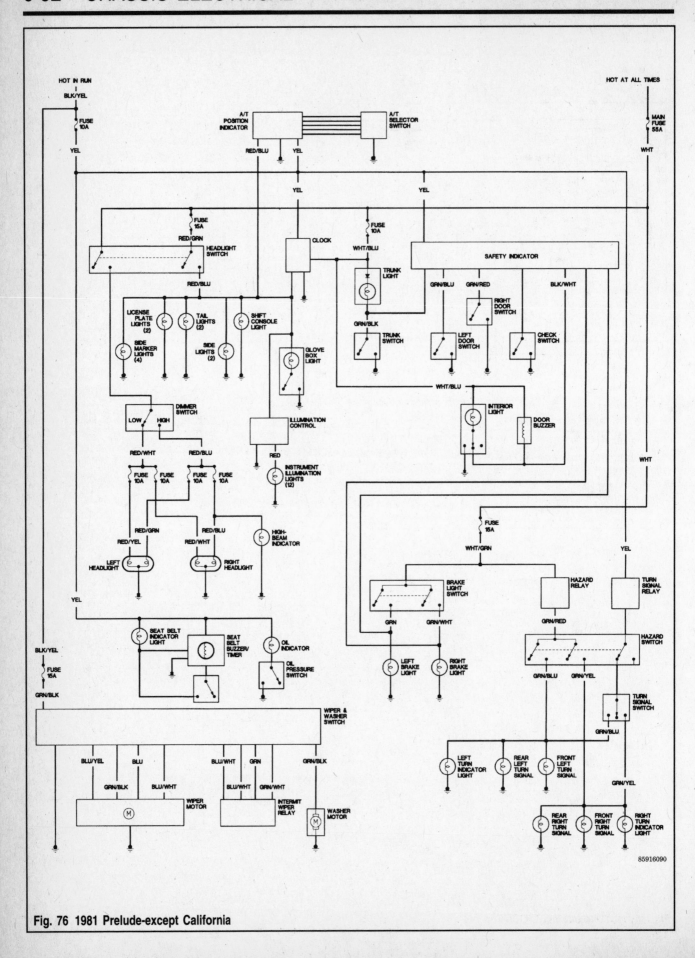

Fig. 76 1981 Prelude-except California

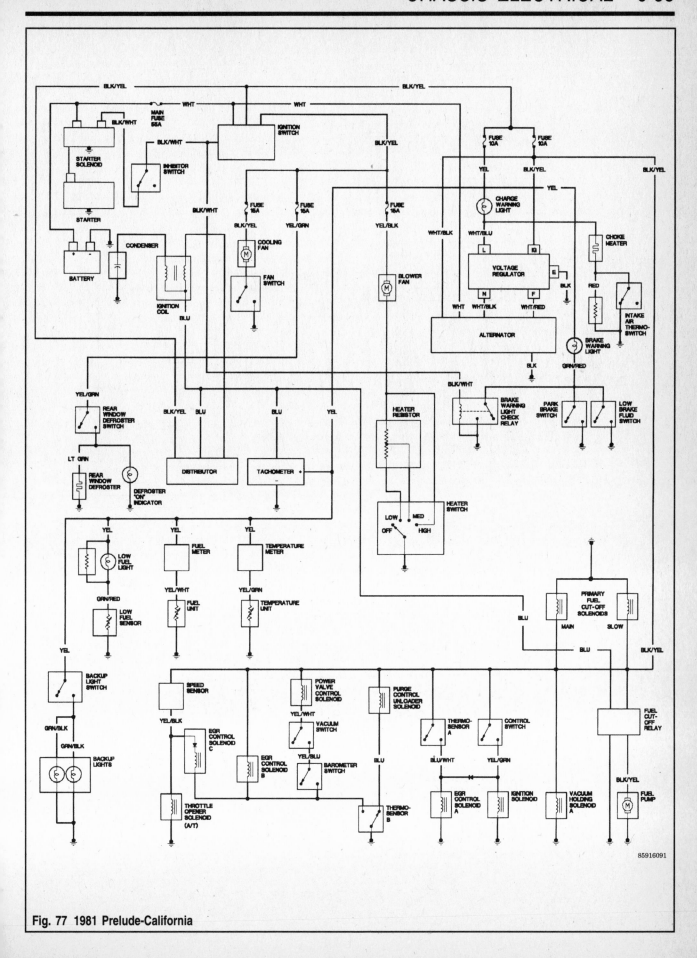

Fig. 77 1981 Prelude-California

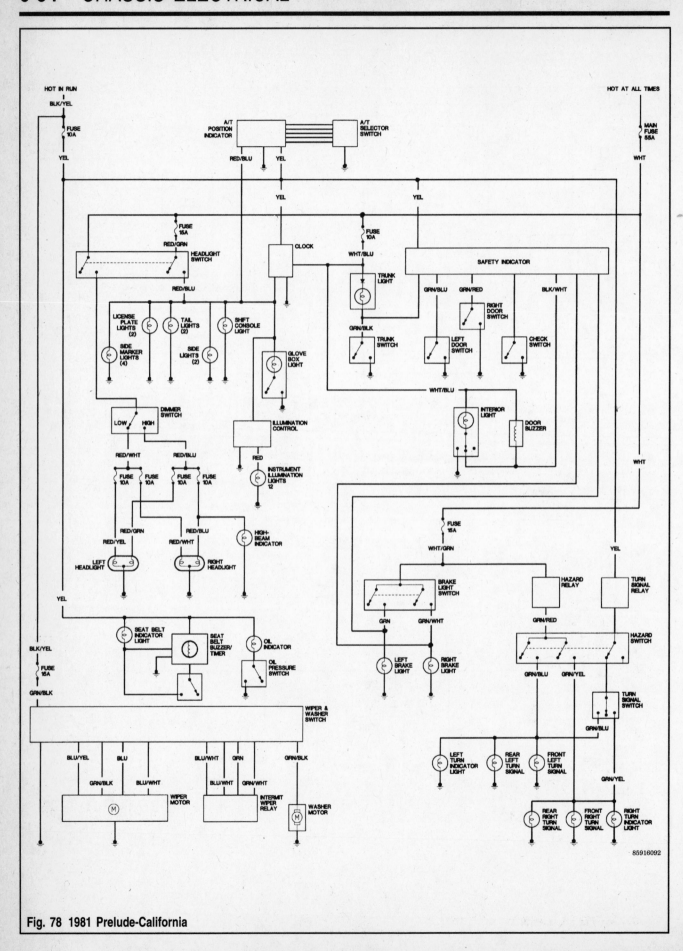

Fig. 78 1981 Prelude-California

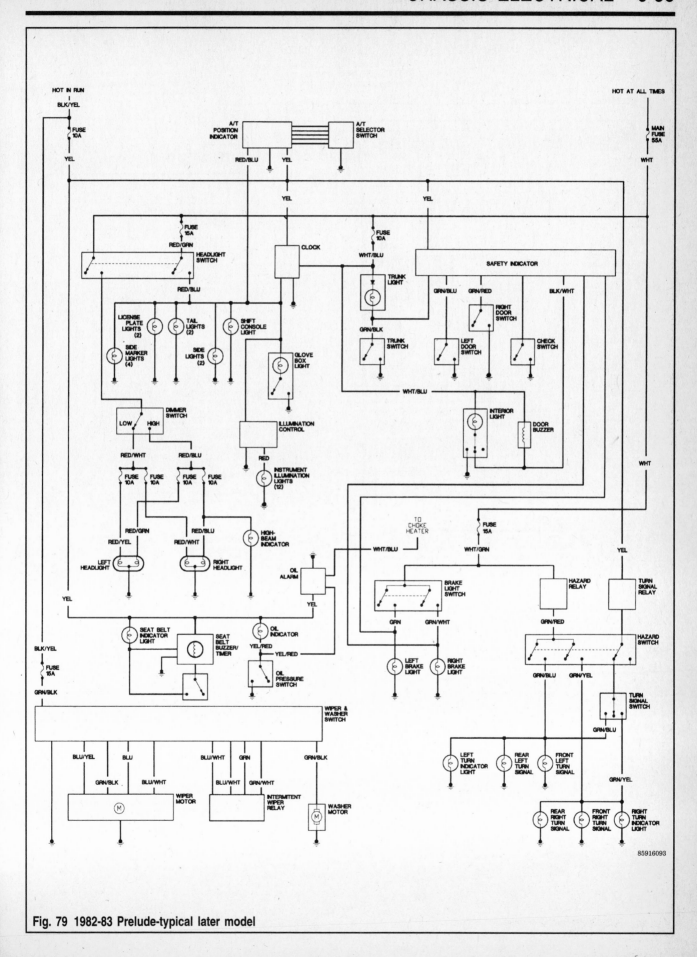

Fig. 79 1982-83 Prelude-typical later model

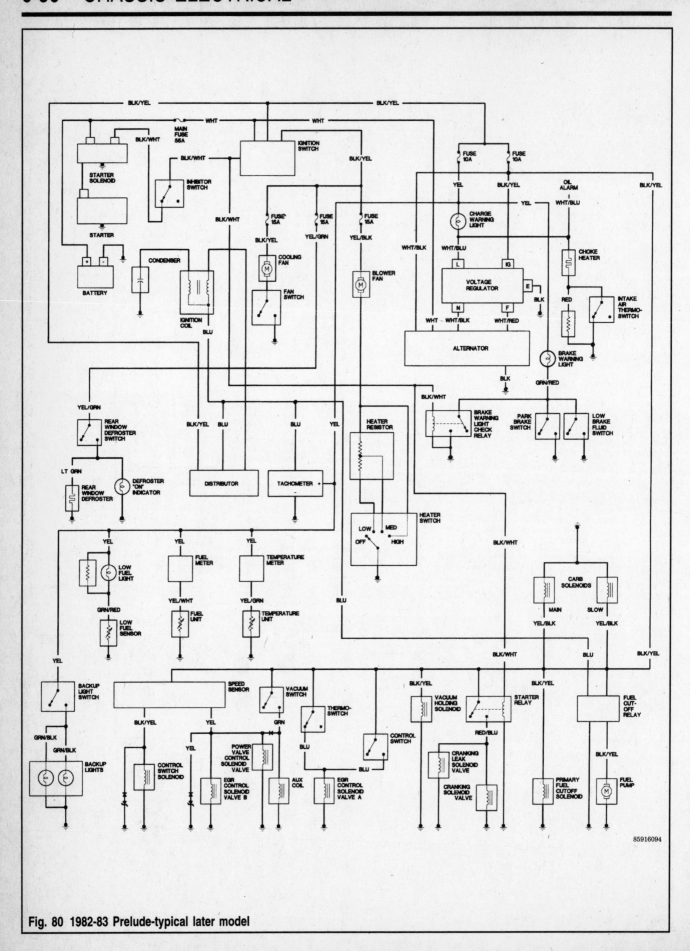

Fig. 80 1982-83 Prelude-typical later model

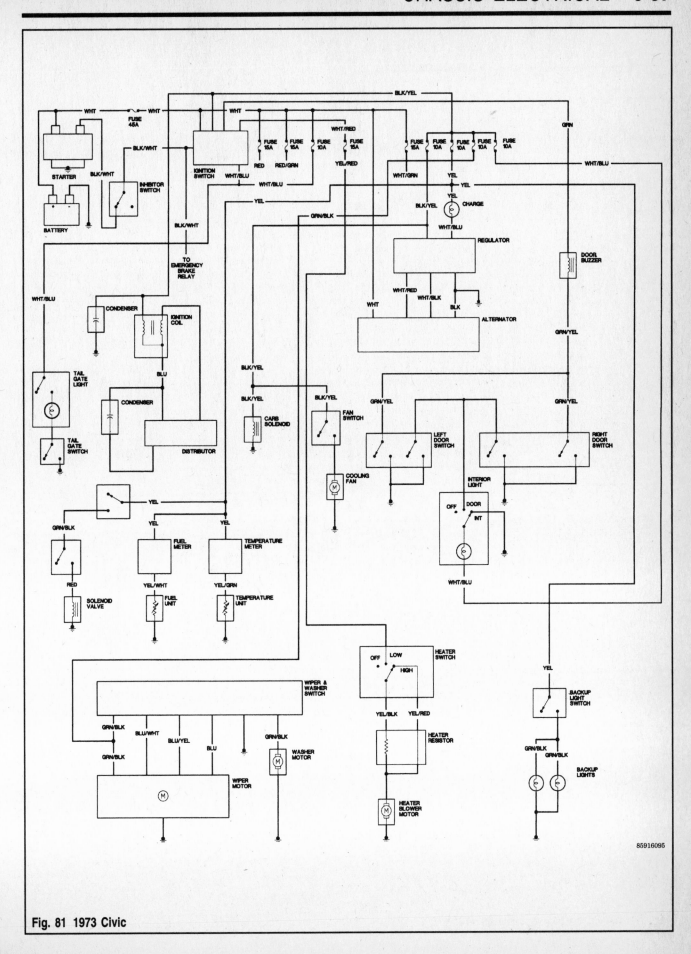

Fig. 81 1973 Civic

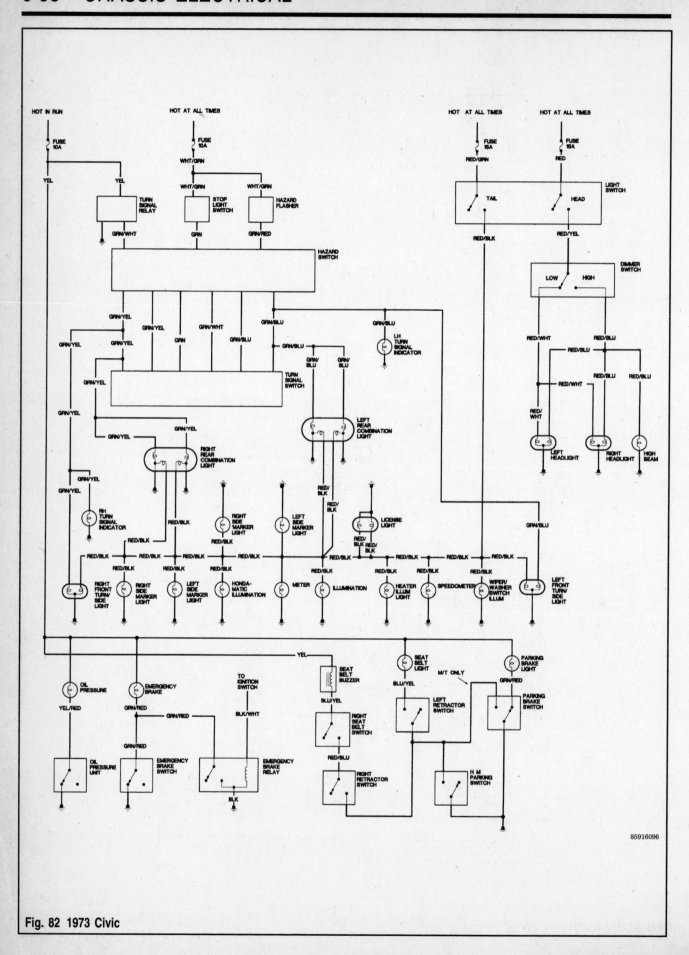

Fig. 82 1973 Civic

85916096

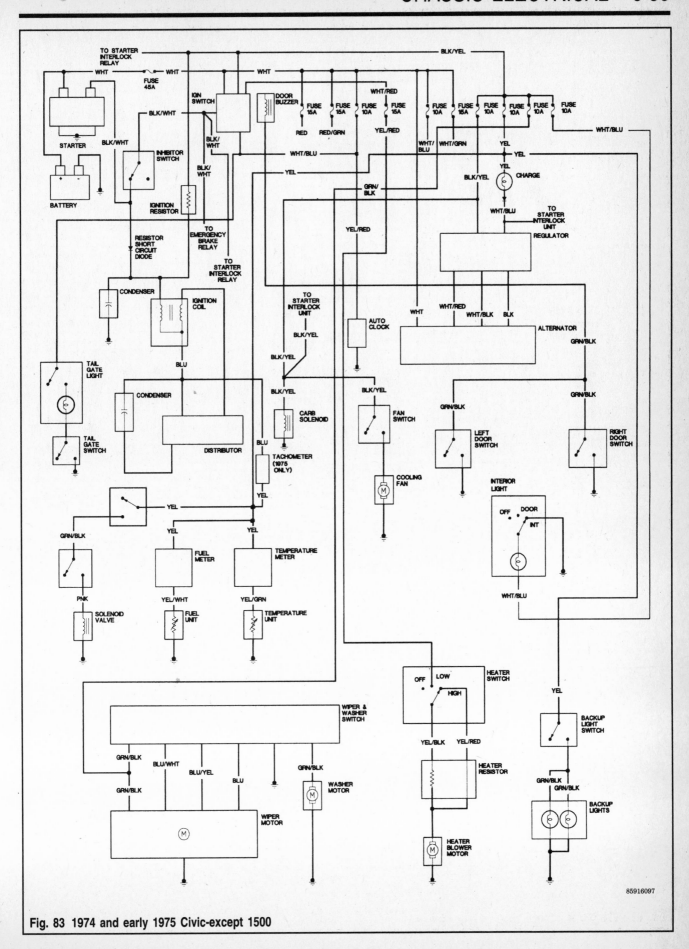

Fig. 83 1974 and early 1975 Civic-except 1500

85916097

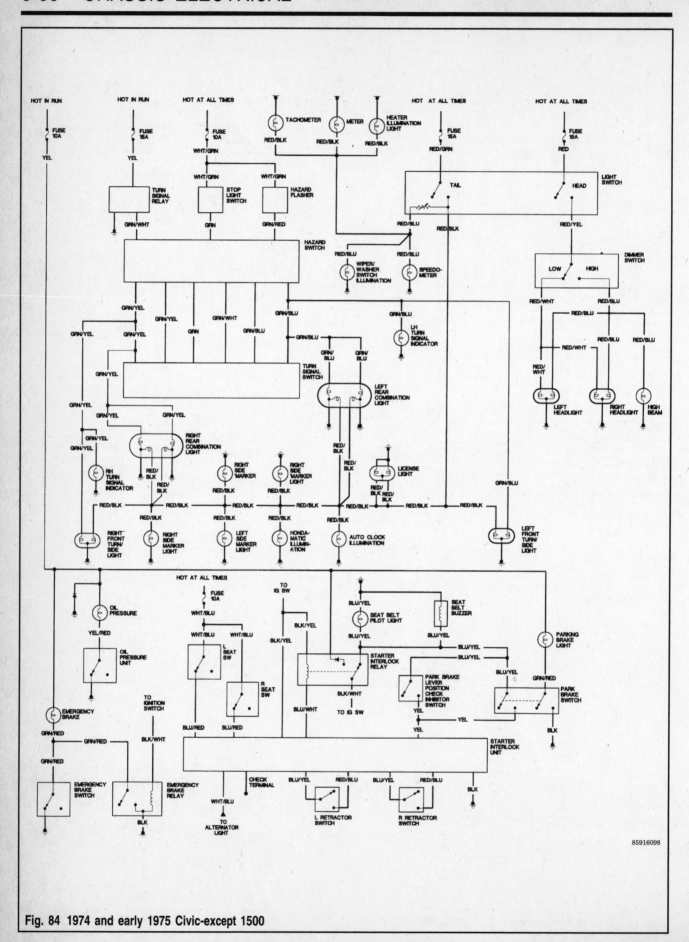

Fig. 84 1974 and early 1975 Civic-except 1500

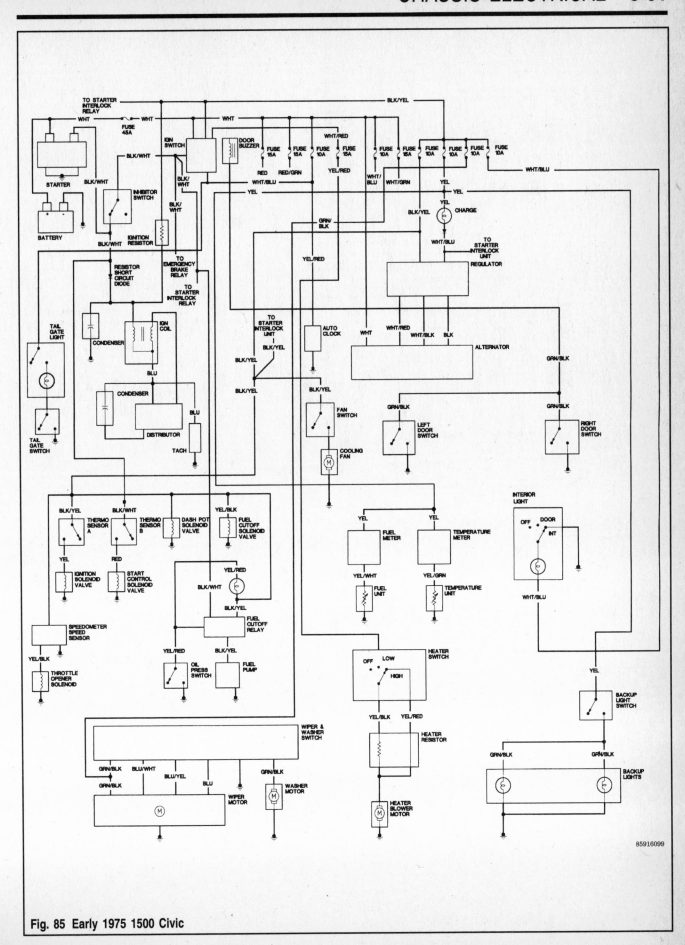

Fig. 85 Early 1975 1500 Civic

85916099

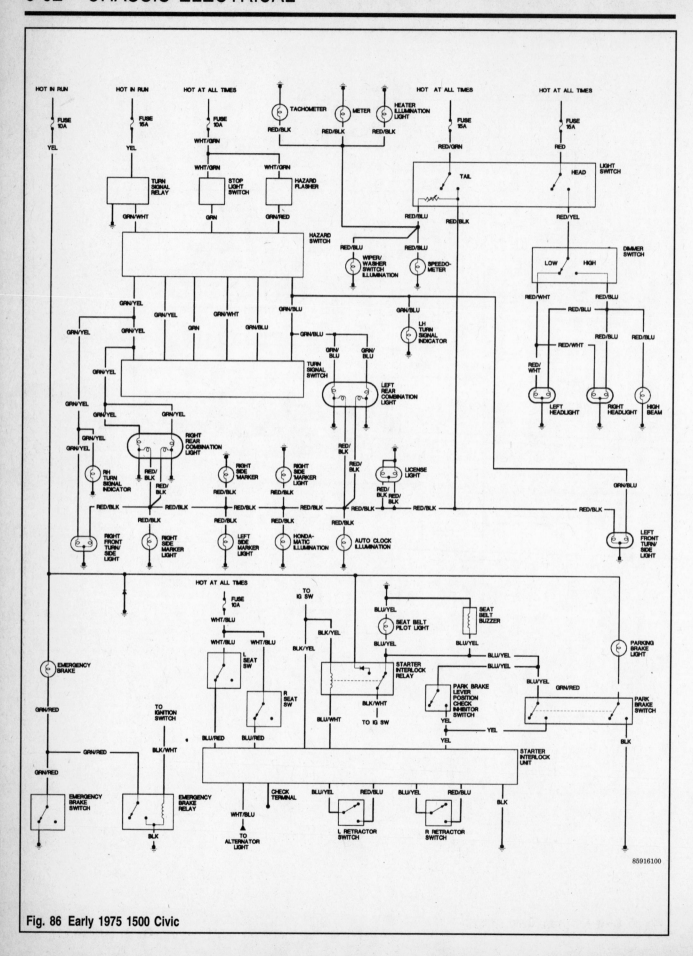

Fig. 86 Early 1975 1500 Civic

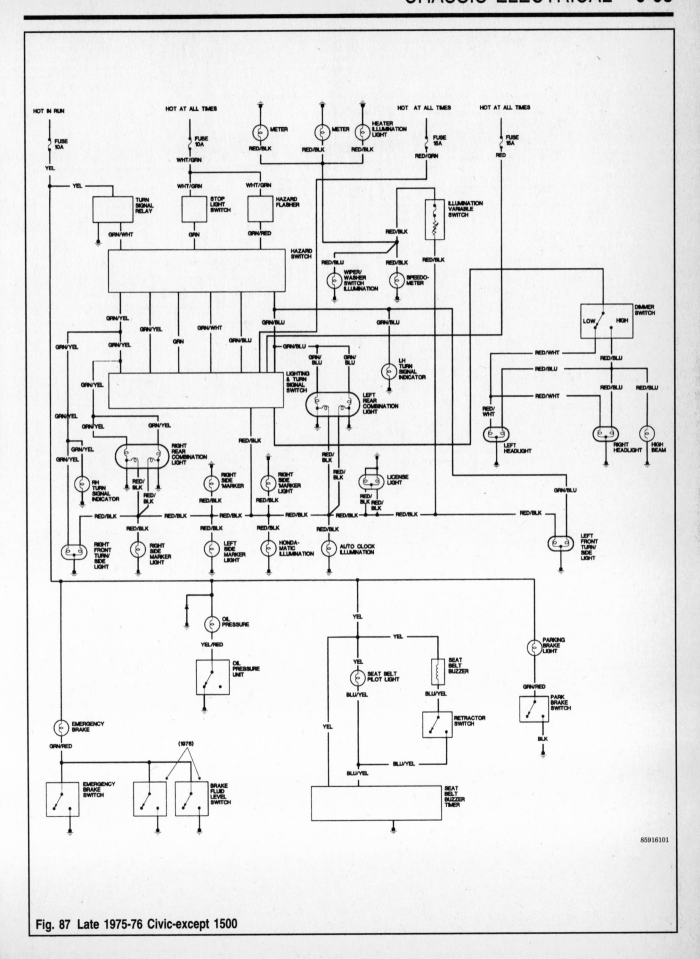

Fig. 87 Late 1975-76 Civic-except 1500

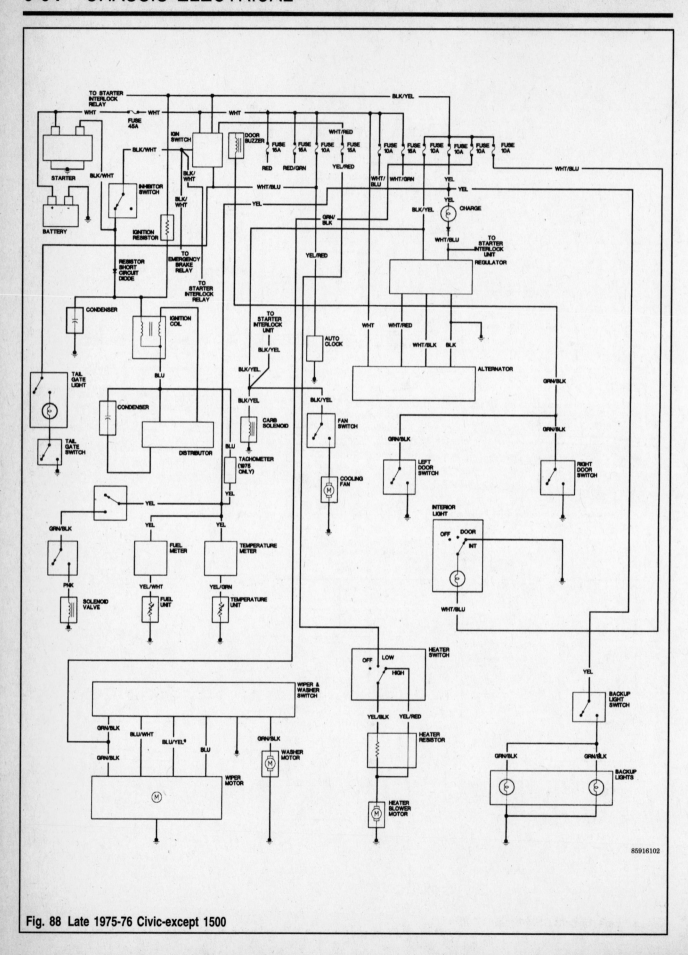

Fig. 88 Late 1975-76 Civic-except 1500

85916102

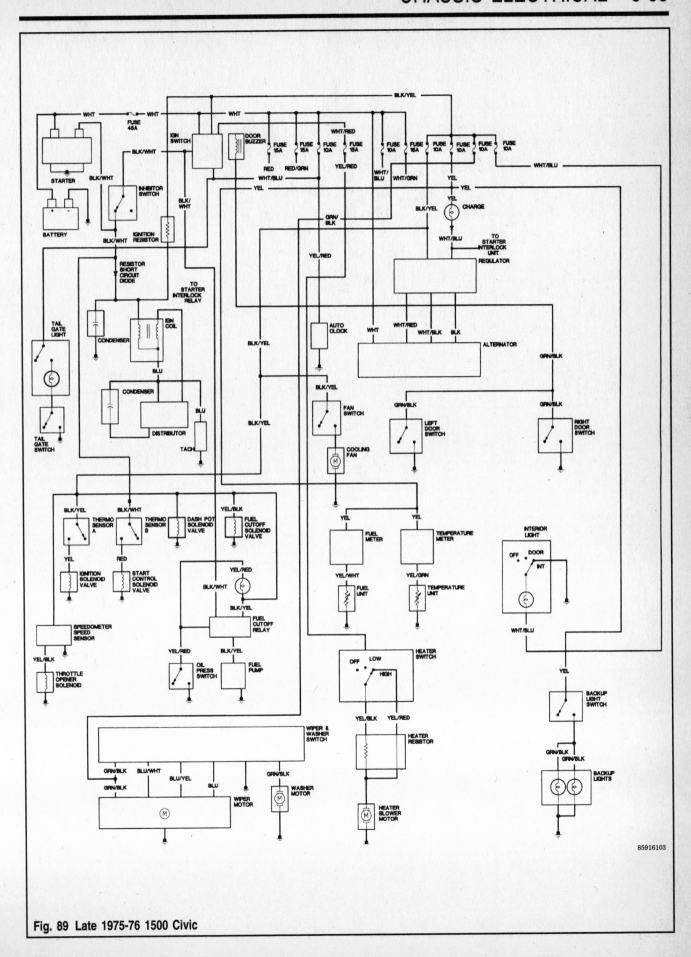

Fig. 89 Late 1975-76 1500 Civic

85916103

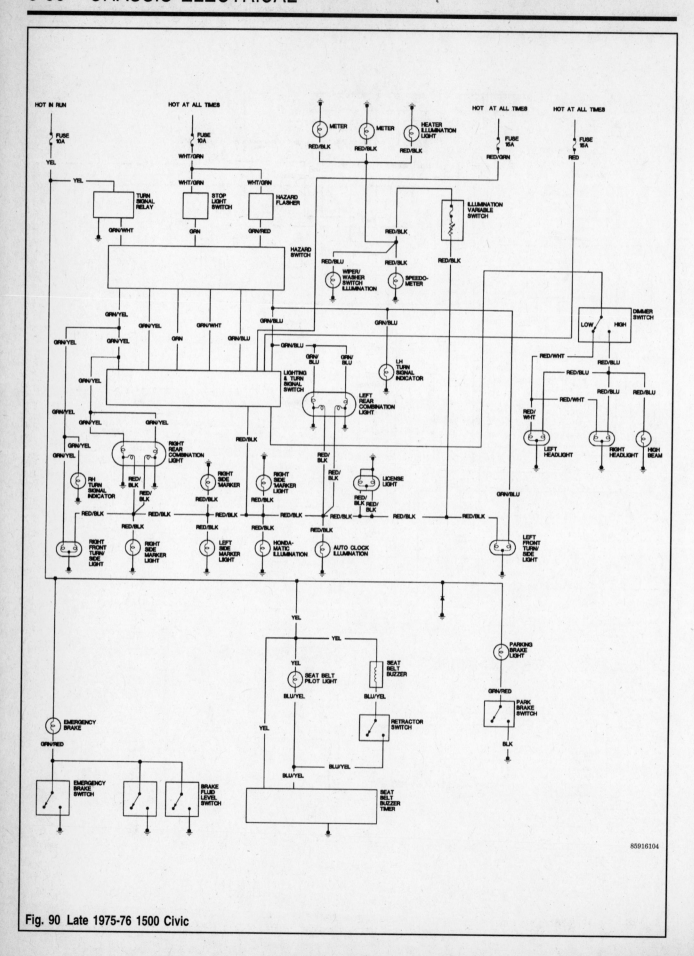

Fig. 90 Late 1975-76 1500 Civic

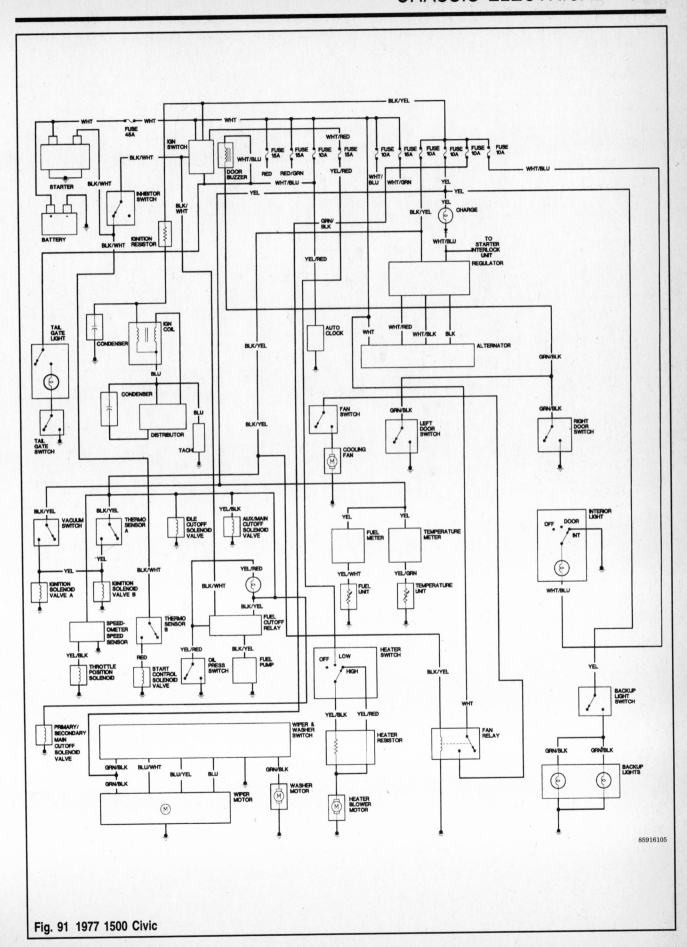

Fig. 91 1977 1500 Civic

85916105

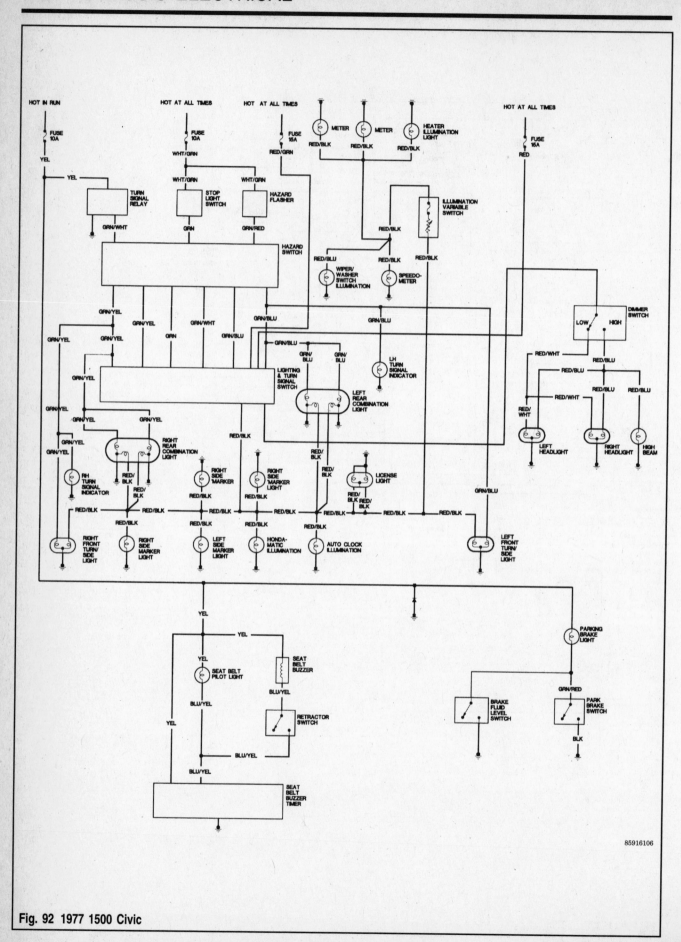

Fig. 92 1977 1500 Civic

85916106

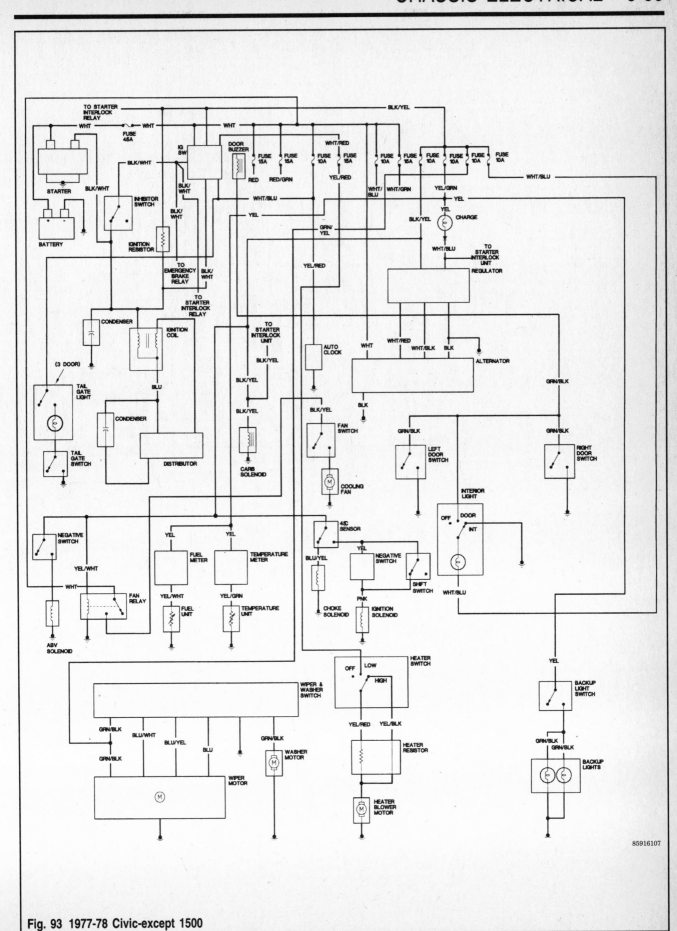

Fig. 93 1977-78 Civic-except 1500

85916107

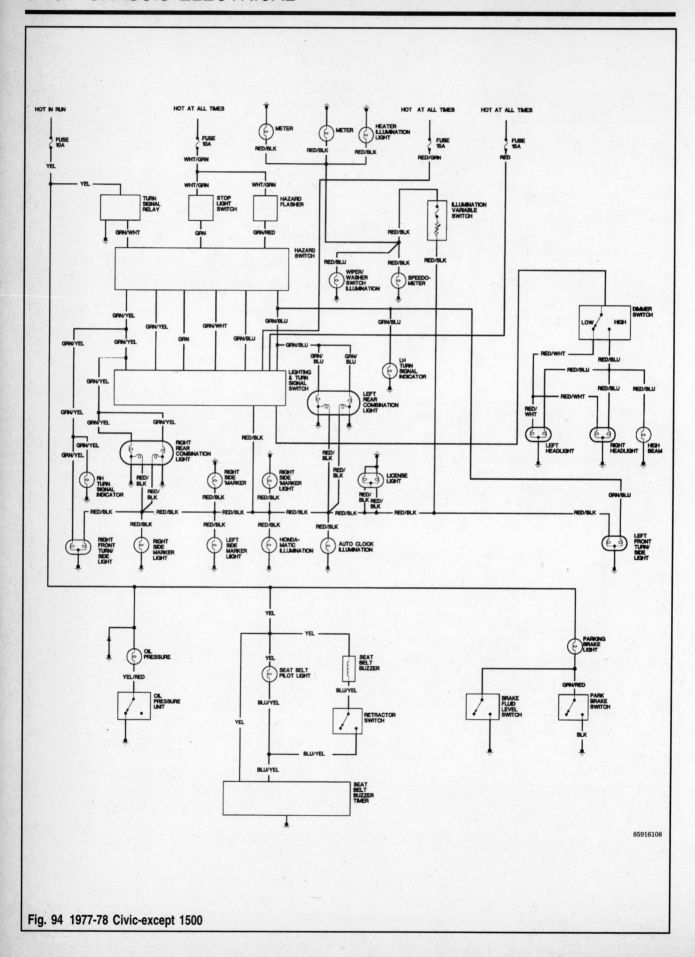

Fig. 94 1977-78 Civic-except 1500

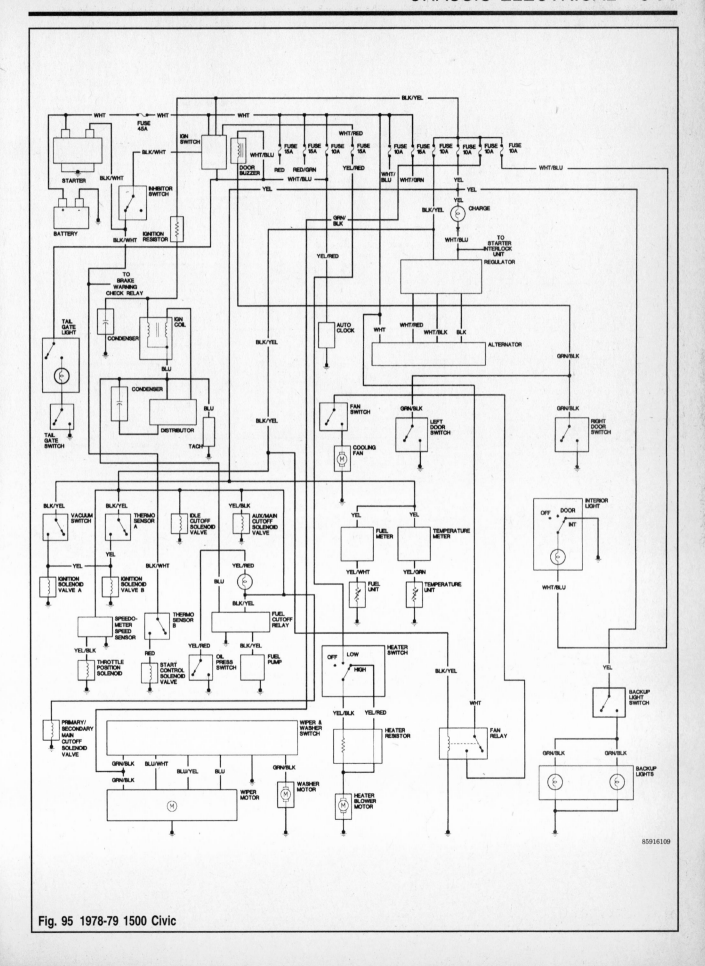

Fig. 95 1978-79 1500 Civic

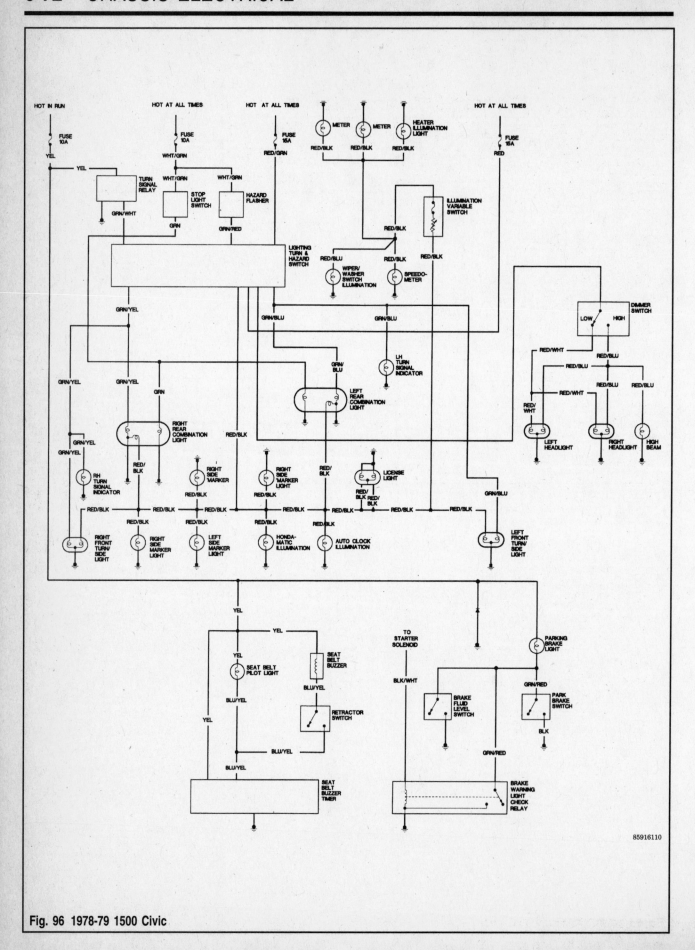

Fig. 96 1978-79 1500 Civic

85916110

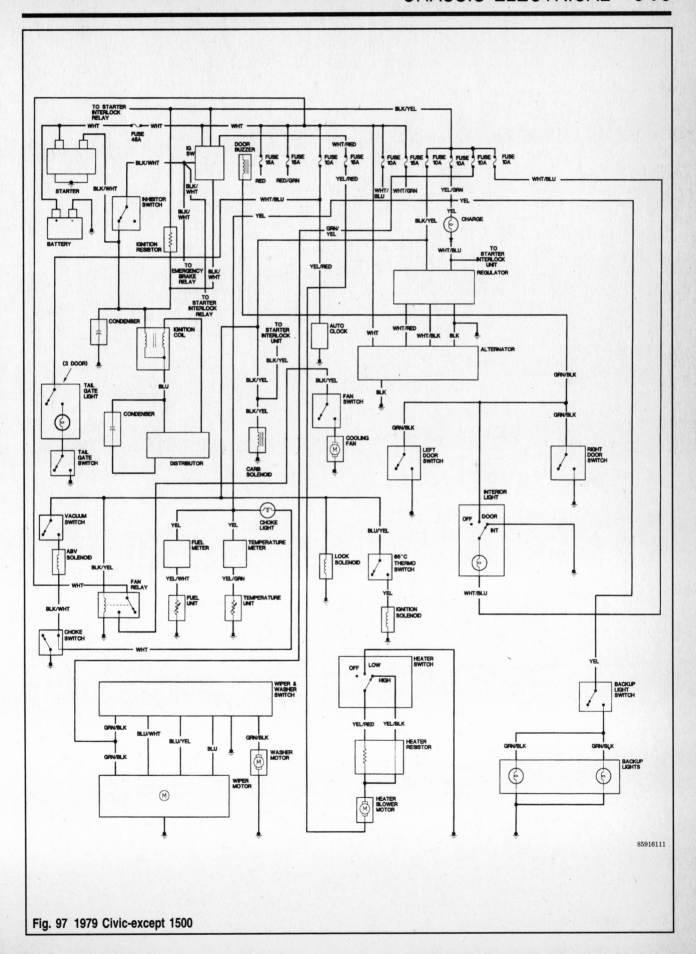

Fig. 97 1979 Civic-except 1500

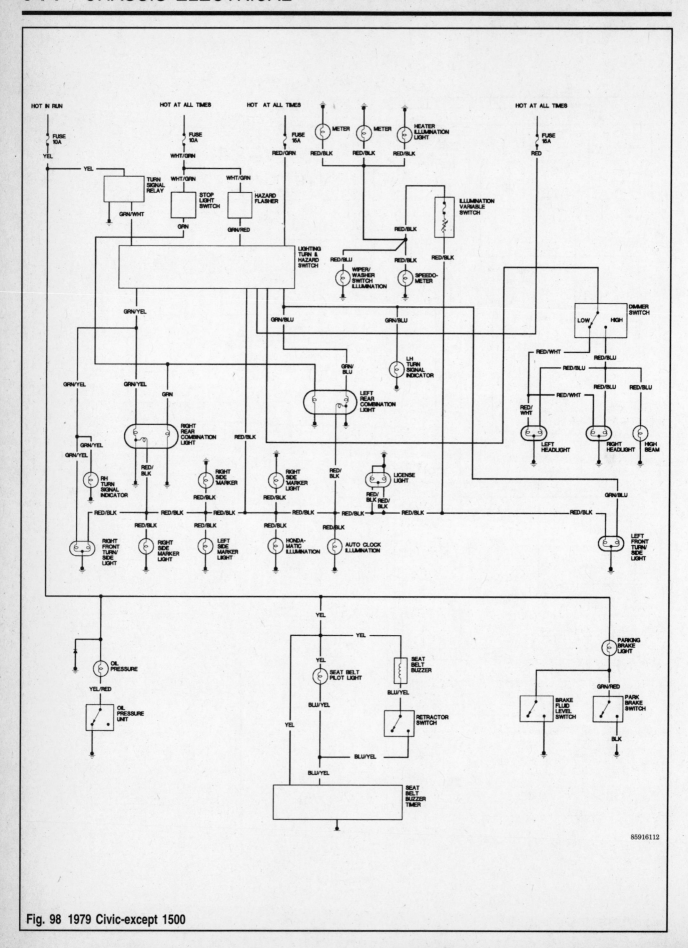

Fig. 98 1979 Civic-except 1500

85916112

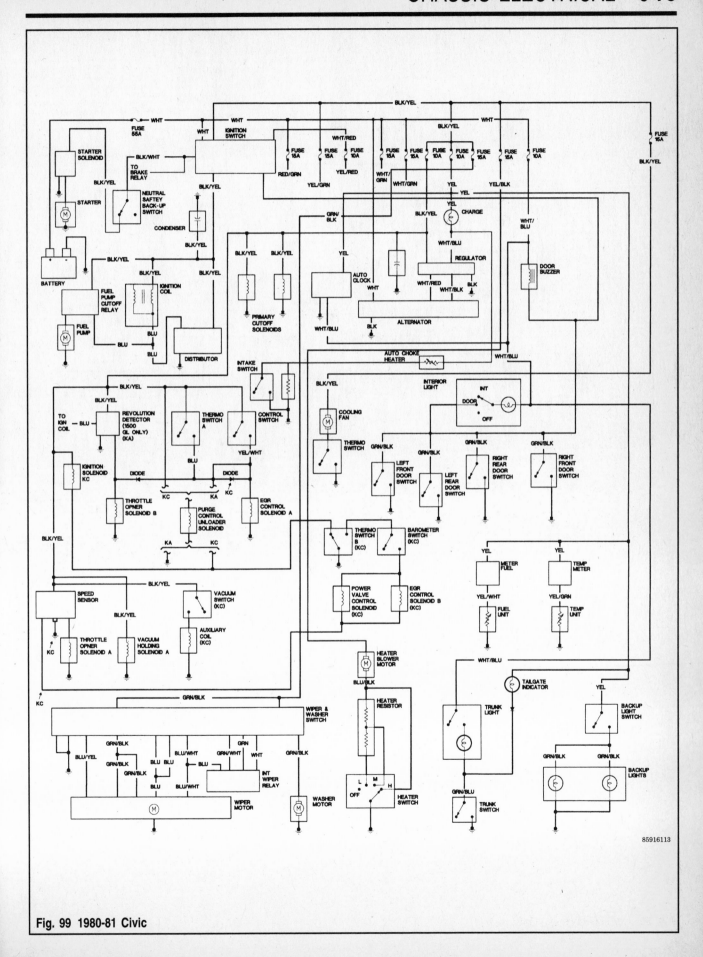

Fig. 99 1980-81 Civic

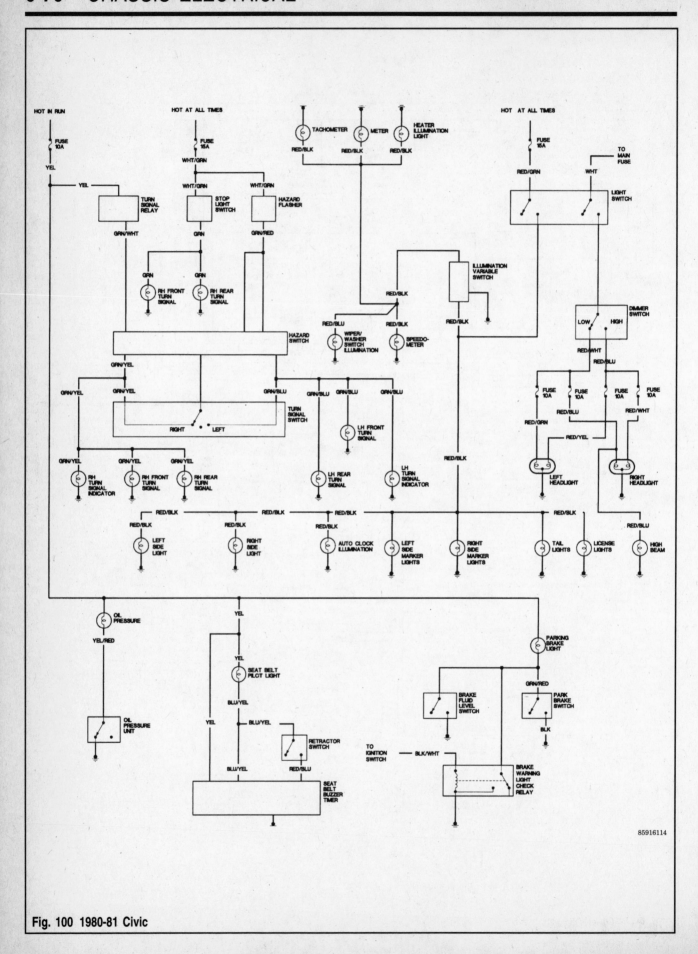

Fig. 100 1980-81 Civic

85916114

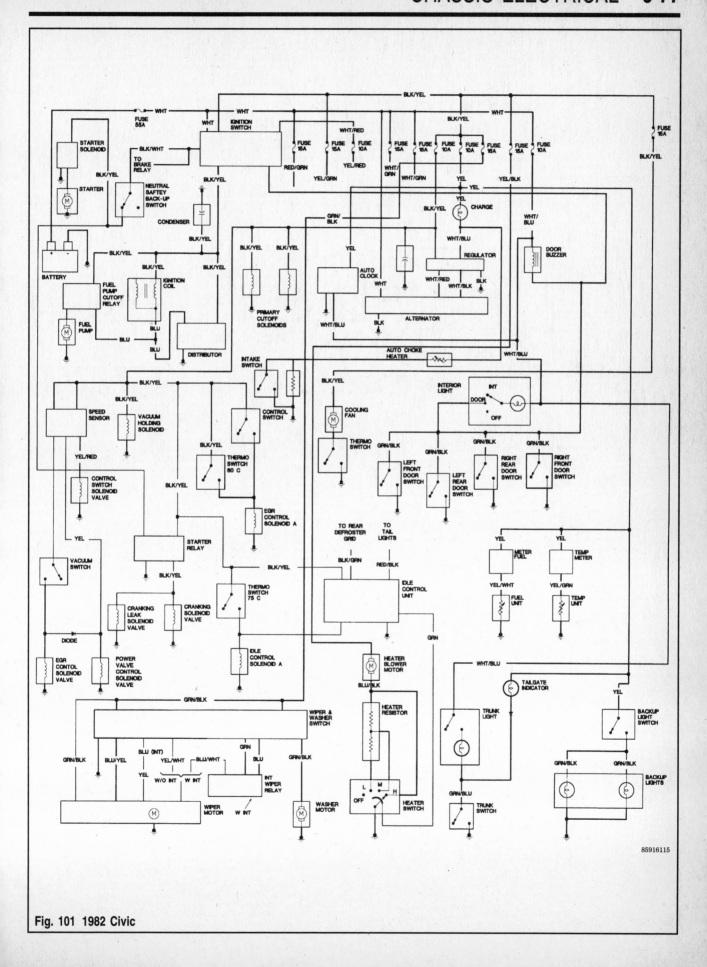

Fig. 101 1982 Civic

85916115

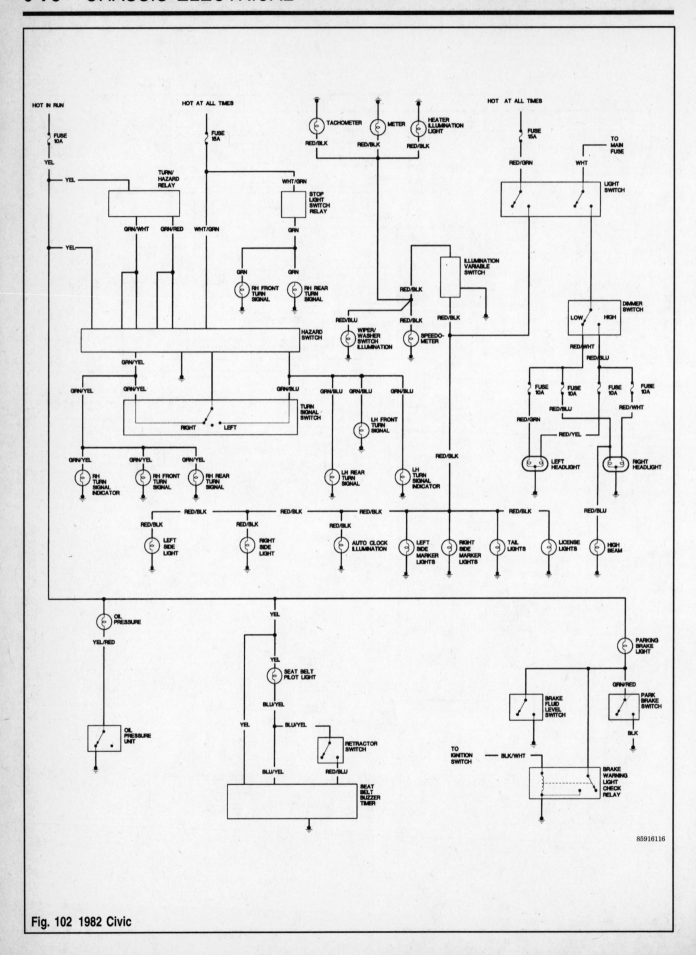

Fig. 102 1982 Civic

85916116

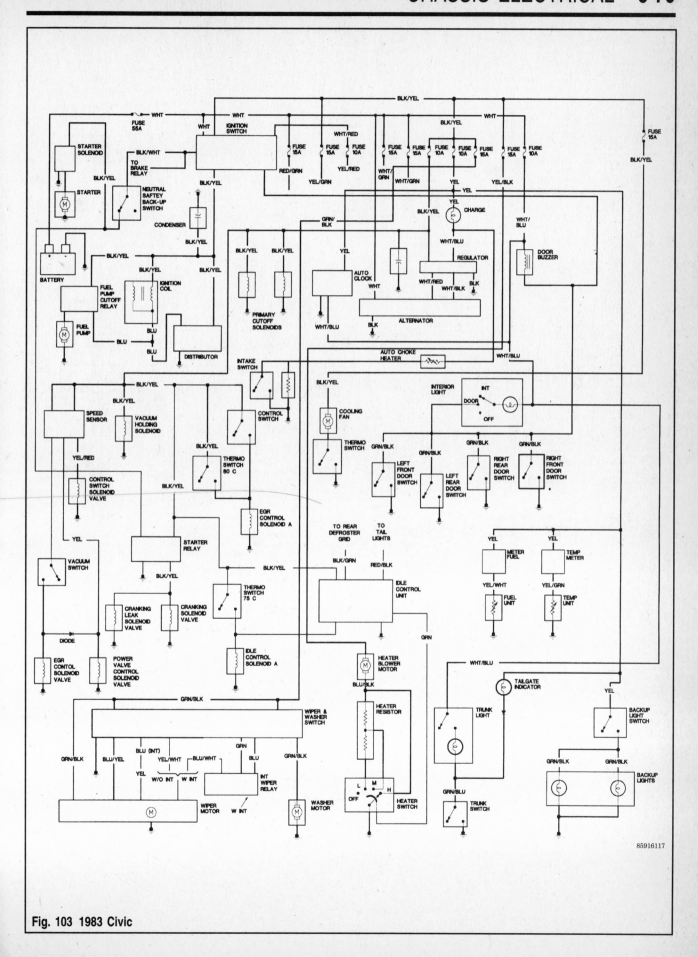

Fig. 103 1983 Civic

85916117

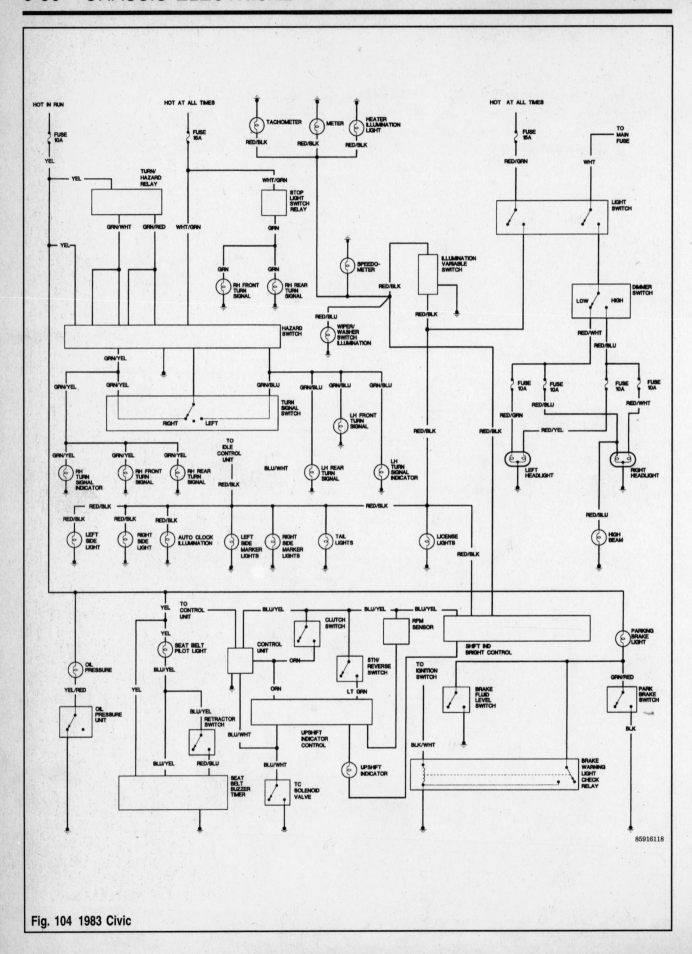

Fig. 104   1983 Civic

7

DRIVE TRAIN

UNDERSTANDING THE MANUAL TRANSAXLE

Because of the way an internal combustion engine breathes, it can produce torque, or twisting force, only within a narrow speed range. Most modern, overhead valve engines must turn at about 2,500 rpm to produce their peak torque. By 4,500 rpm they are producing so little torque that continued increases in engine speed produce no power increases.

The torque peak on overhead camshaft engines is, generally, much higher, but much narrower.

The manual transaxle and clutch are employed to vary the relationship between engine speed and the speed of the wheels so that adequate engine power can be produced under all circumstances. The clutch allows engine torque to be applied to the transaxle input shaft gradually, due to mechanical slippage. The car can, consequently, be started smoothly from a full stop.

The transaxle changes the ratio between the rotating speeds of the engine and the wheels by the use of gears. 4-speed or 5-speed transaxles are most common. The lower gears allow full engine power to be applied to the wheels during acceleration at low speeds.

The clutch drive plate is a thin disc, the center of which is splined to the transaxle input shaft. Both sides of the disc are covered with a layer of material which is similar to brake lining and which is capable of allowing slippage without roughness or excessive noise.

The clutch cover is bolted to the engine flywheel and incorporates a diaphragm spring which provides the pressure to engage the clutch. The cover also houses the pressure plate. The driven disc is sandwiched between the pressure plate and the smooth surface of the flywheel when the clutch pedal is released, thus forcing it to turn at the same speed as the engine crankshaft.

The transaxle contains a mainshaft which passes all the way through the transaxle, from the clutch to the halfshafts. This shaft is separated at one point, so that front and rear portions can turn at different speeds.

Power is transmitted by a countershaft in the lower gears and reverse. The gears of the countershaft mesh with gears on the mainshaft, allowing power to be carried from one to the other. All the countershaft gears are integral with that shaft, while several of the mainshaft gears can either rotate independently of the shaft or be locked to it. Shifting from one gear to the next causes one of the gears to be freed from rotating with the shaft and locks another to it. Gears are locked and unlocked by internal dog clutches which slide between the center of the gear and the shaft. The forward gears usually employ synchronizers; friction members which smoothly bring gear and shaft to the same speed before the toothed dog clutches are engaged.

The clutch is operating properly if:

1. It will stall the engine when released with the vehicle held stationary.

2. The shift lever can be moved freely between 1st and reverse gears when the vehicle is stationary and the clutch disengaged.

A clutch pedal free-play adjustment is incorporated in the linkage. If there is about 25-50mm of motion before the pedal begins to release the clutch, it is adjusted properly. Inadequate free-play wears all parts of the clutch releasing mechanisms and may cause slippage. Excessive free-play may cause inadequate release and hard shifting of gears.

Some clutches use a hydraulic system in place of mechanical linkage. If the clutch fails to release, fill the clutch master cylinder with fluid to the proper level and pump the clutch pedal to fill the system with fluid. Bleed the system in the same way as a brake system. If leaks are located, tighten loose connections or overhaul the master or slave cylinder as necessary.

Front wheel drive cars do not have conventional rear axles or drive shafts. Instead, power is transmitted from the engine to a transaxle, or a combination of transaxle and drive axle, in one unit. Both the transaxle and drive axle accomplish the same function as their counterparts in a front engine/rear axle design. The difference is in the location of the components.

In place of a conventional driveshaft, a front wheel drive design uses two driveshafts, sometimes called halfshafts, which couple the drive axle portion of the transaxle to the wheels. Universal joints or constant velocity joints are used just as they would in a rear wheel drive design.

Manual Transaxle

IDENTIFICATION

The Honda utilizes a transaxle arrangement where the transaxle and the differential are contained within the same housing. Power is transmitted from the engine to the transaxle and in turn, to the differential. The front drive axle halfshafts transfer the power from the differential to the front wheels.

The Civic without the CVCC engine, 1973-80, utilizes a standard design 4-speed, fully synchronized transaxle. The transaxle is located on the right side of the engine, along with the differential. A similar 5-speed is used on Civic and Accord CVCC models in these years. The 5-speed becomes available on all models in 1981-83.

A simple 2-speed, semi-automatic transaxle, Hondamatic, is available on models built 1973-80. As in all automatic transaxles, power is transmitted from the engine to the transaxle through a fluid coupling known as a torque converter. Forward gears are selected simply by moving the shift lever to the proper position — D1 (low speed range) or D2 (high speed range). The gears are engaged through the use of a complex clutch system in each gear range.

In 1981, the Hondamatic was replaced with a more conventional type of automatic transaxle with 3, self-shifting forward ranges. The major difference between this transaxle and the one that preceded it is that it not only shifts by itself but determines, through hydraulic pressures, when shifts are to occur.

In 1983, this transaxle received a 4th gear ratio to improve the cruise fuel economy while maintaining performance at low speeds. This transaxle also locks up the torque converter to eliminate its slip under steady cruise conditions.

MANUAL TRANSAXLE

Adjustments

SHIFT LINKAGE ADJUSTMENT

▶ See Figure 1

All Models

The Honda shift linkage on manual transaxle models 1973-83 is non-adjustable. However, if the linkage is binding, or if there is excessive play, check the linkage bushings and pivot points. Lubricate with light oil, or replace worn bushings as necessary. Always check for smooth operation.

➡**The back-up light switch on these models screws into the rear of the transaxle case. The back-up light switch has a washer that must be replaced for the switch to work properly and to prevent oil leaks.**

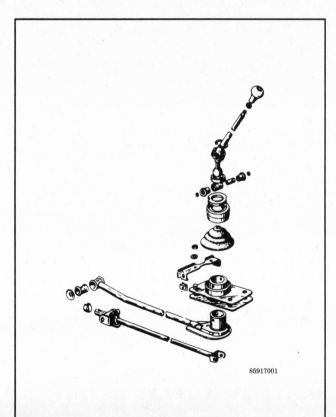

Fig. 1 Exploded view of the gearshift assembly-typical

85917001

Transaxle

REMOVAL & INSTALLATION

▶ See Figure 2

Civic 1973-79

1. Drain the transaxle.
2. Raise and support the front of the vehicle on jackstands.
3. Remove the front wheels.
4. Disconnect the negative battery terminals from the battery and the transaxle case.
5. Disconnect the positive battery terminal from the starter and the wire from the solenoid. Remove the starter.
6. Disconnect the following cables and wires:
    a. Clutch cable at the release arm.
    b. Back-up light switch wires.
    c. Transmission Controlled Spark (TCS) switch wires, if so equipped.
    d. Speedometer cable.

✳✳WARNING

When removing the speedometer cable from the transaxle, it is not necessary to remove the entire cable holder. Remove the end boot (gear holder seal) and the cable retaining clip, then, pull the cable out of the holder. In no way should you disturb the holder, unless it is absolutely necessary.

7. Using a Ball Joint Remover tool, disconnect the left and right lower ball joints from the steering knuckle.
8. Pull on both wheel hubs to disconnect the driveshafts from the differential case.
9. Using a drift punch, drive out the gearshift rod pin (8mm) and disconnect the rod at the transaxle case.
10. Disconnect the gearshift extension from the clutch housing.
11. Screw in the engine hanger bolts to the engine torque rod bolt hole and to the hole just to the left of the distributor. Hook a chain to the bolts and lift the engine just enough to take the weight off the engine mounts.
12. After making sure that the engine is properly supported, remove the two center beam-to-lower engine mount nuts. Remove the center beam and the lower engine mount.
13. Reinstall the center beam (without mount) and lower engine until it rests on the beam.
14. Place a floor jack under the transaxle and loosen the attaching bolts. Using the jack to support the transaxle, slide it away from the engine and lower the jack until the transaxle clears the vehicle.
    To install:
15. Install the transaxle in the vehicle. Reverse all the removal procedures.
16. Be sure to pay attention to the following points:
    a. Tighten all mounting nuts and bolts to their specified torque.

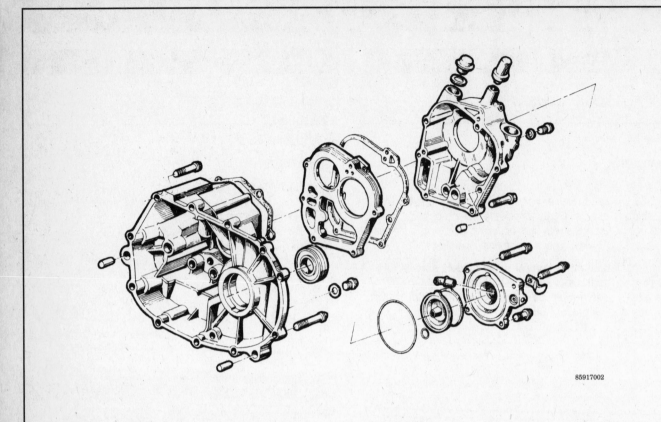

85917002

Fig. 2 5-Speed transaxle housing and related parts

b. Use a new shift rod pin.

c. After installing the driveshafts, attempt to move the inner joint housing in and out of the differential housing. If it moves easily, the driveshaft end clips should be replaced.

d. Make sure that the control cables and wires are properly connected.

e. Be sure the transaxle is refilled to the proper level. Road test the vehicle for proper operation.

Civic 1980-83

1. Disconnect the battery ground.
2. Unlock the steering and place the transaxle in neutral.
3. Disconnect the following wires in the engine compartment:

   a. battery positive cable.

   b. black/white wire from the solenoid.

   c. temperature gauge sending unit wire.

   d. ignition timing thermo-sensor wire.

   e. back-up light switch.

   f. distributor wiring.

   g. transaxle ground cable.

4. Unclip and remove the speedometer cable at the transaxle. Do not disassemble the speedometer gear holder!
5. Remove the clutch slave cylinder with the hydraulic line attached, or disconnect the clutch cable at the release arm.
6. Remove the side and top starter mounting bolts. Loosen the front wheel lug nuts.
7. Apply the parking brake and block the rear wheels. Raise and support the front end of the vehicle. Remove the front wheels.

8. Attach a suitable chain hoist to the rear of the engine then raise the engine slightly to take the weight off of the mounts. Drain the transaxle, then reinstall the drain plug and washer.
9. Remove the splash shields from the underside.
10. Remove the stabilizer bar.
11. Disconnect the left and right lower ball joints and tie end rods, using a ball joint remover.

✳✳CAUTION

Place a floor jack under the lower control arm securely at the ball joint. Otherwise, the lower control arm may jump suddenly away from the steering knuckle as the ball joint is removed!

12. Turn the right steering knuckle out as far as it will go. Place a prybar against the inboard CV-joint, pry the right axle out of the transaxle about ½". This will force the spring clip out of the groove inside the differential gear splines. Pull it out the rest of the way. Repeat this procedure on the other side.
13. Disconnect the shift lever torque rod from the clutch housing.
14. Slide the pin retainer back, drive out the spring pin using a pin punch, then disconnect the shift rod. Remove the bolt from the shift rod clevis, if so equipped.
15. Place a transmission jack under the transaxle and raise the transmission jack securely against the transaxle to take up the weight.

16. Remove the engine torque rods and brackets. Remove the bolts from the front transaxle mount. Remove the transaxle housing bolts from the engine torque bracket.

17. Remove the remaining starter mounting bolts and take out the starter.

18. Remove the remaining transaxle mounting bolts and the upper bolt from the engine damper bracket. Remove the clutch housing bolts from the rear transaxle mounting bracket. Remove the one remaining bolt from the engine.

19. Start backing the transaxle away from the engine and remove the two lower damper bolts.

20. Pull the transaxle clear of the engine and lower the jack.

To install:

21. To ease installation, fabricate two 14mm diameter dowel pins and install them in the clutch housing.

22. Raise the transaxle and slide it onto the dowels. Slide the transaxle onto position aligning the mainshaft splines with the clutch plate.

23. Attach the damper lower bolts when the positioning allows. Tighten both bolts until the clutch housing is seated against the block.

24. Install two lower mounting bolts and torque them to 33 ft. lbs.

25. Install the front and rear torque rod brackets. Torque the front torque rod bolts to 54 ft. lbs., the front bracket bolts to 33 ft. lbs., the rear torque rod bolts to 54 ft. lbs., and the rear bracket bolts to 47 ft. lbs.

26. Remove the transmission jack.

27. Install the starter and torque the mounting bolts to 33 ft. lbs.

28. Turn the right steering knuckle out far enough to fit the end into the transaxle. Use new 26mm spring clips on both axles. Repeat procedure for the other side.

✳✳CAUTION

Make sure that the axles bottom fully so that you feel the spring clip engage the differential.

29. Install the lower ball joints. Torque the nuts to 32 ft. lbs.

30. Install the tie rods. Torque the nuts to 32 ft. lbs.

31. Connect the shift linkage.

32. Connect the shift lever torque rod to the clutch housing and torque the bolt to 7 ft. lbs. (84 inch lbs.).

33. Install the stabilizer bar.

34. Install the lower shields.

35. Install the front wheels and torque the lugs to specifications.

36. Install the remaining starter bolts and torque to 33 ft. lbs.

37. Install the clutch slave cylinder at the release arm.

38. Install the speedometer cable using a new O-ring coated with clean engine oil.

39. Connect all engine compartment wiring.

40. Fill the transaxle with SAE 10W-40 engine oil. Road test the vehicle for proper operation.

Accord 1976-79

1. Drain the transaxle.

2. Raise and support the front of the vehicle on jackstands.

3. Remove the front wheels.

4. Disconnect the negative battery terminals from the battery and the transaxle case.

5. Disconnect the positive battery terminal from the starter and the wire from the solenoid. Remove the starter.

6. Disconnect the following cables and wires:

    a. Clutch cable at the release arm.

    b. Back-up light switch wires.

    c. Transmission Controlled Spark (TCS) switch wires, if so equipped.

    d. Speedometer cable.

✳✳WARNING

When removing the speedometer cable from the transaxle, it is not necessary to remove the entire cable holder. Remove the end boot (gear holder seal) and the cable retaining clip, then, pull the cable out of the holder. In no way should you disturb the holder, unless it is absolutely necessary.

7. Using a Ball Joint Remover tool, disconnect the left and right lower ball joints from the steering knuckle.

8. Pull on both wheel hubs to disconnect the driveshafts from the differential case.

9. Using a drift punch, drive out the gearshift rod pin (8mm) and disconnect the rod at the transaxle case.

10. Disconnect the gearshift extension from the clutch housing.

11. Screw in the engine hanger bolts to the engine torque rod bolt hole and to the hole just to the left of the distributor. Hook a chain to the bolts and lift the engine just enough to take the weight off the engine mounts.

12. After making sure that the engine is properly supported, remove the two center beam-to-lower engine mount nuts. Remove the center beam and the lower engine mount.

13. Reinstall the center beam (without mount) and lower the engine until it rests on the beam.

14. Place a floor jack under the transaxle and loosen the attaching bolts. Using the jack to support the transaxle, slide it away from the engine and lower the jack until the transaxle clears the vehicle.

To install:

15. Install the transaxle in the vehicle. Reverse all the removal procedures.

16. Be sure to pay attention to the following points:

    a. Tighten all mounting nuts and bolts to their specified torque.

    b. Use a new shift rod pin.

    c. After installing the driveshafts, attempt to move the inner joint housing in and out of the differential housing. If it moves easily, the driveshaft end clips should be replaced.

    d. Make sure that the control cables and wires are properly connected.

    e. Be sure the transaxle is refilled to the proper level.
Road test the vehicle for proper operation.

Accord 1980-83

▶ See Figure 3

1. Disconnect the battery ground cable at the battery and the transaxle case.

2. Disconnect the following cables and wires:

    a. Clutch cable at the release arm.

    b. Back-up light switch wires.

c. TCS (Transmission Controlled Spark) switch wires, if so equipped.

d. Black/white wire from the starter solenoid.

3. Release the engine sub wiring harness from the clamp at the clutch housing. Remove the upper two transaxle mounting bolts.

4. Raise the front of the car and support it with safety stands. Drain the transaxle.

5. Remove the front wheels. Disconnect the speedometer cable.

➡When removing the speedometer cable from the transaxle, it is not necessary to remove the entire cable holder. Remove the end boot (gear holder seal), the cable retaining clip and then pull the cable out of the holder. In no way should you disturb the holder, unless it is absolutely necessary.

6. Disconnect the shift lever torque rod from the clutch housing. Remove the bolt from the shift rod clevis.

7. Disconnect the tie rod ball joints and remove them using a suitable ball joint remover.

8. Remove the lower arm ball joint bolt from the right side lower control arm, then using a puller to disconnect the ball joint from the knuckle. Remove the damper fork bolt.

9. Drive out the gearshift rod pin (8mm) with a drift and disconnect the rod at the transaxle case.

10. Disconnect the gearshift extension at the clutch housing.

11. Screw in the engine hanger bolts (see the Engine Removal section) to the engine torque rod bolt hole and to the hole just to the left of the distributor. Hook a chain onto the bolts and lift the engine just enough to take the load off the engine mounts.

12. After making sure that the engine is properly supported, remove the two center beam-to-lower engine mount nuts. Next, remove the center beam, followed by the lower engine mount.

13. Reinstall the center beam (without mount) and lower the engine until it rests on the beam.

14. Place a jack under the transaxle and loosen the 4 attaching bolts. Using the jack to support the transaxle, slide it away from the engine and lower the jack until the transaxle clears the car.

To install:

15. Install the transaxle. Reverse all the removal procedure.

16. Be sure to pay attention to the following points:

a. Tighten all mounting nuts and bolts.

b. Use a new shift rod pin.

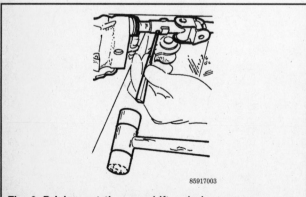

85917003

Fig. 3 Driving out the gearshift rod pin

c. After installing the driveshafts, attempt to move the inner joint housing in and out of the differential housing. If it moves easily, the driveshaft end clips should be replaced.

d. Make sure that the control cables and wires are properly connected.

e. Be sure the transaxle is refilled to the proper level. Road test the vehicle for proper operation.

Prelude 1979-83

1. Disconnect the battery ground cable at the battery and the transaxle case.

2. Disconnect the following cables and wires:

a. Clutch cable at the release arm.

b. Back-up light switch wires.

c. TCS (Transmission Controlled Spark) switch wires, if so equipped.

d. Black/white wire from the starter solenoid.

3. Release the engine sub wiring harness from the clamp at the clutch housing. Remove the upper two transaxle mounting bolts.

4. Raise the front of the car and support it with safety stands. Drain the transaxle.

5. Remove the front wheels. Disconnect the speedometer cable.

➡When removing the speedometer cable from the transaxle, it is not necessary to remove the entire cable holder. Remove the end boot (gear holder seal), the cable retaining clip and then pull the cable out of the holder. In no way should you disturb the holder, unless it is absolutely necessary. For further details, see the Engine Removal section.

6. Disconnect the shift lever torque rod from the clutch housing. Remove the bolt from the shift rod clevis.

7. Disconnect the tie rod ball joints and remove them using a suitable ball joint remover.

8. Remove the lower arm ball joint bolt from the right side lower control arm, then using a puller to disconnect the ball joint from the knuckle. Remove the damper fork bolt.

9. Drive out the gearshift rod pin (8mm) with a drift and disconnect the rod at the transaxle case.

10. Disconnect the gearshift extension at the clutch housing.

11. Screw in the engine hanger bolts to the engine torque rod bolt hole and to the hole just to the left of the distributor. Hook a chain onto the bolts and lift the engine just enough to take the load off the engine mounts.

12. After making sure that the engine is properly supported, remove the two center beam-to-lower engine mount nuts. Next, remove the center beam, followed by the lower engine mount.

13. Reinstall the center beam (without mount) and lower the engine until it rests on the beam.

14. Place a jack under the transaxle and loosen the 4 attaching bolts. Using the jack to support the transaxle, slide it away from the engine and lower the jack until the transaxle clears the car.

To install:

15. Install the transaxle in the vehicle. Reverse all the removal procedure.

16. Be sure to pay attention to the following points:

a. Tighten all mounting nuts and bolts.

b. Use a new shift rod pin.

c. After installing the driveshafts, attempt to move the inner joint housing in and out of the differential housing. If it moves easily, the driveshaft end clips should be replaced.

d. Make sure that the control cables and wires are properly connected.

e. Be sure the transaxle is refilled to the proper level.

OVERHAUL

▶ **See Figures 4, 5, 6 and 7**

4-Speed and 5-Speed Transaxles

➡**Use this general procedure as a guide for this type of repair. Overhaul of a manual transaxle is a complexed and time consuming repair-it is far better to replace the unit with a complete rebuilt assembly.**

DISASSEMBLY

1. Remove the transaxle end cover. Check the transaxle mainshaft and countershaft end-play. End-play should be between 0.0508-0.0762mm. If the clearance is excessive, inspect the ball bearings after transaxle disassembly.

2. Remove the locking tab from the mainshaft locknut. The mainshaft locknut has left hand threads. Place the transaxle in gear and place the proper size wrench on the countershaft to keep it from moving. Remove the mainshaft locknut.

3. Remove the mainshaft bearing and the large snapring.

4. Loosen the 3 shift detent lock ball screws. Remove the screws, springs and balls.

5. Remove the transaxle case bolts. Lightly tap the case with a hammer and drift and separate the case. Do not pry the case apart.

6. Remove the reverse idler gear and shaft. Remove the reverse shift fork.

7. Remove the shift selector assembly. If repair to the shift selector is necessary, disassemble as follows:

a. Remove the two screws and retaining plate. Stake the screws when reinstalling.

b. Push the shift arm into the reverse position (towards the large spring). Then release it.

c. The pivot shaft holds a spring loaded detent. Do not lose the detent ball and spring when removing. Remove the pivot shaft.

d. Remove the interlock bar and shift arms.

e. During reassembly, insert a small prybar into the reverse side (large spring end) of the arm assembly to hold down the detent ball, while inserting the pivot shaft.

8. Remove the shift fork retaining bolts and pull the shift shafts up until they clear the case. Remove the forks and shafts.

➡**When reinstalling the fork retaining bolts, turn the shaft so the threaded portion of the hole is facing away from the bolt.**

9. Remove the mainshaft and countershaft and at the same time by holding the 2 shafts and lightly taping the flywheel end of the mainshaft.

10. Remove the shift rod boot, shift rim, lock washer and bolt. Remove the shift rod and shift arm.

➡**During installation of the shift arm retaining bolt, turn the shaft so that the threaded portion of the hole is facing away from the bolt.**

11. Measure the side clearance of the low gear with a feeler gauge, if the clearance is excessive, replace the thrust plate. Perform the same measurement on the remaining gears, if the clearance is beyond the service limit, replace the bearing race (spacer).

12. If the countershaft must be disassembled to adjust the clearances, or replace gears, remove the locknut by installing the shaft in case and holding the differential securely.

➡**Place the end lugs of the holder in the case and center the lug in the hole of the differential carrier.**

13. Remove the two screws and retaining plate which hold the countershaft bearing. Remove the countershaft bearing with a bearing puller.

14. Clean all component parts thoroughly in the proper solvent.

15. Inspect the surfaces of each gear and blocking ring for roughness or damage. Apply a thin coat of oil to the tapered surfaces of each gear and push them together with a rotating motion. Measure the distance between the ring and gear. Replace all necessary parts. Clearance should be between 3.0-3.5mm.

16. Measure the clearance between the shift forks and synchronizer sleeves. The clearance should be between 1.0-4.5mm. If clearances are excessive, replace the shift forks, synchronizers or both.

17. Ensure that there are no restrictions in the oil holes on the countershaft. Check the splines for wear.

18. Inspect the condition of the mainshaft and countershaft bearing surfaces. Check run-out, gear tooth and spline condition.

19. Check the condition of all the gears. Check the condition of all bearing surfaces.

20. Inspect the bearing race (spacer) of each gear.

21. Replace all questionable parts.

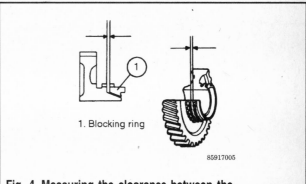

1. Blocking ring

85917005

Fig. 4 Measuring the clearance between the synchronizer ring and gear hub

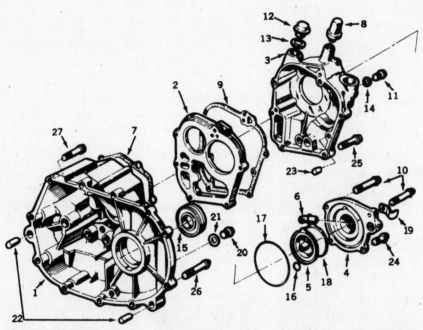

1 Housing, transmission
2 Spacer, transmission housing
3 Cover, transmission
4 Cover, right side
5 Plate, oil barrier
6 Tube, breather
7 Gasket, transmission housing
8 Cap, breather
9 Gasket, transmission case

10 Bolt, flanged, 6 x 85 mm
11 Bolt, oil check
12 Bolt, plug 25 mm
13 Washer, sealing, 25 mm
14 Washer, 8 mm
15 Oil seal, 35 x 56 x 9 mm
16 O-ring, 9.4 x 2.4
17 O-ring, 64.5 x 3
18 O-ring, 42 x 2.4

19 Bracket, wire harness
20 Bolt, drain plug, 14 mm
21 Washer, drain plug, 14 mm
22 Pin, dowel, 14 x 20 mm
23 Pin, dowel, 8 x 14 mm
24 Bolt, flanged, 6 x 20 mm
25 Bolt, flanged, 6 x 45 mm
26 Bolt, flanged, 8 x 40 mm
27 Bolt, flanged, 8 x 45 mm

85917004

Fig. 5 Exploded view of housing and cover assemblies

1. Needle roller bearing set
       plate
2. Needle roller bearing
3. Clutch case
4. Reverse gear shaft
5. Reverse idle gear
6. Reverse shift fork
7. Shift selector assembly
8. Countershaft gear assembly
9. Main shaft
10. First/second fork shaft
11. Reverse fork shaft
12. Third/fourth fork shaft
13. Steel ball
14. Ball set spring
15. Drain plug washer
16. Set ball spring screw
17. Ball bearing
18. Needle roller bearing
19. 48 mm snap ring
20. Ball bearing
21. 62 mm snap ring
22. 23 mm lock nut
23. 20 mm lock nut
24. Transmission rear cover
25. Speedometer gear

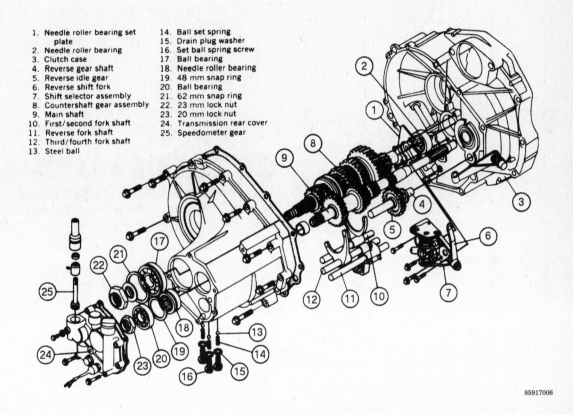

85917006

Fig. 6 Typcial view of the manual transaxle

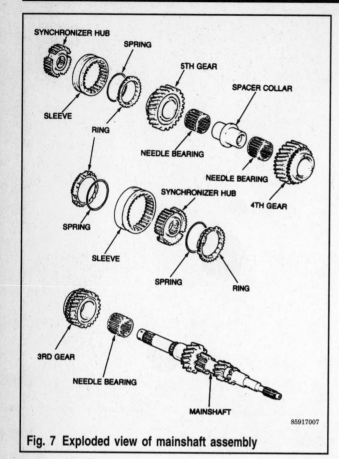

Fig. 7 Exploded view of mainshaft assembly

ASSEMBLY

1. The transaxle should be assembled in the reverse order of disassembly. During assembly, note the following points:

2. Check the differential bearing clearance.

3. Apply a thin coat of oil to all parts before they are installed.

4. Be certain that hub and synchronizer teeth match when they are assembled.

5. The mainshaft and countershaft must be installed at the same time. Next, install the 3rd/4th shift fork and shaft, 1st/2nd shift fork and shaft and then the reverse shaft.

6. When the shift selector assembly is installed, there are two special bolts which must be inserted 1st. These bolts locate the assembly.

7. Lock the mainshaft and countershaft locknuts with a punch.

8. Make sure that the mainshaft and countershaft turn smoothly and that all gears engage freely. Check and be certain that all bolts are properly torqued.

Halfshafts

REMOVAL & INSTALLATION

▶ **See Figures 8, 9, 10, 11, 12, 13, 14, 15, 16, 17, 18 and 19**

All Models

The front driveshaft or halfshaft assembly consists of a sub-axle shaft and a driveshaft or halfshaft with two universal joints.

A constant velocity ball joint is used for both universal joints, which are factory packed with special grease and enclosed in sealed rubber boots. The outer joint cannot be disassembled except for removal of the boot.

1. Remove the hubcap from the front wheel and then remove the center cap.

2. Pull out the 4mm cotter pin and loosen but do not remove the spindle nut.

3. Raise and support the front of the vehicle on jackstands.

4. Remove the wheel lug nuts and the wheel.

5. Remove the spindle nut.

6. Drain the transaxle.

7. Using a Ball Joint Remover tool, remove the lower arm ball joints from the knuckle.

✳✳WARNING

Make sure that a floor jack is positioned securely under the lower control arm, at the ball joint. Otherwise, the lower control arm may 'jump' suddenly away from the steering knuckle as the ball joint is removed.

8. On Prelude model (1983), remove the damper fork bolt, damper locking bolt and the damper fork.

9. To remove the driveshaft, hold the knuckle and pull it toward you. Then slide the driveshaft out of the knuckle. Pry the CV joint (at the transaxle end) out about ½". Prying the axle outward causes an internal lock ring to come out of its locking groove. Pull the inboard joint side of the driveshaft out of the differential case.

To install:

10. Install the driveshaft or halfshaft into the transaxle assembly with a NEW spring locking clip.

11. The splined fitting and clip must fit all the way into position; the clip will engage with a noticeable click. Reverse all the removal procedures.

12. Torque the ball-joint nut to 25 ft. lbs. and always replace the cotter pin. Torque the spindle nut to 108 ft. lbs.

13. If either the inboard or outboard joint boot bands have been removed for inspection or disassembly of the joint (only the inboard joint can be disassembled), be sure to repack the joint with a sufficient amount of bearing grease.

✳✳WARNING

Make sure the CV-joint sub-axle bottoms so that the spring clip may hold the sub-axle securely in the transaxle.

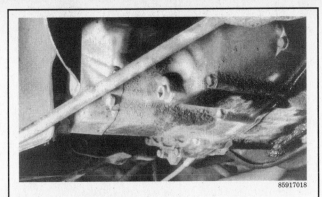

Fig. 8 Drain plug for transaxle

Fig. 9 Removing the center hub cap

Fig. 10 Unstaking the retaining nut

Fig. 11 Removing the lower ball joint assembly

Fig. 12 Separating the lower ball joint

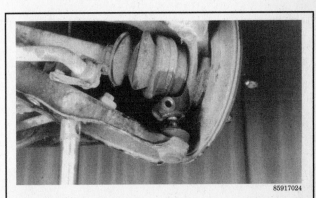

Fig. 13 Note the support under the lower arm assembly

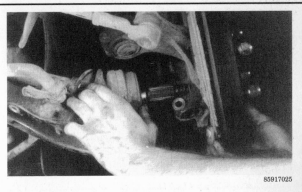

Fig. 14 Removing the halfshaft from the hub assembly

Fig. 15 Removing the halfshaft from the transaxle

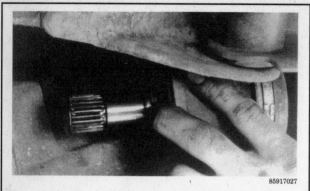

Fig. 16 Note the retaining clip on the halfshaft end

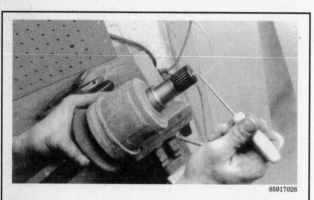

Fig. 17 Removing the retaining clip on the halfshaft

Fig. 18 Installing the halfshaft in the transaxle

Fig. 19 Note the correct position for staking the retaining nut

CV-Joint and CV-Boot

REMOVAL & INSTALLATION

▶ **See Figures 20 and 21**

All Models

1. Raise and safely support the vehicle.
2. Remove the halfshaft.

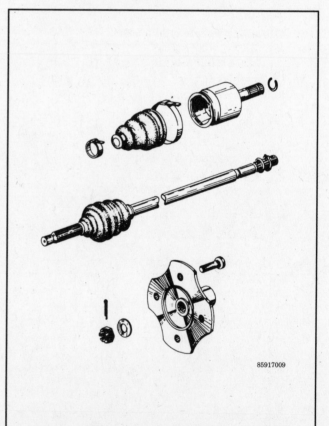

Fig. 20 Exploded view of halfshaft and related parts

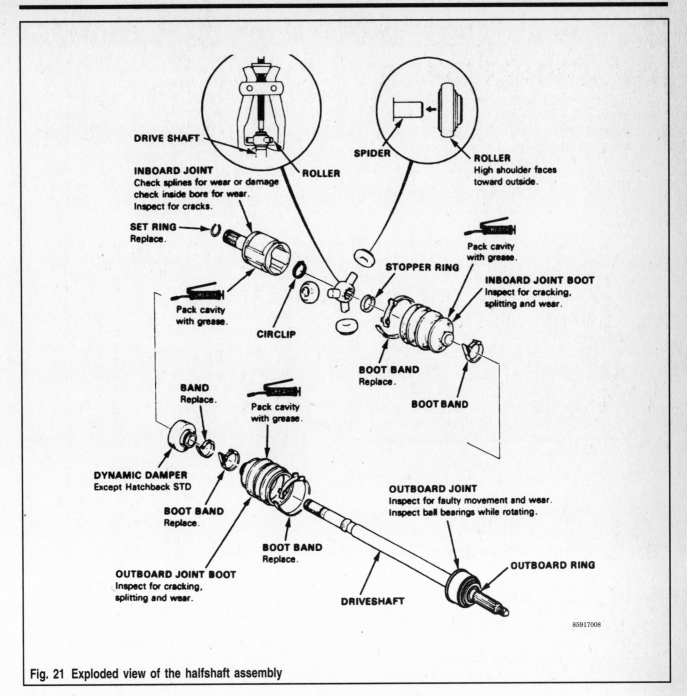

Fig. 21 Exploded view of the halfshaft assembly

3. Place the halfshaft in a suitable holding fixture. Remove the boot bands. If the bands are the welded type, they must be cut to be removed. After removing the bands, push the CV-joint boot away from the end of the halfshaft to gain access to the CV-joint.

4. Remove the CV-joint. Mark the components during disassembly to ensure proper positioning during reassembly.

5. Remove the CV-boot.

6. Installation is the reverse of the removal procedure. Check the CV-joint components for wear prior to installation and replace as necessary.

7. Thoroughly pack the CV-joint and boot with molybdenum disulfide grease. Always install NEW boot bands.

8. Install the halfshaft assembly.

CLUTCH

✳✳CAUTION

The clutch driven disc contains asbestos, which has been determined to be a cancer causing agent. Never clean clutch surfaces with compressed air! Avoid inhaling any dust from any clutch surface! When cleaning clutch surfaces, use a commercially available brake cleaning fluid.

Understanding the Clutch

The purpose of the clutch is to disconnect and connect engine power from the transaxle. A car at rest requires a lot of engine torque to get all that weight moving. An internal combustion engine does not develop a high starting torque (unlike steam engines), so it must be allowed to operate without any load until it builds up enough torque to move the car. Torque increases with engine rpm. The clutch allows the engine to build up torque by physically disconnecting the engine from the transaxle, relieving the engine of any load or resistance. The transfer of engine power to the transaxle (the load) must be smooth and gradual; if it weren't, drive line components would wear out or break quickly. This gradual power transfer is made possible by gradually releasing the clutch pedal. The clutch disc and pressure plate are the connecting link between the engine and transaxle. When the clutch pedal is released, the disc and plate contact each other (clutch engagement), physically joining the engine and transaxle. When the pedal is pushed in, the disc and plate separate (the clutch is disengaged), disconnecting the engine from the transaxle.

The clutch assembly consists of the flywheel, the clutch disc, the clutch pressure plate, the throwout bearing and fork, the actuating linkage and the pedal. The flywheel and clutch pressure plate (driving members) are connected to the engine crankshaft and rotate with it. The clutch disc is located between the flywheel and pressure plate, and splined to the transaxle shaft. A driving member is one that is attached to the engine and transfers engine power to a driven member (clutch disc) on the transaxle shaft. A driving member (pressure plate) rotates (drives) a driven member (clutch disc) on contact and, in so doing, turns the transaxle shaft. There is a circular diaphragm spring within the pressure plate cover (transaxle side). In a relaxed state (when the clutch pedal is fully released), this spring is convex; that is, it is dished outward toward the transaxle. Pushing in the clutch pedal actuates an attached linkage rod. Connected to the other end of this rod is the throwout bearing fork. The throwout bearing is attached to the fork. When the clutch pedal is depressed, the clutch linkage pushes the fork and bearing forward to contact the diaphragm spring of the pressure plate. The outer edges of the spring are secured to the pressure plate and are pivoted on rings so that when the center of the spring is compressed by the throwout bearing, the outer edges bow outward and, by so doing, pull the pressure plate in the same direction - away from the clutch disc. This action separates the disc from the plate, disengaging the clutch and allowing the transaxle to be shifted into another gear. A coil type clutch return spring attached to the clutch pedal arm permits full release of the pedal. Releasing the pedal pulls the throwout bearing away from the diaphragm spring resulting in a reversal of spring position. As bearing pressure is gradually released from the spring center, the outer edges of the spring bow outward, pushing the pressure plate into closer contact with the clutch disc. As the disc and plate move closer together, friction between the two increases and slippage is reduced until, when full spring pressure is applied (by fully releasing the pedal), the speed of the disc and plate are the same. This stops all slipping, creating a direct connection between the plate and disc which results in the transfer of power from the engine to the transaxle. The clutch disc is now rotating with the pressure plate at engine speed and, because it is splined to the transaxle shaft, the shaft now turns at the same engine speed. Understanding clutch operation can be rather difficult at first; if you're still confused after reading this, consider the following analogy. The action of the diaphragm spring can be compared to that of an oil can bottom. The bottom of an oil can is shaped very much like the clutch diaphragm spring and pushing in on the can bottom and then releasing it produces a similar effect. As mentioned earlier, the clutch pedal return spring permits full release of the pedal and reduces linkage slack due to wear. As the linkage wears, clutch free-pedal travel will increase and free-travel will decrease as the clutch wears. Free-travel is actually throwout bearing lash.

The diaphragm spring type clutches used are available in two different designs: flat diaphragm springs or bent spring. The bent fingers are bent back to create a centrifugal boost ensuring quick re-engagement at higher engine speeds. This design enables pressure plate load to increase as the clutch disc wears and makes low pedal effort possible even with a heavy duty clutch. The throwout bearing used with the bent finger design is 32mm long and is shorter than the bearing used with the flat finger design. These bearings are not interchangeable. If the longer bearing is used with the bent finger clutch, free-pedal travel will not exist. This results in clutch slippage and rapid wear.

The transaxle varies the gear ratio between the engine and drive wheels. It can be shifted to change engine speed as driving conditions and loads change. The transaxle allows disengaging and reversing power from the engine to the wheels.

Adjustments

PEDAL HEIGHT

Civic

1976-79

Check the clutch pedal height and if necessary, adjust the upper stop, so that the clutch and brake pedals rest at approximately the same height from the floor. First, be sure that the brake pedal free-play is properly adjusted.

1980-83

The clutch pedal disengagement height should be 30mm minimum from the floor.

Accord and Prelude

1. Pedal height should be 184mm measured from the front of the pedal to the floorboard (mat removed).

2. Adjust by turning the pedal stop bolt in or out until height is correct. Tighten the locknut after adjustment.

FREE PLAY

All Models

Adjust the clutch release lever so that it has 3-4mm on Civic 1973-80 models or 4.4-5.4mm on Civic 1981-83 models of play when you move the clutch release lever at the transaxle with your hand. This adjustment is made at the outer cable housing adjuster, near the release lever on non-CVCC models. Less than 3mm of free-play may lead to clutch slippage, while more than 3mm clearance may cause difficult shifting.

✳✳WARNING

Make sure that the upper and lower adjusting nuts are tightened after adjustment.

On Civic CVCC models, the free-play adjustment is made on the cable at the firewall. Remove the C-clip and then rotate the threaded control cable housing until there is 3-4mm free-play at the release lever. On Accord and Prelude models (1976-81), adjustment is made at the slave cylinder. Simply loosen the lock nut and turn the adjusting nut until the correct free play is obtained. Free play should be 2.0-3.5mm at the release lever. On the 1982-83 Accord and Prelude, adjustment is made on the cable at the firewall. Remove the C-clip and rotate the threaded control cable until 5.0-6.5mm exists at the clutch release lever.

Driven Disc and Pressure Plate

REMOVAL & INSTALLATION

▸ See Figure 22

✳✳CAUTION

The clutch driven disc contains asbestos, which has been determined to be a cancer causing agent. Never clean clutch surfaces with compressed air! Avoid inhaling any dust from any clutch surface! When cleaning clutch surfaces, use a commercially available brake cleaning fluid.

1. Refer to the 'Manual Transaxle, Removal & Installation' procedures in this section and remove the transaxle. Match-mark the flywheel and clutch for reassembly.

2. Using a large pry bar or other fabricated tool, lock the flywheel ring gear. Remove the pressure plate-to-flywheel bolts, the pressure plate and the clutch disc.

➡**Loosen the retaining bolts two turns at a time in a circular pattern. Removing one bolt while the rest are tight may warp the diaphragm spring.**

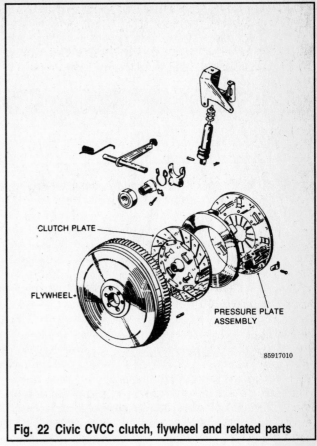

CLUTCH PLATE

FLYWHEEL

PRESSURE PLATE ASSEMBLY

85917010

Fig. 22 Civic CVCC clutch, flywheel and related parts

3. The flywheel can now be removed, if it needs repairing or replacing.

4. To separate the pressure plate from the diaphragm spring, remove the 4 retracting clips.

5. To remove the release, or throw-out, bearing, first straighten the locking tab and remove the 8mm bolt, followed by the release shaft and release arm with the bearing attached.

➡**It is recommended that the release bearing be removed after the release arm has been removed from the casing. Trying to remove or install the bearing with the release arm in the case, will damage the retaining clip.**

6. If a new release bearing is to be installed, separate the bearing from the holder, using a bearing drift.

To install:

7. Assemble and install the clutch and pressure plate assembly in the vehicle. Reverse all the removal procedures.

8. Be sure to pay attention to the following points:

   a. Make sure that the flywheel and the end of the crankshaft are clean before assembling.

   b. When installing the pressure plate, align the mark on the outer edge of the flywheel with the alignment mark on the pressure plate. Failure to align these marks will result in imbalance.

   c. When tightening the pressure plate bolts, use a pilot shaft to center the friction disc; the pilot shaft can be bought at any large auto supply store or fabricated from a wooden dowel. After centering the disc, tighten the bolts two turns at a time, in a circular pattern to avoid warping the diaphragm spring.

d. When installing the release shaft and arm, place a lock tab washer under the retaining bolt.

e. When installing the transaxle, make sure that the mainshaft is properly aligned with the disc spline and the alignment pins are in place, before tightening the case bolts.

Master Cylinder

REMOVAL & INSTALLATION

1. The clutch master cylinder is located on the firewall.
2. Disconnect and plug the hydraulic line at the clutch master cylinder.
3. From under the instrument panel, remove the clutch master cylinder rod-to-clutch pedal arm pin.
4. Remove the clutch master cylinder-to-firewall bolts and the master cylinder.
5. To install, reverse the removal procedures. Refill the master cylinder reservoir and bleed the system.

OVERHAUL

1. Remove the stopper plate snapring.
2. Once the snapring is removed, use compressed air to remove the piston assembly; note the order of all components. The piston assembly is in two parts — the piston and the spring assembly.
3. Inspect the inside of the cylinder bore for rust, pitting or scratching. Light scores or scratches can be removed with a brake cylinder hone. If the bore won't clean up with a few passes of the hone, the entire cylinder will have to be replaced.
4. Replace the interior components with new ones. Overhaul kits will simply be two pieces — a new piston and a new spring assembly. Reassemble them in the correct order. Coat the inside of the cylinder with brake fluid before installing the parts.

AUTOMATIC TRANSAXLE

Understanding Automatic Transaxles

The automatic transaxle allows engine torque and power to be transmitted to the drive wheels within a narrow range of engine operating speeds. The transaxle will allow the engine to turn fast enough to produce plenty of power and torque at very low speeds, while keeping it at a sensible rpm at high vehicle speeds. The transaxle performs this job entirely without driver assistance. The transaxle uses a light fluid as the medium for the transaxle of power. This fluid also works in the operation of various hydraulic control circuits and as a lubricant. Because the transaxle fluid performs all of these three functions, trouble within the unit can easily travel from one part to another. For this reason, and because of the complexity and unusual operating principles of the transaxle, a very sound understanding of the basic principles of operation will simplify troubleshooting.

5. Install the master cylinder and bleed the system.

Slave Cylinder

REMOVAL & INSTALLATION

The slave cylinder is retained by two bolts. To remove the cylinder, simply disconnect the hydraulic line, remove the return spring and the bolts. To install, reverse the removal procedures. Refill the master cylinder and bleed the system.

OVERHAUL

1. There is little you can do to the slave cylinder other than replace the piston and seal inside the cylinder.
2. Using compressed air, blow the piston out of the cylinder; the seal will probably come out with it.
3. Once the piston and seal are removed, check the inside of the cylinder bore for pitting, rust or scratching. The bore can be honed but it's probably not worth the effort. A new slave cylinder would make more sense.

HYDRAULIC CLUTCH SYSTEM BLEEDING

The hydraulic system must be bleed whenever the system has been leaking or repaired. The bleed scew is located on the slave cylinder. Remove the bleed screw dust cap and attach a clear hose to the bleed screw. Immerse the other end of the hose in a clear jar, half filled with clean brake fluid. Fill the clutch master cylinder with new brake fluid. Open the bleed scew slightly and have an assistant depress the clutch pedal slowly. Close the bleed scew when the pedal reaches the end of its travel. Allow the clutch pedal to return slowly. Repeat until all air bubbles are expelled from the system. Replace the dust cap on the slave cylinder. Refill the master cylinder with NEW brake fluid.

THE TORQUE CONVERTER

The torque converter replaces the conventional clutch. It has three functions:
1. It allows the engine to idle with the vehicle at a standstill, even with the transaxle in gear.
2. It allows the transaxle to shift from range to range smoothly, without requiring that the driver close the throttle during the shift.
3. It multiplies engine torque to an increasing extent as vehicle speed drops and throttle opening is increased. This has the effect of making the transaxle more responsive and reduces the amount of shifting required.

The torque converter is a metal case which is shaped like a sphere that has been flattened on opposite sides. It is bolted to the rear end of the engine's crankshaft. Generally, the entire metal case rotates at engine speed and serves as the engine's flywheel.

The case contains three sets of blades. One set is attached directly to the case. This set forms the torus or pump. Another set is directly connected to the output shaft, and forms the turbine. The third set is mounted on a hub which, in turn, is mounted on a stationary shaft through a one-way clutch. This third set is known as the stator.

A pump, which is driven by the converter hub at engine speed, keeps the torque converter full of transaxle fluid at all times. Fluid flows continuously through the unit to provide cooling.

Under low speed acceleration, the torque converter functions as follows:

The torus is turning faster than the turbine. It picks up fluid at the center of the converter and, through centrifugal force, slings it outward. Since the outer edge of the converter moves faster than the portions at the center, the fluid picks up speed.

The fluid then enters the outer edge of the turbine blades. It then travels back toward the center of the converter case along the turbine blades. In impinging upon the turbine blades, the fluid loses the energy picked up in the torus.

If the fluid were now to immediately be returned directly into the torus, both halves of the converter would have to turn at approximately the same speed at all times, and torque input and output would both be the same.

In flowing through the torus and turbine, the fluid picks up two types of flow, or flow in two separate directions. It flows through the turbine blades, and it spins with the engine. The stator, whose blades are stationary when the vehicle is being accelerated at low speeds, converts one type of flow into another. Instead of allowing the fluid to flow straight back into the torus, the stator's curved blades turn the fluid almost 90° toward the direction of rotation of the engine. Thus the fluid does not flow as fast toward the torus, but is already spinning when the torus picks it up. This has the effect of allowing the torus to turn much faster than the turbine. This difference in speed may be compared to the difference in speed between the smaller and larger gears in any gear train. The result is that engine power output is higher, and engine torque is multiplied.

As the speed of the turbine increases, the fluid spins faster and faster in the direction of engine rotation. As a result, the ability of the stator to redirect the fluid flow is reduced. Under cruising conditions, the stator is eventually forced to rotate on its one-way clutch in the direction of engine rotation. Under these conditions, the torque converter begins to behave almost like a solid shaft, with the torus and turbine speeds being almost equal.

THE PLANETARY GEARBOX

The ability of the torque converter to multiply engine torque is limited. Also, the unit tends to be more efficient when the turbine is rotating at relatively high speeds. Therefore, a planetary gearbox is used to carry the power output of the turbine to the halfshafts.

Planetary gears function very similarly to conventional transaxle gears. However, their construction is different in that three elements make up one gear system, and, in that all

three elements are different from one another. The three elements are: an outer gear that is shaped like a hoop, with teeth cut into the inner surface; a sun gear, mounted on a shaft and located at the very center of the outer gear; and a set of three planet gears, held by pins in a ring-like planet carrier, meshing with both the sun gear and the outer gear. Either the outer gear or the sun gear may be held stationary, providing more than one possible torque multiplication factor for each set of gears. Also, if all three gears are forced to rotate at the same speed, the gearset forms, in effect, a solid shaft.

Most modern automatics use the planetary gears to provide either a single reduction ratio of about 1.8:1, or two reduction gears: a low of about 2.5:1, and an intermediate of about 1.5:1. Bands and clutches are used to hold various portions of the gearsets to the transaxle case or to the shaft on which they are mounted. Shifting is accomplished, then, by changing the portion of each planetary gearset which is held to the transaxle case or to the shaft.

THE SERVOS AND ACCUMULATORS

The servos are hydraulic pistons and cylinders. They resemble the hydraulic actuators used on many familiar machines, such as bulldozers. Hydraulic fluid enters the cylinder, under pressure, and forces the piston to move to engage the band or clutches.

The accumulators are used to cushion the engagement of the servos. The transaxle fluid must pass through the accumulator on the way to the servo. The accumulator housing contains a thin piston which is sprung away from the discharge passage of the accumulator. When fluid passes through the accumulator on the way to the servo, it must move the piston against spring pressure, and this action smooths out the action of the servo.

THE HYDRAULIC CONTROL SYSTEM

The hydraulic pressure used to operate the servos comes from the main transaxle oil pump. This fluid is channeled to the various servos through the shift valves. There is generally a manual shift valve which is operated by the transaxle selector lever and an automatic shift valve for each automatic upshift the transaxle provides: i.e., 2-speed automatics have a low/high shift valve, while 3-speeds have a 1-2 valve, and a 2-3 valve.

There are two pressures which effect the operation of these valves. One is the governor pressure which is affected by vehicle speed. The other is the modulator pressure which is affected by intake manifold vacuum or throttle position. Governor pressure rises with an increase in vehicle speed, and modulator pressure rises as the throttle is opened wider. By responding to these two pressures, the shift valves cause the upshift points to be delayed with increased throttle opening to make the best use of the engine's power output.

Most transaxles also make use of an auxiliary circuit for downshifting. This circuit may be actuated by the throttle linkage or the vacuum line which actuates the modulator, or by a cable or solenoid. It applies pressure to a special downshift surface on the shift valve or valves.

The transaxle modulator also governs the line pressure, used to actuate the servos. In this way, the clutches and bands will be actuated with a force matching the torque output of the engine.

Adjustments

SHIFT LINKAGE

Inspection

1. Set the parking brake lever and run the engine at idle speed, while depressing the brake pedal.
2. By moving the shift selector lever slowly forward and backward from the **N** position, make sure that the distance between the **N** and the points where the **D** clutch is engaged for the **2** and **R** positions are the same. The **D** clutch engaging point is just before the slight response is felt. The reverse gears will make a noise when the clutch engages. If the distances are not the same, adjustment is necessary.

Adjustment — 2-Speed

1. Remove the center console screws and it pull away to expose the shift control cable and turnbuckle.
2. Adjust the length of the control cable by turning the turnbuckle, located at the front bottom of the shift lever assembly.

After adjustment, the cable and turnbuckle should twist toward the left (driver's) side of the vehicle when shifted toward the **2** position and toward the right side when shifted into the **R** position.

Adjustment — 3-Speed and 4-Speed
▶ See Figures 23, 24 and 25

1. Remove the shift console.
2. Shift into **REVERSE** and remove the lock-pin from the cable adjuster.
3. With the lock-pin removed, the hole in the adjuster, from which the lock-pin was removed, should be perfectly aligned with the corresponding hole in the shift cable.
4. If they are not perfectly aligned, turn the adjusting nuts as required.
5. Install the lock-pin.

➡**If there is any binding on the lock-pin as it is installed, there is some misalignment. Check and/or adjust as required.**

THROTTLE CABLE ADJUSTMENT

Carbureted Models
▶ See Figures 26 and 27

1. Attach a weight of approximately 3 lbs. to the accelerator pedal. Raise the pedal, then release it, this will allow the weight to remove the normal free play from the throttle cable.
2. Secure the throttle control cable with clamps. Remove the air intake duct.

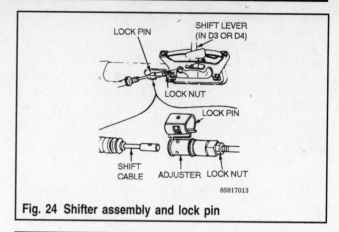

Fig. 24 Shifter assembly and lock pin

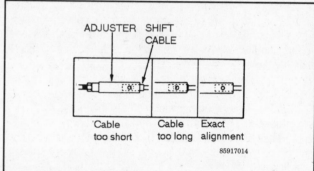

Fig. 25 The cable must be perfectly aligned in the adjuster

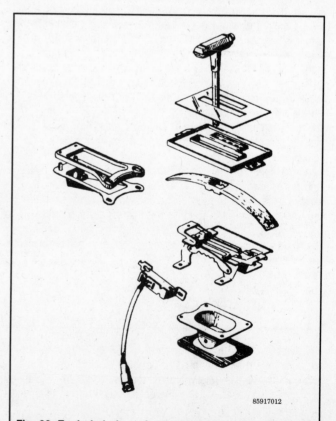

Fig. 23 Exploded view of automatic transaxle shift lever control

3. Lay the end of the throttle control cable over the the shock tower. Adjust the distance between the throttle cable end and the first locknut to 84mm on all models.

4. Insert the end of the throttle control cable into the groove of the throttle control lever. Insert the throttle control cable in the bracket and secure it with the last locknut. Be sure the cable is not kinked or twisted.

5. Check the cable moves freely by depressing the accelerator. Start the engine and check the synchronization between the carburetor and the throttle control cable.

6. The throttle control lever should start to move as the engine speed is increased.

7. If the throttle control lever moves before the engine speed increases, turn the cable top locknut counterclockwise and tighten the bottom locknut.

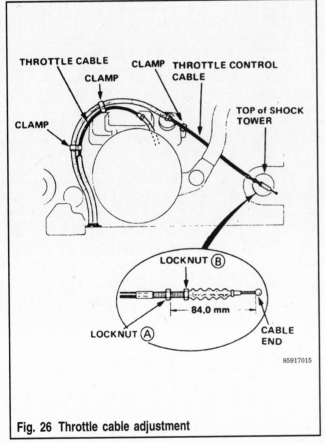

Fig. 26 Throttle cable adjustment

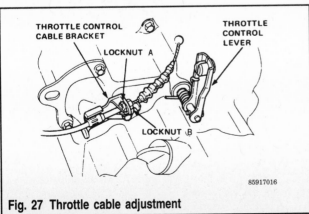

Fig. 27 Throttle cable adjustment

8. If the throttle control lever moves after the engine speed increases, turn the cable top locknut clockwise and tighten the bottom locknut.

Back-Up Light Switch/Neutral Safety Switch

REMOVAL & INSTALLATION

▶ **See Figure 28**

On automatic transaxle vehicles, both the function of the reverse lamps and the neutral safety switch is controlled by the shift position switch at the base of the shift selector assembly. To repalce the shift position switch, firmly set the parking brake and block the wheels. Place the shift selector in Neutral. Remove the console. The shift switch is located on the side of the shift selector, held by 2 bolts or nuts. Disconnect the wiring connector, then remove the switch. When installing the switch, make sure the switch silder is positioned to align with the shifter arm or tab. Install the switch, tighten the retaining nuts or bolts and connect the wiring. Reinstall the console.

After installing the switch, check that the engine starts only in Park or Neutral. The starter should not engage with the shifter in any other position. Check also that the back-up lights (reverse lights) come on when the selector is placed in Reverse.

Transaxle

REMOVAL & INSTALLATION

The automatic transaxle is removed in the same basic manner as the manual transaxle (refer to for Manual Transaxle, Removal & Installation). The following exceptions should be noted during automatic transaxle removal and installation.

1. Remove the center console and control rod pin.

2. Remove the front floor center mat and control cable bracket nuts.

3. Raise and support the front of the vehicle on jackstands.

4. Remove the two selector lever bracket nuts from the front side.

5. Loosen the bolts securing the control cable holder and support beam and disconnect the control cable.

6. Disconnect the transaxle cooler lines from the transaxle.

7. Remove the transaxle together with the engine. Remove the engine mounts and torque converter case cover.

8. Remove the starter motor and separate the transaxle from the engine.

9. To install, reverse the removal procedures. Pay close attention to the following points:

    a. Be sure that the stator hub is correctly located and moves smoothly. The stator shaft can be used for this purpose.

    b. Align the stator, stator shaft, main shaft and torque converter turbine serrations.

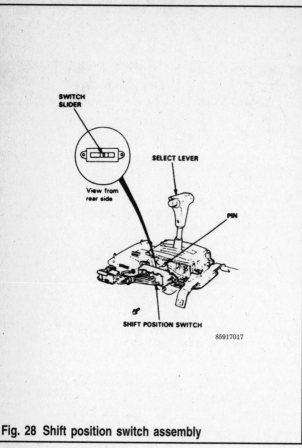

Fig. 28 Shift position switch assembly

c. After installation of the engine/transaxle unit in vehicle, make all required adjustments.

Halfshafts

REMOVAL & INSTALLATION

The front driveshaft assembly consists of a sub-axle shaft and a driveshaft with two universal joints.

A constant velocity ball joint is used for both universal joints, which are factory packed with special grease and enclosed in sealed rubber boots. The outer joint cannot be disassembled except for removal of the boot.

1. Remove the hubcap from the front wheel and then remove the center cap.
2. Pull out the 4mm cotter pin and loosen but do not remove the spindle nut.
3. Raise and support the front of the vehicle on jackstands.
4. Remove the wheel lug nuts and the wheel.
5. Remove the spindle nut.
6. Drain the transaxle.

7. Using a Ball Joint Remover tool, remove the lower arm ball joints from the knuckle.

✳✳WARNING

Make sure that a floor jack is positioned securely under the lower control arm, at the ball joint. Otherwise, the lower control arm may 'jump' suddenly away from the steering knuckle as the ball joint is removed.

8. On Prelude model (1983), remove the damper fork bolt, damper locking bolt and the damper fork.
9. To remove the driveshaft, hold the knuckle and pull it toward you. Then slide the driveshaft out of the knuckle. Pry the CV joint (at the transaxle end) out about ½". Prying the axle outward causes an internal lock ring to come out of its locking groove. Pull the inboard joint side of the driveshaft out of the differential case.

To install:
10. Install the driveshaft or halfshaft into the transaxle assembly with a NEW spring locking clip.
11. The splined fitting and clip must fit all the way into position; the clip will engage with a noticeable click. Reverse all the removal procedures.
12. Torque the ball-joint nut to 25 ft. lbs. and always replace the cotter pin. Torque the spindle nut to 108 ft. lbs.
13. If either the inboard or outboard joint boot bands have been removed for inspection or disassembly of the joint (only the inboard joint can be disassembled), be sure to repack the joint with a sufficient amount of bearing grease.

✳✳WARNING

Make sure the CV-joint sub-axle bottoms so that the spring clip may hold the sub-axle securely in the transaxle.

CV-Joint And CV-Boot

REMOVAL & INSTALLATION

▶ **See Figures 29, 30, 31, 32, 33, 34, 35, 36, 37, 38, 39, 40, 41 and 42**

All Models

1. Raise and safely support the vehicle.
2. Remove the halfshaft.
3. Place the halfshaft in a suitable holding fixture. Remove the boot bands. If the bands are the welded type, they must be cut to be removed. After removing the bands, push the CV-joint boot away from the end of the halfshaft to gain access to the CV-joint.
4. Remove the snapring and the CV-joint from the shaft. Mark the components during disassembly to ensure proper positioning during reassembly.
5. Remove the CV-boot.
6. Installation is the reverse of the removal procedure. Check the CV-joint components for wear prior to installation and replace as necessary.

7. Thoroughly pack the CV-joint and boot with molybdenum disulfide grease. Always install NEW boot bands.

8. Install the halfshaft assembly.

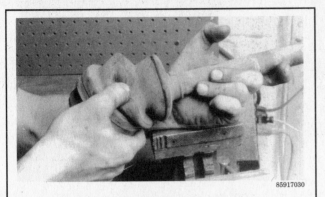

Fig. 29 Check the CV-boot for wear

Fig. 30 Removing the outer band from the CV-boot

Fig. 31 Removing the inner band from the CV-boot

Fig. 32 Positioning the CV-boot

Fig. 33 Check the CV-joint assembly for wear

Fig. 34 Removing the CV-joint housing assembly

Fig. 35 Removing the CV-joint

Fig. 36 Inspecting the CV-joint housing

Fig. 40 Removing the CV-joint assembly

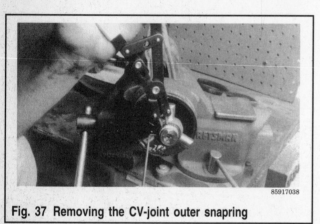

Fig. 37 Removing the CV-joint outer snapring

Fig. 41 Removing the CV-joint inner snapring

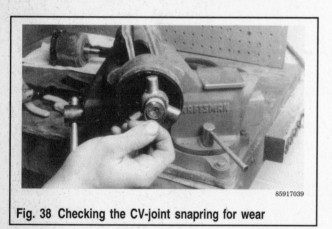

Fig. 38 Checking the CV-joint snapring for wear

Fig. 42 Installing the CV-joint assembly (typical)

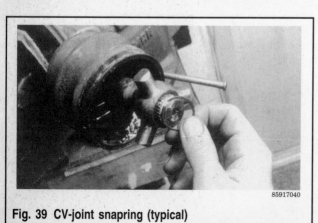

Fig. 39 CV-joint snapring (typical)

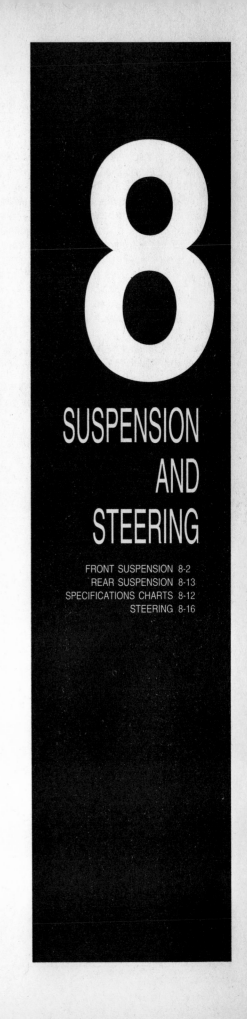

8

SUSPENSION AND STEERING

FRONT SUSPENSION

♦ See Figures 1, 2, 3 and 4

All models, except the 1983 Prelude, use a MacPherson strut type front suspension. Each steering knuckle is suspended by a lower control arm at the bottom and a combined coil spring/shock absorber unit at the top. A front stabilizer bar, mounted between each lower control arm and the body, doubles as a locating rod for the suspension. Caster and camber are not adjustable and are fixed by the location of the strut assemblies in their respective sheet metal towers.

The 1983 Prelude uses a completely redesigned front suspension. A double wishbone system, the lower wishbone consists of a forged transverse link with a locating stabilizer bar. The lower end of the shock absorber has a fork shape to allow the driveshaft to pass through it. The upper arm is located in the wheel well and is twist mounted, angled forward from its inner mount, to clear the shock absorber.

MacPherson Struts

REMOVAL & INSTALLATION

♦ See Figures 5, 6, 7 and 8

1. Raise and support the front of the vehicle on jackstands. Remove the front wheels.

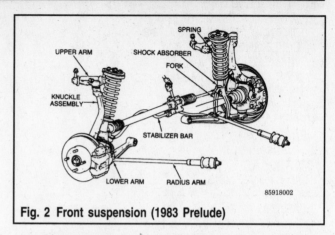

Fig. 2 Front suspension (1983 Prelude)

2. Disconnect the brake pipe at the strut and remove the brake hose retaining clip.

3. Remove the strut-to-steering knuckle bolt (matchmark the assembly) then, push down firmly while tapping it with a hammer until the knuckle is free of the strut.

4. Remove the strut-to-body nuts and the strut from the vehicle.

5. To install, reverse the removal procedures. Be sure to properly match the mating surface of the strut and the knuckle notch.

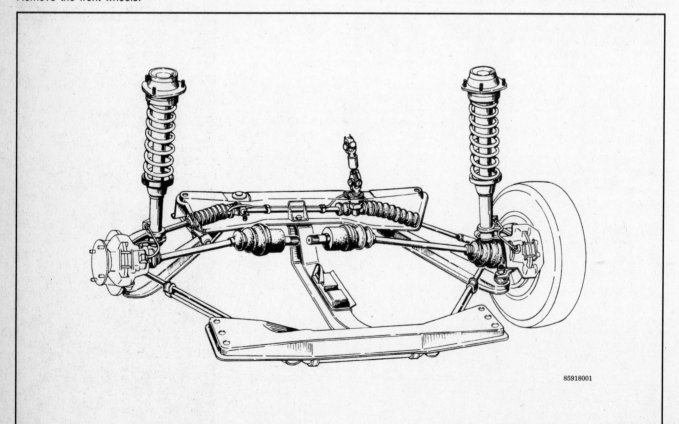

Fig. 1 Front suspension (typical of most models)

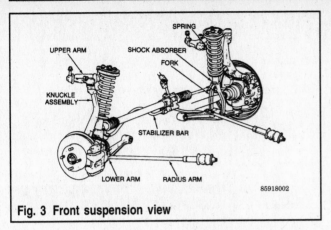

Fig. 3 Front suspension view

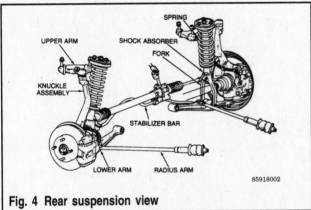

Fig. 5 Front shock assembly mounting-matchmark the assembly before removal

Fig. 6 Front shock assembly upper mounting

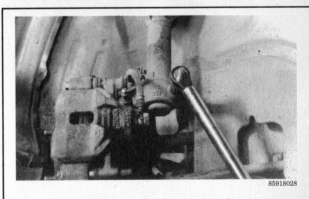

Fig. 7 Front shock assembly lower mounting

Fig. 8 Removing front shock assembly

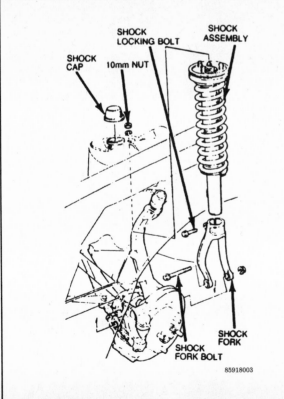

Fig. 4 Rear suspension view

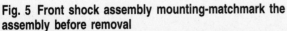

OVERHAUL

▶ **See Figure 9**

1. Disassemble the strut according to the procedure given in the rear strut disassembly section.
2. Remove the rubber cover and the center retaining nuts.
3. Slowly release the compressor and remove the spring.
4. Remove the upper mounting cap, washers, thrust plates, bearings and bushing.

➡**Before discarding any parts, check a parts list to determine which parts are available as replacements.**

5. To reassemble, 1st: pull the strut shaft all the way out, hold it in this position and slide the rubber bumper down the shaft to the strut body. This should hold the shaft in the extended position.
6. Install the spring and its top plate. Make sure the spring seats properly.
7. Install the partially assembled strut in the compressor. Compress the strut until the shaft protrudes through the top plate about 25mm.
8. Now install the bushings, thrust plates, top mounting cap washers and retaining nuts in the reverse order of removal.
9. Once the retaining nut is installed, release the tension on the compressor and loosen the thumbscrew on the bottom plate. Separate the bottom plates and remove the compressor.

INSPECTION

1. Check for wear or damage to bushings and needle bearings.
2. Check for oil leaks from the struts.
3. Check all rubber parts for wear or damage.
4. Bounce the vehicle to check shock absorbing effectiveness. The vehicle should continue to bounce for no more than two cycles. If more than 2 cycles are observed, replace the strut.

Lower Ball Joint

▶ **See Figure 10**

INSPECTION

Check ball joint play as follows:
1. Raise and support the front of the vehicle on jackstands.
2. Using a dial indicator clamp it onto the lower control arm and place the indicator tip on the steering knuckle, near the ball joint.
3. Using a pry bar, place it between the lower control arm and the steering knuckle.
4. Work the ball joint to check for looseness; if the play exceeds 0.5mm, replace the ball joint.

LUBRICATION

1. Remove the screw plug from the bottom of the ball joint and install a grease nipple.
2. Lubricate the ball joint with NLGI No. 2 multipurpose type grease.
3. Remove the nipple and reinstall the screw plug.
4. Repeat for the other ball joint.

REMOVAL & INSTALLATION

All Models

1. Raise and support the front of the vehicle on jackstands.
2. Remove the front wheel.

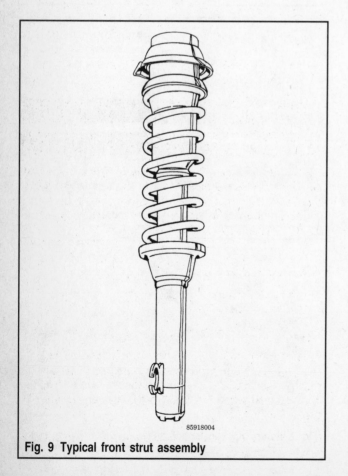

85918004

Fig. 9 Typical front strut assembly

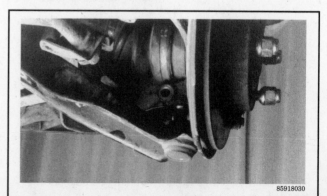

85918030

Fig. 10 View of lower ball assembly

3. Remove the cotter pin and ball joint castle nut.

4. Using a Ball Joint Remover tool, separate the ball joint from the steering knuckle.

5. To install, reverse the removal procedures. Always install a NEW cotter pin. Torque the ball joint nut to 29-35 ft. lbs. Be sure to grease the ball joint once installation is complete.

Upper Control Arm and Bushing

REMOVAL & INSTALLATION

1983 Prelude

1. Raise and support the front of the vehicle safely.

2. Remove the front wheels. Rock the upper ball joint back and forth, replace the upper control arm bushings as follows if there is any play.

3. Remove the self locking nuts, upper control arm bolts and upper control anchor bolts. Separate the upper ball joint using a suitable ball joint separator.

4. Place the upper control arm assembly into a suitable holding fixture and remove the self locking nut, upper arm bolt, upper arm anchor bolts and housing seals.

5. Remove the upper arm collar. Drive out the upper arm bushing, using a suitable drift.

6. Replace the upper control arm bushings, bushing seals and upper control arm collar with new ones. Be sure to coat the ends and the insides of the upper control arm bushings, and the sealing lips of the upper control arm bushing with grease.

7. After Step 6 is completed, apply sealant to the threads and underside of the upper arm bolt heads and self locking nut. Install the upper arm bolt and tighten the self locking nut.

8. To complete installation reverse the removal procedure.

Lower Control Arm and Stabilizer Bar

REMOVAL & INSTALLATION

♦ **See Figures 11 and 12**

1. Raise and support the front of the vehicle on jackstands. Remove the front wheels.

2. Disconnect the lower arm ball joint. Be careful not to damage the seal.

3. Remove the stabilizer bar retaining brackets, starting with the center brackets.

4. Remove the lower arm pivot bolt.

5. Disconnect the radius rod and remove the lower arm.

6. To install, reverse the removal procedures. Be sure to tighten the components to their proper torque. Please refer to the appropriate illustration for torque values.

Knuckle and Spindle

REMOVAL & INSTALLATION

1. Raise and support the front of the vehicle on jackstands. Remove the front wheel.

2. Remove the spindle nut cotter pin and the spindle nut.

3. Remove the brake caliper bolts and the caliper from the steering knuckle. DO NOT allow the caliper to hang by the brake hose, support it with a length of wire.

➡️**In case it is necessary to remove the disc, hub, bearings and/or outer dust seal, use Steps 4 and 5 given below. You will need a hydraulic press for this.**

4. Install a hub puller attachment against the hub with the lug nuts.

5. Attach a slide hammer in the center hole of the attachment and press the hub, with the disc attached, from the steering knuckle.

6. Using the Ball Joint Remover tool, remove the tie rod from the steering knuckle; use care not to damage the ball joint seals.

7. Using the Ball Joint Remover tool, remove the lower arm from the steering knuckle.

8. Loosen the strut-to-steering knuckle lock bolt. Using a hammer, tap the top of the steering knuckle and slide it off the shock.

9. Remove the steering knuckle and hub, if still attached, by sliding the driveshaft out of the hub.

10. To install, reverse the removal procedures. If the hub was removed, visually check the steering knuckle for visible signs of wear and/or damage and the condition of the inner bearing dust seals.

Front Hub and Bearings

❇❇CAUTION

Brake shoes contain asbestos, which has been determined to be a cancer causing agent. Never clean the brake surfaces with compressed air! Avoid inhaling any dust from any brake surface! When cleaning brake surfaces, use a commercially available brake cleaning fluid.

REMOVAL & INSTALLATION

♦ **See Figures 13 and 14**

Except 1982-83 Civic, 1983 Accord and 1982-83 Prelude

➡️**The following procedure for the Honda wheel bearing removal and installation necessitates the use of an hydraulic press. You will have to go to a machine or auto shop equipped with a press. DO NOT attempt this procedure without a press.**

1. Raise and support the front of the vehicle on jackstands. Remove the front wheel.

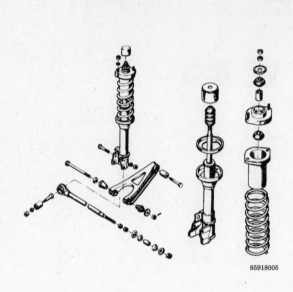

85918005

Fig. 11 Exploded view of the lower control arm assembly

2. Remove the caliper assembly from the brake disc. Separate the tie rod ball joint and lower ball joint from the knuckle.

3. Loosen the front strut-to-steering knuckle bolt. Using a hammer, tap the top of the steering knuckle and slide it off the shock. Remove the steering knuckle/hub assembly by sliding the driveshaft out of the hub.

4. Remove the wheel bearing dust cover on the inboard side of the steering knuckle.

5. Remove the brake disc-to-hub bolts. Remove the splashguard screws and the splashguard.

6. Remove the outer bearing retainer.

7. Using the Special tool No. 07965-6340300 or two support plates and a hydraulic press, support the steering knuckle and remove the wheel bearings. Make sure that the plates do not overlap the outer bearing race. Using the Driver tool No. 07947-6340400 and Handle tool No. 07949-6110000, remove the bearings.

➡**Whenever the wheel bearings are removed, always replace with a new set of bearings and outer dust seal.**

8. Using wheel bearing grease, pack each bearing before installing.

9. Using the Driver tool No. 07947-6340400, the Handle tool No. 07949-6110000 and the Installation Base tool No. 07965-634040, press the bearings into the steering knuckle.

➡**The front wheel bearings are the angular contact type. It is important that they be installed with the manufacturer's markings facing inward.**

10. Press to the hub into the steering knuckle.

11. To complete the installation, reverse the removal procedures.

CLEANING AND REPACKING

1. Clean all old grease from the driveshafts spindles on the vehicle.

2. Remove all old grease from the hub/steering knuckle, then, thoroughly dry and wipe clean all components.

3. When fitting new bearings, you must pack them with wheel bearing grease. To do this, place a glob of grease in your palm, then, holding one of the bearings in your other hand, drag the face of the bearing heavily through the grease. This must be done to work as much grease as possible through the ball bearings and the cage. Turn the bearing and continue to pull it through the grease, until the grease is thoroughly packed between the bearing balls and the cage, all around the bearing. Repeat this operation until all of the bearings are packed with grease.

4. Pack the inside of the rotor and knuckle hub with a moderate amount of grease. DO NOT overload the hub with grease.

5. Apply a small amount of grease to the spindle and to the lip of the inner seal before installing.

6. To install the bearings, check the above procedures. Adjust the spindle nut torque.

1982-83 Civic 1983 Accord 1982 Prelude

1. Pry the lock tab away from the spindle, then loosen the nut. Slightly loosen the lug nuts.

2. Raise the front of the car and support it with safety stands. Remove the front wheel and spindle nut.

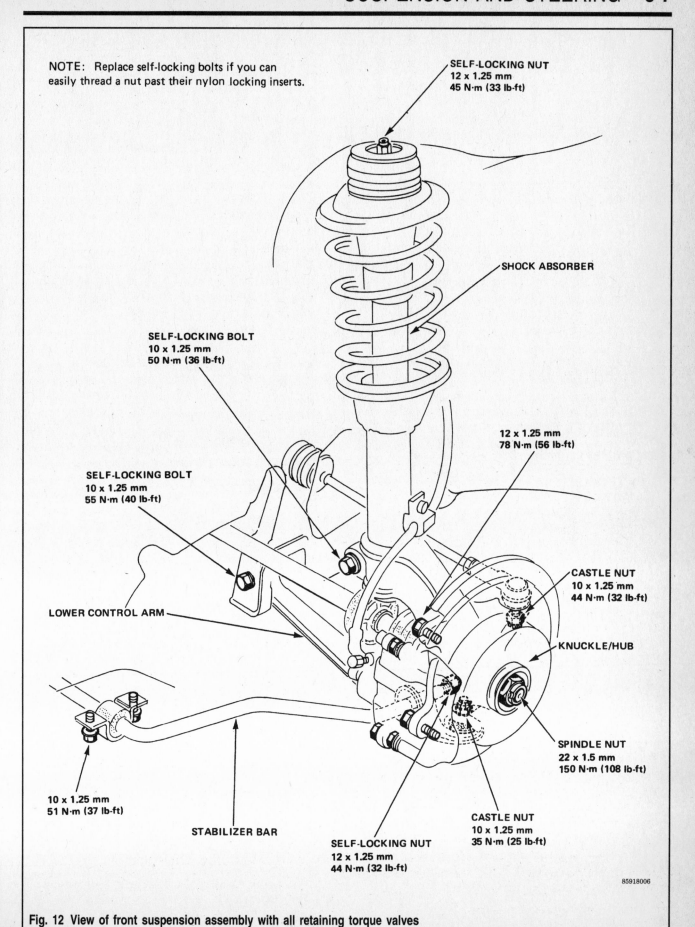

NOTE: Replace self-locking bolts if you can easily thread a nut past their nylon locking inserts.

SELF-LOCKING NUT
12 x 1.25 mm
45 N·m (33 lb-ft)

SHOCK ABSORBER

SELF-LOCKING BOLT
10 x 1.25 mm
50 N·m (36 lb-ft)

12 x 1.25 mm
78 N·m (56 lb-ft)

SELF-LOCKING BOLT
10 x 1.25 mm
55 N·m (40 lb-ft)

CASTLE NUT
10 x 1.25 mm
44 N·m (32 lb-ft)

LOWER CONTROL ARM

KNUCKLE/HUB

SPINDLE NUT
22 x 1.5 mm
150 N·m (108 lb-ft)

10 x 1.25 mm
51 N·m (37 lb-ft)

STABILIZER BAR

SELF-LOCKING NUT
12 x 1.25 mm
44 N·m (32 lb-ft)

CASTLE NUT
10 x 1.25 mm
35 N·m (25 lb-ft)

85918006

Fig. 12 View of front suspension assembly with all retaining torque valves

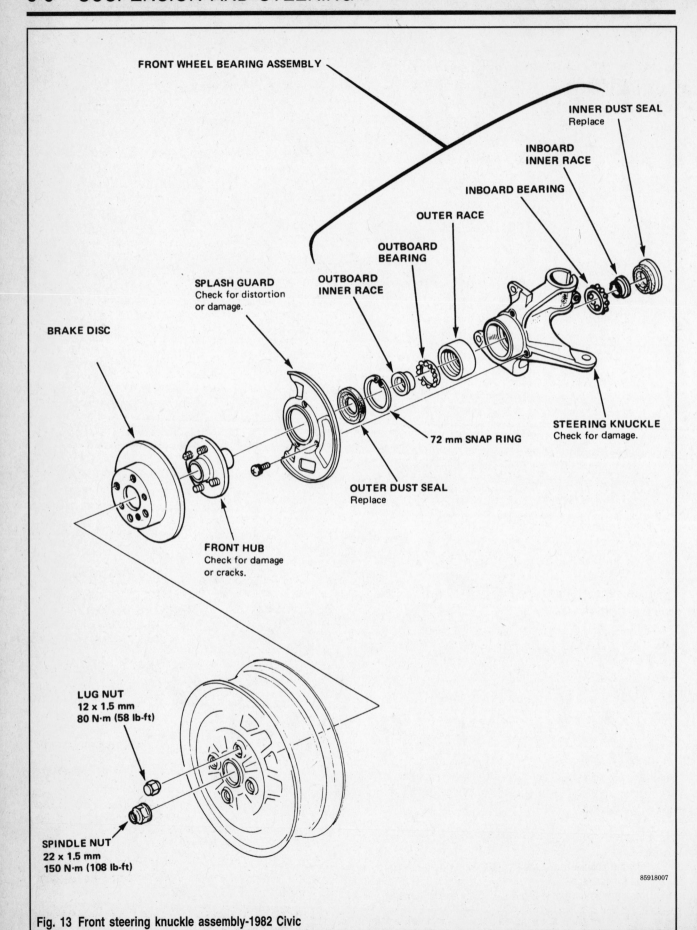

FRONT WHEEL BEARING ASSEMBLY

INNER DUST SEAL
Replace

INBOARD INNER RACE

INBOARD BEARING

OUTER RACE

OUTBOARD BEARING

OUTBOARD INNER RACE

SPLASH GUARD
Check for distortion or damage.

BRAKE DISC

STEERING KNUCKLE
Check for damage.

72 mm SNAP RING

OUTER DUST SEAL
Replace

FRONT HUB
Check for damage or cracks.

LUG NUT
12 x 1.5 mm
80 N·m (58 lb-ft)

SPINDLE NUT
22 x 1.5 mm
150 N·m (108 lb-ft)

85918007

Fig. 13 Front steering knuckle assembly-1982 Civic

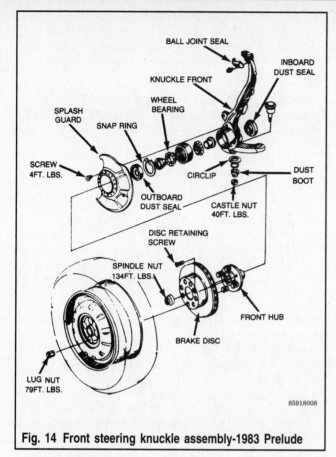

Fig. 14 Front steering knuckle assembly-1983 Prelude

3. Remove the bolts retaining the brake caliper and remove the caliper from the knuckle. Do not let the caliper hang by the brake hose, support it with a length of wire.

4. Remove the disc brake rotor retaining screws (if so equipped). Screw two 8 x 1.25 x 12mm bolts into the disc brake removal holes, and turn the bolts to push the rotor away from the hub.

➡**Turn each bolt only two turns at a time to prevent cocking the disc excessively.**

5. Remove the tie rod from the knuckle using a tie rod end removal tool. Use care not to damage the ball joint seals.

6. Remove the cotter pin from the lower arm ball joint and remove the castle nut.

7. Remove the lower arm from the knuckle using the ball joint remover.

8. Loosen the lockbolt which retains the strut in the knuckle. Tap the top of the knuckle with a hammer and slide it off the shock.

9. Remove the knuckle and hub, if still attached, by sliding the assembly off the driveshaft.

10. Remove the hub from the knuckle using special tools and a hydraulic press.

To Remove the Bearing:

11. Remove the splash guard and the snapring, then remove the outer bearing.

12. Turn the knuckle over and remove the inboard dust seal, bearing and inner race.

13. Press the bearing outer race out of the knuckle using special tools and a hydraulic press.

14. Remove the outboard bearing inner race from the hub using special tools and a bearing puller.

15. Remove the outboard dust seal from the hub.

➡**Whenever the wheel bearings are removed, always replace them with a new set of bearings and outer dust seal.**

To install:

16. Clean all old grease from the driveshafts and spindles on the car.

17. Remove all old grease from the hub and knuckle and thoroughly dry and wipe clean all components.

18. When fitting new bearings, you must pack them with wheel bearing grease. To do this, place a glob of grease in your left palm, then, holding one of the bearings in your right hand, drag the face of the bearing heavily through the grease. This must be done to work as much grease as possible through the ball bearings and the cage. Turn the bearing and continue to pull it through the grease, until the grease is thoroughly packed between the bearing balls and the cage, all around the bearing. Repeat this operation until all of the bearings are packed with grease.

19. Pack the inside of the rotor and knuckle hub with a moderate amount of grease. Do not overload the hub with grease.

20. Apply a small amount of grease to the spindle and to the lip of the inner seal before installing.

21. To install the bearings, press the bearing outer race into the knuckle using the special tools used as above, plus the installing base tool.

22. Install the outboard ball bearing and its inner race in the knuckle.

23. Install the snapring. Pack grease in the groove around the sealing lip of the outboard grease dust seal.

24. Drive the outboard grease seal into the knuckle, using a seal driver and hammer, until it is flush with the knuckle surface.

25. Install the splash guard, then turn the knuckle upside down and install the inboard ball bearing and its inner race.

26. Place the hub in the special tool fixture, then set the knuckle in position on the press and apply downward pressure.

27. Pack grease in the groove around the sealing lip of the inboard dust seal.

28. Drive the dust seal into the knuckle using a seal driver.

29. The remaining step are the reverse of the removal procedure. Use a new spindle nut, and stake after torquing.

1983 Prelude

1. Pry the lock tab away from the spindle, then loosen the nut. Slightly loosen the lug nuts.

2. Raise the front of the car and support it with safety stands. Remove the front wheel and spindle nut.

3. Remove the bolts retaining the brake caliper and remove the caliper from the knuckle. Do not let the caliper hang by the brake hose, support it with a length of wire.

4. Remove the disc brake rotor retaining screws (if so equipped). Screw two 8 x 1.25 x 12mm bolts into the disc brake removal holes, and turn the bolts to push the rotor away from the hub.

➡**Turn each bolt only two turns at a time to prevent cocking the disc excessively.**

5. Remove the tie rod from the knuckle using a tie rod end removal tool. Use care not to damage the ball joint seals.

6. Remove the cotter pin from the lower arm ball joint and remove the castle nut.

7. Remove the lower arm from the knuckle using the ball joint remover.

8. Remove the cotter pin from the upper arm ball joint and remove the castle nut.

9. Remove the upper arm from the knuckle using the ball joint remover.

10. Remove the knuckle and hub by sliding the assembly off of the driveshaft.

11. Remove the two back splash guard screws from the knuckle.

12. Remove the hub from the knuckle using special tools and a hydraulic press.

13. Remove the splash guard, dust seal and the snapring, then remove the outer bearing race.

14. Turn the knuckle over and remove the inboard dust seal, bearing and inner race and bearing.

15. Press the bearing outer race out of the knuckle using special tools and a hydraulic press.

16. Remove the outboard bearing inner race from the hub using special tools and a bearing puller.

17. Remove the outboard dust seal from the hub.

➡**Whenever the wheel bearings are removed, always replace with a new set of bearings and outer dust seal.**

To install:

18. Clean all old grease from the driveshafts spindles on the car.

19. Remove all old grease from the hub and knuckle and thoroughly dry and wipe clean all components.

20. When fitting new bearings, you must pack them with wheel bearing grease. To do this, place a glob of grease in your left palm, then, holding one of the bearings in your right hand, drag the face of the bearing heavily through the grease. This must be done to work as much grease as possible through the ball bearings and the cage. Turn the bearing and continue to pull it through the grease, until the grease is thoroughly packed between the bearing balls and the cage, all around the bearing. Repeat this operation until all of the bearings are packed with grease.

21. Pack the inside of the rotor and knuckle hub with a moderate amount of grease. Do not overload the hub with grease.

22. Apply a small amount of grease to the spindle and to the lip of the inner seal before installing.

23. To install the bearings, press the bearing outer race into the knuckle using the special tools used as above, plus the installing base tool.

24. Install the outboard ball bearing and its inner race in the knuckle.

25. Install the snapring. Pack grease in the groove around the sealing lip of the outboard grease dust seal.

26. Drive the outboard grease seal into the knuckle, using a seal driver and hammer, until it is flush with the knuckle surface.

27. Install the splash guard, then turn the knuckle upside down and install the inboard ball bearing and its inner race.

28. Place the hub in the special tool fixture, then set the knuckle in position on the press and apply downward pressure.

29. Pack grease in the groove around the sealing lip of the inboard dust seal.

30. Drive the dust seal into the knuckle using a seal driver.

31. The remaining steps are the reverse of the removal procedure. Use a new spindle nut, and stake after torquing.

Front End Alignment

▸ **See Figures 15, 16 and 17**

Front wheel alignment (also known as front end geometry) is the position of the front wheels relative to each other and to the vehicle. Correct alignment must be maintained to provide safe, accurate steering, vehicle stability and minimum tire wear. The factors which determine wheel alignment are interdependent. Therefore, when one of the factors is adjusted, the others must be adjusted to compensate.

CASTER

Caster angle is the number of degrees that a line, drawn through the center of the upper and lower ball joints and viewed from the side, can be tilted forward or backward. Positive caster means that the top of the upper ball joint is tilted toward the rear of the vehicle and negative caster means that it is tilted toward the front. A vehicle with a slightly positive caster setting will have its lower ball joint pivot slightly ahead of the tire's center. This will assist the directional stability of the vehicle by causing a drag at the bottom center of the wheel when it turns, thereby, resisting the turn and tending to

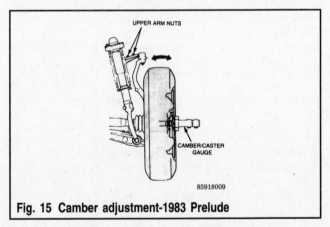

Fig. 15 Camber adjustment-1983 Prelude

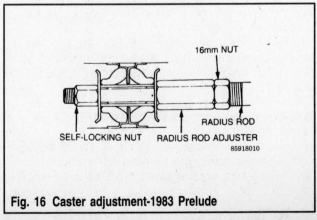

Fig. 16 Caster adjustment-1983 Prelude

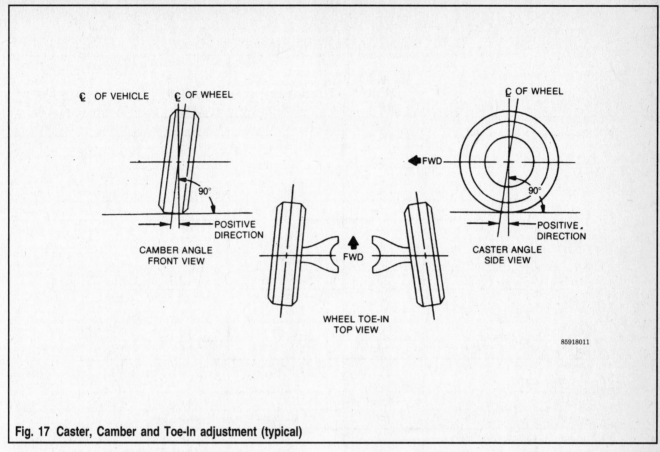

Fig. 17 Caster, Camber and Toe-In adjustment (typical)

hold the wheel steady in whatever direction the vehicle is pointed. Therefore, the vehicle is less susceptible to cross-winds and road surface deviations. A vehicle with too much (positive) caster will be hard to steer and shimmy at low speeds. A vehicle with insufficient (negative) caster may tend to be unstable at high speeds and may respond erratically when the brakes are applied.

CAMBER

Camber angle is the number of degrees that the wheel itself is tilted from a vertical line when viewed from the front. Positive camber means that the top of the wheel is slanted away from the vehicle, while negative camber means that it is tilted toward the vehicle. Ordinarily, a vehicle will have a slight positive camber when unloaded. Then, when the vehicle is loaded and rolling down the road, the wheels will just about be vertical. If you started with no camber at all, then, loading the vehicle would produce a negative camber. Excessive camber (either positive or negative) will produce rapid tire wear, since one side of the tire will be more heavily loaded than the other side.

STEERING AXIS INCLINATION

Steering axis inclination is the number of degrees that a line drawn through the upper and lower ball joints and viewed from

the front, is tilted to the left or the right. This, in combination with caster, is responsible for the directional stability and self-centering of the steering. As the steering knuckle swings from lock-to-lock, the spindle generates an arc, causing the vehicle to be raised when its turned from the straight-ahead position. The reason the vehicle body must rise is straight-forward: since the wheel is in contact with the ground, it cannot move down. However, when it is swung away from the straight-ahead position, it must move either up or down (due to the arc generated by the steering knuckle). Not being able to move down, it must move up. Then, the weight of the vehicle acts against this lift and attempts to return the spindle to the straight-ahead position when the steering wheel is released.

TOE-IN

Toe-in is the difference (in inches) between the front and the rear of the front tires. On a vehicle with toe-in, the distance between the front wheels is less at the front than at the rear. Toe-in is normally only a few fractions of an inch, it is necessary to ensure parallel rolling of the front wheels and to prevent excessive tire wear. As the vehicle is driven at increasingly faster speeds, the steering linkage has a tendency to expand slightly, thereby, allowing the front wheels to turn out and away from each other. Therefore, initially setting the front wheels so that they are pointing slightly inward (toe-in), allows them to turn straight ahead when the vehicle is underway.

WHEEL ALIGNMENT

Year	Model	Caster Range (deg.)	Caster Preferred Setting (deg.)	Camber Range (deg.)	Camber Preferred Setting (deg.)	Toe-in (in.)	Steering Axis Inclination (deg.)
1973	Civic	0–1P	$1/2$P	0–1P	$1/2$P	$1/32$	$9^{5/16}$
1974	Civic exc. SW	0–1P	$1/2$P	0–1P	$1/2$P	$1/32$	$9^{5/16}$
1975	Civic exc. SW	0–1P	$1/2$P	0–1P	$1/2$P	$1/32$	$9^{5/16}$
	Civic SW	0–1P	$1/2$P	0–1P	$1/2$P	$1/32$	$9^{5/16}$
1976	Civic exc. SW	0–1P	$1/2$P	0–1P	$1/2$P	$1/32$	$9^{5/16}$
	Civic SW	0–1P	$1/2$P	0–1P	$1/2$P	$1/32$	$9^{5/16}$
	Accord	1P–3P	2P	$1/4$N–$1^{3/4}$P	$3/4$P	$3/64$	$12^{3/16}$
1977	Civic exc. SW	0–1P	$1/2$P	0–1P	$1/2$P	$1/32$	$9^{5/16}$
	Civic SW	0–1P	$1/2$P	0–1P	$1/2$P	$1/32$	$9^{5/16}$
	Accord	1P–3P	2P	$1/4$N–$1^{3/4}$P	$3/4$P	$3/64$	$12^{3/16}$
1978	Civic exc. SW	0–1P	$1/2$P	0–1P	$1/2$P	$1/32$	$9^{5/16}$
	Civic SW	0–1P	$1/2$P	0–1P	$1/2$P	$1/32$	$9^{5/16}$
	Accord	1P–3P	2P	$1/4$N–$1^{3/4}$P	$3/4$P	$3/64$	$12^{3/16}$
1979	Civic exc. SW	$1/4$P–$1^{1/4}$P	$3/4$P	0–1P	$1/2$P	$3/64$	$9^{5/16}$
	Civic SW	0–1P	$1/2$P	0–1P	$1/2$P	$3/64$	$9^{5/16}$
	Accord	$3/4$P–$1^{3/4}$P	$1^{1/4}$P	0–1P	$1/2$P	$1/32$	$12^{3/16}$
	Prelude	$1/2$P–$2^{1/2}$P	$1^{1/2}$P	1N–1P	0	0	$12^{13/16}$
1980	Civic exc. SW	$3/4$P–$2^{3/4}$P	$1^{3/4}$P	1N–1P	0	0	$12^{15/16}$
	Civic SW	0–2P	1P	1N–1P	0	0	$12^{15/16}$
	Accord	$3/4$P–$1^{3/4}$P	$1^{1/4}$P	0–1P	$1/2$P	$1/32$	$12^{3/16}$
	Prelude	$1/2$P–$2^{1/2}$P	$1^{1/2}$P	1N–1P	0	0	$12^{13/16}$
1981	Civic exc. SW	$3/4$P–$2^{3/4}$P	$1^{3/4}$P	1N–1P	0	0	$12^{5/16}$
	Civic SW	0–2P	1P	1N–1P	0	0	$12^{5/16}$
	Accord	$^{11/16}$P–$2^{11/16}$P	$1^{11/16}$	$^{11/16}$N–$1^{5/16}$P	$5/16$	$3/64$	$12^{1/2}$
	Prelude	$1/2$P–$2^{1/2}$P	$1^{1/2}$P	1N–1P	0	0	$12^{13/16}$
1982	Civic exc. SW	$1^{1/2}$P–$3^{1/2}$P	$2^{1/2}$P	1N–1P	0	0	$12^{11/32}$
	Civic SW	$5/16$P–$2^{5/16}$P	$1^{5/16}$P	1N–1P	0	0	$12^{11/32}$
	Accord	$7/16$P–$2^{7/16}$P	$1^{7/16}$	1N–1P	0	0	$12^{1/2}$
	Prelude	$1/2$P–$2^{1/2}$P	$1^{1/2}$P	1N–1P	0	0	$12^{13/16}$
1983	Civic exc. SW	$1^{1/2}$P–$3^{1/2}$P	$2^{1/2}$P	1N–1P	0	0	$12^{11/32}$
	Civic SW	$5/16$P–$2^{5/16}$P	$1^{5/16}$P	1N–1P	0	0	$12^{11/32}$
	Accord	$7/16$P–$2^{7/16}$P	$1^{7/16}$	1N–1P	0	0	$12^{1/2}$
	Prelude	1N–1P	0	1N–1P	0	0	$6^{13/16}$

85918C01

REAR SUSPENSION

▶ **See Figure 18**

All vehicles, sedan and hatchback models utilize an independent MacPherson strut arrangement for each rear wheel. Each suspension unit consists of a combined coil spring/shock absorber strut, a lower control arm and a radius rod.

Station wagon models use a more conventional leaf spring rear suspension with a solid rear axle. The springs are three-leaf, semi-elliptic types located longitudinally with a pair of telescopic shock absorbers to control rebound. The solid axle and leaf springs allow for a greater load carrying capacity for the wagon over the sedan.

Shock Absorbers — 2WD Station Wagon

REMOVAL & INSTALLATION

1. It is not necessary to raise the vehicle or remove the wheels unless you require working clearance. Unbolt the upper mounting nut and lower bolt and remove the shock absorber. Note the position of the washers and lock washers upon removal.

2. To install, reverse the removal procedures. Be sure the washers and lock washers are installed correctly. Torque the upper mount to 44 ft. lbs. and the lower mount to 33 ft. lbs.

Leaf Springs

REMOVAL & INSTALLATION

▶ **See Figure 19**

Station Wagon Only

1. Raise the rear of the vehicle and support it on stands placed on the frame. Remove the wheels.

2. Remove the shock absorber lower mounting bolt.

3. Remove the nuts from the U-bolt and remove the U-bolts, bump rubber, and clamp bracket.

4. Unbolt the front and rear spring shackle bolts, remove the bolts, and remove the spring.

   To install:

5. First position the spring on the axle and install the front and rear shackle bolts. Apply a soapy water solution to the bushings to ease installation. Do not tighten the shackle nuts yet.

6. Install the U-bolts, spring clamp bracket and bump rubber loosely on the axle and spring.

7. Install the wheels and lower the vehicle. Tighten the front and rear shackle bolts to 33 ft. lbs. Also tighten the U-bolt nuts to 33 ft. lbs., after the shackle bolts have been tightened.

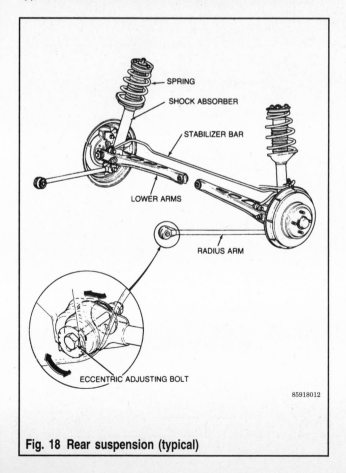

85918012

Fig. 18 Rear suspension (typical)

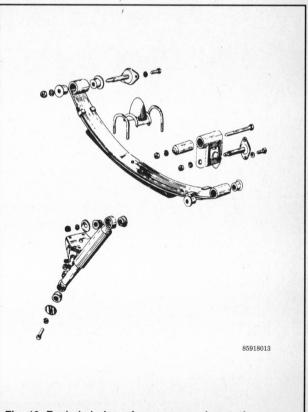

85918013

Fig. 19 Exploded view of rear suspension-station wagon models

8. Install the shock absorber to the lower mount. Tighten to 33 ft. lbs.

MacPherson Struts

REMOVAL & INSTALLATION

▶ **See Figures 20, 21, 22 and 23**

Except 2WD Wagon

1. Raise the rear of the vehicle and support it with safety stands.
2. Remove the rear wheel.
3. Disconnect the brake line at the shock absorber. Remove the retaining clip and separate the brake hose from the shock absorber.
4. Disconnect the parking brake cable at the backing plate lever.
5. Remove the lower strut retaining bolt and hub carrier pivot bolt. To remove the pivot bolt, you first have to remove the castle nut and its cotter pin.
6. Remove the two upper strut retaining nuts and remove the strut from the vehicle.
7. To install, reverse the removal procedure. Be sure to install the top of the strut in the body first. After installation, bleed the brake lines (see Section 9).

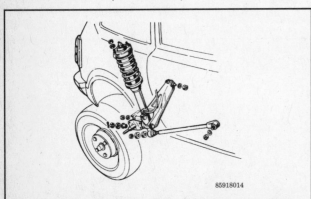

Fig. 20 Rear suspension-sedan and hatchback models

Fig. 21 Lower shock mounting bolt

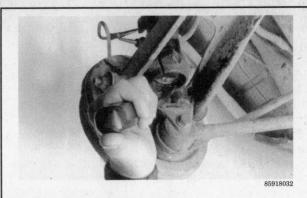

Fig. 22 Removing the rear shock

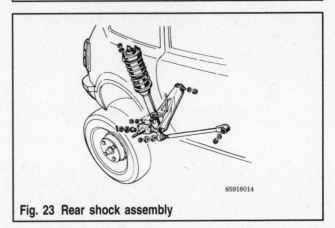

Fig. 23 Rear shock assembly

2WD Wagon

1. Raise the rear of the vehicle and support is securely on stands. Remove the rear wheels.
2. Support the rear axle securely on a floor jack. On each side, remove the damper cover from inside the vehicle; then remove the self-locking nut. To remove the self-locking nut, use an Allen wrench to hold the shock absorber rod.
3. Lower the axle carefully until all spring pressure is released. Remove the self locking bolt from the lower end of the damper. Remove the damper assembly and the spring and upper spring seat above it.
   To install:
4. Install the struts, first fit the upper spring seat into the frame. Install the spring and then the bolt fastening the lower strut to the axle. Just tighten the bolt slightly. Perform this step on both sides.
5. Fit the damper upper rubber mount into the body (on both sides). Then, carefully jack up the axle, making sure the damper shaft fits into the hole in the body far enough that you can install the self-locking retaining nut just far enough so that all threads are engaged. Carefully lower the vehicle.
6. Final tighten the self-locking bolts at the lower ends of the struts to 40 ft. lbs. and the self locking nuts on top to 16 ft. lbs. Install the damper covers.

OVERHAUL

▶ **See Figure 24**

1. Use a coil spring compressor to disassemble the strut. When assembling the compressor onto the strut, the long studs should be installed so that they are flush with the bottom plate and also flush with the retaining nut on the top end. The adjustable plate in the center cup should be screwed all the way in.

2. Insert the strut in the compressor and compress the strut about 2″. Then remove the center retaining nut.

3. Loosen the compressor and remove the strut.

4. Remove the top plate, rubber protector, spring and rubber bumper.

5. To assemble, reverse the removal procedure after checking the shock for oil leaks and all rubber parts for damage, wear or deterioration.

Control Arms

REMOVAL & INSTALLATION

All Models

1. Remove the control arm outboard and inboard pivot bolts.

2. Pull the inboard side of the arm down until it clears the body.

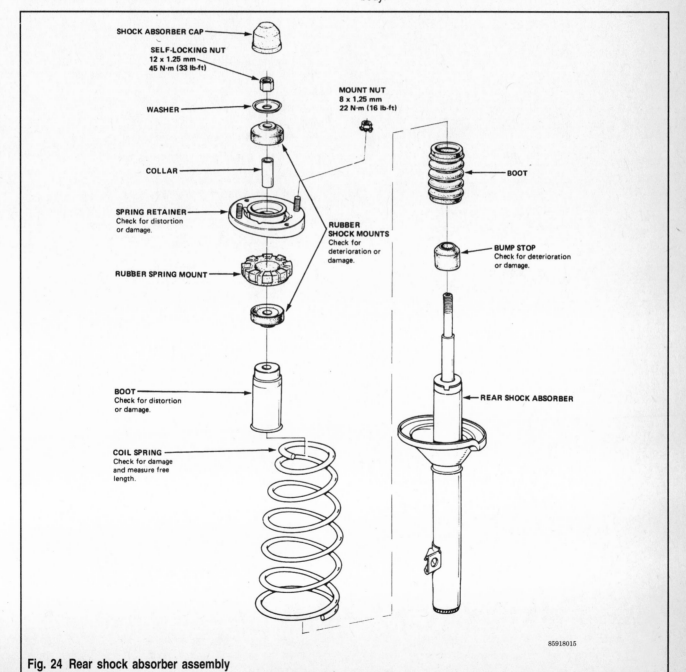

SHOCK ABSORBER CAP

SELF-LOCKING NUT
12 x 1.25 mm
45 N·m (33 lb-ft)

MOUNT NUT
8 x 1.25 mm
22 N·m (16 lb-ft)

WASHER

BOOT

COLLAR

SPRING RETAINER
Check for distortion
or damage.

RUBBER SHOCK MOUNTS
Check for deterioration or damage.

BUMP STOP
Check for deterioration
or damage.

RUBBER SPRING MOUNT

REAR SHOCK ABSORBER

BOOT
Check for distortion
or damage.

COIL SPRING
Check for damage
and measure free
length.

85918015

Fig. 24 Rear shock absorber assembly

3. Slide the arm towards the center of the vehicle until it is free of the hub carrier.

4. To install, reverse the removal procedure. Be sure to check the bushings at each end of the control arm and the control arm for damage and wear.

Rear Wheel Bearings

REPLACEMENT

All Models

1. Slightly loosen the rear lug nuts. Raise the car and support safely on jackstands.

2. Release the parking brake. Remove the rear wheels.

3. Remove the rear bearing hub cap and cotter pin and pin holder.

4. Remove the spindle nut, then pull the hub and drum off the spindle.

5. Drive the outboard and inboard bearing races out of the hub. Punch in a criss-cross pattern to avoid cocking the bearing race in the bore.

6. Clean the bearing seats thoroughly before going on to the next step.

7. Using a bearing driver, drive the inboard bearing race into the hub.

8. Turn the hub over and drive the outboard bearing race in the same way.

To install:

9. Check to see that the bearing races are seated properly.

10. When fitting new bearings, you must pack them with wheel bearing grease. To do this, place a glob of grease in your left palm, then, holding one of the bearings in your right hand, drag the face of the bearing heavily through the grease. This must be done to work as much grease as possible through the ball bearings and the cage. Turn the bearing and continue to pull it through the grease, until the grease is thoroughly packed between the bearing balls and the cage, all

around the bearing. Repeat this operation until all of the bearings are packed with grease.

11. Pack the inside of the hub with a moderate amount of grease. Do not overload the hub with grease.

12. Apply a small amount of grease to the spindle and to the lip of the inner seal before installing.

13. Place the inboard bearings into the hub.

14. Apply grease to the hub seal, and carefully tap into place. Tap in a criss-cross pattern to avoid cocking the seal in the bore.

15. Slip the hub and drum over the spindle, then insert the outboard bearing, hub, washer, and spindle nut.

16. Follow the procedures below under, Adjustment.

ADJUSTMENT

1. Apply grease or oil on the spindle nut and spindle threads.

2. Install and tighten the spindle nut to 18 ft. lbs. and rotate the drum/disc 2-3 turns by hand, then retighten the spindle nut to 18 ft. lbs.

3. Repeat the above step until the spindle nut holds that torque.

4. Loosen the spindle nut to 0 ft. lbs.

➡ **Loosen the nut until it just breaks free, but doesn't turn.**

5. Retorque the spindle nut to 4 ft. lbs.

6. Set the pin holder so the slots will be as close as possible to the hole in the spindle.

7. Tighten the spindle nut just enough to align the slot and hole, then secure it with a NEW cotter pin.

Rear End Alignment

▶ **See Figure 25**

Toe-in is adjustable on the rear wheels of all models except the station wagon. On all models, the toe-in is adjusted by means of a threaded radius rod or by a cam-type adjuster.

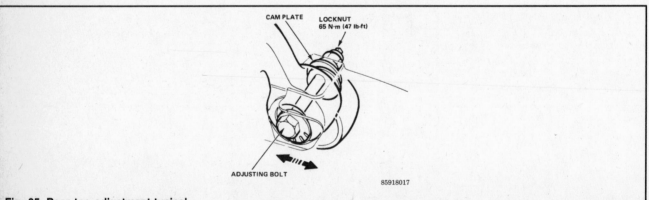

Fig. 25 Rear toe adjustment-typical

STEERING

All vehicles are equipped with rack and pinion steering. Movement of the steering wheel is transmitted through the linkage to the input shaft, which in turn is connected to the

pinion gear. The pinion gear engages the rack and rotation of the pinion, transmitted from the input shaft, causes the rack to move laterally.

Steering Wheel

REMOVAL & INSTALLATION

▶ **See Figure 26**

1. Disconnect the negative battery cable. Using a small pry bar, lift the pad from the steering wheel.
2. Remove the steering wheel retaining nut. Gently hit the backside of each of the steering wheel spokes with equal force from the palms of your hands. Remove the steering wheel assembly. If necessary use a steering wheel type puller tool or equivalent.

✴✴WARNING

Avoid hitting the wheel or the shaft with excessive force. Damage to the shaft could result.

3. To install, reverse the removal procedures. Torque the steering wheel nut to 26-36 ft. lbs.

Combination Switch

REMOVAL & INSTALLATION

1. Refer to the 'Steering Wheel, Removal & Installation' procedures in this section and remove the steering wheel.
2. Disconnect the column wiring harness and coupler.

✴✴WARNING

Be careful not to damage the steering column or shaft.

3. Remove the upper and lower column covers.
4. If equipped cruise control, remove the slip ring.
5. Remove the turn signal canceling sleeve.
6. On later models, remove the switch retaining screws, then, remove the switch.
7. Loosen the turn signal switch cam nut screw and lightly tap its head to permit the cam nut to loosen. Remove the turn signal switch assembly and the steering shaft upper bushing.
To install:
8. Install the switch assembly.

9. When installing the turn signal switch assembly, engage the locating tab on the switch with the notch in the steering column. The steering shaft upper bushing should be installed with the flat side facing the upper side of the column. The alignment notch for the turn signal switch will be centered on the flat side of the bushing.

➡**If the cam nut has been removed on the earlier models, be sure to install it with the small end up.**

10. Reverse all remaining removal steps. Check operation of all related components.

Ignition Switch

REMOVAL & INSTALLATION

▶ **See Figure 27**

1. Disconnect the negative battery cable. Remove the steering column bolts and lower the column from the instrument panel to expose the ignition switch.
2. Remove the steering column housing upper and lower covers.
3. Disconnect the ignition switch wiring at the couplers.
4. The ignition switch assembly is held onto the column by two shear bolts. Using a drill, remove the screws and the ignition switch.
5. To install, reverse the removal procedures. You will have to replace the shear bolts with new ones.

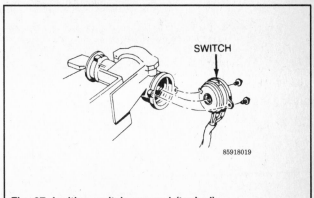

SWITCH

85918019

Fig. 27 Ignition switch removal (typical)

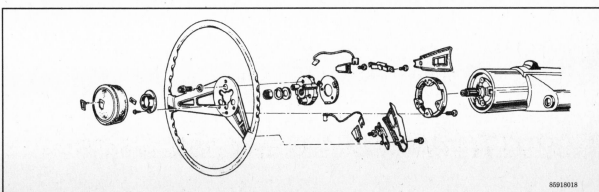

85918018

Fig. 26 Exploded view of steering wheel and related parts

On Accords 1982-83 and Preludes 1983, the mechanical part of the switch does not have to be removed to replace the electrical part.

To remove the electrical part or base of the switch, proceed as follows:

6. Remove the steering column lower cover.
7. Disconnect the electrical connector from the switch.
8. Insert the key and turn it to **LOCK** position.
9. Remove the two switch retaining screws and the switch (base) from the rest of the switch.

Steering Column

REMOVAL & INSTALLATION

▶ **See Figure 28**

1. Dsiconnect the negative battery cable. Refer to the 'Steering Wheel, Removal & Installation' procedures in this section and remove the steering wheel.
2. Disconnect all the steering column wiring.
3. Remove the steering column upper and lower mounting brackets.
4. Remove the bottom bolt on the steering column, then remove the steering column from the car. If necessary, drive tool into the slot in the side of the connector to spread it enough so you can pry it off.
5. To install reverse all the removal procedures. Check steering column and all related parts for proper operation.

Steering Linkage

REMOVAL & INSTALLATION

▶ **See Figures 29, 30, 31, 32, 33, 34, 35, 36 and 37**

Tie Rod Ends

1. Raise and support the front of the vehicle on jackstands. Remove the front wheels.
2. Use a Ball Joint Remover tool, press the tie rod end from the steering knuckle.
3. Remove the tie rod dust seal bellows clamps and move the rubber bellows on the tie rod and rack joints. Disconnect the air tube at the dust seal joint, if so equipped.
4. Straighten the tie rod lockwasher tabs at the tie rod-to-rack joint and remove the tie rod by turning it with a wrench. Record the number of turns necessary to remove the assembly.
5. To install, reverse the removal procedures. Install the assembly the correct number of turns. Always use a new tie rod lockwasher during reassembly. Check front end alignment.

➡ **Fit the locating lugs into the slots on the rack and bend the outer edge of the washer over the flat part of the rod, after the tie rod nut has been properly tightened.**

Manual Steering Gear

TESTING

1. Remove the dust seal bellows retaining bands and slide the dust seals off both sides of the gearbox housing.
2. Turn the front wheels full left and, using your hand, attempt to move the steering rack in an up-down direction.
3. Repeat with the wheel turned full right.
4. If any movement is felt, adjust the steering gearbox.

ADJUSTMENTS

▶ **See Figures 38 and 39**

1. Make sure that the rack is well lubricated.
2. Loosen the rack guide adjusting locknut.
3. Tighten the adjusting screw just to the point where the front wheels cannot be turned by hand.
4. Back off the adjusting screw 45° and hold it in that position while adjusting the locknut.
5. Recheck the play, then, move the wheels lock-to-lock, to make sure that the rack moves freely.
6. Check the steering force by first raising the front wheels and placing them in a straight-ahead position. Using a spring scale, turn the steering wheel, check the steering force; it should be no more than 3.3 lbs.

REMOVAL & INSTALLATION

1. Raise and support the front end on jackstands.
2. Remove the cover panel and steering joint cover. Unbolt and separate the steering shaft at the coupling.
3. Remove the front wheels.
4. Remove the cotter pins and unscrew the castle nuts on the tie rod ends. Using a ball joint tool disconnect the tie rod ends. Lift the tie rod ends out out the steering knuckles.
5. On cars with manual transmissions:
   • Disconnect the shift lever torque rod from the clutch housing.
   • Slide the pin retainer out of the way, drive out the spring pin and disconnect the shift rod.
6. On cars with automatic transmissions, remove the shift cable guide from the floor and pull the shift cable down by hand.
7. Remove the two nut connecting the exhaust header pipe to the exhaust pipe and move the exhaust pipe out of the way.
8. Push the rack all the way to the right and remove the gearbox brackets. Slide the tie rod ends all the way to the right.
9. Drop the gearbox far enough to permit the end of the pinion shaft to come out of the hole in the frame channel, then rotate it forward until the shaft is pointing rearward.
10. Slide the gearbox to the right until the left tie rod clears the exhaust pipe, then drop it down and out of the car to the left.

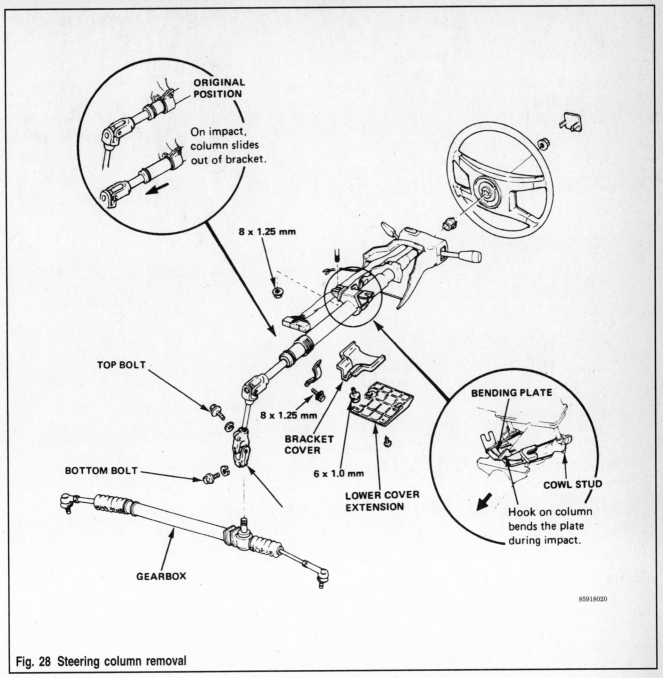

ORIGINAL POSITION

On impact, column slides out of bracket.

8 x 1.25 mm

TOP BOLT

8 x 1.25 mm

BRACKET COVER

BOTTOM BOLT

6 x 1.0 mm

LOWER COVER EXTENSION

GEARBOX

BENDING PLATE

COWL STUD

Hook on column bends the plate during impact.

Fig. 28 Steering column removal

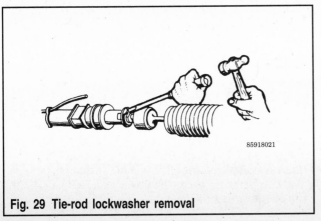

Fig. 29 Tie-rod lockwasher removal

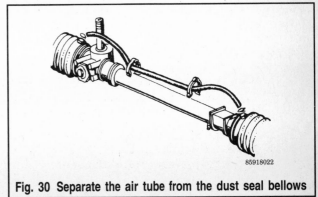

Fig. 30 Separate the air tube from the dust seal bellows

Fig. 31 View tie-rod assembly-note correct installed position

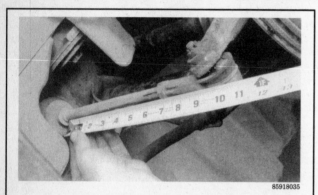

Fig. 32 Record the length of the tie-rod before removal

Fig. 33 Matchmark the tie-rod before removal

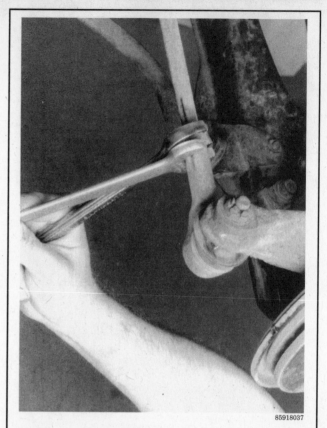

Fig. 34 Loosen the locknut

Fig. 35 Removing the tie-rod end from the knuckle

Fig. 36 Removing the tie-rod

To install:

11. Install the steering rack. Torque the mounting bracket bolts to 29 ft. lbs.

12. On the models equipped with manual transmissions, re-install the pin retainer after driving in the pin and be sure that the projection on the pin retainer is in the hole.

13. Install the tie-rod assemblies.

14. Check front end alignment, if necessary. Road test the vehicle for proper operation.

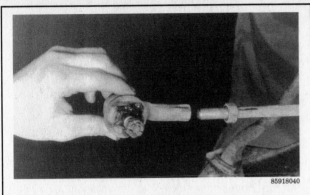

Fig. 37 Tie-rod assembly-correct installation position

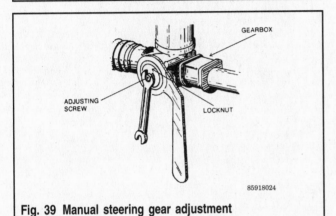

Fig. 39 Manual steering gear adjustment

Power Steering Gear

ADJUSTMENT

Accord & Civic

1. Make sure that the rack is well lubricated.
2. Loosen the rack guide adjusting locknut.
3. Tighten the adjusting screw until it compresses the spring and seats against the guide, then loosen it. Retorque it to 35 inch lbs. then back it off 25°.
4. Hold it in that position while adjusting the locknut to 18 ft. lbs.
5. Recheck the play, and then move the wheels lock-to-lock, to make sure that the rack moves freely.
6. Check the steering force by first raising the front wheels and then placing them in a straight ahead position. Turn the steering wheel with a spring scale to check the steering force. Steering force should be no more than 4 lbs.

Prelude

1. Make sure that the rack is well lubricated.
2. Loosen the rack guide adjusting locknut.
3. Tighten the adjusting screw until it compresses the spring and seats against the guide, then loosen it. Retorque it to 24 inch lbs. then back it off 25°.
4. Hold it in that position while adjusting the locknut to 18 ft. lbs.

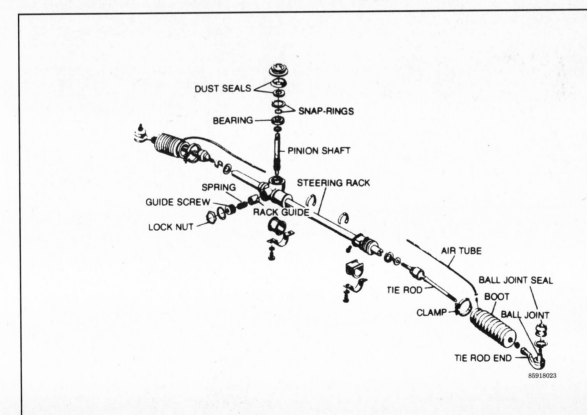

Fig. 38 Manual steering gear assembly

5. Recheck the play, and then move the wheels lock-to-lock, to make sure that the rack moves freely.

6. Check the steering force by first raising the front wheels and then placing them in a straight ahead position. Turn the steering wheel with a spring scale to check the steering force. Steering force should be no more than 4 lbs.

REMOVAL & INSTALLATION

▶ **See Figures 40, 41, 42, 43, 44, 45, 46, 47 and 48**

Accord and Prelude

1. Raise and support the front end on jackstands.
2. Remove the steering shaft joint cover and disconnect the steering shaft at the coupling.
3. Drain the power steering fluid by disconnecting the return hose at the box and running the engine while turning the steering wheel lock to lock until fluid stops draining.
4. Remove the gearbox shield.
5. Remove the front wheels.
6. Using a ball joint tool, disconnect the tie rods from the knuckles.
7. On cars with manual transmissions:
 • Remove the shift extension from the transmission case.
 • Disconnect the gear shift rod from the transmission case by removing the 8mm bolt.
8. On cars with automatic transmissions, remove the control cable clamp.
9. Remove the center beam.

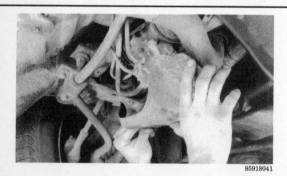
Fig. 40 Removing the shield or cover from the power steering gear assembly

Fig. 41 Removing the hydraulic lines from power steering gear assembly

Fig. 42 Removing the sway bar, if necessary for power steering gear removal

Fig. 43 Removing the exhaust system for power steering gear removal

Fig. 44 View of the power steering gear assembly mounting

Fig. 45 View of the steering rack (inner components)

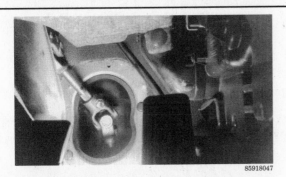

Fig. 46 View of the steering column to steering rack connecting point

Fig. 47 View of the dust cover at the bottom of the steering column assembly-note warning on the cover

10. Disconnect the exhaust header pipe at the manifold.

11. Remove the exhaust header pipe joint nuts.

12. Disconnect the hydraulic lines at the steering control until.

13. Shift the tie rods all the way right.

14. Remove the gearbox mounting bolts.

15. Slide the gearbox right so that the left tie rod clears the bottom of the rear beam. Remove the gearbox.

To install:

16. Install the steering rack in the steering coupling. Torque the mounting bracket bolts to 29 ft. lbs.

17. On the models equipped with manual transmissions, reinstall the pin retainer after driving in the pin and be sure that the projection on the pin retainer is in the hole.

18. Install the hydraulic lines and exhaust components.

Fig. 48 Checking the power steering fluid

19. Install the tie-rod assemblies. Refill the fluid level.

20. Check front end alignment, if necessary. Road test the vehicle for proper operation.

➡Some Accord and Prelude models may experience a power steering moan noise. This noise comes from the power steering rack and is usually heard on hard left turns. The corrective action to be taken in this case is to remove and replace the old power steering control valve with the new improved control valve available from the manufacturer.

Civic

1. Raise and support the front end on jackstands.

2. Remove the cover panel and steering joint cover. Unbolt and separate the steering shaft at the coupling.

3. Drain the power steering fluid by disconnecting the return hose at the box and running the engine while turning the steering wheel lock to lock until fluid stops draining. Remove the gearbox shield. Remove the front wheels.

4. Remove the cotter pins and unscrew the castle nuts on the tie rod ends. Using a ball joint tool disconnect the tie rod ends. Lift the tie rod ends out of the steering knuckles.

5. On cars with manual transmissions:
  • Disconnect the shift lever torque rod from the clutch housing.
  • Slide the pin retainer out of the way, drive out the spring pin and disconnect the shift rod.

6. On cars with automatic transmissions, remove the shift cable guide from the floor and pull the shift cable down by hand.

7. Remove the two nuts connecting the exhaust header pipe to the exhaust pipe and move the exhaust pipe out of the way. Disconnect the three hydraulic lines from the control unit.

8. Push the rack all the way to the right and remove the gearbox brackets. Slide the tie rod ends all the way to the right.

9. Drop the gearbox far enough to permit the end of the pinion shaft to come out of the hole in the frame channel, then rotate it forward until the shaft is pointing rearward.

10. Slide the gearbox to the right until the left tie rod clears the exhaust pipe, then drop it down and out of the car to the left.

To install:

11. Install the steering rack in the steering gear coupling. Torque the mounting bracket bolts to 29 ft. lbs.

12. On the models equipped with manual transmissions, re-install the pin retainer after driving in the pin and be sure that the projection on the pin retainer is in the hole.

13. Install the hydraulic lines and exhaust components.

14. Install the tie-rod assemblies. Refill the fluid level.

15. Check front end alignment, if necessary. Road test the vehicle for proper operation.

Power Steering Pump

REMOVAL & INSTALLATION

1. Using a drain pan, disconnect the cooler return hose from the reservoir and drain the fluid. Start the engine and allow it to run at fast idle. Turn the steering wheel from lock-to-lock several times, until the fluid stops running from the hose. Turn **OFF** the engine and discard the fluid. Reattach the hose.

2. Disconnect the inlet and outlet hoses from the pump.

3. Remove the drive belt.

4. Remove the bolts and the pump.

5. To install, reverse the removal procedures. Adjust the drive belt tension.

6. Refill the reservoir with fresh fluid, to the Full mark. Use only genuine Honda power steering fluid or equivalent. Bleed the power steering system.

BELT ADJUSTMENT

1. Loosen the adjuster arm bolt.

2. Move the pump, until the belt can be depressed approximately 15mm at the midpoint between the two pulleys under moderate thumb pressure. If the tension adjustment is being made on a new belt, the deflection should only be about 11mm, to allow for the initial stretching of the belt.

There is a raised bump on the top of the adjusting arm. If the belt has stretched to the point where the adjustment bolt is at or beyond the bump, the belt should be replaced.

BLEEDING

1. Check and/or refill the power steering reservoir.

2. Start the engine and operate it at fast idle.

3. Turn the steering wheel from side-to-side several times, lightly contacting the stops; this will bleed the system of air.

4. Check the reservoir level and add fluid if necessary.

TORQUE SPECIFICATIONS

Component	U.S.	Metric
Lower Ball joint nut	25 ft. lbs.	35 Nm
Front spindle nut	108 ft. lbs.	150 Nm
Steering wheel	36 ft. lbs.	50 Nm
Steering column	16 ft. lbs.	22 Nm
Steering column to steering rack	22 ft. lbs.	30 Nm
Tie-rod end	32 ft. lbs.	44 Nm
Lower arm to frame	40 ft. lbs.	55 Nm
Stabilizer bar	32 ft. lbs.	44 Nm
Stabilizer bar bracket	37 ft. lbs.	51 Nm
Front and rear shock lower mounting	36 ft. lbs.	50 Nm
Rear lower control arm	40 ft. lbs.	55 Nm

85918C09

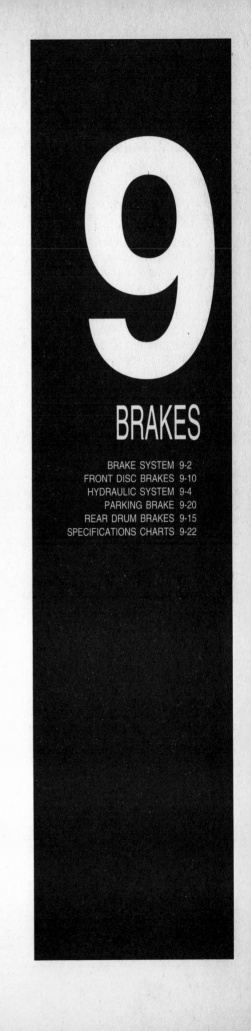

9
BRAKES

BRAKE SYSTEM

Understanding the Brakes

HYDRAULIC SYSTEM

▶ **See Figure 1**

The brake pedal operates a hydraulic system that is used for 2 reasons. First, fluid under pressure can be carried to all parts of the vehicle by small hoses or metal lines without taking up a lot of room or causing routing problems. Second, the hydraulic fluid offers a great mechanical advantage — little foot pressure is required on the pedal, but a great deal of pressure is generated at the wheels.

The brake pedal is linked to a piston in the brake master cylinder, which is filled with hydraulic brake fluid. The master cylinder consists of a cylinder, containing a small piston and a fluid reservoir.

Modern master cylinders are actually 2 separate cylinders. These systems are called a dual circuit, because the front cylinder is connected to the front brakes and the rear cylinder to the rear brakes; some vehicles are connected diagonally. The 2 cylinders are actually separated, allowing for emergency stopping power should one part of the system fail.

The entire hydraulic system from the master cylinder to the wheels is full of hydraulic brake fluid. When the brake pedal is depressed, the pistons in the master cylinder are forced to move, exerting tremendous force on the fluid in the lines. The fluid has nowhere to go and forces the wheel cylinder piston (drum brakes) or caliper pistons (disc brakes) to exert pressure on the brake shoes or pads. The resulting friction between the brake shoe and wheel drum or the brake pad and disc slows the vehicle and eventually stops it.

Also attached to the brake pedal is a switch which lights the brake lights as the pedal is depressed. The lights stay **ON** until the brake pedal is released and returns to its normal position.

Each wheel cylinder in a drum brake system contains 2 pistons, one at either end, which push outward in opposite directions. In disc brake systems, the wheel cylinders are part of the caliper; there can be as many as 4 or as few as 1. Whether disc or drum type, all pistons use some type of rub-

ber seal to prevent leakage around the piston and a rubber dust boot seals the outer ends of the wheel cylinders against dirt and moisture.

When the brake pedal is released, a spring pushes the master cylinder pistons back to their normal position. Check valves in the master cylinder piston allow fluid to flow toward the wheel cylinders or calipers as the piston returns. As the brake shoe return springs pull the brake shoes back to the released position, excess fluid returns to the master cylinder through compensating ports, which have been uncovered as the pistons move back. Any fluid that has leaked from the system will also be replaced through the compensating ports.

All dual circuit brake systems use a switch to activate a light, warning of brake failure. The switch is located in a valve mounted near the master cylinder. A piston in the valve receives pressure on each end from the front and rear brake circuits. When the pressures are balanced, the piston remains stationary but when one circuit has a leak, greater pressure during the application of the brakes will force the piston to one side or the other, closing the switch and activating the warning light.

Disc brake systems also have a metering valve to prevent the front disc brakes from engaging before the rear brakes have contacted the drums. This ensures that the front brakes will not normally be used alone to stop the vehicle. A proportioning valve is also used to limit pressure to the rear brakes to prevent rear wheel lock-up during hard braking.

DRUM BRAKES

Drum brakes use two brake shoes mounted on a stationary backing plate. These shoes are positioned inside a circular cast iron drum which rotates with the wheel assembly. The shoes are held in place by springs; this allows them to slide toward the drums (when they are applied) while keeping the linings and drums in alignment. The shoes are actuated by a wheel cylinder which is usually mounted at the top of the backing plate. When the brakes are applied, hydraulic pressure forces the wheel cylinder's two actuating links outward. Since these links bear directly against the top of the brake shoes, the tops of the shoes are forced outward against the inner side of the drum. This action forces the bottoms of the two shoes to contact the brake drum by rotating the entire assembly slightly (known as servo action). When pressure within the wheel cylinder is relieved, return springs pull the shoes back away from the drum.

Most modern drum brakes are designed to self-adjust during application when the vehicle is moving in reverse. This motion causes both shoes to rotate very slightly with the drum, rocking an adjusting lever. The self-adjusters are only intended to compensate for normal wear. Although the adjustment is 'automatic', there is a definite method to actuate the self-adjuster, which is done during normal driving. Driving the vehicle in reverse and applying the brakes usually activates the automatic adjusters. If the brake pedal was low, you should be able to feel an increase in the height of the brake pedal.

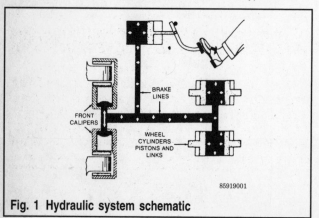

BRAKE LINES

FRONT CALIPERS

WHEEL CYLINDERS PISTONS AND LINKS

85919001

Fig. 1 Hydraulic system schematic

DISC BRAKES

Instead of the traditional expanding brakes that press outward against a circular drum, disc brake systems utilize a cast iron disc with brake pads positioned on either side of it. Braking effect is achieved in a manner similar to the way you would squeeze a spinning disc between your fingers. The disc (rotor) is a one-piece casting with cooling fins between the two braking surfaces. This enables air to circulate between the braking surfaces making them less sensitive to heat buildup and more resistant to fade. Dirt and water do not affect braking action since contaminants are thrown off by the centrifugal action of the rotor or scraped off by the pads. Also, the equal clamping action of the two brake pads tends to ensure uniform, straight-line stops. All disc brakes are inherently self-adjusting. There are three general types of disc brake:

1. A fixed caliper, 4-piston type.
2. A floating caliper, single piston type.
3. A sliding caliper, single piston type.

The fixed caliper design uses two pistons mounted on either side of the rotor (in each side of the caliper). The caliper is mounted rigidly and does not move.

The sliding and floating designs are quite similar and often considered as one. The pad on the inside of the rotor is moved into contact with the rotor by hydraulic force. The caliper, which is not held in a fixed position, moves slightly, bringing the outside pad into contact with the rotor. There are various methods of attaching floating calipers; some pivot at the bottom or top and some slide on mounting bolts.

POWER BRAKE BOOSTERS

Power brakes operate just as standard brake systems except in the actuation of the master cylinder pistons. A vacuum diaphragm is located behind the master cylinder and assists the driver in applying the brakes, reducing both the effort and travel he must put into moving the brake pedal.

The vacuum diaphragm housing is connected to the intake manifold by a vacuum hose. A check valve at the point where the hose enters the diaphragm housing ensures that during periods of low manifold vacuum brake assist vacuum will not be lost.

Depressing the brake pedal closes off the vacuum source and allows atmospheric pressure to enter on one side of the diaphragm. This causes the master cylinder pistons to move and apply the brakes. When the brake pedal is released, vacuum is applied to both sides of the diaphragm and return springs return the diaphragm and master cylinder pistons to the released position. If the vacuum fails, the brake pedal rod will butt against the end of the master cylinder actuating rod and direct mechanical application will occur as the pedal is depressed.

The hydraulic and mechanical problems that apply to conventional brake systems also apply to power brakes.

Honda uses a dual hydraulic system, with the brakes connected diagonally. In other words, the right front and left rear brakes are on the same hydraulic line and the left front and right rear are on the other line. This has the added advantage of front disc emergency braking, should either of the hydraulic systems fail. The diagonal rear brake serves to counteract the sway from single front disc braking.

A leading/trailing drum brake is used for the rear brakes, with disc brakes for the front. All Honda's are equipped with a brake warning light, which is activated when a defect in the brake system occurs.

Adjustments

REAR DRUM BRAKE ADJUSTMENT

Early Models

➡On later models, when the brake drum or rear brake system has been serviced, depress brake pedal several times to set self-adjusting brakes before adjusting parking cable. On all models make sure the parking brake cable is properly adjusted.

1. Block the front wheels and release the parking brake. Raise and support the rear of the vehicle on jackstands.
2. Depress the brake pedal 2-3 times and release.
3. The adjuster (if so equipped) is located on the inboard side, underneath the control arm. Turn the adjuster clockwise until the wheel no longer turns.
4. Back off the adjuster two (2) clicks and turn the wheel to see if the brake shoes are dragging. If they are dragging, back off the adjuster one more click.

BRAKE PEDAL FREE-PLAY

Free-play is the distance the pedal travels from the stop (brake light switch) until the pushrod actuates the master cylinder.

To check free-play, first measure the distance (with the carpet removed) from the floor to the brake pedal. Then disconnect the return spring and again measure the distance from the floor to the brake pedal. The difference between the two measurements is the pedal free-play. The specified free-play is 1.0-5.0mm. Free-play adjustment is made by loosening the locknut on the brake light switch and rotating the switch body until the specified clearance is obtained.

❋❋WARNING

If there is no free-play, the master cylinder pistons will not return to their stops. This can block the compensating ports, which will prevent the brake pads and linings from returning fully when the pedal is released. This will result in rapid brake burn-up. Free-play provides a safety factor against normal rubber swell and expansion or deflection of body parts and pedal linkage.

Brake Light Switch

REMOVAL, INSTALLATION & ADJUSTMENT

▶ See Figure 2

1. Disconnect the negative battery cable. Locate the switch under the dash area at the top of the brake pedal mount.
2. Disconnect the electrical leads from the switch. Remove the nut from the switch and unscrew the switch from its mount.
3. Install the new switch in position and connect the electrical lead.
4. Connect the negative battery cable. Adjust the switch (unscrew the switch from its mount and reposition) as necessary to make the brake lights come on with the brake pedal is depressed and the the lights to go off when the pedal is not depressed.

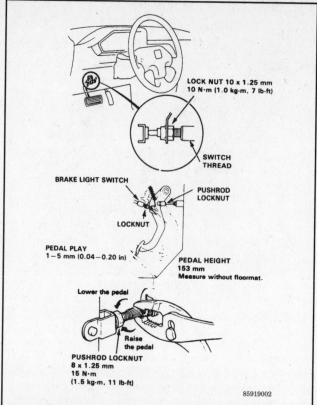

LOCK NUT 10 x 1.25 mm
10 N·m (1.0 kg-m, 7 lb-ft)

SWITCH THREAD

BRAKE LIGHT SWITCH

PUSHROD LOCKNUT

LOCKNUT

PEDAL PLAY
1—5 mm (0.04—0.20 in)

PEDAL HEIGHT
153 mm
Measure without floormat.

Lower the pedal

Raise the pedal

PUSHROD LOCKNUT
8 x 1.25 mm
15 N·m
(1.5 kg-m, 11 lb-ft)

85919002

Fig. 2 Brake pedal height, free play and brake light switch adjustment

HYDRAULIC SYSTEM

▶ See Figure 3

The hydraulic system is composed of the master cylinder and brake booster, the brake lines, the brake pressure differential valve(s), the wheel cylinders (drum brakes) and calipers (disc brakes).

The master cylinder serves as a brake fluid reservoir and (along with the booster) as a hydraulic pump. Brake fluid is stored in the two sections of the master cylinder. Each section corresponds to each part of the dual braking system. This tandem master cylinder is required by Federal law as a safety device.

When the brake pedal is depressed, it moves a piston mounted in the bottom of the master cylinder. The movement of this piston creates hydraulic pressure in the master cylinder. This pressure is carried to the wheel cylinders or the calipers by brake lines, passing through the pressure differential or proportioning valve.

When the hydraulic pressure reaches the wheels, after the pedal has been depressed, it enters the wheel cylinders or calipers. Here it comes into contact with a piston(s). The hydraulic pressure causes the piston(s) to move, which moves the brake shoes or pads (disc brakes), causing them to contact the drums or rotors (disc brakes). Friction between the brake shoes and the drums causes the vehicle to slow. There is a relationship between the amount of pressure that is applied to the brake peal and the amount of force which moves

the brake shoes against the drums. Therefore, the harder the brake pedal is depressed, the quicker the vehicle will stop.

Since the hydraulic system is one which operates on fluids, air is a natural enemy of the brake system. Air in the hydraulic system retards the passage of hydraulic pressure from the master cylinder to the wheels. Anytime a hydraulic component below the master cylinder is opened or removed, the system must be bled of air to ensure proper operation. Air trapped in the hydraulic system can also cause the brake warning light to turn ON, even though the system has not failed. This is especially true after repairs have been performed on the system.

Dual Proportioning Valve

REMOVAL & INSTALLATION

▶ See Figure 4

The brake proportioning valve is located in the engine compartment, bolted to the firewall or inner fender well on the passenger side (most vehicles). The valve is not to be repaired, replace it as an assembly.

1. Locate the valve and disconnect the brake fluid lines. Plug all lines.
2. Remove the mounting bolts and remove the valve.

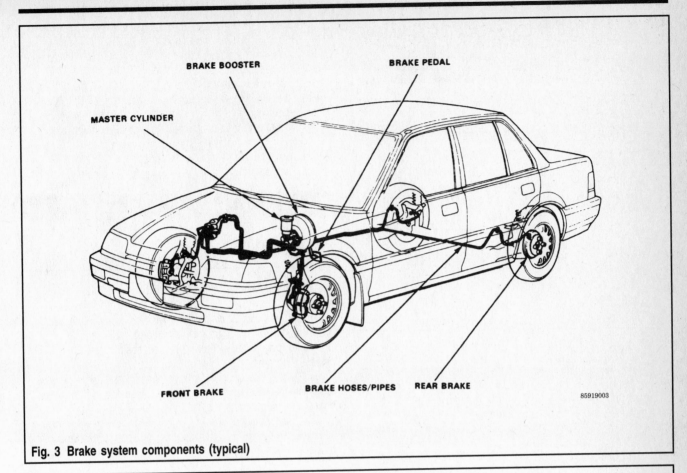

MASTER CYLINDER

BRAKE BOOSTER

BRAKE PEDAL

FRONT BRAKE

BRAKE HOSES/PIPES

REAR BRAKE

85919003

Fig. 3 Brake system components (typical)

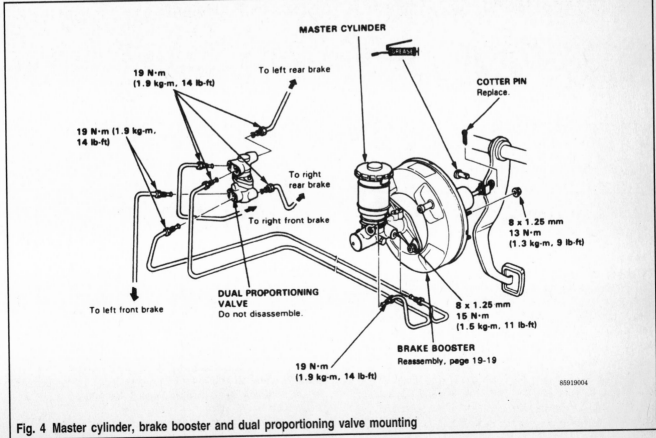

MASTER CYLINDER

19 N·m
(1.9 kg-m, 14 lb-ft)

To left rear brake

19 N·m (1.9 kg-m,
14 lb-ft)

COTTER PIN
Replace.

To right
rear brake

To right front brake

8 x 1.25 mm
13 N·m
(1.3 kg-m, 9 lb-ft)

To left front brake

DUAL PROPORTIONING
VALVE
Do not disassemble.

8 x 1.25 mm
15 N·m
(1.5 kg-m, 11 lb-ft)

BRAKE BOOSTER
Reassembly, page 19-19

19 N·m
(1.9 kg-m, 14 lb-ft)

85919004

Fig. 4 Master cylinder, brake booster and dual proportioning valve mounting

3. To install, reverse the removal procedures. Bleed the brake system.

Master Cylinder

REMOVAL & INSTALLATION

▶ See Figure 5

Before removing the master cylinder, cover the body surfaces with fender covers and rags to prevent damage to painted surfaces by brake fluid.

1. Disconnect the brake lines from the master cylinder.
2. Remove the master cylinder-to-vacuum booster attaching bolts and the master cylinder from the vehicle.
3. To install, reverse the removal procedures. Bleed the brake system.

OVERHAUL

▶ See Figures 6, 7, 8, 9, 10, 11, 12, 13 and 14

1. Remove the fluid reservoir caps and floats, then, drain the reservoirs.
2. Loosen the retaining clamps and remove the reservoirs.
3. Remove the primary piston stop bolt.
4. Remove the piston retaining clip, washer and the primary piston.
5. Wrap a rag around the end of the master cylinder, so that it blocks the bore. Hold your finger over the stop bolt hole and direct a small amount of compressed air into the primary outlet. This should slide the primary piston to the end of the master cylinder bore, so it can be removed.
6. Remove the two union caps, washers, check valves and springs.
7. For overhaul procedures, check the following:
   a. Clogged orifices in the pistons and cylinder.
   b. Damage to the reservoir attaching surface.
   c. Damage to the check valves.
   d. Wear or damage to the piston cups.

Fig. 5 Removing the master cylinder assembly

85919016

   e. The clearance between the master cylinder bore and the pistons. The clearance should be 0.020-0.127mm.
8. To assemble of the master cylinder, reverse the disassembly procedures. Be sure to check the following:
   a. The check valves and piston cups should be replaced when the master cylinder is assembled, regardless of their condition.
   b. Apply a thin coat of brake fluid to the pistons before installing. When installing the pistons, push in while rotating to prevent damage to the piston cups.
   c. Tighten the union cap and stop bolts securely.

Power Brake Booster

INSPECTION

A preliminary check of the vacuum booster can be made as follows:

1. Depress the brake pedal several times using normal pressure. Make sure that the pedal height does not vary.
2. Hold the pedal in the depressed position and start the engine. The pedal should drop slightly.
3. Hold the pedal in the above position and stop the engine. The pedal should stay in the depressed position for approximately 30 seconds.
4. If the pedal does not drop when the engine is started or rises after the engine is stopped, the booster is not functioning properly.

REMOVAL & INSTALLATION

1. Disconnect the vacuum hose. Mark the hose ends to denote positioning so it can be reinstalled correctly, if hose ends are reversed the booster will not work properly.
2. Disconnect the brake lines from the master cylinder.
3. Remove the brake pedal-to-booster link pin and the booster-to-firewall nuts. The pushrod and nuts are located inside the vehicle on the passenger side, under the dash.
4. Remove the booster with the master cylinder attached.
5. To install, reverse the removal procedures. Bleed the brake system.

Brake Hoses And Pipes

REMOVAL & INSTALLATION

▶ See Figures 15 and 16

All brake lines and hoses should be checked for rust, holes, kinks, tears and any sign of deterioration. Any hose showing these signs should be replaced. Always replace brake hose or lines with parts specifically designed for the braking system. Parts that are not designed for brake systems can fail under the extreme pressures that are present in the system.

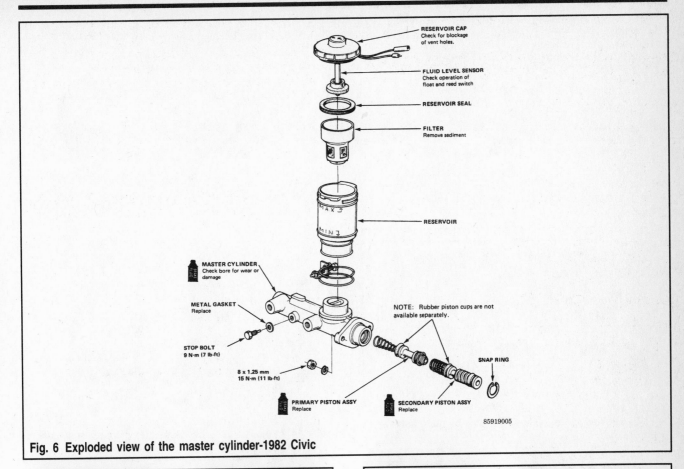

RESERVOIR CAP
Check for blockage
of vent holes.

FLUID LEVEL SENSOR
Check operation of
float and reed switch

RESERVOIR SEAL

FILTER
Remove sediment

RESERVOIR

MASTER CYLINDER
Check bore for wear or
damage

METAL GASKET
Replace

STOP BOLT
9 N·m (7 lb-ft)

8 x 1.25 mm
15 N·m (11 lb-ft)

PRIMARY PISTON ASSY
Replace

NOTE: Rubber piston cups are not
available separately.

SNAP RING

SECONDARY PISTON ASSY
Replace

85919005

Fig. 6 Exploded view of the master cylinder-1982 Civic

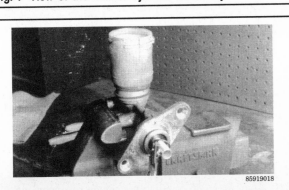

85919017

Fig. 7 View of the master cylinder assembly in vise

85919019

Fig. 9 Removing the washer of the master cylinder

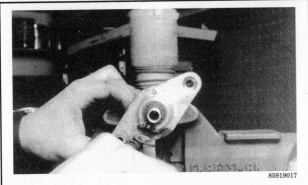

85919018

**Fig. 8 Removing the outer retaining snapring of the
master cylinder**

85919020

Fig. 10 Removing the spacer of the master cylinder

Fig. 11 Removing the piston retaining bolt of the master cylinder

Fig. 12 Removing the piston assembly of the master cylinder

Fig. 13 Removing the piston assembly of the master cylinder

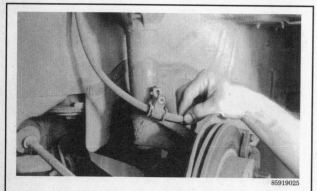

Fig. 15 Front brake hose retaining location

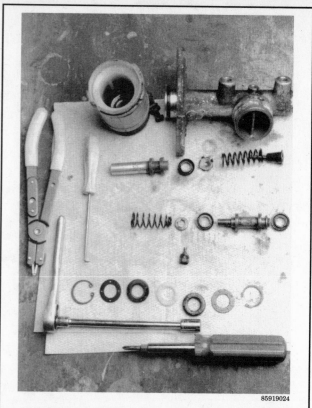

Fig. 14 Exploded view of the master cylinder assembly and necessary tools

Fig. 16 Rear brake line retaining location

The brake system lines can be replaced by disconnecting them at their mounting points along the underside of the vehicle and at the components that they attach to. Tighten brake lines-to-brake hoses to 10 ft. lbs. The brake hoses, which are rubber are located at each wheel. They can be replaced by disconnecting them from the brake line and then from the caliper or wheel cylinder. Tighten all brake hose-to-wheel cylinder fittings to 14 ft. lbs. Brake hose-to-caliper connection should be tightened to 25 ft. lbs. Always bleed the brake system after replacing any components.

➡ If the new metal line requires bending, do so gently using a pipe bending tool. Do not attempt to bend the tubing by hand.

BRAKE LINE FLARING

Use only brake line tubing approved for automotive use; never use copper tubing. Whenever possible, try to work with brake lines that are already cut to the length needed. These lines are available at most auto parts stores and have machine made flares, the quality of which is hard to duplicate with most of the available inexpensive flaring kits.

When the brakes are applied, there is a great amount of pressure developed in the hydraulic system. An improperly formed flare can leak with resultant loss of stopping power. If you have never formed a double-flare, take time to familiarize yourself with the flaring kit; practice forming double-flares on scrap tubing until you are satisfied with the results.

The following procedure applies to most commercially available double-flaring kits. If these instructions differ in any way from those in your kit, follow the instructions in the kit.

1. Cut the brake line to the necessary length using a tubing cutter.

2. Square the end of the tube with a file and chamfer the edges.

3. Insert the tube into the proper size hole in the bar until the end of the tube sticks out the thickness of the single flare adapter. Tighten the bar wing nuts tightly so the tube cannot move.

4. Place the single flare adapter into the tube and slide the bar into the yoke.

5. Position the yoke screw over the single flare adapter and tighten it until the bar is locked in the yoke. Continue tightening the yoke screw until the adapter bottoms on the bar. This should form the single flare.

➡**Make sure the tube is not forced out of the hole in the bar during the single flare operation. If it is, the single flare will not be formed properly and the procedure must be repeated from Step 1.**

6. Loosen the yoke screw and remove the single flare adapter.

7. Position the yoke screw over the tube and tighten until the taper contacts the single flare and the bar is locked in the yoke. Continue tightening to form the double flare.

➡**Make sure the tube is not forced out of the hole in the bar during the double flare operation. If it is, the double flare will not be formed properly and the procedure must be repeated from Step 1.**

8. Loosen the screw and remove the bar from the yoke. Remove the tube from the bar.

9. Check the flare for cracks or uneven flaring. If the flare is not perfect, cut it off and begin again at Step 1.

Flushing And Bleeding

▶ **See Figures 17, 18 and 19**

When it is necessary to flush the brake hydraulic system because of parts replacement or fluid contamination, the following procedure should be observed:

1. Loosen the wheel cylinder bleeder screw. Drain the brake fluid by pumping the brake pedal. Pump the pedal until all of the old fluid has been pumped out and replaced by new fluid.

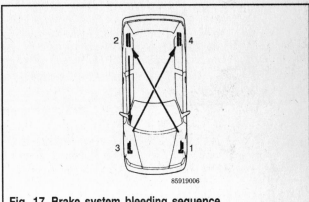

85919006

Fig. 17 Brake system bleeding sequence

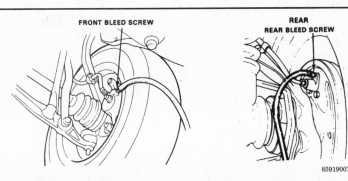

85919007

Fig. 18 Hose connected to bleeder-used in bleeding the brake system, the end of the hose submerged in a jar of clean brake fluid

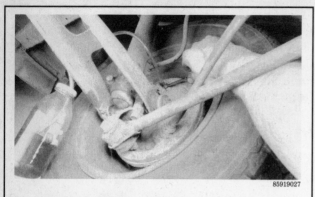

Fig. 19 Brake bleeding procedure

2. The flushing procedure should be performed in the following sequence:
   a. Bleed the left front brake.
   b. Bleed the right rear brake.
   c. Bleed the right front brake.
   d. Bleed the left rear brake.

FRONT DISC BRAKES

The major components of the disc brake system are the brake pads, the caliper and the rotor (disc). The caliper is similar in function to the wheel cylinder used with drum brakes and the rotor is similar to the brake drum used in drum brakes.

The major difference between drum brakes and disc brakes is that with drum brakes, the wheel cylinder forces the brake shoes out against the brake drum to stop the vehicle, while with disc brakes, the caliper forces the brake pads inward to squeeze the rotor and stop the vehicle. The biggest advantage of disc brakes over drum brakes is that the caliper and brake pads enclose only a small portion of the rotor, leaving the rest of it exposed to outside air. This aids in rapid heat dissipation, reducing brake fade and throws off water fast.

✳✳CAUTION

Brake shoes contain asbestos, which has been determined to be a cancer causing agent. Never clean the brake surfaces with compressed air! Avoid inhaling any dust from any brake surface! When cleaning brake surfaces, use a commercially available brake cleaning fluid.

Brake Pads

INSPECTION

The disc pads should be replaced when approximately 2mm lining thickness remains (thickness of lining material only). If lining thickness varies between inner and outer brake pads check the brake caliper. The disc brake pads are always replaced as a set (both front wheels).

3. Bleed the back of the master cylinder before the front, through the two bleed valves.

4. To bleed the master cylinder and brake system (start with the wheel farthest away from the master cylinder) fasten one end of a plastic tube onto the bleed valve and immerse the other end in a clear jar filled with brake fluid. Pump brake pedal slowly, hold pedal down and open bleed valve (1/4 turn open) then close the valve. When air bubbles cease to emerge from the end of the tubing, the bleeding is completed. Be sure to keep the fluid reservoir filled at all times during the bleeding process (bleed all 4 wheels-start with the wheel farthest away from the the master cylinder and work toward it) so air does not enter the system.

✳✳WARNING

Brake fluid is adversely affected by contamination from dirt, automotive petroleum products and water. Contaminants can plug parts of the hydraulic system, causing rapid wear or swelling of rubber parts and lower the boiling point of the fluid. KEEP FLUID CLEAN.

REMOVAL & INSTALLATION

1973-78 Models
▶ See Figures 20, 21 and 22

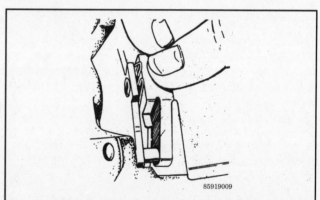

Fig. 20 Removing the pad retaining clip (early models)

Fig. 21 Removing the retaining pin springs (early models)

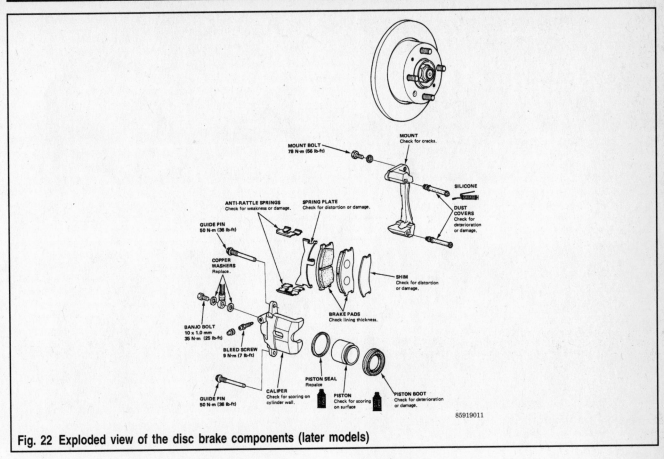

Fig. 22 Exploded view of the disc brake components (later models)

1. Raise and support the vehicle on jackstands. Remove the wheels.

2. After removing the wheel, remove the pad retaining clip which is fitted in the holes of the pad retaining pins.

3. Using a pair of pliers, remove the two retaining pins and fitting springs. When removing them, care must be taken to prevent the springs from flying apart.

4. The front brake pad can be removed, together with the shim, after removing the springs and pins. If the pads are difficult to remove, open the bleeder valve and move the caliper in the direction of the piston. The pads will become loose and can be easily removed.

➡ After the pads are removed, the brake pedal must not be touched.

The disc pads should be replaced when approximately 2mm lining thickness remains (thickness of lining material only).

To provide space for installing the pad, loosen the bleed valve and push the inner piston back into the cylinder. Also push back the outer piston by applying pressure to the caliper. After providing space for the pads, close the bleed valve and insert the pad. Insert a shim behind each pad with the arrow on the shim pointing up. Incorrect installation of the shims can cause squealing brakes. Bleed brake system.

1979-83 Models

▶ See Figures 23, 24, 25, 26, 27, 28 and 29

1. Raise and support the vehicle on jackstands. Remove the wheels.

2. Remove the lower caliper support pin and pivot the caliper up, away from the rotor.

3. Remove the pads, shim and anti-rattle spring.

To install:

4. Clean all points where the shoes and shim touch the caliper and mount. Apply a thin film of silicone grease to the cleaned areas.

5. Place the anti-rattle springs in position.

Fig. 23 View of the front disc brake assembly

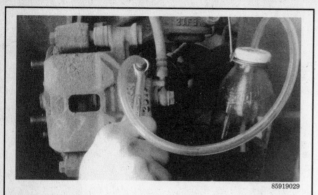

Fig. 24 Opening the bleeder valve-front brake caliper

Fig. 25 Compressing the front brake caliper

Fig. 26 Removing the mounting bolt or pin-front brake caliper

Fig. 27 Removing the mounting bolt

Fig. 28 Removing the front disc brake pad

Fig. 29 Removing the front disc brake pads

6. Install the pads with the shim against the outside shoe.

7. Loosen the bleed screw slightly and push in the caliper piston to allow mounting of the caliper over the rotor. Tighten the bleed screw.

8. Pivot the caliper down over the rotor and install the lower support pin. Tighten the pin to 13 ft. lbs.

Brake Caliper

REMOVAL & INSTALLATION

◆ See Figures 30, 31, 32 and 33

1. Raise and support the front of the vehicle on jackstands. Remove the front wheels.

2. Loosen the brake line from the wheel cylinder.

3. The caliper housing is mounted to the steering knuckle with two bolts located behind the cylinder. Remove these bolts and the caliper.

To install:

4. Reverse the removal procedures. Be sure to inspect all parts before installing and bleed the brake system before operating the vehicle.

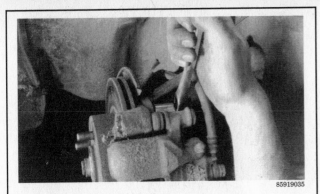

Fig. 30 Removing the caliper retaining bolts

Fig. 31 Removing the caliper brake hose retaining bolt

Fig. 32 Removing the caliper assembly

Fig. 33 Do not let the caliper assembly hang on the brake hose-support it

OVERHAUL

♦ See Figures 34, 35, 36, 37, 38, 39, 40 and 41

➡Wash all parts in brake fluid. DO NOT use cleaning solvent or gasoline.

1. Remove the inner and outer pad springs and pin clips, then, the pins and pads.

➡The springs are different, so note the location and method of installation before removing.

2. Push the yoke toward the rear (inboard side) of the cylinder, until it is free to separate the yoke from the cylinder. You may have to tap lightly with a plastic hammer (where the mounting bolts are located) to remove the cylinder. Exercise extreme care to avoid damaging the cylinder body. If only the cylinder body moves, without the outer piston, a gentle tap on the piston should loosen it.

3. To dismantle the cylinder, first remove the retaining rings at both ends of the cylinder with a screwdriver, being careful not to damage the rubber boot.

4. Both pistons can be removed from the cylinder body either by pushing through one end with a wooden rod or by blowing compressed air into the cylinder inlet port.

➡If the wheel cylinder pistons are removed for any reason, the piston seals must be replaced.

5. Using a small pry bar, remove the piston seals, installed on the inside of the cylinder at both ends.

6. Inspect the caliper operation. If the lining wear differs greatly between the inner and outer pads, the caliper may be unable to move properly due to rust an dirt on the sliding surfaces. Clean the sliding part of the caliper and apply brake grease.

➡All brake parts are critical items. If there is any question as to the serviceability of any brake part — replace it.

7. Check the piston-to-cylinder clearance. The specified clearance is 0.020-0.127mm. Also check the pistons and cylinder bore for scuffing and scratching.

8. Check the dust covers, retaining rings, nylon retainers and all other parts for wear or damage.

9. To reassemble the caliper, reverse the removal procedures. Bleed the brake system.

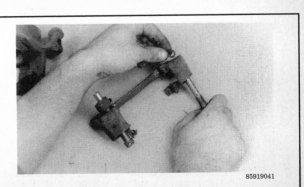

Fig. 34 View of the mounting bolts or pins and related parts of brake caliper

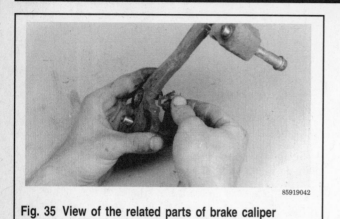

Fig. 35 View of the related parts of brake caliper

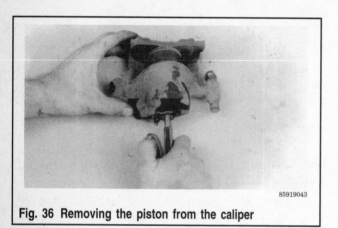

Fig. 36 Removing the piston from the caliper

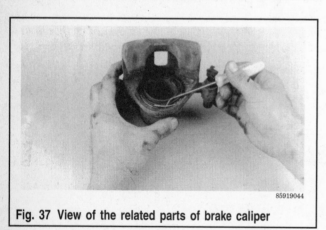

Fig. 37 View of the related parts of brake caliper

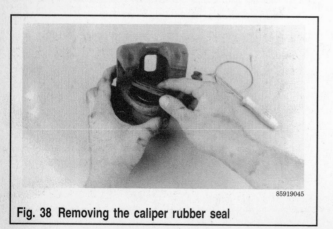

Fig. 38 Removing the caliper rubber seal

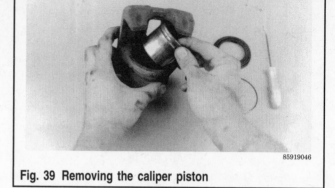

Fig. 39 Removing the caliper piston

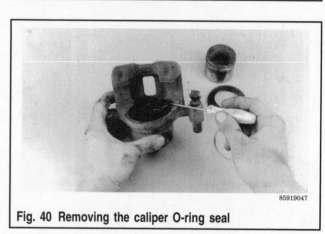

Fig. 40 Removing the caliper O-ring seal

Fig. 41 Removing the caliper mounting dust boots

Brake Disc (Rotor)

REMOVAL & INSTALLATION

1973-79 Civic and 1979-81 Accord Models

➡The following procedure for the brake disc removal necessitates the use of a hydraulic press. You will have to go to a machine or auto shop equipped with a press; DO NOT attempt this procedure without a press.

1. Raise and support the front of the vehicle on jackstands. Remove the front wheels.
2. Remove the center spindle nuts.

3. Remove the caliper assembly; DO NOT let the caliper assembly hang by the brake hose.

4. Use a slide hammer with a hub puller attachment or a conventional hub puller, to extract the hub with the disc attached.

5. Remove the four bolts and separate the hub from the disc.

6. Remove the steering knuckle from the vehicle.

7. Remove the wheel bearings from the knuckle.

➡**If, for any reason, the hub is removed, the front wheel bearings must be replaced.**

8. Install the bearings and hub using a press. To install the disc, you have to use a hydraulic press for both the bearings and the hub. After installing the bearings (see below), install the front hub using the Special Base tool No. 07965-6340300 and Drift tools No. 07965-6340100 and 07965-6340200. Position the hub with the steering knuckle under the base and press it through the base.

9. Install the remaining components reversing the steps of removal.

1980-83 Civic, 1982-83 Accord and 1979-83 Prelude Models
◗ **See Figure 42**

1. Raise and support the front of the vehicle on jackstands. Remove the front wheels.

2. Remove the caliper assembly; DO NOT let the caliper assembly hang by the brake hose.

3. Remove the retaining screw from the brake rotor and remove the rotor from the hub.

4. To install the disc, reverse the removal procedure.

85919040

Fig. 42 Removing the brake disc

INSPECTION

1. The brake disc develops circular scores after long or even short usage when there is frequent braking. Excessive scoring not only causes a squealing brake, but also shortens the service life of the brake pads. However, light scoring of the disc surface, will result from normal use and is not detrimental to brake operation.

➡**Differences in the left and right disc surfaces can result in uneven braking.**

2. Disc runout is the movement of the disc from side-to-side. Position a dial indicator in the middle of the pad wear area and turn the disc, while checking the indicator. If disc runout exceeds 0.15mm, replace the disc.

3. Disc parallelism is the measurement of variations in disc thickness at several locations on the disc circumference. To measure parallelism, place a mark on the disc and measure the disc thickness with a micrometer. Repeat this measurement at eight (8) equal increments on the circumference of the disc. If the measurements vary, replace the disc. Refer to a local automotive machine shop if necessary.

REAR DRUM BRAKES

✳✳CAUTION

Brake shoes contain asbestos, which has been determined to be a cancer causing agent. Never clean the brake surfaces with compressed air! Avoid inhaling any dust from any brake surface! When cleaning brake surfaces, use a commercially available brake cleaning fluid.

All vehicles employ a leading/trailing type of drum brake, in which there are two curved brake shoes supported by an anchor plate and wheel cylinder. When the brake pedal is depressed and hydraulic pressure is delivered to the wheel cylinder, the wheel cylinder expands to force the shoes against the drum.

Friction between the brake shoes and the drum causes the vehicle to slow and stop. When the brake pedal is released, the brake shoe return springs move the brakes away from the drum. If the lining on the brakes becomes contaminated or the lining/drum becomes grooved, the engagement of the brakes and drum will become very harsh, causing the brakes to lock up and/or squeal. If the brake shoes on one wheel contact the drum before the same action occurs in the other wheels, the brakes will pull to one side when applied.

Brake Drums

REMOVAL & INSTALLATION

◗ **See Figures 43 and 44**

1. Raise and support the rear of the vehicle on jackstands. Remove the rear wheels. Make sure that the parking brake is **OFF**.

2. Remove the bearing cap, cotter pin and the castle nut or spindle nut.

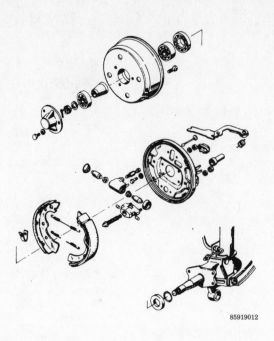

85919012

Fig. 43 Rear drum brake assembly-Early models

3. Pull off the rear brake drum. If the drum is difficult to remove, use a brake drum puller or a front hub puller and slide hammer.

4. To install, reverse the removal procedures. Torque the rear hub nut to 83 ft. lbs. (Civic 1973-79 early models).

5. On the Accord, Prelude and Civic (1980-83 late models), which have tapered roller bearings, use the following procedure:

   a. Torque the hub nut to 18 ft. lbs.

   b. Rotate the drum by hand several times and loosen the nut.

   c. Torque the nut to 4 ft. lbs.

   d. If the spindle nut is not aligned with the hole in spindle, tighten the nut just enough to align the nut and the hole.

   e. Insert the cotter pin holder and a NEW cotter pin.

INSPECTION

Check the drum for cracks and the inner surface of the shoe for excessive wear and damage. The inner diameter (I.D.) of the drum should be no more than specifications, nor should the drum be more than 0.10mm out-of-round. Refer to a local automotive machine shop if necessary.

Brake Shoes

INSPECTION

The brake shoes should be replaced when heat cracks are visible or approximately 2mm of lining thickness remains (thickness of lining material only). The brake shoes are always replaced as a set (both rear wheels). If necessary leave one side connected to use as a guide for this repair.

REMOVAL & INSTALLATION

▶ **See Figures 45, 46, 47, 48, 49, 50, 51, 52, 53, 54, 55, 56, 57 and 58**

➡**Manufacturing numbers on brake shoes face towards outside. Apply brake grease on wear points on the brake backing plate. Move the self-adjuster to fully released position before reinstalling the brake drum.**

1. Refer to the 'Brake Drum, Removal & Installation' procedures in this section and remove the brake drum.

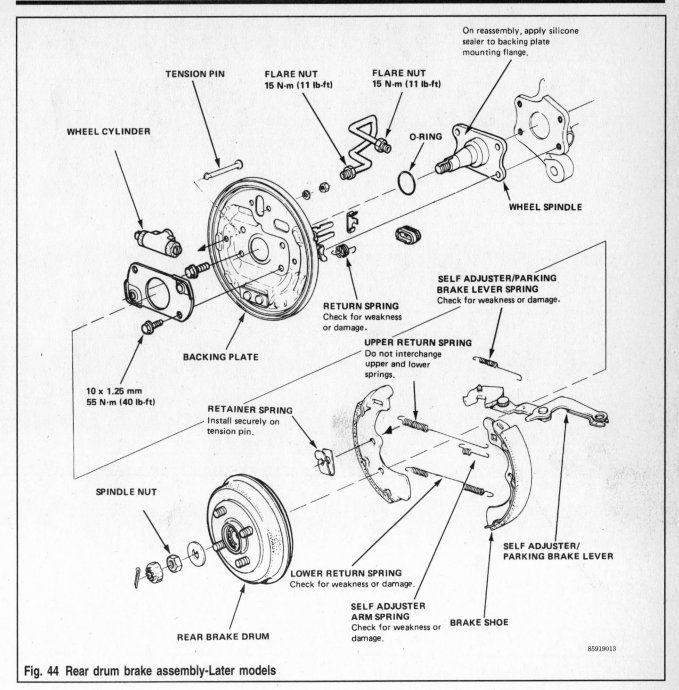

On reassembly, apply silicone sealer to backing plate mounting flange.

TENSION PIN

FLARE NUT 15 N·m (11 lb-ft)

FLARE NUT 15 N·m (11 lb-ft)

O-RING

WHEEL CYLINDER

WHEEL SPINDLE

SELF ADJUSTER/PARKING BRAKE LEVER SPRING
Check for weakness or damage.

RETURN SPRING
Check for weakness or damage.

UPPER RETURN SPRING
Do not interchange upper and lower springs.

BACKING PLATE

10 x 1.25 mm
55 N·m (40 lb-ft)

RETAINER SPRING
Install securely on tension pin.

SPINDLE NUT

SELF ADJUSTER/ PARKING BRAKE LEVER

LOWER RETURN SPRING
Check for weakness or damage.

SELF ADJUSTER ARM SPRING
Check for weakness or damage.

BRAKE SHOE

REAR BRAKE DRUM

85919013

Fig. 44 Rear drum brake assembly-Later models

2. Remove the tension pin clips, the two brake return springs and the brake shoes. If you are installing new shoes, back off the adjusters.

✳✳WARNING

The upper and lower brake shoe return springs on the sedan are different and should not be interchanged. The upper spring is designed so that the spring coils are lo-

cated on the outboard side of the shoe, while the lower spring is designed so that its coils are located on the inboard side of the shoe with the crossbar facing downward.

3. To install, reverse the removal procedure. Be sure to check the self-adjuster assembly for free and proper operation and the brake lining for grease spots (sand paper brake shoes lightly, if necessary). Bleed and adjust the brake system.

Fig. 45 Removing the spindle retaining nut cover

Fig. 49 Removing the rear brake return springs

Fig. 46 Removing the wheel bearing washer

Fig. 50 Removing the wheel cylinder retaining bolts

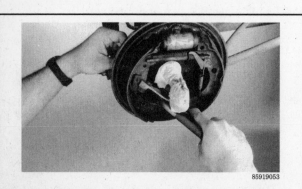

Fig. 47 Removing the rear brake drum assembly

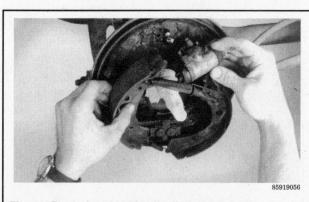

Fig. 51 Removing the wheel cylinder assembly

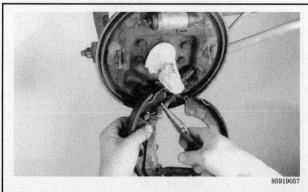

Fig. 48 Removing the rear brake shoe hold down springs

Fig. 52 Removing the brake shoe-to-parking brake lever

Fig. 53 View of the rear brakes with related hardware and parts

Fig. 54 View of the rear brake drum with related parts

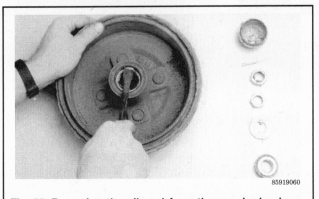

Fig. 55 Removing the oil seal from the rear brake drum

Fig. 56 Installing the rear oil seal in the rear brake drum

Fig. 57 Installing the rear oil seal in the rear brake drum-note position of seal driver tool

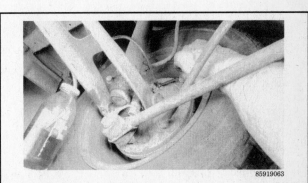

Fig. 58 Bleed rear brakes after installing the new brake shoes for a complete brake job

Wheel Cylinders

REMOVAL & INSTALLATION

1. Refer to the 'Brake Shoes, Removal & Installation' procedures in this section and remove the brake shoes.
2. Disconnect the parking brake cable and brake lines from the backing plate; be sure to have a drip pan to catch the brake fluid.
3. Remove the two wheel cylinder-to-backing plate nuts and the wheel cylinder.
4. To install, reverse the removal procedures. When assembling, apply a thin coat of grease to the grooves of the wheel cylinder piston and the sliding surfaces of the backing plate.

OVERHAUL

▶ See Figure 59

Remove the wheel cylinder dust seals from the grooves to permit the removal of the cylinder pistons, refer to the necessary illustration.

Wash all parts in fresh brake fluid and check the cylinder bore and pistons for scratches and other damage, replacing where necessary.

When assembling the wheel cylinder, apply a coat of brake fluid to the pistons, piston cups and cylinder walls.

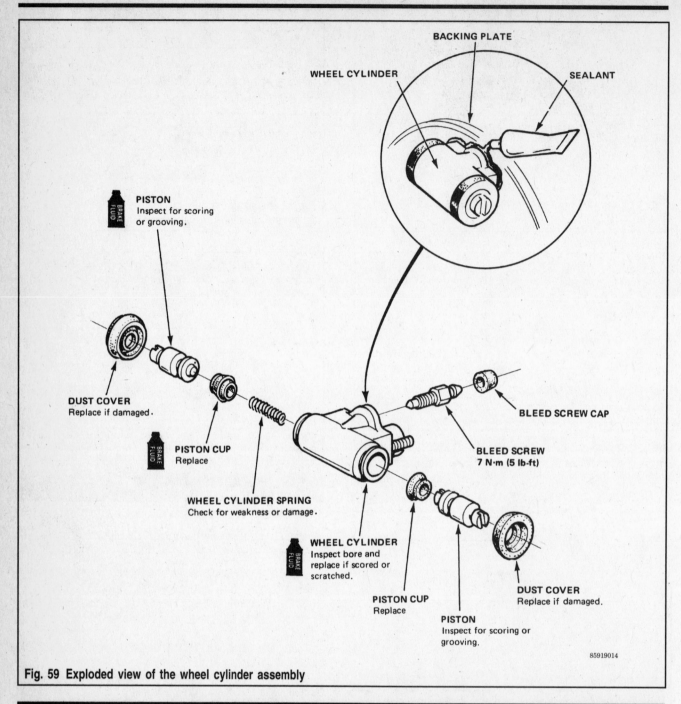

PISTON
Inspect for scoring or grooving.

DUST COVER
Replace if damaged.

PISTON CUP
Replace

WHEEL CYLINDER SPRING
Check for weakness or damage.

WHEEL CYLINDER
Inspect bore and replace if scored or scratched.

PISTON CUP
Replace

PISTON
Inspect for scoring or grooving.

DUST COVER
Replace if damaged.

BLEED SCREW CAP

BLEED SCREW
7 N·m (5 lb-ft)

BACKING PLATE

WHEEL CYLINDER

SEALANT

85919014

Fig. 59 Exploded view of the wheel cylinder assembly

PARKING BRAKE

▶ **See Figures 61 and 60**

Cable

The parking brake is a mechanical type which applies braking force to the rear wheels, through the rear brake shoes. The cable, which is attached to the tail end of the parking brake lever, extends to the equalizer and to the both rear brakes. When the lever is pulled, the cable becomes taut, pulling the parking brake arms fitted to the brake shoes.

REMOVAL & INSTALLATION

1. Remove the adjusting nut from the equalizer mounted on the rear axle or in the console (Accord 1982-83 and Prelude 1983) and separate the cable from the equalizer.

2. Set the parking brake to a fully released position and remove the cotter pin from the side of the brake lever.

Fig. 60 Removing the parking brake cable from the rear brake backing plate

3. After removing the cotter pin, pull out the pin which connects the cable and the lever.

4. Detach the cable from the guides at the front and right side of the fuel tank, then, remove the cable.

5. To install, grease the cable/guides and reverse the removal procedures.

ADJUSTMENT

➡When the brake drum has been serviced, depress brake pedal several times to set self-adjusting brakes before adjusting parking brake cable. Block the front wheels before starting this service procedure, if necessary.

Inspect the following items:

1. Check the ratchet for wear.

2. Check the cables for wear or damage and the cable guide and equalizer for looseness.

3. Check the equalizer cable where it contacts the equalizer and apply grease (if necessary).

4. Check the rear brake adjustment.

The rear wheels should be locked when the handbrake lever is pulled 1-5 notches (1973-78 models) or 3-7 notches (1979-83 models). Adjustment is made by lifting the lever one notch and turning the nut located at the equalizer, between the rear lower control arms or console assembly.

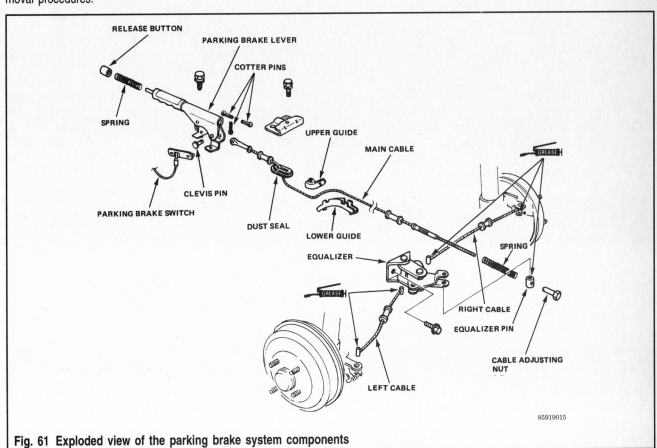

Fig. 61 Exploded view of the parking brake system components

BRAKE SPECIFICATIONS

Year	Model	Lug Nut Torque (ft. lbs.)	Brake Disc		Standard Brake Drum Diameter	Minimum Lining Thickness	
			Minimum Thickness	Maximum Runout		Front	Rear
1973	Civic	51–65	0.354	0.006	7.066	0.063	0.079
	Civic Wagon	51–65	0.449	0.006	7.087	0.300	0.079
1974	Civic	51–65	0.354	0.006	7.066	0.063	0.079
	Civic Wagon	51–65	0.449	0.006	7.087	0.300	0.079
1975	Civic	51–65	0.354	0.006	7.066	0.063	0.079
	Civic Wagon	51–65	0.449	0.006	7.087	0.300	0.079
1976	Civic	51–65	0.354	0.006	7.066	0.063	0.079
	Civic Wagon	51–65	0.449	0.006	7.087	0.300	0.079
	Accord	51–65	0.433	0.006	7.080	0.063	0.079
1977	Civic	51–65	0.354	0.006	7.066	0.063	0.079
	Civic Wagon	51–65	0.449	0.006	7.087	0.300	0.079
	Accord	51–65	0.433	0.006	7.080	0.063	0.079
1978	Civic	51–65	0.354	0.006	7.066	0.063	0.079
	Civic Wagon	51–65	0.449	0.006	7.087	0.300	0.079
	Accord	51–65	0.433	0.006	7.080	0.063	0.079
1979	Civic	51–65	0.354	0.006	7.066	0.063	0.079
	Civic Wagon	51–65	0.449	0.006	7.087	0.300	0.079
	Accord	51–65	0.413	0.006	7.080	0.063	0.079
	Prelude	80	0.413	0.006	7.087	0.063	0.079
1980	Civic	51–65	①	0.006	7.066	0.063	0.079
	Civic Wagon	51–65	①	0.006	7.870	0.063	0.079
	Accord	51–65	0.413	0.006	7.080	0.063	0.079
	Prelude	80	0.413	0.006	7.080	0.063	0.079
1981	Civic	51–65	①	0.006	7.066	0.063	0.079
	Civic Wagon	51–65	①	0.006	7.870	0.063	0.079
	Accord	51–65	0.413	0.006	7.080	0.063	0.079
	Prelude	80	0.413	0.006	7.080	0.063	0.079
1982	Civic	51–65	①	0.006	7.066	0.063	0.079
	Civic Wagon	51–65	①	0.006	7.870	0.063	0.079
	Accord	51–65	0.600	0.006	7.870	0.063	0.079
	Prelude	80	0.413	0.006	7.080	0.063	0.079
1983	Civic	51–65	①	0.006	7.066	0.063	0.079
	Civic Wagon	51–65	①	0.006	7.870	0.063	0.079
	Accord	80	0.600	0.006	7.870	0.063	0.079
	Prelude	80	0.670	0.006	7.870	0.120	0.080

① 1980–83 1300 4 spd: 0.350
  1980–83 1300 5 spd: 0.390
  1980–82 1500: 0.394
  1983 1500: 0.590

85919c01

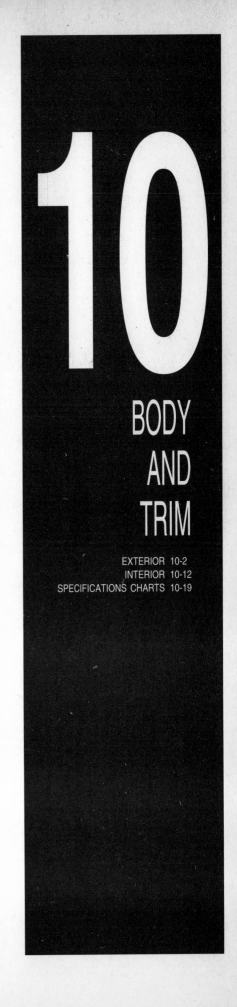

10

BODY AND TRIM

EXTERIOR

Doors

REMOVAL & INSTALLATION

▶ **See Figure 1**

Front and Rear

1. Place a jack or stand beneath the door assembly to support its weight.

➡**Place a rag at lower edge of the door and jack or stand to prevent damage to painted surface.**

2. Remove door without hinge.
3. Remove the door hinge.
4. Installation is in the reverse order of removal. Check door for proper fit and operation.

➡**When installing hinge, coat the hinge link with recommended multipurpose grease.**

ADJUSTMENT

▶ **See Figures 2 and 3**

Front and Rear

Proper door alignment can be obtained by adjusting the door hinge and door lock striker. The door hinge and striker can be moved up and down fore and aft in enlarged holes by loosening the attaching bolts.

➡**The door should be adjusted for an even and parallel fit for the door opening and surrounding body panels.**

Hood

REMOVAL & INSTALLATION

1. Open the hood and protect the body with covers to protect the painted surfaces.
2. Mark the hood hinge locations on the hood for proper reinstallation.
3. Holding both sides of the hood, unscrew the bolts securing the hinge to the hood. This operation requires a helper.
4. Installation is the reverse of removal. Check hood for proper fit and operation.

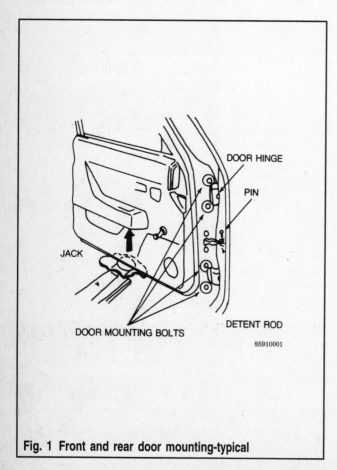

Fig. 1 Front and rear door mounting-typical

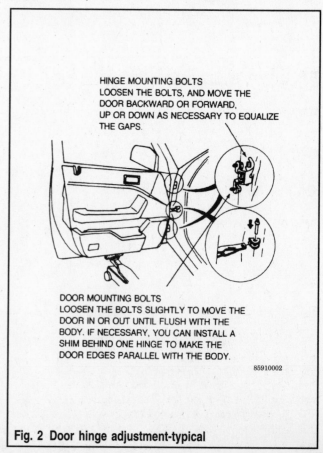

Fig. 2 Door hinge adjustment-typical

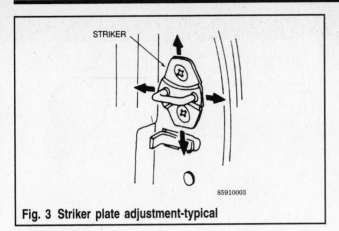

Fig. 3 Striker plate adjustment-typical

ALIGNMENT

▶ **See Figure 4**

The hood can be adjusted with bolts attaching the hood to the hood hinges, hood lock mechanism and hood bumpers. Adjust the hood for an even fit between the front fenders.

1. Adjust the hood fore and aft by loosening the bolts attaching the hood to the hinge and repositioning hood.
2. Loosen the hood bumper lock nuts and lower bumpers until they do not contact the front of the hood when the hood is closed.
3. Set the striker at the center of the hood lock, and tighten the hood lock securing bolts temporarily.
4. Raise the two hood bumpers until the hood is flush with the fenders.
5. Tighten the hood lock securing bolts after the proper adjustment has been obtained.

Trunk Lid

REMOVAL & INSTALLATION

▶ **See Figure 5**

1. Open the trunk lid and position a cloth or cushion to protect the painted areas.
2. Mark the trunk lid hinge locations or trunk lid for proper reinstallation.
3. Support the trunk lid by hand and remove the bolts attaching the trunk lid to the hinge. Then remove the trunk lid.
4. Installation is the reverse of removal. Check truck lid for proper fit and operation.

ALIGNMENT

1. Loosen the trunk lid hinge attaching bolts until they are just loose enough to move the trunk lid.
2. Move the trunk lid for and aft to obtain a flush fit between the trunk lid and the rear fender.
3. To obtain a snug fit between the trunk lid and weatherstrip, loosen the trunk lid lock striker attaching bolts enough to move the lid, working the striker up and down and from side to side as required.

4. After the adjustment is made tighten the striker bolts securely.

Power Trunk and Liftgate System

The power liftgate release system consists of a release switch (usually found on the dash panel), a wiring harness, lock solenoid and linkage rods. The power trunk system consists of a push button release switch (usually found in the glove box), a door latch solenoid and the necessary wiring.

REMOVAL & INSTALLATION

Trunk Opener Latch

1. Pry the cover off the trunk opener handle. Remove the door sill molding.
2. Remove the trunk opener. Disconnect the link from the trunk lid lock cylinder.
3. Remove the trunk latch molding bolts. Disconnect all electrical connections.
4. Loosen the trunk opener cable lock nut and remove the cable end from the slot in the trunk lock. Tie a wire to the trunk end of the cable before removing it, so the new cable can be pulled in.
5. Pull off the door opening trim and pull the cable out between the quarter panel and body.
6. Install a new cable, as required.
7. Install the remaining components by installing in reverse order of removal.

COMPONENT TESTING

Power Trunk Latch Test

There should be continuity between the G/BI lead and the ground when the trunk lid is open and no continuity when the trunk lid is closed.

Power Tailgate Switch Test

There should be continuity between the switch terminals when the switch is in the **ON** position and no continuity when the switch is in the **OFF** position.

Power Tailgate Solenoid Test

Using a suitable ohmmeter, check for continuity between the terminal and the solenoid body ground. There should be continuity. If there is no continuity, replace the solenoid.

Manual Hatchback or Tailgate Lid

REMOVAL & INSTALLATION

▶ **See Figure 6**

1. Open the lid and disconnect the rear defogger harness if so equipped.
2. Mark the hinge locations on the lid for proper relocation.

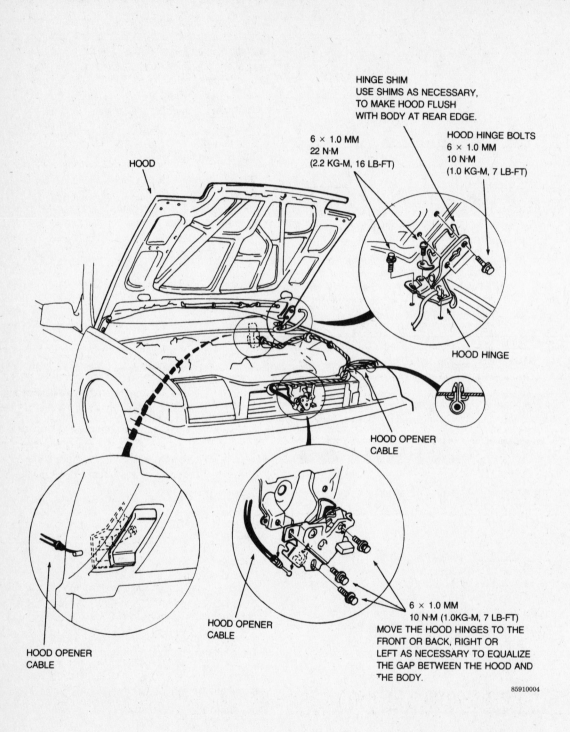

HINGE SHIM
USE SHIMS AS NECESSARY,
TO MAKE HOOD FLUSH
WITH BODY AT REAR EDGE.

6 × 1.0 MM
22 N·M
(2.2 KG-M, 16 LB-FT)

HOOD HINGE BOLTS
6 × 1.0 MM
10 N·M
(1.0 KG-M, 7 LB-FT)

HOOD

HOOD HINGE

HOOD OPENER
CABLE

HOOD OPENER
CABLE

HOOD OPENER
CABLE

6 × 1.0 MM
10 N·M (1.0KG-M, 7 LB-FT)
MOVE THE HOOD HINGES TO THE
FRONT OR BACK, RIGHT OR
LEFT AS NECESSARY TO EQUALIZE
THE GAP BETWEEN THE HOOD AND
THE BODY.

85910004

Fig. 4 Hood replacement and adjustment

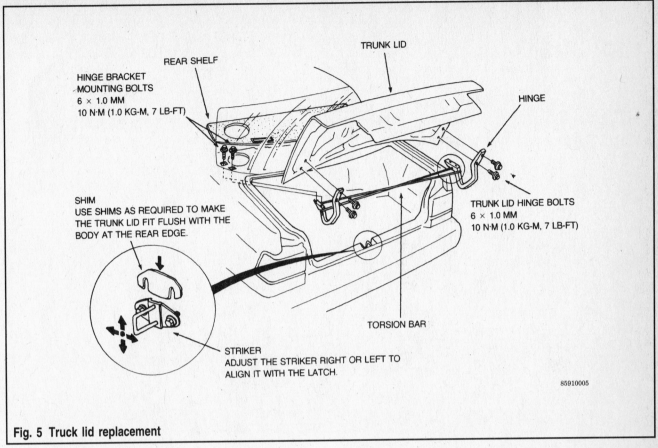

Fig. 5 Truck lid replacement

3. Position rags between the roof and the upper end of the lid to prevent scratching the paint.

4. Support the lid and remove the support bolts the the hinge retaining bolts and remove the lid.

5. Installation is the reverse of removal. Check hatchback or tailgate lid for proper fit and operation.

➡**Be careful not to scratch the lift support rods. A scratched rod may cause oil or gas leakage**

ALIGNMENT

1. Open the hatchback lid.
2. Loosen the lid hinge to body attaching bolts until they are just loose enough to move the lid.
3. Move the lid up and down to obtain a flush fit between the lid and the roof.
4. After adjustment is completed tighten the hinge attaching bolts securely.

Electric Sunroofs

The sunroof is operated by a switch, which is usually located on the left side of the instrument panel. The system is consists of the sunroof switch, motor drive cables and relay(s), which are located in a fuse/relay junction block in the engine compartment.

Several fuses, located in a fuse/relay junction block in the engine compartment and dash fuse box, are used to power/protect the system. The sunroof can be closed manually,

(should it be necessary) by removing the headliner plug, insert the handle and turn the gear to close the sunroof.

➡**The sunroof assembly is equipped with water drain tubes. It is important to keep these drain tubes open. So it is recommended to blow compressed air through the drain tubes at regular intervals, in order to keep the drain tubes clear.**

ADJUSTMENTS

Sunroof Glass

The roof molding should be even with the glass weather strip, to within 1.0mm ± 1.5mm all the way around. If it is not, slide the sunshade back and follow this procedure.

1. Pry the plug out of the glass mount bracket cover, remove the screw, then slide the cover off to the rear.
2. Loosen the mount bracket nuts and install shims between the glass frame and bracket. Repeat this on the other side if necessary.

Side Clearance

If the glass weather strip fits too tightly against the roof molding on either side when closed, slide the sunshade back and follow this procedure.

1. Pry the plug out of each mount bracket cover, remove the screw, then slide the cover off to the rear.
2. Loosen all 8 mount bracket nuts. Move the glass right or left as necessary and tighten the mount bracket nuts.

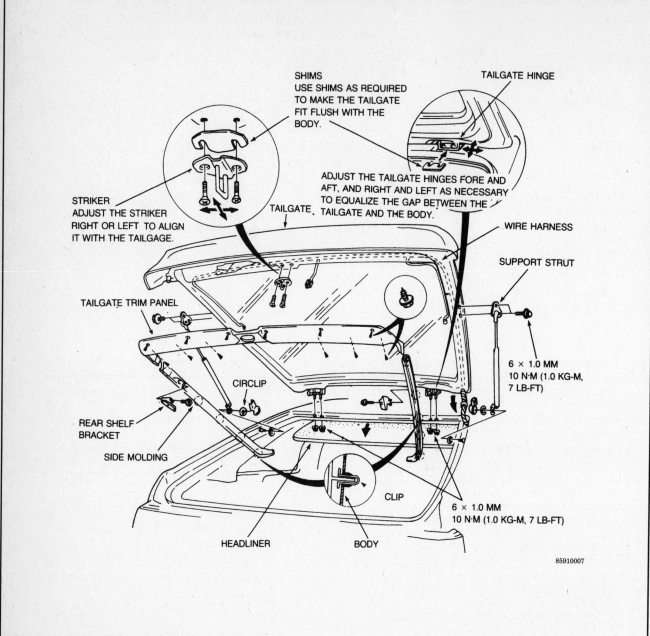

Fig. 6 Hatch replacement-typical

Rear Edge Closing

Open the glass approximately 1 ft., then close it to check where the rear edge begins to rise. If it rises too soon and seat too tightly against the roof molding or too late and does not seat tightly enough, adjust as follows:

1. Open the glass fully. Remove the rail covers from both sides and loosen the lift-up guide screws.

2. Move the guide forward or backward, then tighten the screws and recheck the roof closing. The guides have notches 1.5mm each and can be adjusted 2 notches forward or backward.

REMOVAL & INSTALLATION

Sunroof Glass and Sunshade

1. Slide the sunshade all the way back. Pry the plug out of each mount bracket cover, remove the screw, then slide the cover off to the rear.

2. Close the glass fully. Remove the nuts from the front and rear mounts on both sides.

3. Remove the glass by lifting it up and pulling it towards the front of the vehicle. Once the glass is removed, pull the sunshade out. When removing the sunshade, it is correct to bend the sunshade slightly to aid in the removal.

4. Installation is the reverse order of the removal procedure. Check operation of assembly.

Sunroof Motor, Drain Tube and Frame

▶ **See Figure 7**

1. Remove the headliner from inside of the vehicle.
2. Remove the sunroof motor by removing 2 bolts and 3 nuts from the bottom of the motor mount plate. Disconnect the motor wire harness at the connector and remove the motor.
3. Slide back the drain tube clamps and remove the drain tubes. Remove the 11 mounting bolts from the sunroof frame and remove the frame from the vehicle.
4. To install, insert the frame's rear pins into the body holes, then install the rest of the assembly in the reverse order of the removal procedure.

➡**Before installing the sunroof motor, measure the effort required to close the sliding panel using a suitable spring scale. If the load is over 22 lbs., check the side clearance and the glass height adjustment. Be sure when using the spring scale to protect the leading edge of the sunroof with a shop rag.**

Sunroof Cable Replacement

With the sun roof out of the vehicle, remove the guide rail mounting nuts, lift off the guide rails and remove the cables with the rear mounts attached. Be sure to fill the groove in each grommet with a suitable sealant and apply a suitable grease to the inner cable.

Wind Deflector

A gap between the deflector seal and roof molding will cause wind noise when driving at high speed with the roof opening.

1. Open the sunroof and pry the rail covers off of both sides. Loosen the deflector mounting nuts. The wind deflector can be adjusted 2.0mm forward or backward.
2. Adjust the deflector forward or backward so that the edge of its seal touches the roof molding evenly.
3. The height of the deflector when opened can not be adjusted. If it is damaged or deformed, replace it.

Sunroof Rear Mount Bracket Disassembly

1. Remove the side guides from the rear mount brackets. It is advisable to replace the guides with new ones whenever they are disassembled.
2. Pry the E-clip off of the pin and remove the rear mount bracket from the cable.
3. Assembly is the reverse order of the disassembly procedure.

COMPONENT TESTING

➡**The terminal identification for the sunroof relay should be marked above each terminal on the relay.**

Sunroof Relay

5-PIN RELAY

1. Remove relay from dash relay holder.
2. Check for continuity between terminals **B** and **C**.
3. Apply battery voltage to terminal **E** and ground terminal **F**.
4. Check for continuity between terminals **A** and **C**.
5. If either test fails, replace relay.

4-PIN RELAY

1. Remove relay from dash relay holder.
2. There should be no continuity between terminals **A** and **B**.
3. Apply battery voltage to terminal **C** and ground terminal **D**.
4. There should be continuity between terminals **A** and **B**.
5. If either test fails, replace relay.

Sunroof Closing Force Check (With The Motor Installed)

1. After installing all removed parts, using a second person, have them hold the switch to close the sunroof while measuring the force required to stop the sunroof with a suitable spring scale.
2. Read the force on the scale as soon as the glass stops moving, then immediately release the switch and spring scale. The closing force should be 44-56 lbs.
3. If the force required to stop the sunroof is not within specifications, adjust it, by turning the sunroof motor clutch adjusting nut. Turn clockwise to increase the force and counterclockwise to decrease the force.
4. After the proper adjustment has been made, install a new lockwasher and bend it against the flat on the adjusting nut.

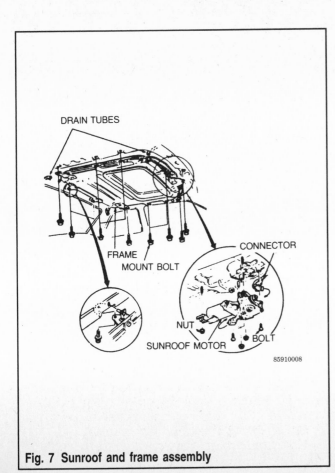

DRAIN TUBES

FRAME MOUNT BOLT

CONNECTOR

NUT

SUNROOF MOTOR · BOLT

85910008

Fig. 7 Sunroof and frame assembly

Bumpers

REMOVAL & INSTALLATION

▶ **See Figures 8 and 9**

Front and Rear

1. Disconnect all electrical connectors at bumper assembly if so equipped.
2. Remove bumper mounting bolts and bumper assembly.
3. Remove shock absorbers from bumper (if so equipped).

✳✳CAUTION

The shock absorber is filled with a high pressure gas and should not be disassembled, drilled or exposed to an open flame.

4. Install shock absorbers (if so equipped) and bumper in reverse order of removal.

Grille

REMOVAL & INSTALLATION

▶ **See Figure 10**

1. Remove radiator grille bracket bolts.

➡ **Some models use clips to hold the radiator grille assembly to the vehicle.**

2. Remove radiator grille from the vehicle.
3. To install reverse the removal procedures.

➡ **The radiator grille assembly is made of plastic, thus never use excessive force to remove it.**

Outside Mirrors

REMOVAL & INSTALLATION

Manual

▶ **See Figure 11**

1. Remove control knob handle.
2. Remove door corner finisher panel.
3. Remove mirror body attaching screws, and then remove mirror body

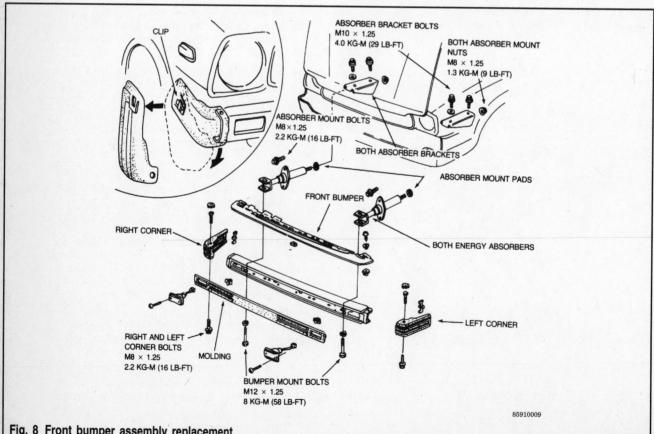

85910009

Fig. 8 Front bumper assembly replacement

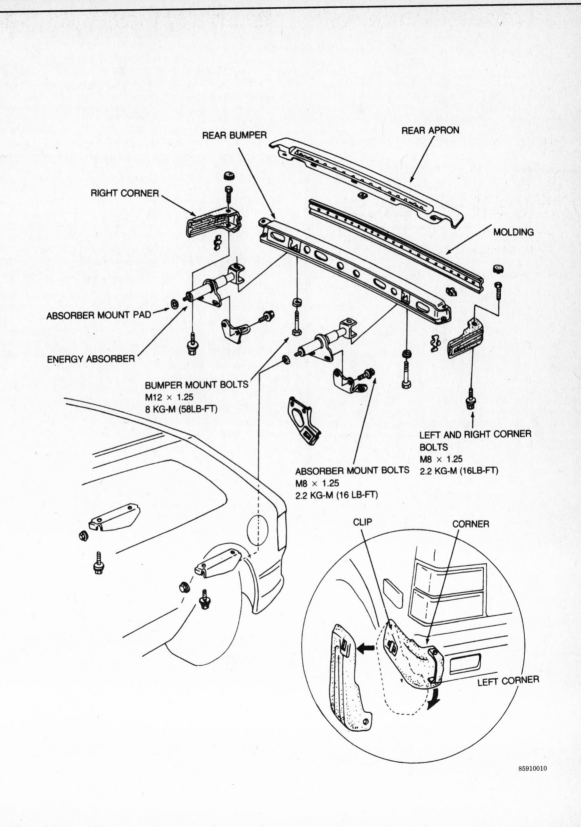

REAR BUMPER

REAR APRON

RIGHT CORNER

MOLDING

ABSORBER MOUNT PAD

ENERGY ABSORBER

BUMPER MOUNT BOLTS
M12 × 1.25
8 KG-M (58LB-FT)

LEFT AND RIGHT CORNER
BOLTS
M8 × 1.25
2.2 KG-M (16LB-FT)

ABSORBER MOUNT BOLTS
M8 × 1.25
2.2 KG-M (16 LB-FT)

CLIP

CORNER

LEFT CORNER

85910010

Fig. 9 Rear bumper assembly replacement

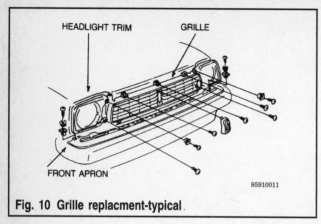

Fig. 10 Grille replacment-typical

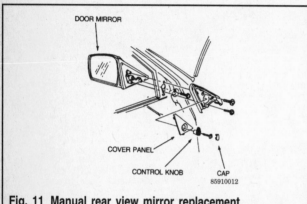

Fig. 11 Manual rear view mirror replacement

4. Installation is in the reverse order of removal.

➡**Apply sealer to the rear surface of door corner finisher panel during installation to prevent water leak.**

Power

▶ See Figure 12

1. Remove door corner finisher panel.
2. Remove mirror body attaching screws, and then remove mirror body
3. Disconnect the electrical connection.

➡**It may be necessary to remove the door trim panel to gain access to the electrical connection.**

4. Installation is in the reverse order of removal. Check power mirror for proper operation.

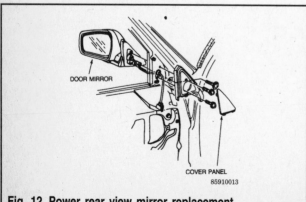

Fig. 12 Power rear view mirror replacement

Power Mirror Switch

The power mirrors are controlled by a single switch assembly, located on the instrument panel. The motors that operate the mirrors are part of the mirror assembly and cannot be replaced separately.

The mirror switch consists of a left-right change over select knob and control knobs. The switch is ready to function only when the ignition switch is in the **ACC** or **ON** position. Movement of the mirror is accomplished by the motors, located in the mirror housing.

REMOVAL & INSTALLATION

1. Disconnect the negative battery cable.
2. Remove the lower instrument panel trim cover.
3. Remove the screw retaining the switch and, using a small pry bar, remove the switch from the instrument panel.
4. Disconnect the electrical lead and remove the switch from the vehicle.
   To install:
5. Connect the electrical lead to the switch and push it into the instrument panel.
6. Install the retaining screw and install the lower trim panel.
7. Connect the battery cable.

Mirror Assembly

1. Disconnect the negative battery cable.
2. Remove the door panel.
3. Disconnect the electrical leads from the mirror harness connector.
4. Using a small pry bar, remove the mirror cover panel lid.
5. Remove the 2 screws retaining the mirror cover panel and remove the cover panel.
6. While holding the mirror assembly, remove the mounting screws and remove the mirror assembly.
   To install:
7. Position the mirror assembly and install the mounting screws.
8. Install the cover panel and the cover panel lid. Attach the wiring harness connector.
9. Install the door panel. Connect the negative battery cable.

Diagnosis and Testing

COMPONENT TESTING

▶ See Figures 13, 14 and 15

Power Mirror Switch

Remove the switch from the instrument panel. Check for continuity between the terminals in each switch position.

Mirror Assembly

1. Remove the door trim panel and disconnect the electrical lead to the mirror.

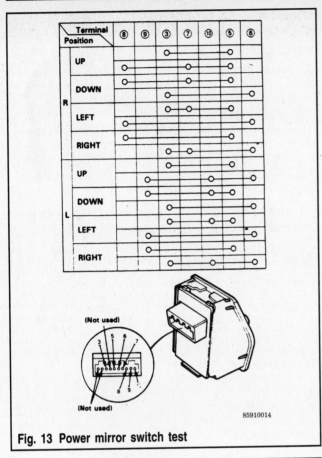

Fig. 13 Power mirror switch test

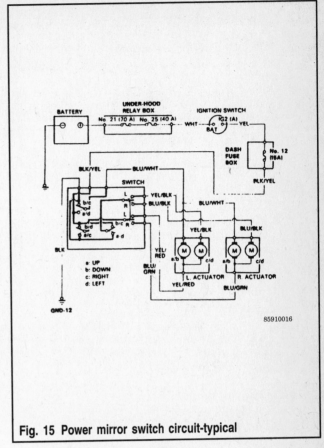

Fig. 15 Power mirror switch circuit-typical

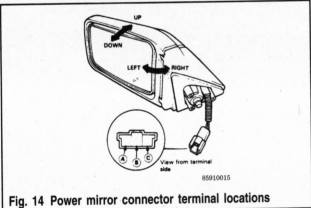

Fig. 14 Power mirror connector terminal locations

2. Test the mirror operation using the following procedures:

  a. Tilt up: connect 12V power source to the **C** terminal and ground the **B** terminal.

  b. Tilt down: connect 12V power source to the **B** terminal and ground the **C** terminal.

  c. Swing right: connect 12V power source to the **A** terminal and ground the **B** terminal.

  d. Swing left: connect 12V power source to the **B** terminal and ground the **A** terminal.

3. If the mirror does not operate properly in any of these tests, replace the assembly.

Antenna

REMOVAL & INSTALLATION

1. Remove antenna mounting nut or screws.
2. Disconnect the antenna lead at the radio.
3. Tie a cord to the end on the antenna lead.
4. Remove antenna from vehicle while fishing out the cord.
5. Installation is in the reverse order of removal. Use the cord to pull the new antenna lead through the body. Check operation of the radio.

INTERIOR

Dashboard

REMOVAL & INSTALLATION

All Models

1. Disconnect the negative battery cable. Remove the fuse box cover and mounting nut.
2. Lower the steering column assembly.
3. Mark and disconnect all electrical wiring.
4. Remove the heater panel trim plate.
5. Remove the heater control bracket mounting screws. Remove the speaker grille plate.
6. Disconnect the speedometer cable and tachometer if so equipped.
7. Remove the 2 bolt hole plugs from both sides of the dashbaord assembly.
8. Remove all retaining bolts. Lift the dashboard up as you pull it out to remove it from the guide pin.
To install:
9. Make sure the dashboard hangs on the guide pin correctly.
10. Reconnect the speedometer cable.
11. Install the dashboard assembly and temporarily tighten all retaining bolts.
12. Reconnect all electrical wiring. Install the heater trim plate.
13. Install the steering column in the correct position. Install the fuse box cover.
14. Reconnect the battery cable all check all electrcial; related items, roadtest the vehicle to check the speedometer.

Door Panel, Glass and Regulator

REMOVAL & INSTALLATION

▶ **See Figure 16**

Front and Rear

1. Remove the regulator handle by pushing the set pin spring.
2. Remove the arm rest, door inside handle escutcheon and door lock.
3. Remove the door finisher and sealing screen.
4. On some models it may be necessary to remove the outer door molding.
5. Lower the door glass with the regulator handle until the regulator-to-glass attaching bolts appear at the access holes in the door inside panel.
6. Raise the door glass and draw it upwards.
7. Remove the regulator attaching bolts and remove the regulator assembly through the large access hole in the door panel.

To install:
8. Position and install the window regulator assembly in the door.
9. Connect all mounting bolts and check for proper operation.
10. Adjust the window if necessary and install the door trim panel.
11. Install all the attaching components to the door panel.
12. Install the window regulator handle. Check operation of the window and lock assembly.

Manual Door Locks

REMOVAL & INSTALLATION

1. Remove the door panel and sealing screen.
2. Remove the lock cylinder from the rod by turning the resin clip.
3. Loosen the nuts attaching the outside door handle and remove the outside door handle.
4. Remove the screws retaining the inside door handle and door lock, and remove the door lock assembly from the hole in the inside of the door.
5. Remove the lock cylinder by removing the retaining clip.
To install:
6. Install the lock cylinder and clip to the door.
7. Install the door lock assembly and handles.
8. Install door panel and all attaching parts. Check operation of manual door lock.

Power Door Locks

The power door locking system consists of switches, actuators and relays. Control switch(es) are used to operate the system. Actuators are used to raise and lower the door lock buttons. These actuators are mounted inside the door assembly and are electrically operated once the switch is depressed. A control unit or functional relay is used to allow the system to regulate current, to function and to align all the actuators and switches with one another.

Some vehicles incorporate a central unlocking system that automatically unlocks all the doors of the vehicle once the key is inserted in the door from the outside of the vehicle.

REMOVAL & INSTALLATION

Door Lock Switch
▶ **See Figure 17**

CIVIC, ACCORD AND PRELUDE

1. Disconnect the negative battery cable.
2. Remove the door panel retaining screws.
3. Lift the door panel up and disconnect all the electrical connections required to separate the door panel from the door.

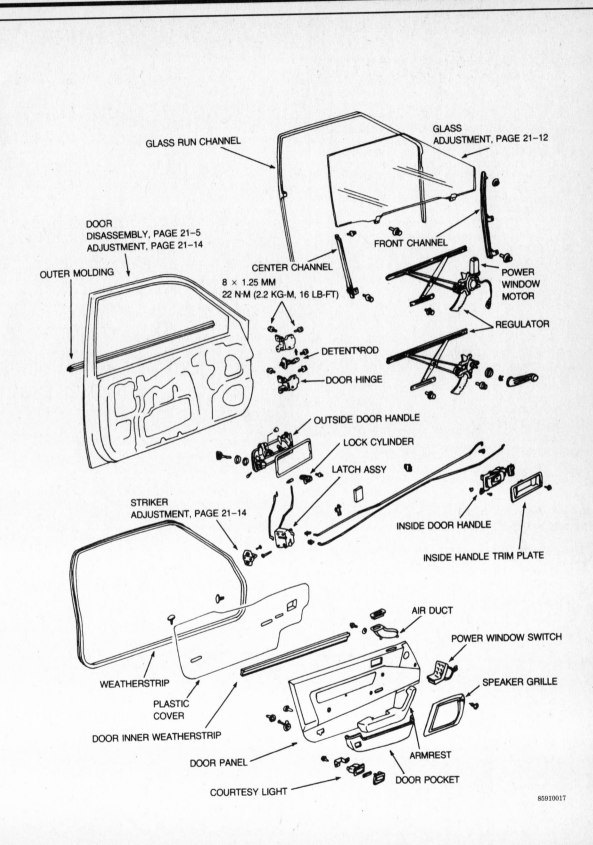

GLASS RUN CHANNEL

GLASS ADJUSTMENT, PAGE 21-12

FRONT CHANNEL

DOOR
DISASSEMBLY, PAGE 21-5
ADJUSTMENT, PAGE 21-14

OUTER MOLDING

CENTER CHANNEL
8 × 1.25 MM
22 N·M (2.2 KG-M, 16 LB-FT)

POWER WINDOW MOTOR

REGULATOR

DETENT ROD

DOOR HINGE

OUTSIDE DOOR HANDLE

LOCK CYLINDER

LATCH ASSY

INSIDE DOOR HANDLE

INSIDE HANDLE TRIM PLATE

STRIKER
ADJUSTMENT, PAGE 21-14

AIR DUCT

POWER WINDOW SWITCH

SPEAKER GRILLE

WEATHERSTRIP

PLASTIC COVER

DOOR INNER WEATHERSTRIP

DOOR PANEL

COURTESY LIGHT

ARMREST

DOOR POCKET

85910017

Fig. 16 Exploded view of the door, regulator and lock assembly

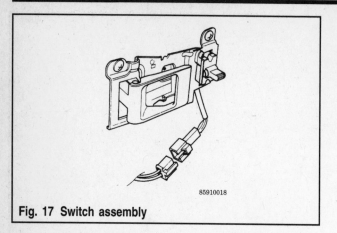

Fig. 17 Switch assembly

4. Remove the door panel from the vehicle. Remove the switch assembly from its mounting.

5. Installation is the reverse of the removal procedure.

Door Lock Actuator

▶ **See Figure 18**

CIVIC, ACCORD AND PRELUDE

1. Disconnect the negative battery cable.
2. Remove the door panel.
3. Disconnect the actuator electrical connector. Disconnect the required linkage rods.
4. Remove the actuator assembly retaining screws. Remove the actuator assembly from the vehicle.
5. Installation is the reverse of the removal procedure.

Door Key Switch

▶ **See Figure 19**

PRELUDE

1. Disconnect the negative battery cable.
2. Remove the door panel.
3. Disconnect the electrical connections from the door key assembly.
4. Remove the door key assembly retaining clip. Remove the switch from its mounting.
5. Installation is the reverse of the removal procedure.

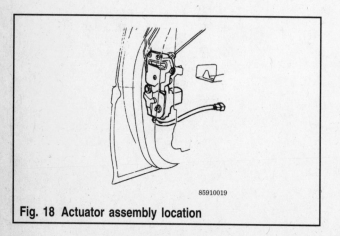

Fig. 18 Actuator assembly location

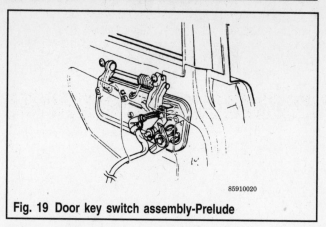

Fig. 19 Door key switch assembly-Prelude

Door Lock Relay

▶ **See Figures 20, 21, 22, 23 and 24**

CIVIC AND PRELUDE

1. Disconnect the negative battery cable.
2. Remove the left side door panel on Civic. Remove the right side door panel on Prelude.
3. Disconnect the relay electrical connectors.
4. Remove the relay retaining screws. Remove the relay from its mounting.
5. Installation is the reverse of the removal procedure.

ACCORD

1. Disconnect the negative battery cable.

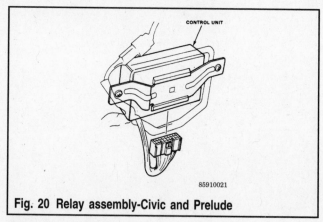

Fig. 20 Relay assembly-Civic and Prelude

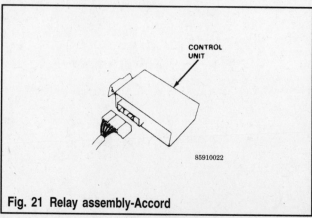

Fig. 21 Relay assembly-Accord

2. Remove the right side front seat retaining bolts. Lift the seat and disconnect all the electrical connectors.

3. Remove the relay retaining screws. Remove the relay from its mounting under the right seat.

4. Installation is the reverse of the removal procedure.

Power Windows

REMOVAL & INSTALLATION

Motor and Regulator

ACCORD, CIVIC, PRELUDE

1. Remove the trim plate and the speaker.

2. Remove the screws attaching the armrest.

3. Remove the door trim panel by removing the attaching screws and the clips then pull it upward.

4. Lower the door glass until the mounting bolts can be seen.

5. Disconnect the power window harnesses, remove the screws then the armrest.

6. Support the glass and remove the glass to regulator attaching bolts.

7. Remove the regulator mounting bolts, then take out the regulator through the lower hole in the door.

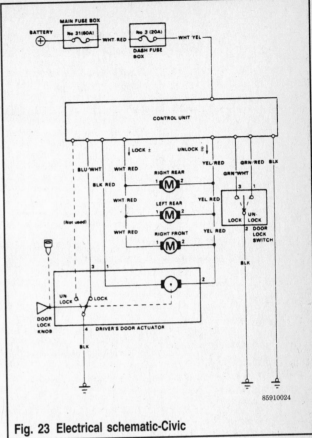

Fig. 23 Electrical schematic-Civic

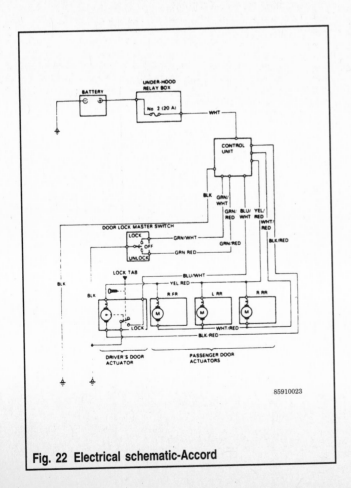

Fig. 22 Electrical schematic-Accord

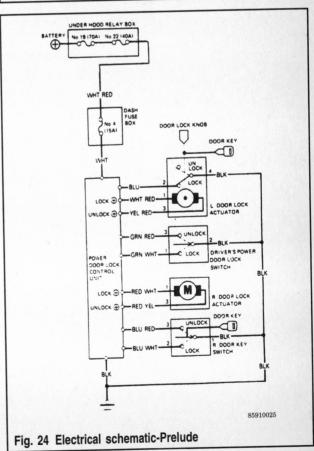

Fig. 24 Electrical schematic-Prelude

8. With the regulator removed from the door panel, remove the attaching bolts and the motor from the regulator.

✴✴CAUTION

The regulator gear will move suddenly when the motor is removed, because the regulator spring is tensioned against the gear.

9. Install the window regulator assembly.
10. Install the glass.
11. Connect the power window harnesses and install the armrest.
12. Install the door trim panel.
13. Install speaker and trim panel. Check for proper operation.

Windshield and Rear Glass

REMOVAL & INSTALLATION

1. Remove rear view mirror, if necessary.
2. Remove the cowl cover (front glass) and all necessary glass mouldings.
3. Cut the urethane bonding from around the glass. Separate the windshield from the vehicle.

To install:

4. Clean the windshield area of all old sealer. Clean the support spacers and reposition them on the studs.
5. Place the replacement windshield in the opening and position it in the center of the opening. Mark the glass at the supports, once it is centered.
6. Remove the glass, clean the inside of the glass. Apply clear glass primer in a 1 inch path around perimeter of glass and wiper with clean cloth.
7. Apply a 15mm path of blackout primer around the top and sides of the glass. Apply a 1 inch path to the bottom of the glass. Allow 3 minutes drying time.
8. Position the glass bonding compression spacers around the opening for the glass.
9. Apply a 12mm bead of urethane around the inside of the opening.
10. Install the glass in the correct position, aligning the marks made earlier. Push the glass until it bottoms on the spacers and is flush with its mounting.
11. Clean excess sealer from the glass. Install the necessary mouldings.
12. Install all necessary components.
13. After the sealer has cured (the more time the better-do not drive the vehicle unit the glass sealer has dry and cured) water test the glass for leaks.

Stationary Glass

REMOVAL & INSTALLATION

All of the fixed glass in the vehicle is removed and installed in the same manner as the windshield and rear glass.

Inside Rear View Mirror

REMOVAL & INSTALLATION

▶ See Figure 25

1. Remove rear view mirror mounting bolt cover.
2. Remove rear view mirror mounting bolts.
3. Remove mirror.
4. Installation is in the reverse order of removal.

Seats

REMOVAL & INSTALLATION

Front
▶ See Figure 26

1. Remove front seat mounting bolts
2. Remove front seat assembly.
3. Installation is in the reverse order of removal.

Rear
▶ See Figure 27

1. Remove rear seat cushion mounting bolts.
2. Remove screw attaching luggage floor carpet.

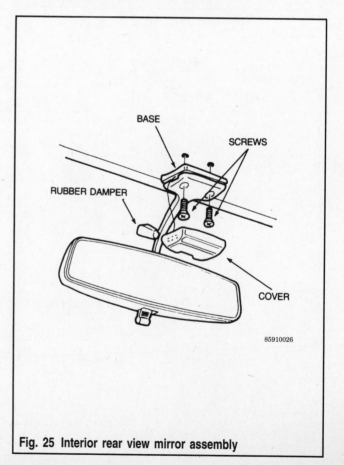

Fig. 25 Interior rear view mirror assembly

3. Remove rear seat back by tilting forward and pulling straight up.

➡**On hatchback models the rear seat back is remove similar as above.**

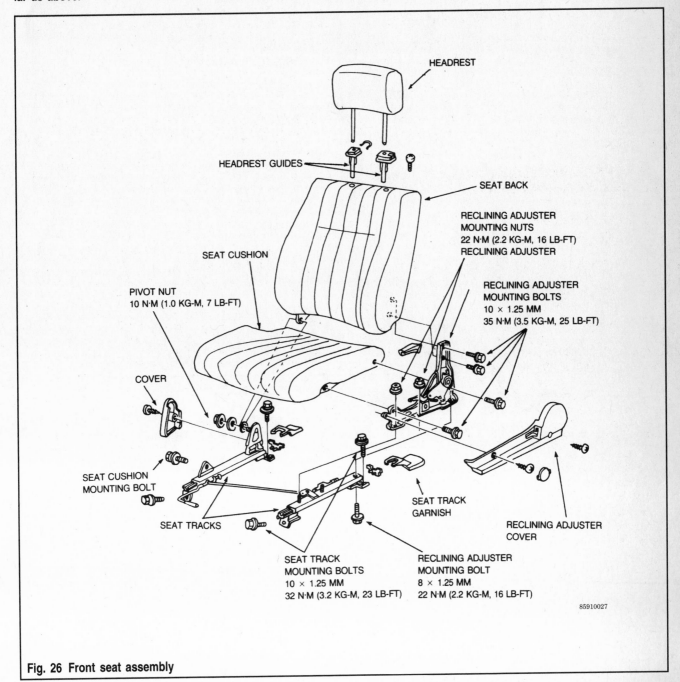

Fig. 26 Front seat assembly

HEADREST

HEADREST GUIDES

SEAT BACK

RECLINING ADJUSTER
MOUNTING NUTS
22 N·M (2.2 KG-M, 16 LB-FT)
RECLINING ADJUSTER

RECLINING ADJUSTER
MOUNTING BOLTS
10 × 1.25 MM
35 N·M (3.5 KG-M, 25 LB-FT)

SEAT CUSHION

PIVOT NUT
10 N·M (1.0 KG-M, 7 LB-FT)

COVER

SEAT CUSHION
MOUNTING BOLT

SEAT TRACKS

SEAT TRACK
MOUNTING BOLTS
10 × 1.25 MM
32 N·M (3.2 KG-M, 23 LB-FT)

SEAT TRACK
GARNISH

RECLINING ADJUSTER
MOUNTING BOLT
8 × 1.25 MM
22 N·M (2.2 KG-M, 16 LB-FT)

RECLINING ADJUSTER
COVER

85910027

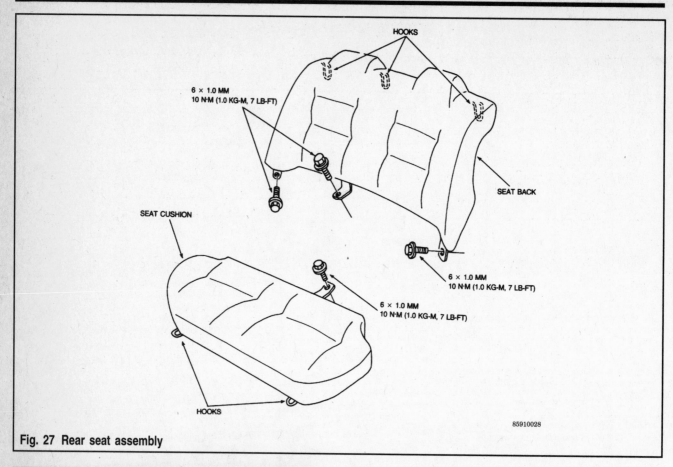

Fig. 27 Rear seat assembly

Seat Belt System

REMOVAL & INSTALLATION

Front

1. Remove the seat cushion, as required.
2. Remove the quarter trim panel or center trim panel.
3. Remove the cover from the upper anchor bolt and remove the 17mm bolt. Slide the seat forward and remove the lower anchor (17mm) bolts.
4. Installation is the reverse of the removal procedure. Torque all the anchor retaining bolts to 23 ft. lbs.

Rear

1. Remove the rear seat cushion.
2. Remove the rear seat belt anchor bolts.
3. Remove the retractor anchor bolts, then remove the retractors.

To install:

4. Install the rear seat belt retractors and bolts, then torque the bolts to 23 ft. lbs.
5. Install each seat belt anchor plate with its belt facing the rear of the car so when you torque the bolt, the plate and belt will come around to an angle of about 45 degrees above horizontal.
6. Install the rear seat cushion.

TORQUE SPECIFICATIONS

Component	U.S.	Metric
Door hinge mounting bolts	16 ft. lbs.	22 Nm
Rear seat belt mounting	23 ft. lbs.	32 Nm
Front seat belt mounting	23 ft. lbs.	32 Nm
Front bumper bolts	58 ft. lbs.	80 Nm
Rear bumper bolts	58 ft. lbs.	80 Nm
Hood hinge	16 ft. lbs.	22 Nm
Hood latch assembly	7 ft. lbs.	10 Nm
Trunk hinge	16 ft. lbs.	22 Nm
Trunk latch assembly	7 ft. lbs.	10 Nm

85910C09

AIR/FUEL RATIO: The ratio of air to gasoline by weight in the fuel mixture drawn into the engine.

AIR INJECTION: One method of reducing harmful exhaust emissions by injecting air into each of the exhaust ports of an engine. The fresh air entering the hot exhaust manifold causes any remaining fuel to be burned before it can exit the tailpipe.

ALTERNATOR: A device used for converting mechanical energy into electrical energy.

AMMETER: An instrument, calibrated in amperes, used to measure the flow of an electrical current in a circuit. Ammeters are always connected in series with the circuit being tested.

AMPERE: The rate of flow of electrical current present when one volt of electrical pressure is applied against one ohm of electrical resistance.

ANALOG COMPUTER: Any microprocessor that uses similar (analogous) electrical signals to make its calculations.

ARMATURE: A laminated, soft iron core wrapped by a wire that converts electrical energy to mechanical energy as in a motor or relay. When rotated in a magnetic field, it changes mechanical energy into electrical energy as in a generator.

ATMOSPHERIC PRESSURE: The pressure on the Earth's surface caused by the weight of the air in the atmosphere. At sea level, this pressure is 14.7 psi at 32{248}F (101 kPa at 0{248}C).

ATOMIZATION: The breaking down of a liquid into a fine mist that can be suspended in air.

AXIAL PLAY: Movement parallel to a shaft or bearing bore.

BACKFIRE: The sudden combustion of gases in the intake or exhaust system that results in a loud explosion.

BACKLASH: The clearance or play between two parts, such as meshed gears.

BACKPRESSURE: Restrictions in the exhaust system that slow the exit of exhaust gases from the combustion chamber.

BAKELITE: A heat resistant, plastic insulator material commonly used in printed circuit boards and transistorized components.

BALL BEARING: A bearing made up of hardened inner and outer races between which hardened steel balls roll.

BALLAST RESISTOR: A resistor in the primary ignition circuit that lowers voltage after the engine is started to reduce wear on ignition components.

BEARING: A friction reducing, supportive device usually located between a stationary part and a moving part.

BIMETAL TEMPERATURE SENSOR: Any sensor or switch made of two dissimilar types of metal that bend when heated or cooled due to the different expansion rates of the alloys. These types of sensors usually function as an on/off switch.

BLOWBY: Combustion gases, composed of water vapor and unburned fuel, that leak past the piston rings into the crankcase during normal engine operation. These gases are removed by the PCV system to prevent the buildup of harmful acids in the crankcase.

BRAKE PAD: A brake shoe and lining assembly used with disc brakes.

BRAKE SHOE: The backing for the brake lining. The term is, however, usually applied to the assembly of the brake backing and lining.

BUSHING: A liner, usually removable, for a bearing; an anti-friction liner used in place of a bearing.

CALIPER: A hydraulically activated device in a disc brake system, which is mounted straddling the brake rotor (disc). The caliper contains at least one piston and two brake pads. Hydraulic pressure on the piston(s) forces the pads against the rotor.

CAMSHAFT: A shaft in the engine on which are the lobes (cams) which operate the valves. The camshaft is driven by the crankshaft, via a belt, chain or gears, at one half the crankshaft speed.

CAPACITOR: A device which stores an electrical charge.

CARBON MONOXIDE (CO): A colorless, odorless gas given off as a normal byproduct of combustion. It is poisonous and extremely dangerous in confined areas, building up slowly to toxic levels without warning if adequate ventilation is not available.

CARBURETOR: A device, usually mounted on the intake manifold of an engine, which mixes the air and fuel in the proper proportion to allow even combustion.

CATALYTIC CONVERTER: A device installed in the exhaust system, like a muffler, that converts harmful byproducts of combustion into carbon dioxide and water vapor by means of a heat-producing chemical reaction.

CENTRIFUGAL ADVANCE: A mechanical method of advancing the spark timing by using flyweights in the distributor that react to centrifugal force generated by the distributor shaft rotation.

CHECK VALVE: Any one-way valve installed to permit the flow of air, fuel or vacuum in one direction only.

CHOKE: A device, usually a moveable valve, placed in the intake path of a carburetor to restrict the flow of air.

CIRCUIT: Any unbroken path through which an electrical current can flow. Also used to describe fuel flow in some instances.

CIRCUIT BREAKER: A switch which protects an electrical circuit from overload by opening the circuit when the current flow exceeds a predetermined level. Some circuit breakers must be reset manually, while most reset automatically

COIL (IGNITION): A transformer in the ignition circuit which steps up the voltage provided to the spark plugs.

COMBINATION MANIFOLD: An assembly which includes both the intake and exhaust manifolds in one casting.

COMBINATION VALVE: A device used in some fuel systems that routes fuel vapors to a charcoal storage canister instead of venting them into the atmosphere. The valve relieves fuel tank pressure and allows fresh air into the tank as the fuel level drops to prevent a vapor lock situation.

COMPRESSION RATIO: The comparison of the total volume of the cylinder and combustion chamber with the piston at BDC and the piston at TDC.

CONDENSER: 1. An electrical device which acts to store an electrical charge, preventing voltage surges.
2. A radiator-like device in the air conditioning system in which refrigerant gas condenses into a liquid, giving off heat.

CONDUCTOR: Any material through which an electrical current can be transmitted easily.

CONTINUITY: Continuous or complete circuit. Can be checked with an ohmmeter.

COUNTERSHAFT: An intermediate shaft which is rotated by a mainshaft and transmits, in turn, that rotation to a working part.

CRANKCASE: The lower part of an engine in which the crankshaft and related parts operate.

CRANKSHAFT: The main driving shaft of an engine which receives reciprocating motion from the pistons and converts it to rotary motion.

CYLINDER: In an engine, the round hole in the engine block in which the piston(s) ride.

CYLINDER BLOCK: The main structural member of an engine in which is found the cylinders, crankshaft and other principal parts.

CYLINDER HEAD: The detachable portion of the engine, fastened, usually, to the top of the cylinder block, containing all or most of the combustion chambers. On overhead valve engines, it contains the valves and their operating parts. On overhead cam engines, it contains the camshaft as well.

DEAD CENTER: The extreme top or bottom of the piston stroke.

DETONATION: An unwanted explosion of the air/fuel mixture in the combustion chamber caused by excess heat and compression, advanced timing, or an overly lean mixture. Also referred to as "ping".

DIAPHRAGM: A thin, flexible wall separating two cavities, such as in a vacuum advance unit.

DIESELING: A condition in which hot spots in the combustion chamber cause the engine to run on after the key is turned off.

DIFFERENTIAL: A geared assembly which allows the transmission of motion between drive axles, giving one axle the ability to turn faster than the other.

DIODE: An electrical device that will allow current to flow in one direction only.

DISC BRAKE: A hydraulic braking assembly consisting of a brake disc, or rotor, mounted on an axle, and a caliper assembly containing, usually two brake pads which are activated by hydraulic pressure. The pads are forced against the sides of the disc, creating friction which slows the vehicle.

DISTRIBUTOR: A mechanically driven device on an engine which is responsible for electrically firing the spark plug at a predetermined point of the piston stroke.

DOWEL PIN: A pin, inserted in mating holes in two different parts allowing those parts to maintain a fixed relationship.

DRUM BRAKE: A braking system which consists of two brake shoes and one or two wheel cylinders, mounted on a fixed backing plate, and a brake drum, mounted on an axle, which revolves around the assembly.

DWELL: The rate, measured in degrees of shaft rotation, at which an electrical circuit cycles on and off.

ELECTRONIC CONTROL UNIT (ECU): Ignition module, module, amplifier or igniter. See Module for definition.

ELECTRONIC IGNITION: A system in which the timing and firing of the spark plugs is controlled by an electronic control unit, usually called a module. These systems have no points or condenser.

ENDPLAY: The measured amount of axial movement in a shaft.

ENGINE: A device that converts heat into mechanical energy.

EXHAUST MANIFOLD: A set of cast passages or pipes which conduct exhaust gases from the engine.

FEELER GAUGE: A blade, usually metal, of precisely predetermined thickness, used to measure the clearance between two parts.

FIRING ORDER: The order in which combustion occurs in the cylinders of an engine. Also the order in which spark is distributed to the plugs by the distributor.

FLOODING: The presence of too much fuel in the intake manifold and combustion chamber which prevents the air/fuel mixture from firing, thereby causing a no-start situation.

FLYWHEEL: A disc shaped part bolted to the rear end of the crankshaft. Around the outer perimeter is affixed the ring gear. The starter drive engages the ring gear, turning the flywheel, which rotates the crankshaft, imparting the initial starting motion to the engine.

FOOT POUND (ft.lb. or sometimes, ft. lbs.): The amount of energy or work needed to raise an item weighing one pound, a distance of one foot.

FUSE: A protective device in a circuit which prevents circuit overload by breaking the circuit when a specific amperage is present. The device is constructed around a strip or wire of a lower amperage rating than the circuit it is designed to protect. When an amperage higher than that stamped on the fuse is present in the circuit, the strip or wire melts, opening the circuit.

GEAR RATIO: The ratio between the number of teeth on meshing gears.

GENERATOR: A device which converts mechanical energy into electrical energy.

HEAT RANGE: The measure of a spark plug's ability to dissipate heat from its firing end. The higher the heat range, the hotter the plug fires.

HUB: The center part of a wheel or gear.

HYDROCARBON (HC): Any chemical compound made up of hydrogen and carbon. A major pollutant formed by the engine as a byproduct of combustion.

HYDROMETER: An instrument used to measure the specific gravity of a solution.

INCH POUND (in.lb. or sometimes, in. lbs.): One twelfth of a foot pound.

INDUCTION: A means of transferring electrical energy in the form of a magnetic field. Principle used in the ignition coil to increase voltage.

INJECTOR: A device which receives metered fuel under relatively low pressure and is activated to inject the fuel into the engine under relatively high pressure at a predetermined time.

INPUT SHAFT: The shaft to which torque is applied, usually carrying the driving gear or gears.

INTAKE MANIFOLD: A casting of passages or pipes used to conduct air or a fuel/air mixture to the cylinders.

JOURNAL: The bearing surface within which a shaft operates.

KEY: A small block usually fitted in a notch between a shaft and a hub to prevent slippage of the two parts.

MANIFOLD: A casting of passages or set of pipes which connect the cylinders to an inlet or outlet source.

MANIFOLD VACUUM: Low pressure in an engine intake manifold formed just below the throttle plates. Manifold vacuum is highest at idle and drops under acceleration.

MASTER CYLINDER: The primary fluid pressurizing device in a hydraulic system. In automotive use, it is found in brake and hydraulic clutch systems and is pedal activated, either directly or, in a power brake system, through the power booster.

MODULE: Electronic control unit, amplifier or igniter of solid state or integrated design which controls the current flow in the ignition primary circuit based on input from the pick-up coil. When the module opens the primary circuit, the high secondary voltage is induced in the coil.

NEEDLE BEARING: A bearing which consists of a number (usually a large number) of long, thin rollers.

OHM:(Ω) The unit used to measure the resistance of conductor to electrical flow. One ohm is the amount of resistance that limits current flow to one ampere in a circuit with one volt of pressure.

OHMMETER: An instrument used for measuring the resistance, in ohms, in an electrical circuit.

OUTPUT SHAFT: The shaft which transmits torque from a device, such as a transmission.

OVERDRIVE: A gear assembly which produces more shaft revolutions than that transmitted to it.

OVERHEAD CAMSHAFT (OHC): An engine configuration in which the camshaft is mounted on top of the cylinder head and operates the valve either directly or by means of rocker arms.

OVERHEAD VALVE (OHV): An engine configuration in which all of the valves are located in the cylinder head and the camshaft is located in the cylinder block. The camshaft operates the valves via lifters and pushrods.

OXIDES OF NITROGEN (NOx): Chemical compounds of nitrogen produced as a byproduct of combustion. They combine with hydrocarbons to produce smog.

OXYGEN SENSOR: Used with the feedback system to sense the presence of oxygen in the exhaust gas and signal the computer which can reference the voltage signal to an air/fuel ratio.

PINION: The smaller of two meshing gears.

PISTON RING: An open ended ring which fits into a groove on the outer diameter of the piston. Its chief function is to form a seal between the piston and cylinder wall. Most automotive pistons have three rings: two for compression sealing; one for oil sealing.

PRELOAD: A predetermined load placed on a bearing during assembly or by adjustment.

PRIMARY CIRCUIT: Is the low voltage side of the ignition system which consists of the ignition switch, ballast resistor or resistance wire, bypass, coil, electronic control unit and pick-up coil as well as the connecting wires and harnesses.

PRESS FIT: The mating of two parts under pressure, due to the inner diameter of one being smaller than the outer diameter of the other, or vice versa; an interference fit.

RACE: The surface on the inner or outer ring of a bearing on which the balls, needles or rollers move.

REGULATOR: A device which maintains the amperage and/or voltage levels of a circuit at predetermined values.

RELAY: A switch which automatically opens and/or closes a circuit.

RESISTANCE: The opposition to the flow of current through a circuit or electrical device, and is measured in ohms. Resistance is equal to the voltage divided by the amperage.

RESISTOR: A device, usually made of wire, which offers a preset amount of resistance in an electrical circuit.

RING GEAR: The name given to a ring-shaped gear attached to a differential case, or affixed to a flywheel or as part a planetary gear set.

ROLLER BEARING: A bearing made up of hardened inner and outer races between which hardened steel rollers move.

ROTOR: 1. The disc-shaped part of a disc brake assembly, upon which the brake pads bear; also called, brake disc.
2. The device mounted atop the distributor shaft, which passes current to the distributor cap tower contacts.

SECONDARY CIRCUIT: The high voltage side of the ignition system, usually above 20,000 volts. The secondary includes the ignition coil, coil wire, distributor cap and rotor, spark plug wires and spark plugs.

SENDING UNIT: A mechanical, electrical, hydraulic or electromagnetic device which transmits information to a gauge.

SENSOR: Any device designed to measure engine operating conditions or ambient pressures and temperatures. Usually electronic in nature and designed to send a voltage signal to an on-board computer, some sensors may operate as a simple on/off switch or they may provide a variable voltage signal (like a potentiometer) as conditions or measured parameters change.

SHIM: Spacers of precise, predetermined thickness used between parts to establish a proper working relationship.

SLAVE CYLINDER: In automotive use, a device in the hydraulic clutch system which is activated by hydraulic force, disengaging the clutch.

SOLENOID: A coil used to produce a magnetic field, the effect of which is produce work.

SPARK PLUG: A device screwed into the combustion chamber of a spark ignition engine. The basic construction is a conductive core inside of a ceramic insulator, mounted in an outer conductive base. An electrical charge from the spark plug wire travels along the conductive core and jumps a preset air gap to a grounding point or points at the end of the conductive base. The resultant spark ignites the fuel/air mixture in the combustion chamber.

SPLINES: Ridges machined or cast onto the outer diameter of a shaft or inner diameter of a bore to enable parts to mate without rotation.

TACHOMETER: A device used to measure the rotary speed of an engine, shaft, gear, etc., usually in rotations per minute.

THERMOSTAT: A valve, located in the cooling system of an engine, which is closed when cold and opens gradually in response to engine heating, controlling the temperature of the coolant and rate of coolant flow.

TOP DEAD CENTER (TDC): The point at which the piston reaches the top of its travel on the compression stroke.

TORQUE: The twisting force applied to an object.

TORQUE CONVERTER: A turbine used to transmit power from a driving member to a driven member via hydraulic action, providing changes in drive ratio and torque. In automotive use, it links the driveplate at the rear of the engine to the automatic transmission.

TRANSDUCER: A device used to change a force into an electrical signal.

TRANSISTOR: A semi-conductor component which can be actuated by a small voltage to perform an electrical switching function.

TUNE-UP: A regular maintenance function, usually associated with the replacement and adjustment of parts and components in the electrical and fuel systems of a vehicle for the purpose of attaining optimum performance.

TURBOCHARGER: An exhaust driven pump which compresses intake air and forces it into the combustion chambers at higher than atmospheric pressures. The increased air pressure allows more fuel to be burned and results in increased horsepower being produced.

VACUUM ADVANCE: A device which advances the ignition timing in response to increased engine vacuum.

VACUUM GAUGE: An instrument used to measure the presence of vacuum in a chamber.

VALVE: A device which control the pressure, direction of flow or rate of flow of a liquid or gas.

VALVE CLEARANCE: The measured gap between the end of the valve stem and the rocker arm, cam lobe or follower that activates the valve.

VISCOSITY: The rating of a liquid's internal resistance to flow.

VOLTMETER: An instrument used for measuring electrical force in units called volts. Voltmeters are always connected parallel with the circuit being tested.

WHEEL CYLINDER: Found in the automotive drum brake assembly, it is a device, actuated by hydraulic pressure, which, through internal pistons, pushes the brake shoes outward against the drums.

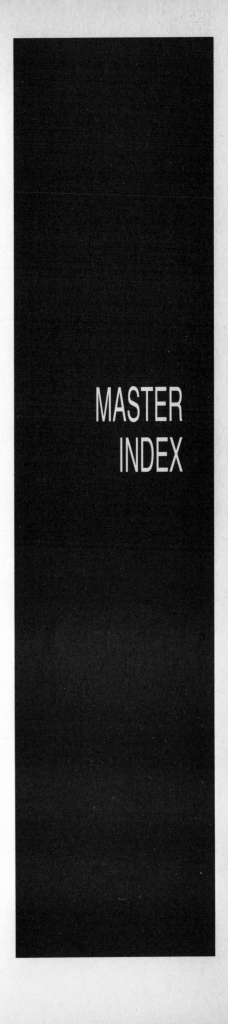

MASTER

INDEX